A BOOK OF DISCOVERY

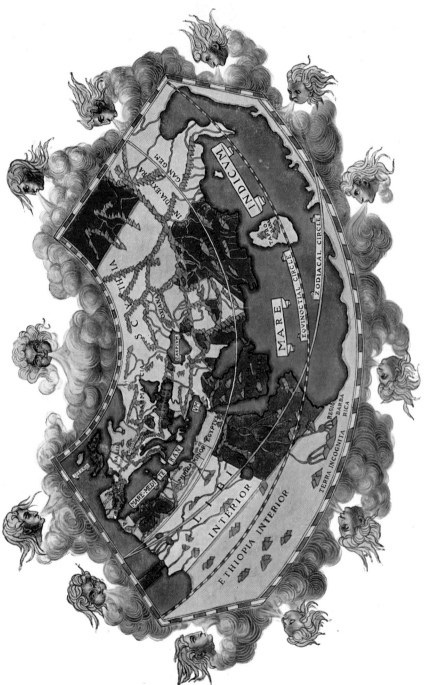

PTOLEMY'S MAP OF THE WORLD, ORIGINALLY DRAWN ABOUT A.D. 150.

Taken from the first printed edition of 1472 (the first book to have printed maps) and the famous Rome edition of 1508. It is only necessary to compare this map with the mythical geography represented in a mediæval map, such as the Hereford map of the world, made *eleven centuries* later, to recognise the extraordinary accuracy and scientific value of Ptolemy's geography.

A BOOK OF
DISCOVERY

THE HISTORY OF THE WORLD'S EXPLORATION, FROM THE EARLIEST TIMES TO THE FINDING OF THE SOUTH POLE

By M. B. SYNGE, F.R.Hist.S.

AUTHOR OF "THE STORY OF THE WORLD"
"A SHORT HISTORY OF SOCIAL LIFE IN ENGLAND" ETC.

*FULLY ILLUSTRATED FROM AUTHENTIC SOURCES
AND WITH MAPS*

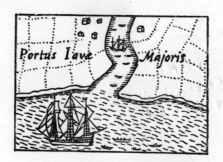

THE *GOLDEN HIND*
(*From the Chart of "Drake's Voyages"*)

NEW YORK
G. P. PUTNAM'S SONS
LONDON: T. C. & E. C. JACK, Ltd.

INTRODUCTION

" Hope went before them, and the world was wide."

SUCH was the spirit in which the exploration of the world was accomplished. It was the inspiration that carried men of old far beyond the sunrise into those magic and silent seas whereon no boat had ever sailed. It is the incentive of those to-day with the wander-thirst in their souls, who travel and suffer in the travelling, though there are fewer prizes left to win. But

" The reward is in the doing,
And the rapture of pursuing
Is the prize."

"To travel hopefully," says Stevenson, "is a better thing than to arrive." This would explain the fact that this Book of Discovery has become a record of splendid endurance, of hardships bravely borne, of silent toil, of courage and resolution unequalled in the annals of mankind, of self-sacrifice unrivalled and faithful lives laid ungrudgingly down. Of the many who went forth, the few only attained. It is of these few that this book tells.

"All these," says the poet in Ecclesiastes — "all these were honoured in their generation, and were the glory of their times . . . their name liveth for evermore."

But while we read of those master - spirits who

succeeded, let us never forget those who failed to achieve.

"Anybody might have found it, but the Whisper came to Me."

Enthusiasm too was the secret of their success. Among the best of crews there was always some one who would have turned back, but the world would never have been explored had it not been for those finer spirits who resolutely went on—even to the death.

This is what carried Alexander the Great to the "earth's utmost verge," that drew Columbus across the trackless Atlantic, that nerved Vasco da Gama to double the Stormy Cape, that induced Magellan to face the dreaded straits now called by his name, that made it possible for men to face without flinching the ice-bound regions of the far North.

"There is no land uninhabitable, nor sea unnavigable," asserted the men of the sixteenth century, when England set herself to take possession of her heritage in the North. Such an heroic temper could overcome all things. But the cost was great, the sufferings intense.

"Having eaten our shoes and saddles boiled with a few wild herbs, we set out to reach the kingdom of gold," says Orellana in 1540.

"We ate biscuit, but in truth it was biscuit no longer, but a powder full of worms,—so great was the want of food, that we were forced to eat the hides with which the mainyard was covered; but we had also to make use of sawdust for food, and rats became a great delicacy," related Magellan, as he led his little ship across the unknown Pacific.

Again, there is Franklin returning from the Arctic coast, and stilling the pangs of hunger with "pieces of singed hide mixed with lichen," varied with "the horns and bones of a dead deer fried with some old shoes."

The dangers of the way were manifold.

For the early explorers had no land map or ocean chart to guide them, there were no lighthouses to warn the strange mariner of dangerous coast and angry surf, no books of travel to relate the weird doings of fierce and inhospitable savages, no tinned foods to prevent the terrible scourge of sailors, scurvy. In their little wooden sailing ships the men of old faced every conceivable danger, and surmounted obstacles unknown to modern civilisation.

> " Now strike your Sails ye jolly Mariners,
> For we be come into a quiet Rode."

For the most part we are struck with the light-hearted ness of the olden sailor, the shout of gladness with which men went forth on these hazardous undertakings, knowing not how they would arrive, or what might befall them by the way, went forth in the smallest of wooden ships, with the most incompetent of crews, to face the dangers of unknown seas and unsuspected lands, to chance the angry storm and the hidden rock, to discover inhospitable shores and savage foes. Founded on bitter experience is the old saying—

> " A Passage Perilous makyth a Port Pleasant."

For the early navigators knew little of the art of navigation.

Pytheas, who discovered the British Isles, was " a great mathematician." Diego Cam, who sailed to the mouth of the Congo, was " a knight of the King's household." Sir Hugh Willoughby, " a most valiant gentleman." Richard Chancellor, " a man of great estimation for many good parts of wit in him." Anthony Jenkinson, a " resolute and intelligent gentleman." Sir Walter Raleigh, an Elizabethan courtier, and so forth.

It has been obviously impossible to include all the famous names that belong to the history of exploration.

Most of these explorers have been chosen for some definite new discovery, some addition to the world's geographical knowledge, or some great feat of endurance which may serve to brace us to fresh effort as a nation famous for our seamen. English navigators have been afforded the lion's share in the book, partly because they took the lion's share in exploring, partly because translations of foreign travel are difficult to transcribe. Most of these stories have been taken from original sources, and most of the explorers have been allowed to tell part of their own story in their own words.

Perhaps the most graphic of all explorations is that written by a native of West Australia, who accompanied an exploring party searching for an English lad named Smith, who had been starved to death.

" Away, away, away, away ; we reach the water of Djunjup ; we shoot game. Away, away, away through a forest away, through a forest away ; we see no water. Through a forest away, along our tracks away ; hills ascending, then pleasantly away, away, through a forest away. We see a water—along the river away—a short distance we go, then away, away, away through a forest away. Then along another river away, across the river away. Still we go onwards, along the sea away, through the bush away, then along the sea away. We sleep near the sea. I see Mr. Smith's footsteps ascending a sandhill; onwards I go regarding his footsteps. I see Mr. Smith dead. Two sleeps had he been dead; greatly did I weep, and much I grieved. In his blanket folding him, we scraped away the earth. The sun had inclined to the westward as we laid him in the ground."

The book is illustrated with reproductions from old maps—old primitive maps, with a real Adam and Eve standing in the Garden of Eden, with Pillars of Hercules guarding the Straits of Gibraltar, with Paradise in the east, a realistic Jerusalem in the centre, the island of Thule in the north, and St. Brandon's Isles of the Blest in the west.

Beautifully coloured were the maps of the Middle Ages, " joyous charts all glorious with gold and vermilion, compasses and crests and flying banners, with mountains of red and gold." The seas are full of ships—" brave beflagged vessels with swelling sails." The land is ablaze with kings and potentates on golden thrones under canopies of angels. While over all presides the Madonna in her golden chair."

The Hereford Mappa Mundi, drawn in the thirteenth century on a fine sheet of vellum, circular in form, is among the most interesting of the mediæval maps. It must once have been gorgeous, with its gold letters and scarlet towns, its green seas and its blue rivers. The Red Sea is still red, but the Mediterranean is chocolate brown, and all the green has disappeared. The mounted figure in the lower right-hand corner is probably the author, Richard de Haldingham. The map is surmounted by a representation of the Last Judgment, below which is Paradise as a circular island, with the four rivers and the figures of Adam and Eve. In the centre is Jerusalem. The world is divided into three — Asia, "Affrica," and Europe. Around this earth-island flows the ocean. America is, of course, absent ; the East is placed at Paradise and the West at the Pillars of Hercules. North and South are left to the imagination.

And what of the famous map of Juan de la Cosa, once pilot to Columbus, drawn in the fifteenth century, with St. Christopher carrying the infant Christ across the water, supposed to be a portrait of Christopher Columbus carrying the gospel to America ? It is the first map in which a dim outline appears of the New World.

The early maps of "Apphrica" are filled with camels

and unicorns, lions and tigers, veiled figures and the turrets and spires of strange buildings—

> " Geographers in Afric maps
> With savage pictures fill their gaps."

"Surely," says a modern writer,—"surely the old cartographer was less concerned to fill his gaps than to express the poetry of geography."

And to-day, there are still gaps in the most modern maps of Africa, where one-eleventh of the whole area remains unexplored. Further, in Asia the problem of the Brahmaputra Falls is yet unsolved; there are shores untrodden and rivers unsurveyed.

"God hath given us some things, and not all things, that our successors also might have somewhat to do," wrote Barents in the sixteenth century. There may not be much left, but with the words of Kipling's *Explorer* we may fitly conclude—

> "Something hidden. Go and find it. Go and look
> behind the Ranges—
> Something lost behind the Ranges. Lost and
> waiting for you. Go!"

Thanks are due to Mr. S. G. Stubbs for valuable assistance in the selection and preparation of the illustrations, which, with few exceptions, have been executed under his directions.

CONTENTS

CONTENTS

CONTENTS

CONTENTS

COLOURED ILLUSTRATIONS

BLACK & WHITE ILLUSTRATIONS

Acknowledgment is due to the courtesy of Mr. John Murray and the *Illustrated London
News* for the photograph taken at the South Pole, facing page 544; to Admiral Peary for
that taken at the North Pole, facing page 534; and to Sir Ernest Shackleton and Mr.
Heinemann for the colour-plate of the *Nimrod*. Permissions have also been granted by
Mr. John Murray (for illustrations from Livingstone's books and Admiral M'Clintock's *Voyage
of the Fox*); by Messrs. Macmillan (for the colour-plate of the Polos leaving Venice, from the
Bodleian); and by Messrs. Sampson, Low, Marston, & Co. (for illustrations from Sir H. M.
Stanley's books).

LIST OF ILLUSTRATIONS
IN THE TEXT

xix

A BOOK OF DISCOVERY

CHAPTER I

A LITTLE OLD WORLD

No story is complete unless it begins at the very beginning.
But where is the beginning? Where is the dawn of
geography—the knowledge of our earth? What was
it like before the first explorers made their way into
distant lands? Every day that passes we are gaining
fresh knowledge of the dim and silent past.

Every day men are patiently digging in the old heaps
that were once the sites of busy cities, and, as a result of
their unwearying toil, they are revealing to us the life-
stories of those who dwelt therein; they are disclosing
secrets writ on weather-worn stones and tablets, bricks
and cylinders, never before even guessed at.

Thus we read the wondrous story of ancient days, and
breathlessly wonder what marvellous discovery will thrill
us next.

For the earliest account of the old world—a world
made up apparently of a little land and a little water—
we turn to an old papyrus, the oldest in existence, which
tells us in familiar words, unsurpassed for their exquisite
poetry and wondrous simplicity, of that great dateless
time so full of mystery and awe.

" In the beginning God created the heaven and the
earth. And the earth was waste and void; and darkness

was upon the face of the deep: and the spirit of God moved upon the face of the waters. . . . And God said, Let there be a firmament in the midst of the waters, and let it divide the waters from the waters. And God . . . divided the waters which were under the firmament from the waters which were above the firmament. . . . And God said, Let the waters under the heaven be gathered into one place, and let the dry land appear. . . . And God called the dry land Earth; and the gathering together of the waters called he Seas."

Thus beautifully did the children of men express their earliest idea of the world's distribution of land and water.

THE GARDEN OF EDEN WITH ITS FOUR RIVERS.
From the Hereford Map of the World.

And where, on our modern maps, was this little earth, and what was it like? Did trees and flowers cover the land? Did rivers flow into the sea? Listen again to the old tradition that still rings down the ages—

"And the Lord God planted a garden eastward in Eden . . . and a river went out of Eden to water the garden; and from thence it was parted, and became four heads. The name of the first is Pison . . . and the name of the second river is Gihon; the name of the third river is Hiddekel (Tigris). And the fourth river is Euphrates."

Now look at a modern map of Asia. Between Arabia and Persia there is a long valley watered by the Tigris and Euphrates, rivers which rise in Armenia and flow into the Persian Gulf. This region was the traditional "cradle of the human race." Around and beyond was a great world, a world with great surging seas, with lands of trees and flowers, a world with continents and lakes and bays and capes, with islands and mountains and rivers.

There were vast deserts of sand rolling away to right and to left; there were mountains up which no man had climbed; there were stormy seas over which no ship had ever sailed. But these men of old had never explored far. They believed that their world was just a very little world with no other occupants than themselves. They believed it to be flat, with mountains at either end on which rested a solid metal dome known as the "firmament."

In this shining circle were windows, in and out of which the sun would creep by day and the moon and stars by night. And the whole of this world was, they thought, balanced on the waters. There was water above, the "waters that be above the firmament," and water below, and water all round.

Long ages pass away. Let us look again at the green

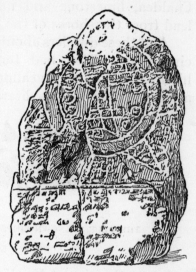

BABYLONIAN MAP OF THE WORLD
ON CLAY.

Showing the ocean surrounding the world and the position of Babylon on the Euphrates. In the British Museum.

valley of the Euphrates and Tigris. It has been called the "nursery of nations"—names have been given to various regions round about, and cities have arisen on the banks of the rivers. Babylonia, Mesopotamia, Chaldea, Assyria — all these long names belonged to this region, and around each centres some of the most interesting history and legend in the world.

Rafts on the river and caravans on the land carried

merchandise far and wide—men made their way to the
" Sea of the Rising Sun," as they called the Persian Gulf,
and to the " Sea of the Setting Sun," as they called
the Mediterranean. They settled on the shores of the
Caspian Sea, on the shores of the Black Sea, on the shores
of the Red Sea. They carried on magnificent trade—
cedar, pine, and cypress were brought from Lebanon to
Chaldea, limestone and marble from Syria, copper and
lead from the shores of the Black Sea.

And these dwellers about Babylonia built up a wonderful
civilisation. They had temples and brick-built houses,
libraries of tablets revealing knowledge of astronomy and
astrology; they had a literature of their own. Suddenly

THE OLDEST KNOWN SHIPS : BETWEEN 6000 AND 5000 B.C.

From a pre-Egyptian vase-painting.

from out the city of Ur (Kerbela), near the ancient mouth
of the Euphrates, appears a traveller. There had doubtless
been many before, but records are scanty and hard to
piece together, and a detailed account of a traveller with
a name is very interesting.

" Abram went . . . forth to go into the land of Canaan.
. . . And Abram journeyed, going on still toward the
South. And there was a famine in the land. And
Abram went down into Egypt to sojourn there." He
would have travelled by the chief caravan routes of
Syria into Egypt. Here about the fertile mouth of the
Nile he would have found an ancient civilisation as
wonderful as that to which he was accustomed in Baby-

lonia. It was a grain-growing country, and when there was famine in other lands, there was always " corn in Egypt "—thanks to the mighty life-giving Nile.

But we must not linger over the old civilisation, over the wonderful Empire governed by the Pharaohs or kings, first from Memphis (Cairo) and then from the hundred-gated Thebes ; must not linger over these old pyramid builders, the temple, sphinxes, and statues of ancient Egypt. Before even Abram came into their country we find the Egyptians famous for their shipping and navigation. Old pictures and tombs recently discovered tell us this.

On the coast of the Red Sea they built their long, narrow ships, which were rowed by some twenty paddlers on either side, and steered by three men standing in the stern. With one mast and a large sail they flew before the wind. They had to go far afield for their wood; we find an Egyptian being sent " to cut down four forests in the South in order to build three large vessels . . . out of acacia wood."

Petrie tells us of an Egyptian sailor who was sent to Punt or Somaliland " to fetch for Pharaoh sweet-smelling spices." He was shipwrecked on the way, and this is the account of his adventures—

" ' I was going,' he relates, ' to the mines of Pharaoh and I went down on the sea on a ship with a hundred and fifty sailors of the best of Egypt, whose hearts were stronger than lions. They had said that the wind would be contrary, or that there would be none. But as we approached the land the wind rose and threw up high waves. As for me, I seized a piece of wood; but those who were in the vessel perished, without one remaining. A wave threw me on an island; after that I had been three days alone without a companion beside my own heart, I laid me in a thicket, and the shadow covered me. I found figs and grapes, all manner of good herbs, berries and grain, melons of all kinds, fishes and birds. I lighted a fire and I made a burnt-offering unto the gods. Suddenly I heard a noise as of thunder, which I thought to be that of a wave of the sea. The trees shook and the earth was moved. I uncovered my eyes and I saw that a serpent drew near; his body was as if overlaid with gold, and his colour as that of true lazuli.'

" ' What has brought thee here, little one, to this isle, which is in the sea and of which the shores are in the midst of the waves ? ' asked the serpent.

" The sailor told his story kneeling on his knees, with his face bowed to the ground.

" ' Fear not, little one, and make not thy face sad,' continued the serpent, ' for it is God who has brought thee to this isle of the blest, where nothing is lacking and which is filled with all good things. Thou shalt be four months in this isle. Then a ship shall come from thy land with sailors, and thou shalt go to thy country. As for me, I am a prince of the land of Punt. I am here with my brethren and children around me; we are seventy-five serpents, children and kindred.'

" Then the grateful sailor promised to bring all the treasures of Egypt back to Punt, and ' I shall tell of thy presence unto Pharaoh; I shall make him to know of thy greatness,' said the Egyptian stranger.

" But the strange prince of Punt only smiled.

" ' Thou shalt never more see this isle,' he said; ' it shall be changed into waves.' "

Everything came to pass as the serpent said. The ship came, gifts were lavished on the sailor from Egypt, perfumes of cassia, of sweet woods, of cypress, incense, ivory tusks, baboons, and apes, and thus laden he sailed home to his own people.

Long centuries after this we get another glimpse at

the land of Punt. This time it is in the reign of Queen
Hatshepsu, who sent a great trading expedition into this
famous country. Five ships started from Thebes, sailing
down the river Nile and probably reaching the Red Sea
by means of a canal. Navigation in the Red Sea was
difficult; the coast was steep and inhospitable; no rivers
ran into it. Only a few fishing villages lay along the coasts
used by Egyptian merchants as markets for mother-of-
pearl, emeralds, gold, and sweet-smelling perfumes.

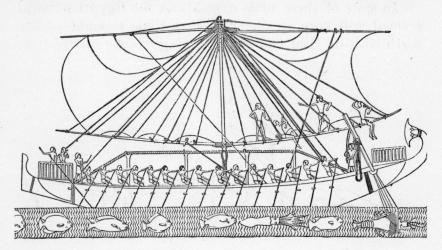

EGYPTIAN SHIP OF THE EXPEDITION TO PUNT, ABOUT 1600 B.C.
From a rock-carving at Der el Bahari.

Thence the ships continued their way, the whole voyage
taking about two months. Arrived at Punt, the Egyptian
commander pitched his tents upon the shore, to the great
astonishment of the inhabitants.

"Why have ye come hither unto this land, which the
people of Egypt know not?" asked the Chief of Punt.
"Have ye come through the sky? Did ye sail upon the
waters or upon the sea?"

Presents from the Queen of Egypt were at once laid
before the Chief of Punt, and soon the seashore was alive

with people.   The ships were drawn up, gang-planks were
very heavily laden with " marvels of the country of Punt."
There were heaps of myrrh, resin, of fresh myrrh trees,
ebony and pure ivory, cinnamon wood, incense, baboons,
monkeys, dogs, natives, and children.   " Never was the
like brought to any king of Egypt since the world stands."
And the ships voyaged safely back to Thebes with all their
booty and with pleasant recollections of the people of
Somaliland.

In spite of these little expeditions the Egyptian world
seemed still very small.   The Egyptians thought of the
earth with its land and sea as a long, oblong sort of box,

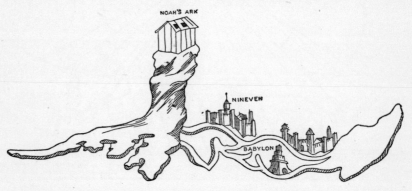

THE ARK ON ARARAT AND THE CITIES OF NINEVEH AND BABYLON.
From Leonardo Dati's map of 1422.

the centre of which was Egypt.   The sky stretched over
it like an iron ceiling, the part toward the earth being
sprinkled with lamps hung from strong cables lighted by
night and extinguished by day.   Four forked trunks of
trees upheld the sky roof.   But lest some storm should
overthrow these tree trunks there were four lofty peaks
connected by chains of mountains.   The southern peak
was known as the " Horn of the Earth," the eastern, the
" Mountain of Birth," the western, the " Region of Life,"
the southern was invisible.   And why ?   Because they

thought the Great Sea, the " Very Green," the Mediterranean, lay between it and Egypt. Beyond these mountain peaks, supporting the world, rolled a great river, an ocean stream, and the sun was as a ball of fire placed on a boat and carried round the ramparts of the world by the all-encircling water.

So we realise that the people living in Babylonia about the river Euphrates, and those living in Egypt about the river Nile, had very strange ideas about the little old world around them.

CHAPTER II

EARLY MARINERS

THE law of the universe is progress and expansion, and this little old world was soon discovered to be larger than men thought.

Now in Syria—the highway between Babylonia and Egypt—dwelt a tribe of dusky people known as Phœnicians. Some have thought that they were related to our old friends in Somaliland, and that long years ago they had migrated north to the seacoast of that part of Syria known as Canaan.

Living on the seashore, washed by the tideless Mediterranean, they soon became skilful sailors. They built ships and ventured forth on the deep; they made their way to the islands of Cyprus and Crete and thence to the islands of Greece, bringing back goods from other countries to barter with their less daring neighbours. They reached Greece itself and cruised along the northern coast of the Great Sea to Italy, along the coast of Spain to the Rock of Gibraltar, and out into the open Atlantic.

How their little sailing boats lived through the storms of that great ocean none may know, for Phœnician records are lost, but we have every reason to believe that they reached the northern coast of France and brought back tin from the islands known to them as the Tin Islands. In their home markets were found all manner of strange things from foreign unknown lands, discovered by these master mariners—the admiration of the ancient world.

"The ships of Tarshish," said the old poet, "did sing of thee in thy market, and thou wast replenished and made very glorious in the midst of the seas; thy rowers have brought thee into great waters; the east wind hath broken thee in the midst of the seas."

All the world knew of the Phœnician seaports, Tyre and Sidon. They were as famous as Memphis and Thebes on the Nile, as magnificent as Nineveh on the Tigris and Babylon on the Euphrates. Men spoke of the "renowned city of Tyre," whose merchants were as princes, whose "traffickers" were among the

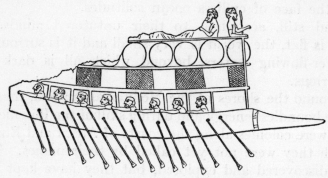

A PHŒNICIAN SHIP, ABOUT 700 B.C.
From a bas-relief at Nineveh.

honourable of the earth. "O thou that art situate at the entry of the sea," cries the poet again, when the greatness of Tyre was passing away, "which art a merchant of the people from many isles. . . . Thy borders are in the midst of the seas; thy builders have perfected thy beauty. They have made all thy shipboards of fir trees . . . they have taken cedars of Lebanon to make masts for thee. Of the oaks of Basan have they made thy oars. . . . Fine linen with broidered work from Egypt was that which thou spreadest forth to be thy sail. . . . The inhabitants of Sidon . . . were thy mariners; thy wise men were thy pilots."

As time goes on, early groups round the Euphrates and the Nile continue, but new nations form and grow, new cities arise, new names appear. Centuries of men live and die, ignorant of the great world that lies about them—" Lords of the eastern world that knew no west."

England was yet unknown, America undreamt of, Australia still a desolate island in an unknown sea. The burning eastern sun shone down on to vast stretches of desert-land uninhabited by man, great rivers flowed through dreary swamps unrealised, tempestuous waves beat against their shores, and melancholy winds swept over the face of endless ocean solitudes.

And still, according to their untutored minds, the world is flat, the world is very small and it is surrounded by ever-flowing waters, beyond which all is dark and mysterious.

Around the shores of the Mediterranean Sea, revealed by the boundless energy and daring skill of the Phœnicians, there were colonies along the coasts of Africa and Europe, though they were not yet called by their names. They have discovered and explored, but they have kept their information to themselves, and they have specially refused to divulge their voyages to the Greeks.

A story is told at a later date than this of a Phœnician shipmaster who was bound for the Tin Islands, when he suddenly discovered that he was being followed by a strange ship evidently bent on finding out where these unknown islands lay. The Phœnician purposely ran his ship on to a shoal in order to keep the secret of the discovery. When he returned home his conduct was upheld by the State!

But though the Phœnicians have left us no record of their travels and voyages, they had been the carriers of knowledge, and it was from them that the Greeks learnt of " the extreme regions of the world " and of the dim "far west." Indeed, it is highly probable that from the Phœnicians they got material for their famous legend of the Argonauts and their adventures in the Black Sea. Though the story is but legendary, and it has been added to with the growing knowledge of the world, yet it gives an idea of the perils that beset the sailors of those remote ages and of their limitations.

And again we must remind ourselves that both the Phœnicians and early Greeks had, like the Egyptians and Babylonians, childish ideas as to the form of the earth. To them it was a circular plane, encircled by the ocean, which they believed to be a broad, deep-running river flowing round and round the world. Into this ocean stream ran all the rivers and seas known to them. Over the earth was raised a solid firmament of bronze in which the stars were set, and this was supported on tall pillars "which kept the heaven and the earth asunder."

The whole delightful story of the Argonauts can be read in Kingsley's "Heroes." It is the story of brave men who sailed in the ship *Argo*, named after the great shipbuilder Argos, to bring back the Golden Fleece from Colchis in the Black Sea.

Nowhere in all the history of exploration have we a more poetical account of the launching of a ship for distant lands: "Then they have stored her well with food and water, and pulled the ladder up on board, and settled themselves each man to his oar and kept time to Orpheus' harp; and away across the bay they rowed southward, while the people lined the cliffs; and the women wept while the men shouted at the starting of that gallant crew." They chose a captain, and the choice fell on Jason, "because he was the wisest of them all"; and they rowed on "over the long swell of the sea, past Olympus, past the wooded bays of Athos and the sacred isle; and they came past Lemnos to the Hellespont, and so on into the Propontis, which we call Marmora now." So they came to the Bosphorus, the "land then as now of bitter blasts, the land of cold and misery," and a great battle of the winds took place.

Then the Argonauts came out into the open sea—the Black Sea. No Greek had ever crossed it, and even the

— Track of the Argo to Colchis
--------- Return Voyage of the Argonauts according to Orpheus
— · — · — · — · — · Pindar
— · · — · · — · · Apollonius

A MAP OF THE VOYAGE ON THE ARGONAUTS.

Drawn according to the principal classical traditions. The voyage through the ocean which, according to the ancient idea, surrounded the world will be especially noted.

heroes, for all their courage, feared "that dreadful sea and its rocks and shoals and fogs and bitter freezing storms," and they trembled as they saw it "stretching out before them without a shore, as far as the eye could see."

Wearily they sailed on past the coast of Asia; they passed Sinope and the cities of the Amazons, the warlike women of the east, until at last they saw the "white snow peaks hanging glittering sharp and bright above the clouds. And they knew that they were come to Caucasus at the end of all the earth—Caucasus, the highest of all mountains, the father of the rivers of the East. And they rowed three days to the eastward, while the Caucasus rose higher hour by hour, till they saw the dark stream of Phasis rushing headlong to the sea and, shining above the treetops, the golden roofs of the Child of the Sun."

How they reached home no man knows. Some say they sailed up the Danube River and so came to the Adriatic, dragging their ship over the snowclad Alps. Others say they sailed south to the Red Sea and dragged their ship over the burning desert of North Africa. More than once they gave themselves up for lost, " heart-broken with toil and hunger," until the brave helmsman cried to them, " Raise up the mast and set the sail and face what comes like men."

After days and weeks on the " wide wild western sea " they sailed by the coast of Spain and came to Sicily, the " three-cornered island," and after numerous adventures they reached home once more. And they limped ashore weary and worn, with long, ragged beards and sunburnt cheeks and garments torn and weather-stained. No strength had they left to haul the ship up the beach. They just crawled out and sat down and wept, till they could weep no more. For the houses and trees were all altered, and all the faces which they saw were strange ; and their joy was swallowed up in sorrow while they thought of their youth and all their labour, and the gallant comrades they had lost. And the people crowded round and asked them, " Who are you that sit weeping here ? "

" We are the sons of your princes, who sailed away many a year ago. We went to fetch the Golden Fleece and we have brought it back." Then there was shouting and laughing and weeping, and all the kings came to the shore, and they led the heroes away to their homes and bewailed the valiant dead. Old and charming as is the story of the Argonauts, it is made up of travellers' tales, probably told to the Greeks by the Phœnicians of their adventures on unknown seas.

The wanderings of Ulysses by the old Greek poet Homer shows us that, though they seldom ventured beyond the Mediterranean Sea, yet the Greeks were dimly conscious of an outer world beyond the recognised limits. They still dreamt that the earth was flat, and that the ocean stream flowed for ever round and round it. There were no maps or charts to guide the intrepid mariners who embarked on unknown waters.

The siege of Troy, famous in legend, was over, and the heroes were anxious to make their way home. Ulysses was one of the heroes, and he sailed forth from Asia Minor into the Ægean Sea. But contrary winds drove him as far south as Cape Malea.

" Now the gatherer of the clouds," he says, in telling his story, " aroused the North Wind against our ships with a terrible tempest, and covered land and sea alike with clouds, and down sped night from heaven. Thus the ships were driven headlong, and their sails were torn to shreds by the might of the wind. So we lowered the sails into the hold in fear of death, and rowed the ships landward apace."

Throughout all ages Cape Malea has been renowned for sudden and violent storms, dreaded by early mariners as well as those of later times.

" Thence for nine whole days was I borne by ruinous winds over the teeming deep ; but on the tenth day we set foot on the land of the lotus-eaters who eat a flowery food."

Now ten days' sail to the south would have brought

Ulysses to the coast of North Africa, and here we imagine the lotus-eaters dwelt. But their stay was short. For as soon as the mariners tasted the " honey-sweet fruit of the lotus " they forgot their homes, forgot their own land, and only wanted to stay with the " mild-eyed melancholy lotus-eaters."

> "They sat them down upon the yellow sand,
> Between the sun and moon upon the shore;
> And sweet it was to dream of Fatherland,
> Of child, and wife, and slave; but evermore
> Most weary seem'd the sea, weary the oar,
> Weary the wandering fields of barren foam.
> Then someone said: ' We will return no more';
> And all at once they sang, ' Our island home
> Is far beyond the wave; we will no longer roam.'"

" Therefore," said Ulysses, " I led them back to the ships, weeping and sore against their will, and dragged them beneath the benches. Soon they embarked and, sitting orderly, they smote the grey sea water with their oars. Thence we sailed onward, stricken at heart. And we came to the land of the Cyclops."

No one knows exactly where the land of the Cyclops is. Some think it may be Sicily and the slopes of Mount Etna facing the sea.

The famous rock of Scylla and whirlpool of Charybdis, known to the ancients as two sea-monsters, near the Straits of Messina, next claimed his attention. Let us see how Ulysses passed them.

" We began to sail up the narrow strait," he says, lamenting. " For on the one side lay Scylla and on the other mighty Charybdis sucking down the salt sea water. Like a cauldron on a great fire she would seethe up through all her troubled deeps, and overhead the spray fell on the top of either cliff—the rock around roared horribly, and pale fear gat hold on my men. Toward her, then, we

2

looked, fearing destruction ; but Scylla meanwhile caught
from out my hollow ships six of my company. They
cried aloud in their agony, and there she devoured them
shrieking at her gates, they stretching forth their hands to
me in their death struggles. And the most pitiful thing
was this, that mine eyes have seen of all my travail in
searching out the paths of the sea."

Some have thought that the terrifying stories of Scylla,
Charybdis, and the Cyclops were stories invented by the
Phœnicians to frighten travellers of other nations away
from the sea that they wished to keep for themselves
for purposes of trade.

It would take too long to tell of the great storm that
destroyed the ships and drowned the men, leaving Ulysses
to make a raft on which he drifted about for nine days,
blown back to Scylla and Charybdis and from thence to
the island of Ogygia, " in the centre of the sea." Finally
he reached his home in Ithaca so changed, so aged and
weather-worn, that only his dog Argus recognised him.

This, very briefly, is Homer's world-picture of a bygone
age, when those who were seized with a thirst for travel
sailed about the Mediterranean in their primitive ships,
landing on unnamed coasts, cruising about unknown
islands, meeting strange people, encountering strange
adventures.

It all reads like an old fairy tale to us to-day, for
we have our maps and charts and know the where-
abouts of every country and island about the tideless
Mediterranean.

"THE UNROLLING OF THE CLOUDS"—I.

The world as known at the time of Homer.

CHAPTER III

IS THE WORLD FLAT?

STILL, although the men of ancient time were learning fast about the land and sea, they were woefully ignorant. Hesiod, a Greek poet, who lived seven hundred and fifty years before the Christian era, declared that the world was flat, and the ocean stream or the " perfect river," as he called it, flowed round and round, encompassing all things.

Still, there was something beyond the water—something dim, mysterious, unknowable. It might be the " Islands of the Blest "; it might be the " sacred isle." One thing he asserted firmly: " Atlas upholds the broad Heaven . . . standing on earth's verge with head and unwearied hands," while the clear-voiced Hesperides guarded their beautiful golden apples "beyond the waters of Ocean."

> " Hesperus and his daughters three
> That sung about the golden tree."

But who thinks now of the weary Titan doomed for ever to support the ancient world on his head and hands, when the atlas of to-day is brought forth for a lesson in geography ?

About this time comes a story—it may be fact or it may be fiction—that the Phœnicians had sailed right round Africa. The voyage was arranged by Neco, an enterprising Egyptian king, who built his ships in the Red Sea in the year 613 B.C. The story is told by Herodotus, the Greek traveller, many years afterwards.

"Libya," he says, "is known to be washed on all sides by the sea, except where it is attached to Asia. This discovery was first made by Neco, the Egyptian king, who sent a number of ships manned by Phœnicians with orders to make for the Pillars of Hercules (now known as the Straits of Gibraltar), and return to Egypt through them and by the Mediterranean Sea. The Phœnicians took their departure from Egypt by way of the Erythræan Sea, and so sailed into the Southern Ocean. When autumn came (it is supposed they left the Red Sea in August) they went ashore, wherever that might happen to be, and, having sown a tract of land with corn, waited until the grain was fit to cut. Having reaped it, they set sail, and thus it came to pass that two whole years went by, and it was not till the third year that they doubled the Pillars of Hercules and made good their voyage home. On their return they declared (I, for my part, says Herodotus, do not believe them, but perhaps others may) that in sailing round Libya they had the sun upon their right hand. In this way was the extent of Libya first discovered."

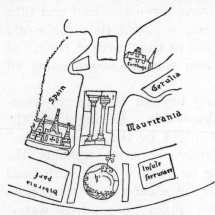

THE PILLARS OF HERCULES, AS SHOWN IN A MEDIÆVAL MAP.

Higden's Map of the World, 1360 A.D.

To modern students, who have learnt more of Phœnician enterprise, the story does not seem so incredible as it did to Herodotus; and a modern poet, Edwin Arnold, has dreamed into verse a delightful account of what this voyage may have been like.

Ithobal of Tyre, Chief Captain of the seas, standing

before Neco, Pharaoh and King, Ruler of Nile and its
lands, relates the story of his two years' voyage, of the
strange things he saw, of the hardships he endured, of
the triumphant end. He tells how, with the help of
mechanics from Tarshish, Tyre, and Sidon, he built
three goodly ships, "Ocean's children," in a "wind-
less creek" on the Red Sea, how he loaded them with
cloth and beads, "the wares wild people love," food-flour
for the ship, cakes, honey, oil, pulse, meal, dried fish and
rice, and salted goods. Then the start was made down
the Red Sea, until at last "the great ocean opened"
east and south to the unknown world and into the great
nameless sea, by the coast of that "Large Land whence
none hath come" they sailed.

Ithobal had undertaken no light task; contrary
winds, mutiny on board, want of fresh water, all the
hardships that confront the mariner who pilots his crews
in search of the unknown. Strange tribes met them on
the coast and asked them whither they went.

> "We go as far as the sun goes
> As far as the sea rolls, as far as the stars
> Shine still in sky. To find for mighty Pharaoh what his world
> Holds hidden."

South and ever south they sailed, "day after day
and night succeeding night, close clinging to the
shore." New stars appeared, lower and lower sank the
sun, moons rose and waned, and still the coast stretched
southwards till they reached a "Cape of Storms" and
found the coast was turning north. And now occurred
that strange phenomenon mentioned by Herodotus, that
while sailing westwards the sun was on their right
hand. "No man had seen that thing in Syria or in
Egypt."

A year and a half had now passed away since they

left home, but onward to the north they now made
their way, past the mouth of the golden waters (Orange
River), past the Congo, past the Niger, past the island of
Gorillas described by Hanno, who explored the west coast
under Neco either before or after this time, until at last
the little Phœnician ships sailed peacefully into the
Mediterranean Sea.

> " Here is the Ocean-Gate.   Here is the Strait
> Twice before seen, where goes the Middle Sea
> Unto the Setting Sun and the Unknown—
> No more unknown, Ithobal's ships have sailed
> Around all Africa.   Our task is done.
> These are the Pillars, this the Midland Sea.
> The road to Tyre is yonder.   Every wave
> Is homely.   Yonder, sure, Old Nilus pours
> Into this Sea, the Waters of the World,
> Whose secret is his own and thine and mine."

It will ever remain one of the many disputed points
in early geography whether
or not Africa was circum-
navigated at this early date.
If the Phœnicians did ac-
complish such a feat they
kept their experiences a
secret as usual, and the early
maps gave a very wrong idea
of South Africa.   On the
other hand, we know they
had good seaworthy ships in
advance of their neighbours.

THE PILLARS OF HERCULES, AS SHOWN
IN THE ANGLO-SAXON MAP OF THE
WORLD, TENTH CENTURY.

" I remember," says Xenophon, " I once went aboard
a Phœnician ship, where I observed the best example of
good order that I ever met with ; and especially it was
surprising to observe the vast numbers of implements
which were necessary for the management of such a small
vessel.   What numbers of oars, stretchers, ship-hooks,

and spikes were there for bringing the ship in and out of the harbour! What numbers of shrouds, cables, ropes, and other tackling for the ship! What a vast quantity of provisions were there for the sustenance and support of the sailors!" Captain and sailors knew where everything was stowed away on board, and " while the captain stood upon the deck, he was considering with himself what things might be wanting in his voyage, what things wanted repair, and what length of time his provisions would last; for, as he observed to me, it is no proper time, when the storm comes upon us, to have the necessary

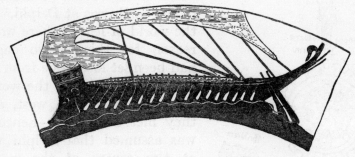

A GREEK GALLEY ABOUT 500 B.C.
From a vase-painting.

implements to seek, or to be out of repair, or to want them on board; for the gods are never favourable to those who are negligent or lazy; and it is their goodness that they do not destroy us when we are diligent."

There is an old story which says that one day the Greeks captured a Phœnician ship and copied it. However this may be, the Greeks soon became great colonisers themselves, and we have to thank a Greek philosopher living in Miletus, on the coast of Asia Minor, for making the first map of the ancient world. Of course, the Babylonians and Egyptians had made maps thousands of years before this, but this Greek-Anaximander introduced the idea of map-making to the astonished world about the year 580 B.C. What was the map like? It was "a bronze tablet, whereupon the whole circuit of the Earth was engraved with all its seas and rivers."

This is all we know. But this map-making Greek was famous for another idea in advance of his time. He used to study the heavens and the earth, and after much study he made up his mind that the earth was round and not flat. He taught that the world hung free in the midst of the universe, or rather in the midst of the waters. The centre of the earth was at Delphi. In the world of legend there was a reason for this. Two eagles had been let loose, one from the eastern extremity of the world, the other from the west, and they met at Delphi—hence it was assumed that Delphi was at the centre of the world. And Delphi at this time was such a wonderful city. On the slopes of Mount Parnassus it stood high on a rock—on the heights stood the temple of Apollo with its immense riches,

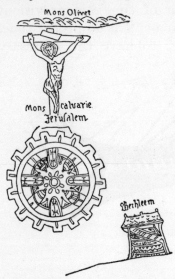

JERUSALEM, THE CENTRE OF THE WORLD.
From the Hereford Map of the World, thirteenth century.

its golden statue of the great god, and its ever-smoking fire of wood.

In the same way, in those days of imperfect geography, as we hear of Delphi being the centre of the Greek world, so we hear of Jerusalem being considered the central point of the world.

"This is Jerusalem," says Ezekiel, "in the midst of the nations and countries that are round about her."

In the Mappa Mundi (thirteenth century) in Hereford Cathedral, Jerusalem is still the centre of the earth.

Following close on these ideas came another. It, too, came from Miletus, now famous for its school of thought and its searchers after truth.

A *Tour of the World* is the grand-sounding title of the work of Hecatæus, who wrote it about 500 years B.C. It contains an account of the coast and islands of the Mediterranean Sea and an outline of all the lands the Greeks thought they knew. In the fragments that have come down to us, the famous old geographer divides both his work and the world into two parts. One part he calls Europe, the other Asia, in which he includes Africa bounded by the river Nile. He held that these two parts were equal. They were divided from one another by the Mediterranean Sea, the Black Sea, and the Caspian Sea, while round the whole flat world still flowed the everlasting ocean stream.

CHAPTER IV

HERODOTUS—THE TRAVELLER

THE greatest traveller of olden times now comes upon the scene—Herodotus, the Greek, the "Father of History."

He is a traveller as well as a writer. He has journeyed as one eager for knowledge, with a "hungry heart" and a keen, observant eye. He tells us what he has seen with his eyes, what he has heard with his ears. He insists that the world is flat, he acknowledges that it is divided into two parts—Europe and Asia; but he can afford to laugh at those who draw maps of the world "without any sense to guide them," in which they make the whole world round as if drawn with a pair of compasses, with the ocean stream running round it, making Europe and Asia of equal size.

His first journey is to Egypt.

"I speak at length about Egypt," he says, "because it contains more marvellous things than any other country—things too strange for words. Not only is the climate different from that of the rest of the world and the rivers unlike any other rivers, but the people also, in most of their manners and customs, reverse the common practice of mankind. The women are employed in trade and business, while the men stay at home to spin and weave. Other nations in weaving throw the woof up the warp, but an Egyptian throws it down. In other countries, sons are constrained to make provision for their parents; in Egypt it is not only the sons, but the daughters. In other countries the priests have long hair; in Egypt their heads are shaven. Other nations fasten their ropes and hooks to the outside of their sails, but the Egyptians to the inside. The Greeks write and read from left to right, but the Egyptians from right to left."

After sailing for some seven hundred miles up the river Nile from the coast, past Heliopolis, the once famous city of Ancient Egypt, past Memphis, the old capital, past Thebes, with its hundred gates, to Elephantine, the "ivory island," opposite to what is now Assuan, he is more than ever puzzled about its course and the reason of its periodical floods.

"Concerning the nature of the river, I was not able to gain any information from the priests. I was particularly anxious to learn from them why the Nile, at the commencement of the summer solstice, begins to rise and continues to increase for a hundred days—and why, as soon as that number is past, it forthwith retires and contracts its stream, continuing low during the whole of the winter until the summer solstice comes round again. On none of these points could I obtain any explanation from the inhabitants, though I made every inquiry."

The sources of the Nile entirely baffled Herodotus as they baffled many another later explorer long years after he had passed away. "Of the sources of the Nile no one can give any account, since the country through which it passes is desert and without inhabitants," he explains, his thirst for knowledge unsatisfied. Some priest volunteers this explanation. On the frontiers of Egypt are two high mountain-peaks called Crophi and Mophi; in an unfathomable abyss between the two rose the Nile. But Herodotus does not believe in Crophi and Mophi; he inclines to the idea that the Nile rises away in the west and flows eastward right across Libya.

He travelled a little about Libya himself, little realising

the size of the great continent of Africa through which he passed. Many a strange tale of these unknown parts did he relate to his people at home. He had seen the tallest and handsomest race of men in the world, who lived to the age of one hundred and twenty years—gold was so abundant that it was used even for the prisoners' chains— he had seen folks who lived on meat and milk only, never having seen bread or wine.

Some thirty days' journey from the land of the lotus-eaters he had found tribes who hunted with four-horse

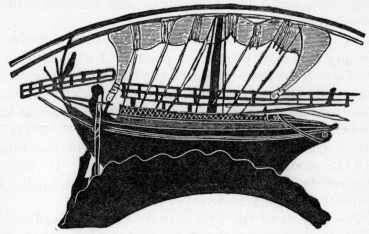

A MERCHANT-SHIP OF ATHENS, ABOUT 500 B.C.
From a vase-painting.

chariots and whose oxen walked backwards as they grazed, because their horns curve outwards in front of their heads, and if they moved forwards these horns would stick in the ground.

Right across the desolate sandy desert of the north, Herodotus seems to have made his way. The "region of the wild beasts" must have been truly perilous, "for this is the tract," he says, "in which huge serpents are found, and the lions, the elephants, the bears, and the horned asses."

He also tells us of antelopes, gazelles, asses, foxes, wild sheep, jackals, and panthers. There is no end to the quaint sights he records. Here is a tribe whose wives drive the chariots to battle, here another who paint themselves red and eat honey and monkeys, another who grow their hair long on the right side of their heads and shave it close on the left. Back through Egypt to Syria went our observant traveller, visiting the famous seaport of Tyre on the way. " I visited the temple of Hercules at that place and found two pillars, one of pure gold, the other of emerald, shining with great brilliancy at night." That temple was already two thousand three hundred years old.

Herodotus makes some astounding statements about various parts of the world. He asserts that a good walker could walk across Asia Minor, from north to south, in five days, a distance we know now to be three hundred miles ! He tells us that the Danube rises in the Pyrenees Mountains and flows right through Europe till it empties its waters into the Black Sea, giving us a long and detailed account of a country he calls Scythia (Russia) with many rivers flowing into this same Black Sea.

But here we must leave the old traveller and picture him reading aloud to his delighted hearers his account of his discoveries and explorations, discussing with the learned Greeks of the day the size and wonders of the world as they imagined it.

News travelled slowly in these bygone days, and we know the Phœnicians were very fond of keeping their discoveries secret, but it seems strange to think that Herodotus never seems to have heard the story of Hanno the Carthaginian, who coasted along the west of North Africa, being the first explorer to reach the place we know as " Sierra Leone."

Hanno's " Periplus," or the " Coasting Survey of Hanno," is one of the few Phœnician documents that has lived through the long ages. In it the commander of the expedition himself tells his own story. With an idea of colonising, he left Carthage—the most famous of the Phœnician colonies—with sixty ships containing an enormous number of men and women.

"When we had set sail," says Hanno shortly, "and passed the pillars (of Hercules) after two days' voyage, we founded the first city. Below this city lay a great plain. Sailing thence westward we came to a promontory of Libya thickly covered with trees. Here we built a temple to the Sea-god and proceeded thence half a day's journey eastward, till we reached a lake lying not far from the sea and filled with abundance of great reeds. Here were feeding elephants and a great number of other wild animals. After we had gone a day's sail beyond the lakes we founded cities near to the sea."

Making friends with the tribes along the coast, they reached the Senegal River. Here they fell in with "savage men clothed with the skins of beasts," who pelted them with stones so that they could not land. Past Cape Verde they reached the mouth of the Gambia, "great and broad and full of crocodiles and river-horses," and thence coasted twelve days to the south and again five days to the south, which brought them to Sierra Leone—the Lion Mountain as it was called long years after by the Portuguese.

Here Hanno and his party landed, but as night approached they saw flames issuing from the island and heard the sound of flutes and cymbals and drums and the noise of confused shouts.

"Great fear then came upon us; we sailed therefore quickly thence much terrified, and passing on for four days found at night a country full of fire. In the middle was a lofty fire, greater than all the rest, so that it seemed to touch the stars. When day came on we found that this was a great mountain which they called the chariot of the

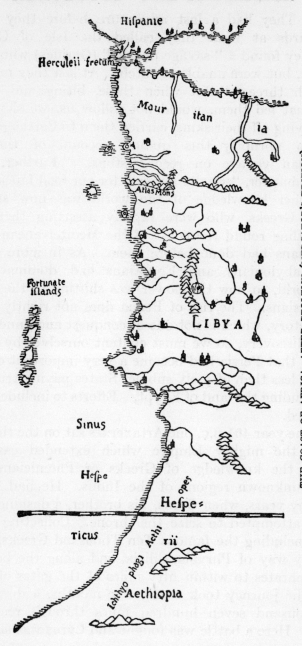

Hispanie

Herculeii fretum

Maur itan ia

Atlas Mons

Fortunate iſlands

LIBYA

Sinus

Heſpe opes

Heſpes

Ticus Achi rii

Ichthyo phagi

Ichthyo phagi Aethiopia

THE COAST OF AFRICA, AFTER PTOLEMY (MERCATOR'S EDITION).

This map shows the extent of Hanno's voyage from the Pillars of Hercules, past the Equator, to what is now called Sierra Leone gods." They had a last adventure before they turned homewards at what they called the Isle of Gorillas. Here they found a " savage people " (Gorillas) whom they pursued, but were unable to catch. At last they managed to catch three. " But when these, biting and tearing those that led them, would not follow us, we slew them and, flaying off their skins, carried them to Carthage."

Then abruptly this quaint account of the only Phœnician voyage on record stops. " Further," says the commander, " we did not sail, for our food failed us."

Further knowledge of the world was now supplied by the Greeks, who were rapidly asserting themselves and settling round the coast of the Mediterranean as the Phœnicians had done before them. As in more ancient days Babylonians and Egyptians had dominated the little world, so now the power was shifting to the Greeks and Persians. The rise of Persia does not rightly belong to this story, which is not one of conquest and annexation, but of discovery, so we must content ourselves by stating the fact that Persia had become a very important country with no less than fifty-six subject States paying tribute to her, including the land of Egypt. Efforts to include Greece had failed.

In the year 401 B.C. one Artaxerxes sat on the throne of Persia, the mighty Empire which extended eastwards beyond the knowledge of Greeks or Phœnicians, even to the unknown regions of the Indus. He had reigned for many years, when Cyrus, his brother, a dashing young prince, attempted to seize the throne. Collecting a huge army, including the famous Ten Thousand Greeks, he led them by way of Phrygia, Cilicia, and along the banks of the Euphrates to within fifty miles of the gates of Babylon. The journey took nearly five months, a distance of one thousand seven hundred miles through recognised tracks. Here a battle was fought and Cyrus was slain.

It was midwinter when the Ten Thousand Greeks who had followed their leader so loyally through the plains of Asia Minor found themselves friendless and in great danger in the very heart of the enemy's country.

How Xenophon—a mere Greek volunteer, who had accompanied the army from the shores of Asia Minor—rose up and offered to lead his countrymen back to Greece is a matter of history. It would take too long to tell in detail how they marched northward through the Assyrian plains, past the neighbourhood of Nineveh, till they reached the mountain regions which were known to be inhabited by fierce fighters, unconquered even by the powerful Persians.

Up to this time their line of retreat had followed the " royal road " of merchants and caravans. Their only chance of safety lay in striking north into the mountains inhabited by this warlike tribe who had held out amid their wild and rugged country against the Persians themselves. They now opposed the Greeks with all their might, and it took seven days of continuous fighting to reach the valley which lay between them and the high tableland of Armenia. They crossed the Tigris near its source, and a little farther on they also crossed the Euphrates not far from its source, so they were informed by the Armenians. They now found themselves some five or six thousand feet above sea-level and in the midst of a bitter Armenian winter. Snow fell heavily, covering all tracks, and day after day a cold north-east wind, " whose bitter blast was torture," increased their sufferings as they ploughed their way on and on through such depths of snow as they had never seen before.

Many died of cold and hunger, many fell grievously sick, and others suffered from snow-blindness and frostbite.

But Xenophon led his army on, making his notes of

3

the country through which they were toiling, measuring distances by the day's march, and at last one day when the soldiers were climbing a steep mountain, a cry, growing louder and more joyous every moment, rent the air—

" Thalassa ! Thalassa ! The sea ! The sea ! "

True enough, on the distant horizon, glittering in the sunlight, was a narrow silver streak of sea—the Black Sea—the goal of all their hopes. The long struggle of five months was over ; they could sail home now along the shores of the Black Sea. They had reached the coast near the spot Colchis, where the Argonauts landed to win the Golden Fleece long centuries before.

In a work known as the *Anabasis*, Xenophon wrote the adventures of the Ten Thousand Greeks, and no geographical explorer ever recorded his travels through unknown countries more faithfully than did the Greek leader of twenty-three hundred years ago.

CHAPTER V

ALEXANDER THE GREAT EXPLORES INDIA

STILL greater light was shed on the size of the world by Alexander the Great on his famous expedition to India, by which he almost doubled the area of the world known to the people of his time. It was just sixty years after Xenophon had made his way right across Asia to the shores of the Black Sea when Alexander resolved to break, if possible, the power of the Persians.

The great Persian Empire extended from the shores of the Mediterranean right away to the east, far beyond the knowledge of the Greeks. Indeed, their knowledge of the interior of Asia was very imperfect, and Alexander's expedition was rather that of an explorer than of a conqueror. How he overthrew the Persians and subdued an area as large as Europe in the space of twelve years reads like a romance rather than fact, and it is not for us to tell the story in detail. Rather let us take up the story, after Alexander has fought and conquered the Persians twice, besieged Tyre, taken the Phœnician fleet, occupied Egypt, marched across the desert and crossed the Euphrates, passed over the plain and followed the Tigris to near Nineveh, where he crossed that river too, fought another famous battle over the Persians, which decided the fate of King and Monarchy and opened to him the capitals of Babylon and Susa, wherein the immense treasures of the Persian Empire were stored. King of all Asia. he sat on the throne of the Persian kings under a golden canopy in the palace of Persepolis.

So far the whole expedition was over country known, if imperfectly, to the Greeks. Now we have to follow the conquering hero more closely as he leads us into an unknown land away to the east, known as " the farthest region of the inhabited world towards the east, beyond which lies the endless sandy desert void of inhabitants." And all the while the great land of India lay beyond, and beyond again was China, and away far over the ocean sea lay America—and they knew it not.

Alexander was a young man yet, only twenty-six. It was four years since he had left Europe, and in that short time he had done wonders. He had conquered the whole eastern half of the Persian Empire. Now he resolutely turned his face to the unknown east and started forth on an expedition of exploration.

Following the main highway from Media, which to-day leads from Teheran, capital of modern Persia, into the land of the Turkomans and the borders of Russia, he found himself between the great salt desert and the mountains, which to-day mark the frontier of Persia. Suddenly, to his great surprise, the Caspian Sea came into sight. It seemed about the same size as the Black Sea, and he concluded it was connected with the Sea of Azof, though the men of his day were certain enough that it was the most northern of four great gulfs connected with the outer ocean which flowed round the world.

Onwards towards the east he marched with his great army. To conciliate the tribes through which he passed, he adopted Persian dress. This annoyed his Greek countrymen, but, " as they admired his other virtues, they thought he might be suffered to please himself a little and enjoy his vanity."

Arrived at the modern boundary between Persia, Afghanistan, and Russia, he and his men pushed on across Afghanistan, by the caravan route that had long existed from the shores of the Caspian, by modern Herat, Kandahar,[1] which still bears the conqueror's name, and Kabul to India. Their way lay through deep snow, deeper than they had ever seen before; and by the time they had reached the mountains of Kabul it was midwinter.

Between Alexander and India still lay the lofty range of the Hindu Koosh or Indian Caucasus. But before going south toward India, he turned northwards to explore the unknown country which lay about the river Oxus. They found the Oxus, a mighty stream, swollen with melting snows. There were no boats and no wood to build them, so Alexander pioneered his men across in "life-preservers" made out of their leather tent coverings and stuffed with straw. This river impressed the Greeks even more than the Euphrates and Tigris, as it impressed many an explorer and poet since these early days. Let us recall Matthew Arnold's famous description of the Oxus, now seen for the first time by the Greeks.

> "But the majestic river floated on,
>   Out of the mist and hum of that low land,
>   Into the frosty starlight, and there moved
>
> .   .   .   .   .
>
>   Brimming, and bright, and large; then sands begin
> To hem his watery march and dam his streams,
> And split his currents; that for many a league
> The shorn and parcell'd Oxus strains along
> Through beds of sand and matted rushy isles—
> Oxus, forgetting the bright speed he had,
> In his high mountain-cradle in Pamere,
> A foil'd circuitous wanderer—till at last
> The long'd for dash of waves is heard, and wide
> His luminous home of waters opens, bright
> And tranquil, from whose floor the new-bathed stars
> Emerge, and shine upon the Aral Sea."

Here in this valley the Greeks met more determined opposition than they had yet encountered since entering

---

[1] Kandahar = Alexandria in a modern form..

Asia, and over two years were occupied in reducing this single district (now Bokhara and Turkestan) to submission, though it was only some three hundred and fifty miles square, and in one single year Alexander had conquered a kingdom over one thousand miles in width.

It was not till the spring of 327 B.C. that he was ready to cross the Hindu Koosh and begin the great expedition into India. The night before the start Alexander discovered that his troops were now so heavily laden with spoils that they were quite unfit for the long march. So in the early morning, when they were all ready to start, he suddenly set fire to his own baggage, and, giving orders that all his men were to do the same, the army started for the passes of the lofty mountain range. And—

> ". . . as a troop of pedlars from Kabul
> Cross underneath the Indian Caucasus,
> That vast sky neighbouring mountain of milk snow;
> Crossing so high, that, as they mount, they pass
> Long flocks of travelling birds dead on the snow,
> Choked by the air, and scarce can they themselves
> Slake their parch'd throats with sugar'd mulberries—
> In single file they move, and stop their breath,
> For fear they should dislodge the o'erhanging snows."

The banks of the river of Kabul were reached at last. Sending part of the army by the now famous Kyber Pass toward the Indus, Alexander himself undertook to subdue the mountain tribes and get control of the Chitral passes. The shepherds of this region opposed him vigorously, but swiftly and pitilessly the King of Asia sacked their peaceful homes, and city after city fell to him as he advanced towards the boundaries of Kashmir.

At last the valley of the Indus was reached. A bridge of boats was hastily thrown over, and Alexander and his army passed to the other side.

Porus, the ruler of the country between the Indus

and the river Hydaspes (Jehlam), sent presents of welcome
to the invader, including three thousand animals for sacrifice, ten thousand sheep, thirty elephants, two hundred
talents of silver, and seven hundred horsemen. The new
king was also greeted with presents of ivory and precious
stones. Even from far Kashmir came greetings to Alexander, whose fame was spreading rapidly. He now
entered the Punjab, the " Land of the Five Rivers." But
on the other side of the river Hydaspes a different reception awaited him.

There the king (Porus) had assembled a sturdy, well-
disciplined troop to dispute the passage of the river, which
still separated the new King of Asia from his territory.
But under cover of a mighty thunderstorm Alexander
contrived to cross, though the river was rushing down
yellow and fierce after the rains. Secretly the Greeks put
together their thirty-oared galleys hidden in a wood, and
utterly surprised Porus by landing on the other side. In
their strange wanderings the Greeks had fought under
varying conditions, but they had never faced elephants
before. Nevertheless, they brilliantly repulsed an on-
slaught of these animals, who slowly retreated, "facing the
foe, like ships backing water, and merely uttering a shrill,
piping sound." Despite the elephants the old story was
repeated, civilised arms triumphed over barbarians, and
the army of Porus was annihilated, his chariots shattered,
and thirty-three thousand men slain.

The kingdom beyond the Hydaspes was now Alexander's. Ordering a great fleet of rafts and boats to be
built for his proposed voyage to the mouth of the Indus,
he pushed on to complete the conquest of the Five Stream
Land, or the Punjab — the last province of the great
Persian Empire. This was India—all that was known at
this time. The India of the Ganges valley was beyond
the knowledge of the Western world—the Ganges itself

unknown to the Persians. And Alexander saw no reason to change his mind.

" The great sea surrounds the whole earth," he stoutly maintained.

But when he reached the eastern limit of the Punjab and heard that beyond lay a fertile land " where the inhabitants were skilled in agriculture, where there were elephants in yet greater abundance and men were superior in stature and courage," the world stretched out before him in an unexpected direction, and he longed to explore farther, to conquer new and utterly unknown worlds!

But at last his men struck. They were weary, some were wounded, some were ill; seventy days of incessant rain had taken the heart out of them.

" I am not ignorant, soldiers," said Alexander to the hesitating troops, " that during the last few days the natives of this country have been spreading all sorts of rumours to work upon your fears. The Persians in this way sought to terrify you with the gates of Cilicia, with the plains of Mesopotamia, with the Tigris and Euphrates, and yet this river you crossed by a ford and that by means of a bridge. By my troth, we had long ago fled from Asia could fables have been able to scare us. We are not standing on the threshold of our enterprise, but at the very close. We have already reached the sunrise and the ocean, and unless your sloth and cowardice prevent, we shall thence return in triumph to our native land, having conquered the earth to its remotest bounds. I beseech you that ye desert not your king just at the very moment when he is approaching the limits of the inhabited world."

But the soldiers, " with their heads bent earthwards," stood in silence. It was not that they *would* not follow him beyond the sunset; they *could* not. Their tears began to flow, sobs reached the ears of Alexander, his anger turned to pity, and he wept with his men.

" Oh, sir," at last cried one of his men, " we have done and suffered up to the full measure of the capacity of mortal nature. We have traversed seas and lands, and know them better than do the inhabitants themselves. We are standing now almost on the earth's utmost verge, and yet you are preparing to go in quest of an India unknown even to the Indians themselves. You would fain root out, from their hidden recesses and dens, a race of men that herd with snakes and wild beasts, so that you may traverse as a conqueror more regions than the sun surveys. But while your courage will be ever growing, our vigour is fast waning to its end. See how bloodless be our bodies, pierced with how many wounds and gashed with how many scars! Our weapons are blunt, our armour worn out! We have been driven to assume the Persian dress! Which of us has a horse? We have conquered all the world, but are ourselves destitute of all things."

The conqueror was at last conquered. The order to turn back was reluctantly given by the disappointed king and leader. It was received with shouts of joy from the mixed multitudes of his followers, and the expedition faced for home. Back they marched through the new lands where no less than two thousand cities had owned his sway, till they came to the banks of the river where the ships were building. Two thousand boats were ready, including eighty thirty-oared galleys.

It was now September 326 B.C.

Nearchus from Crete was made Admiral of the new fleet, which at dawn one October morning pushed out upon the river Hydaspes and set sail downstream towards the unknown sea, Alexander standing proudly on the prow of the royal galley. The trumpets rang out, the oars moved, and the strange argosy, " such as had never been seen before in these parts," made its way down the unknown river to the unknown sea. Natives swarmed to the banks of the river to wonder at the strange sight, marvelling specially to see horses as passengers on board ! The greater part of the army followed the ships on land, marching along the shores. At last the waters of the Hydaspes mingled with those of the Indus, and onwards down this great river floated the Persian fleet. Alexander had no pilots, no local knowledge of the country, but with his " unquenchable ambition to see the ocean and reach the boundaries of the world," he sailed on, "ignorant of everything on the way they had to pass." In vain they asked the natives assembled on the banks how far distant was the sea ; they had never heard of the sea ! At last they found a tide mixing its salt waters with the fresh. Soon a flood-tide burst upon them, forcing back the current of the river, and scattering the fleet. The sailors of the tideless Mediterranean knew nothing of the rise and fall of tides. They were in a state of panic and consternation. Some tried to push off their ships with long poles, others tried to row against the incoming tide ; prows were dashed against poops, oars were broken, sterns were bumped, until at last the sea had flowed over all the level land near the river mouth.

Suddenly a new danger appeared ! The tide turned and the sea began to recede. Further misfortunes now befell the ships. Many were left high and dry ; most of them were damaged in some way or another. Alexander sent horsemen to the seashore with instructions to watch for the return of the tide and to ride back in haste so that the fleet might be prepared.

Thus they got safely out to sea on the next high tide.

Alexander's explorations were now at an end. Leaving Nearchus to explore the seacoast at the mouth of the Indus, he left the spot near where the town of Hyderabad now stands, and turned his face toward the home he was never to reach. We must not linger over his terrible coast journey through the scorching desert of Beluchistan the billows of sand, the glare of the barren sea, the awful thirst, the long hungry marches of forty miles a day under the burning Eastern sun.

Our story is one of discovery, and we must turn to Nearchus, Admiral of the fleet, left behind at the mouth of the Indus to explore the coast to the Persian Gulf, where he was to meet Alexander if possible. Shortly

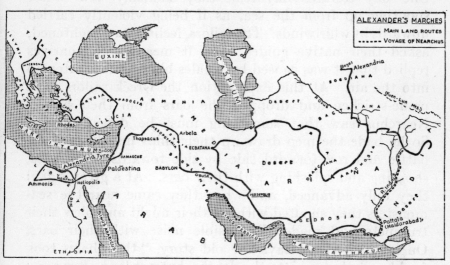

A SKETCH-MAP OF ALEXANDER'S CHIEF EXPLORATORY MARCHES FROM ATHENS TO HYDERABAD AND GAZA.

The dotted line shows the course of Nearchus' voyage down the river Indus, along the northern shores of the Indian Ocean, and up the Persian Gulf to Babylonia.

after the fleet had emerged from the mouth of the Indus a violent south-west monsoon began to blow and Nearchus was obliged to seek shelter in a harbour, which he called the port of Alexander, but which to-day is known as Karachi, the most western seaport of India. The waters of the Indian Ocean were quite unknown to the Greeks, and they could only coast along in sight of land, anchoring at different points for the men to land and get water and food. Past the wild barren shores of Beluchistan they made their way; the natives subsisted on fish entirely even as they do to-day—even their huts being made of fish bones and their bread of pounded fish.

They had but one adventure in their five months' cruise to the Persian Gulf, but we have a graphic account of how the terrified Greeks met a shoal of whales and how they frightened the whales away. Here is the story. One day towards daybreak they suddenly saw water spouting up from the sea, as if being violently carried upwards by whirlwinds. The sailors, feeling very frightened, asked their native guides what it meant. The natives replied that it was caused by whales blowing the water up into the air. At this explanation the Greek sailors were panic-stricken and dropped the oars from their hands. Nearchus saw that something must be done at once. So he bade the men draw up their ships in line as if for battle and row forward side by side towards the whales, shouting and splashing with their oars. At a given signal they duly advanced, and when they came near the sea-monsters they shouted with all their might and blew their trumpets and made all possible noise with their oars. On hearing which, says the old story, " the whales took fright and plunged into the depths, but not long after came to the surface again close to the sterns of the vessels and once more spouted great jets of water. Then the sailors shouted aloud at their happy and unlooked-for escape," and Nearchus was cheered as the saviour of the fleet. It is not uncommon to-day for steamers bound from Aden to Bombay to encounter what is called a " school of whales " similar to those which alarmed the fleet of Nearchus in the year 323 B.C.

The expedition was completely successful and Nearchus pioneered his fleet to the mouth of the Euphrates.

But the death of Alexander the Great and the confusion

that followed set back the advance of geographical
discovery in this direction for some time.

Alexandria — one of the many towns founded by
Alexander—had become the world centre of the learned
from Europe, Asia, and Africa. Its position was unrivalled. Situated at the mouth of the Nile, it commanded the Mediterranean Sea, while by means of the
Red Sea it held easy communication with India and Arabia.

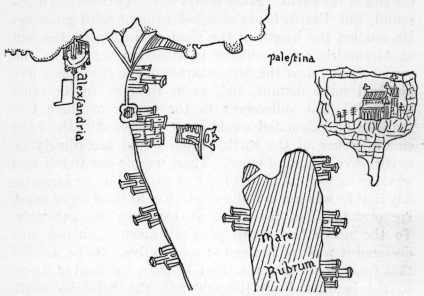

ALEXANDRIA IN PIZZIGANI'S MAP, FOURTEENTH CENTURY.
The river with the buildings on its bank is the Nile.

When Egypt had come under the sway of Alexander,
he had made one of his generals ruler over that country,
and men of intellect collected there to study and to
write. A library was started, and a Greek, Eratosthenes,
held the post of librarian at Alexandria for forty years,
namely, from 240–196 B.C. During this period he made
a collection of all the travels and books of earth description—the first the world had ever known—and stored them

in the Great Library of which he must have felt so justly proud. But Eratosthenes did more than this. He was the originator of Scientific Geography. He realised that no maps could be properly laid down till something was known of the size and shape of the earth.

By this time all men of science had ceased to believe that the world was flat; they thought of it as a perfect round, but fixed at the centre in space. Many had guessed at the size of the earth. Some said it was forty thousand miles round, but Eratosthenes was not content with guessing. He studied the length of the shadow thrown by the sun at Alexandria and compared it with that thrown by the sun at Syene, near the first cataract of the Nile, some five hundred miles distant, and, as he thought, in the same longitude. The differences in the length of these two shadows he calculated would represent one-fiftieth of the circumference of the earth, which would accordingly be twenty-five thousand miles. There was no one to tell him whether he had calculated right or wrong, but we know to-day that he was wonderfully right. But he must know more. He must find out how much of this earth was habitable. To the north and south of the known countries men declared it was too hot or too cold to live. So he decided that from north to south, that is, from the land of Thule to the land of Punt (Somaliland), the habitable earth stretched for some three thousand eight hundred miles, while from east to west — that is, from the Pillars of Hercules (Straits of Gibraltar) to India—would be some eight thousand miles. All the rest was ocean. Ignoring the division of the world into three continents, he divided it into two, north and south, divided by the Mediterranean and by a long range of mountains intersecting the whole of Asia.

Then the famous librarian drew a map of the world for his library at Alexandria, but it has perished with all the rest of the valuable treasure collected in this once celebrated city. We know that he must have made a great many mistakes in drawing a map of his little island world which measured eight thousand miles by three thousand eight hundred miles. It must have been quaintly arranged. The Caspian Sea was connected with a Northern Ocean, the Danube sent a tributary to the Adriatic, there was no Bay of Biscay, the British Isles lay in the wrong direction, Africa was not half its right size, the Ganges flowed into the Eastern Ocean, Ceylon was a huge island stretching east and west, while across the whole of Asia a mountain chain stretched in one long unbroken line. And yet, with all his errors, he was nearer the truth than men three centuries later.

CHAPTER VI

PYTHEAS FINDS THE BRITISH ISLES

FOR some centuries past men had been pushing eastward, and to west, vast lands lay unexplored, undreamt of, amongst them a little far-off island " set in a silver sea." Pytheas was the first explorer to bring the world news of the British Isles.

About the time that Alexander was making his way eastward through Persia, Pytheas was leaving the Greek colony of Marseilles for the west and north. The Phœnicians, with their headquarters at Carthage, had complete command of the mineral trade of Spain—the Mexico of the ancient world. They knew where to find the gold and silver from the rivers—indeed, they said that the coast, from the Tagus to the Pyrenees, was " stuffed with mines of gold and silver and tin." The Greeks were now determined to see for themselves—the men of Carthage should no longer have it all their own way. Where were these tin islands, kept so secret by the master-mariners of the ancient world ?

A committee of merchants met at Marseilles and engaged the services of Pytheas, a great mathematician, and one who made a study of the effect of the moon on the tides. All sorts of vague rumours had reached the ears of Pytheas about the northern regions he was about to visit. He would discover the homes of the tin and amber merchants, he would find the people who lived " at the back of the north wind," he would reach a land of perpetual sunshine, where swans sang like nightingales and life was one unending banquet.

So Pytheas, the mathematician of Marseilles started off on his northern trip. Unfortunately, his diary and book called *The Circuit of the Earth* have perished, and our story of geographical discovery is the poorer. But these facts have survived.

The ships first touched at Cadiz, the " Tyre of the West," a famous port in those days, where Phœnician merchants lived, " careless and secure " and rich. This was the limit of Greek geographical knowledge ; here were the Pillars of Hercules, beyond which all was dim and mysterious and interesting. Five days' sail, that is to say, some three hundred miles along the coast of Spain, brought Pytheas to Cape St. Vincent.

He thought he was navigating the swift ocean river flowing round the world. He was, therefore, surprised to find as he rounded the Cape that the current had ceased, or, in his own words, the " ebb came to an end." Three days more and they were at the mouth of the Tagus. Near this part of the coast lay the Tin Islands, according to Greek ideas, though even to-day their exact locality is uncertain. Pytheas must have heard the old tradition that the Cassiterides were ten in number and lay near each other in the ocean, that they were inhabited by people who wore black cloaks and long tunics reaching to the feet, that they walked with long staves and subsisted by their cattle. They led a wandering life ; they bartered hides, tin, and lead with the merchants in exchange for pottery, salt, and implements of bronze.

That these islands had already been visited by Himilco the Carthaginian seems fairly certain. He had started from Cadiz for the north when Hanno started for the south. From the Tin Islands his fleet had ventured forth into the open sea. Thick fogs had hidden the sun and

4

the ships were driven south before a north wind till they reached, though they did not know it, the Sargasso Sea, famous for its vast plains of seaweed, through which it was difficult to push the ships.

" Sea animals," he tells us, " crept upon the tangled weed." It has been thought that with a little good fortune Himilco might have discovered America two thousand years before the birth of Columbus. But Himilco returned home by the Azores or Fortunate Islands, as they were called.

Leaving the Tin Islands, Pytheas voyaged on to Cape Finisterre, landing on the island of Ushant, where he found a temple served by women priests who kept up a perpetual fire in honour of their god. Thence Pytheas sailed prosperously on up the English Channel till he struck the coast of Kent. Britain, he announced, was several days' journey from Ushant, and about one hundred and seventy miles to the north. He sailed round part of the coast, making notes of distances, but these are curiously exaggerated. This was not unnatural, for the only method of determining distance was roughly based on the number of miles that a ship could go in an hour along the shore. Measuring in this primitive fashion, Pytheas assures us that Britain is a continent of enormous size, and that he has discovered a " new world." It is, he says, three cornered in shape, something like the head of a battleaxe. The south side, lying opposite the coast of France, is eight hundred and thirty-five miles in length, the eastern coast is sixteen hundred and sixty-five miles, the western two thousand two hundred and twenty-two— indeed, the whole country was thought to be over four thousand miles in circumference. These calculations must have been very upsetting to the old geographers of that age, because up to this time they had decided that the whole world was only three thousand four hundred miles long and six thousand eight hundred broad.

He tells us that he made journeys into the interior of Britain, that the inhabitants drink mead, and that there is an abundance of wheat in the fields.

" The natives," he says, " collect the sheaves in great barns and thrash out the corn there, because they have so little sunshine that an open thrashing-place would be of little use in that land of clouds and rain." He seems to have voyaged north as far as the Shetland Islands, but he never saw Ireland.

Having returned from the north of the Thames, Pytheas crossed the North Sea to the mouth of the Rhine, a passage which took about two and a half days. He gives a pitiable account of the people living on the Dutch coast and their perpetual struggle with the sea. The natives had not learnt the art of making dykes and embankments. A high tide with a wind setting toward the shore would sweep over the low-lying country and swamp their homes. A mounted horseman could barely gallop from the rush and force of these strong North Sea tides.

But the Greek geographers would not believe this; they only knew the tideless Mediterranean, and they thought Pytheas was lying when he told of the fierce northern sea. Pytheas sailed past the mouth of the Elbe, noting the amber cast upon the shore by the high spring tides. But all these interesting discoveries paled before the famous land of Thule, six days' voyage north of Britain, in the neighbourhood of the frozen ocean. Grand excitement reigned among geographers when they heard of Thule, and a very sea of romance rose up around the name. Had Pytheas indeed found the end of the world? Was it an island? Was it mainland? In the childhood of the world, when so little was known and so much imagined, men's minds caught at the name of Thule—

Ultima Thule—far-away Thule, and weaved round it
many and beautiful legends.   But to-day we ask : Was it
Iceland ?   Was it Lapland ?   Was it one of the Shetland
Isles ?

"Pytheas said that the farthest parts of the world
are those which lie about Thule, the northernmost of the
Britannic Isles, but he never said whether Thule was an
island or whether the world was habitable by man as
far as that point.   I should think myself "—the speaker

NORTH BRITAIN AND THE ISLAND OF THULE.
From Mercator's edition of Ptolemy's map.

is Strabo, a famous Greek traveller who wrote seventeen
books of geography — "I should think myself that the
northern limit of habitude lies much farther to the south,
for the writers of our age say nothing of any place beyond
Ireland, which is situate in front of the northern parts of
Britain." Pytheas said that Thule was six days' sail
north of Britain. "But who in his senses would believe
this ?" cries Strabo again. "For Pytheas, who described Thule, has been shown to be the falsest of men.
A traveller, starting from the middle of Britain and going

five hundred miles to the north, would come to a country somewhere about Ireland, where living would be barely possible."

The first account of the Arctic regions likewise reads like pure romance to the ignorant and untravelled. "After one day's journey to the north of Thule," says Pytheas, "men come to a sluggish sea, where there is no separation of sea, land, and air, but a mixture of these elements like the substance of jelly-fish, through which one can neither walk nor sail." Here the nights were very short, sometimes only two hours, after which the sun rose again. This, in fact, was the "Sleeping Palace of the Sun."

With all this wealth of discovery, Pytheas returned home by the Bay of Biscay to the mouth of the Gironde; thence he sailed up the Garonne, and from the modern town of Bordeaux he reached Marseilles by an overland journey.

CHAPTER VII

JULIUS CÆSAR AS EXPLORER

OUR next explorer is Julius Cæsar. As Alexander the Great had combined the conqueror with the explorer, so now history repeats itself, and we find the Roman Cæsar not only conquering, but exploring. It was Cæsar who first dispelled the mist that lay over the country about the French Seine, the German Rhine, the English Thames —Cæsar who gives us the first graphic account of crossing the English Channel from France to England. Pytheas had hinted at the fog-bound lands of the north—Cæsar brought them into the light of day.

Since the days of Alexander the centre of Empire had shifted from Greece to Rome, and Rome was now conquering and annexing land, as Persia had done in the olden days. Hence it was that Julius Cæsar was in the year 58 B.C. appointed Governor of a new province recently brought under Roman sway, stretching from the Alps to the Garonne and northward to the Lake of Geneva, which at this time marked the frontier of the Roman Empire. Cæsar made no secret of his intentions to subdue the tribes to the north of his province and bring all Gaul under the dominion of Rome. His appointment carried with it the command of four legions, including some twenty thousand soldiers. His chance soon came, and we find Cæsar, with all the ability of a great commander, pushing forward with his army into the very heart of France one hundred and fifty miles beyond the Roman frontier.

On the banks of the river Saône he defeated a large body of Celtic people who were migrating from Switzerland to make their homes in the warmer and roomier plains at the foot of the Pyrenees.

While the defeated Celts returned to their chilly homes among the mountains, victorious Cæsar resolved to push on at the head of his army toward the Rhine, where some German tribes under a " ferocious headstrong savage " threatened to overrun the country. After marching through utterly unknown country for three days, he heard that fresh swarms of invaders had crossed the Rhine, intending to occupy the more fertile tracts on the French side. They were making for the town we now call Besançon—then, as now, strongly fortified, and nearly surrounded by the river Doubs. By forced marches night and day, Cæsar hastened to the town and took it before the arrival of the invaders.

Accounts of the German tribes even now approaching were brought in by native traders and Gaulish chiefs, until the Roman soldiers were seized with alarm. Yes, said the traders, these Germans were " men of huge stature, incredible valour, and practised skill in wars ; many a time they had themselves come across them, and had not been able to look them in the face or meet the glare of their piercing eyes."

The Romans felt they were in an unknown land, about to fight against an unknown foe. Violent panic seized them, " completely paralysing every one's judgment and nerve." Some could not restrain their tears ; others shut themselves up in their tents and bemoaned their fate. " All over the camp men were making their wills," until Cæsar spoke, and the panic ceased. Seven days' march brought them to the plain of Alsace, some fifty miles from the Rhine. A battle was fought with the German tribes, and " the enemy all turned tail and did not cease their flight until they reached the Rhine." Some swam across, some found boats, many were killed by the Romans in hot pursuit.

For the first time Romans beheld the German Rhine —that great river that was to form a barrier for so long between them and the tribes beyond. But Cæsar's exploration was not to end here. The following year found him advancing against the Belgæ—tribes living between the Rhine and the Seine. In one brilliant campaign he subdued the whole of north-eastern Gaul from the Seine to the Rhine. Leaving Roman soldiers in the newly conquered country, he returned to his province, and was some eight hundred miles away when he heard that a general rebellion was breaking out in that part we now know as Brittany. He at once ordered ships to be built on the Loire, "which flows into the ocean," oarsmen to be trained, seamen and pilots assembled.

The spring of 56 B.C. found Cæsar at the seat of war. His ships were ready on the Loire. But the navy of the Veneti was strong. They were a sea-going folk, who knew their own low rocky coast, intersected by shallow inlets of the sea; they knew their tides and their winds. Their flat-bottomed boats were suitable to shallows and ebbing tides. Bows and stern stood high out of the water to resist heavy seas and severe gales; the hulls were built of oak. Leather was used for sails to withstand the violent ocean storms. The long Roman galleys were no match for these, and things would have gone badly had not Cæsar devised a plan for cutting the enemy's rigging with hooks " sharpened at the end and fixed to long poles." With these, the Romans cut the rigging of the enemy's ships forming the fleet of Brittany ; the sails fell and the ships were rendered useless. One after another they were easily captured, and at sunset the victory lay with the Romans.

The whole of Gaul, from the Rhine to the Pyrenees, seemed now subdued. Cæsar had conquered as he explored, and the skill of his well-disciplined army triumphed everywhere over the untrained courage of the barbarian tribes.

Still, the German tribes were giving trouble about the country of the Rhine, and in the words of the famous *Commentaries,* " Cæsar was determined to cross the Rhine, but he hardly thought it safe to cross in boats. Therefore, although the construction of a bridge presented great difficulties on account of the breadth, swiftness, and depth of the stream, he nevertheless thought it best to make the attempt or else not cross at all." Indeed, he wanted to impress the wild German people on the other side with a sense of the vast power of the Roman Empire. The barbarian tribes beyond must, indeed, have been impressed with the skill of the Roman soldier. For in ten days the bridge was completed : timber had been hewn from the forest, brought to the banks of the Rhine, worked into shape, piles driven into the bed of the river, beams laid across. And Cæsar led his army in triumph to the other side. They stood for the first time in the land of the Germans, near the modern town of Coblenz, and after eighteen days on the farther side, they returned to Gaul, destroying the bridge behind them.

Cæsar had now a fresh adventure in view. He was going to make his way to Britain. The summer of 55 B.C. was passing, and " in these parts, the whole of Gaul having a northerly trend, winter sets in early," wrote Cæsar afterwards. There would be no time to conquer, but he could visit the island, find out for himself what the people were like, learn about harbours and landing-places, " for of all this the Greeks knew practically nothing. No one, indeed, readily undertakes the voyage to Britain except traders, and even they know nothing of it except the coast."

Cæsar summoned all the traders he could collect and inquired the size of the island, what tribes dwelt there, their names, their customs, and the shortest sea passage. Then he sent for the ships which had vanquished the fleet of Brittany the previous year; he also assembled some eighty merchant ships on the northern coast of Gaul, probably not very far from Calais.

It was near the end of August, when soon after midnight the wind served and he set sail. A vision of the great Roman—determined, resolute—rises before us as, standing on the deck of the galley, he looks out on to the dark waters of the unknown sea bound for the coast of England. After a slow passage the little fleet arrived under the steep white cliffs of the southern coast about nine o'clock next morning. Armed forces of barbarians stood on the heights above Dover, and, finding it impossible to land, Cæsar gave orders to sail some seven miles farther along the coast, where they ran the ships aground not far from Deal.

But the visit of the Romans to Britain on this occasion lasted but three days, for a violent storm scattered the ships with the horses on board.

" The same night," says Cæsar, " it happened to be full moon, which generally causes very high tides in the ocean, a fact of which our men were not aware."

Indeed, we may well believe that a night of full moon and an unusually high tide would be a mystery to those children of the Mediterranean. Their ships had been beached and were lying high and dry when the rapidly rising tide overwhelmed them. Cables were broken, anchors lost, panic ensued.

But Cæsar's glory lay in overcoming obstacles, and it is well known how he got his troops and ships safely back across the Channel, and how preparations were hurried on in Gaul for a second invasion of Britain. This is not the place for the story of his campaign. He was the first to raise the curtain on the mysterious islands discovered by Pytheas.

> " Far to the west, in the ocean wide,
>   Beyond the realm of Gaul, a land there lies,
>   Sea-girt it lies, where giants dwelt of old."

Cæsar's remarks on this new-found land are interesting for us to-day. He tells us of " a river called the Thames, about eight miles from the sea." " The interior of Britain," he says, "is inhabited by a people who, according to tradition, are aboriginal. The population is immense; homesteads closely resembling those of the Gauls are met with at every turn, and cattle are very numerous. Gold coins are in use, or iron bars of fixed weight. Hares, fowls, and geese they think it wrong to taste; but they keep them for pastime or amusement. The climate is more equable than in Gaul, the cold being less severe. The island is triangular in shape, one side being opposite Gaul. One corner of this side, by Kent —the landing-place for almost all ships from Gaul—has an easterly, and the lower one a westerly, aspect. The extent of this side is about five hundred miles. The second trends off towards Spain. Off the coast here is Ireland, which is considered only half as large as Britain. Half-way across is an island called ' Man,' and several smaller islands also are believed to be situated opposite this coast, in which there is continuous night for thirty days. The length of this side is eight hundred miles. Thus the whole island is two thousand miles in circumference. The people of the interior do not, for the most part, cultivate grain, but live on milk and flesh-meat, and clothe themselves with skins. All Britons, without exception, stain themselves with woad, which produces a bluish tint. They wear their hair long."

Cæsar crossed the Thames. "The river can only be forded at one spot," he tells us, "and there with difficulty." Farther he did not go. And so this is all that was known of Britain for many a long year to come.

CHAPTER VIII

STRABO'S GEOGRAPHY

STRABO wrote his famous geography near the beginning of the Christian era, but he knew nothing of the north of England, Scotland, or Wales. He insisted on placing Ireland to the north, and scoffed at Pytheas' account of Thule.

And yet he boasted a wider range than any other writer on geography, " for that those who had penetrated farther towards the West had not gone so far to the East, and those on the contrary who had seen more of the East had seen less of the West."

Like Herodotus, Strabo had travelled himself from Armenia and western Italy, from the Black Sea to Egypt and up the Nile to Philæ. But his seventeen volumes —vastly important to his contemporaries—read like a romance to us to-day, and a glance at the map laid down according to his descriptions is like a vague and distorted caricature of the real thing. And yet, according to the men of his times, he " surpasses all the geographical writings of antiquity, both in grandeur of plan and in abundance and variety of its materials."

Strabo has summed up for us the knowledge of the ancient world as it was in the days of the Emperor Cæsar Augustus of the great Roman Empire, as it was when in far-off Syria the Christ was born and the greater part of the known earth was under the sway of Rome.

A wall-map had already been designed by order of Augustus to hang in a public place in Rome—the heart

of the Empire—so that the young Romans might realise
the size of their inheritance, while a list of the chief places
on the roads, which, radiating from Rome, formed a net-

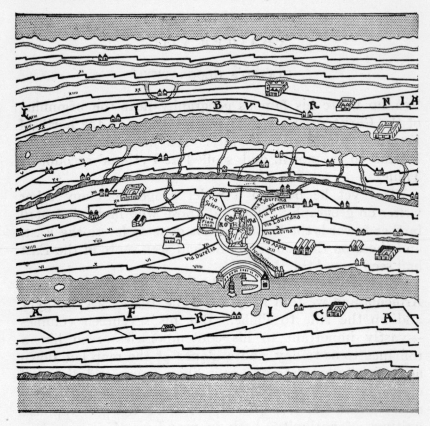

A PORTION OF AN OLD ROMAN MAP OF THE WORLD, SHOWING THE ROADS
THROUGH THE EMPIRE, RIVERS, MOUNTAINS, AND THE SURROUNDING SEAS.

This is a portion—a few inches—taken from the famous Peutinger Table, a long strip
map on parchment, of the fourth century, derived from Augustan maps according to
the measurements of Cæsar Augustus Agrippa. It will be noticed how the roads,
beginning with the Twelve Ways, which start from Rome in the centre, go in
straight lines over all obstacles to the towns of the Empire. Distances are marked
in stadia (about ⅛ mile).

work over the Empire, was inscribed on the Golden
Milestone in the Forum.

We may well imagine with what keen interest the schoolmen of Alexandria would watch the extension of the Roman Empire. Here Strabo had studied, here or at Rome he probably wrote his great work toward the close of a long life. He has read his Homer and inclines to take every word he says as true. Herodotus he will have none of.

"Herodotus and other writers trifle very much," he asserts, "when they introduce into their histories the marvellous like an interlude of some melody."

In like manner he disbelieves poor Pytheas and his accounts of the land of Ultima Thule and his marvellous walks through Britain, while he clings to the writings of Eratosthenes.

But in common with them all Strabo believes the world to be one vast island, surrounded on all sides by ocean into which the rivers flow, and the Caspian Sea and Persian Gulf are but inlets. So is also the Mediterranean or "Our Sea," as he prefers to call it. This earth-island reaches north to south, from Ireland, "barely habitable on account of the cold," to the cinnamon country (Somaliland), "the most southerly point of the habitable earth." From west to east it stretches from the Pillars of Hercules right "through the middle of Our Sea" to the shores of Asia Minor, then across Asia by an imaginary chain of mountains to an imaginary spot where the Ganges, lately discovered, emptied its waters into the world-surrounding ocean stream.

The breadth of the habitable earth is three thousand miles, the length about seven thousand—a little world, indeed, with the greater world lying all around it, still undreamt of by the old student of geography and the traveller after truth.

He begins his book with a detailed account of southern Spain. He tells of her two hundred towns. "Those best known are situated on the rivers, estuaries, and seas ; but the two which have acquired the greatest name and importance are Cordova and Cadiz. After these Seville is the most noted. . . . A vast number of people dwell along the Guadalquivir, and you may sail up it almost a hundred and twenty miles from the sea to Cordova and the places a little higher up. The banks and little inlets of this river are cultivated with the greatest diligence. The eye is also delighted with groves and gardens, which in this district are met with in the highest perfection. For fifty miles the river is navigable for ships of considerable size, but for the cities higher up smaller vessels are employed, and thence to Cordova river - boats. These are now constructed of planks joined together, but they were formerly made out of a single trunk. A chain of mountains, rich in metal, runs parallel to the Guadalquivir, approaching the river, sometimes more, sometimes less, toward the north."

He grows enthusiastic over the richness of this part of southern Spain, famous from ancient days under the name of Tartessus for its wealth. " Large quantities of corn and wine are exported, besides much oil, which is of the first quality, also wax, honey, and pitch . . . the country furnishes the timber for their shipbuilding. They have likewise mineral salt and not a few salt streams. A considerable quantity of salted fish is exported, not only from hence, but also from the remainder of the coast beyond the Pillars. Formerly they exported large quantities of garments, but they now send the unmanufactured wool remarkable for its beauty. The stuffs manufactured are of incomparable texture. There is a superabundance of cattle and a great variety of game, while on the other hand there are certain little hares which burrow in the ground (rabbits). These creatures destroy both seeds and trees by gnawing their roots. They are met with throughout almost the whole of Spain. It is said that formerly the inhabitants of Majorca and Minorca sent a deputation to the Romans requesting that a new land might be given them, as they were quite driven out of their country by these animals, being no longer able to stand against their vast multitudes." The seacoast on the Atlantic side abounds in fish, says Strabo. "The congers

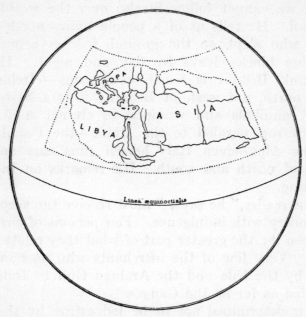

THE WORLD-ISLAND ACCORDING TO STRABO, 18 A.D.

The blank space within the circle is one vast sea surrounding the world.

are quite monstrous, far surpassing in size those of Our Sea. Shoals of rich fat tunny fish are driven hither from the seacoast beyond. They feed on the fruit, of stunted oak, which grows at the bottom of the sea and produces very large acorns. So great is the quantity of fruit, that at the season when they are ripe the whole coast on either side of the Pillars is covered with acorns thrown up by the tides. The tunny fish become gradually thinner, owing

5

to the failure of their food as they approach the Pillars from the outer sea."

He describes, too, the metals of this wondrous land— gold, silver, copper, and iron. It is astonishing to think that in the days of Strabo the silver mines employed forty thousand workmen, and produced something like £900 a day in our modern money!

But we cannot follow Strabo over the world in all his detail. He tells us of a people living north of the Tagus, who slept on the ground, fed on acorn-bread, and wore black cloaks by day and night. He does not think Britain is worth conquering — Ireland lies to the north, not west, of Britain; it is a barren land full of cannibals and wrapped in eternal snows — the Pyrenees run parallel to the Rhine—the Danube rises near the Alps—even Italy herself runs east and west instead of north and south. His remarks on India are interesting.

"The reader," he says, "must receive the accounts of this country with indulgence. Few persons of our nation have seen it; the greater part of what they relate is from report. Very few of the merchants who now sail from Egypt by the Nile and the Arabian Gulf to India have proceeded as far as the Ganges."

He is determined not to be led astray by the fables of the great size of India. Some had told him it was a third of the whole habitable world, some that it took four months to walk through the plain only. "Ceylon is said to be an island lying out at sea seven days' sail from the most southerly parts of India. Its length is about eight hundred miles. It produces elephants."

Strabo died about the year 21 A.D., and half a century passed before Pliny wrote *An Account of Countries, Nations, Seas, Towns, Havens, Mountains, Rivers, Distances, and Peoples who now Exist or Formerly Existed.*

Strange to say, he never refers in the most distant way to his famous predecessor Strabo. He has but little to add to the earth-knowledge of Strabo. But he gives us a fuller account of Great Britain, based on the fresh discoveries of Roman generals.

CHAPTER IX

THE ROMAN EMPIRE AND PLINY

In the year 43 A.D. the Emperor Claudius resolved to send an expedition to the British coast, lying amid the mists and fog of the Northern Ocean.

A gigantic army landed near the spot where Cæsar had landed just a hundred years before. The discovery and conquest of Britain now began in real earnest. The Isle of Wight was overrun by Romans; the south coast was explored. Roman soldiers lost their lives in the bogs and swamps of Gloucestershire. The eastern counties, after fierce opposition, submitted at the last. The spirit of Caractacus and Boadicea spread from tribe to tribe and the Romans were constantly assailed. But gradually they swept the island. They reached the banks of the river Tyne; they crossed the Tweed and explored as far as the Firths of Clyde and Forth. From the coast of Galloway the Romans beheld for the first time the dim outline of the Irish coast. In the year 83 A.D. Agricola, a new Roman commander, made his way beyond the Firth of Forth.

"Now is the time to penetrate into the heart of Caledonia and to discover the utmost limits of Britain," cried the Romans, as they began their advance to the Highlands of Scotland. While a Roman fleet surveyed the coasts and harbours, Agricola led his men up the valley of the Tay to the edge of the Highlands, but he could not follow the savage Caledonians into their rugged and inaccessible mountains. To the north of Scotland they never penetrated, and no part of Ireland ever came under Roman sway, in that air "the Roman eagle never fluttered." The Roman account of Britain at this time is interesting. "Britain," says Tacitus, "the largest of all the islands which have come within the knowledge of the Romans, stretches on the east towards Germany, on the west towards Spain, and on the south it is even within sight of France. . . . The Roman fleet, at this period first sailing round this remotest coast, gave certain proof that Britain was an island, and at the same time discovered and subdued the Orkney Islands, till then unknown. Thule was also distinctly seen, which winter and eternal snow had hitherto concealed. . . . The sky in this country is deformed by clouds and frequent rains; but the cold is never extremely rigorous. The earth yields gold and silver and other metals—the ocean produces pearls."

The account of Ireland is only from hearsay. "This island," continues Tacitus, "is less than Britain, but larger than those of Our Sea. Situated between Britain and Spain and lying commodiously to the Bay of Biscay, it would have formed a very beneficial connection between the most powerful parts of the Empire. Its soil, climate, and the manners and dispositions of its inhabitants are little different from those of Britain. Its ports and harbours are better known from the concourse of merchants for the purposes of commerce."

Not only the British Isles, but a good deal of the wild North Sea and the low-lying coast on the opposite side were explored by Roman ships and Roman soldiers. Cæsar had crossed the Rhine; he had heard of a great forest which took a man four months to cross, and in 16 A.D. a Roman general, Drusus, penetrated into the interior of Germany. Drusus crossed the Rhine near the coast, made his way across the river Weser, and reached the banks of the Elbe. But the fame of Drusus rests mainly on his navigation of the German Ocean or North Sea in a Roman fleet. Near the mouth of the Rhine a thousand ships were quickly built by expert Romans. "Some were short, with narrow stern and prow and broad in the middle, the easier to endure the shock of the waves; some had flat bottoms that without damage they might run aground; many were fitted for carrying horses and provisions, convenient for sails and swift with oars."

The Roman troops were in high spirits as they launched their splendid fleet on the Northern Ocean and sailed prosperously to the mouth of the Elbe, startling the Frisians into submission. But no friendliness greeted them on the farther side of the river. The Germans were ready to defend their land, and further advance was impossible. Returning along the northern coast, the Romans got a taste of the storms of this northern ocean, of which they were in such complete ignorance.

"The sea, at first calm," says Tacitus, "resounded with the oars of a thousand ships; but presently a shower of hail poured down from a black mass of clouds, at the same time storms raging on all sides in every variety, the billows rolling now here, now there, obstructed the view and made it impossible to manage the ships. The whole expanse of air and sea was swept by a south-west wind, which, deriving strength from the mountainous regions of Germany, its deep rivers and boundless tract of clouded atmosphere, and rendered still harsher by the rigour of the neighbouring north, tore away the ships, scattered and drove them into the open ocean or upon islands dangerous from precipitous rocks or hidden sandbanks. Having got a little clear of these, but with great difficulty, the tide turning and flowing in the same direction as that in which the wind blew, they were unable to ride at anchor or bale out the water that broke in upon them; horses, beasts of burthen, baggage, even arms were thrown overboard to lighten the holds of the ships, which took in water at their sides, and from the waves, too, running over them.   Around were either shores inhabited by enemies, or a sea so vast and unfathomable as to be supposed the limit of the world and unbounded by lands.   Part of the fleet was swallowed up; many were driven upon remote islands, where the men perished through famine.   The galley of Drusus or, as he was hereafter called, Germanicus, alone reached the mouth of the Weser.   Both day and night, amid the rocks and prominences of the shore, he reproached himself as the author of such overwhelming

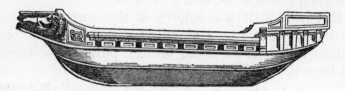

HULL OF A ROMAN MERCHANT-SHIP.

From a Roman model in marble at Greenwich.

destruction, and was hardly restrained by his friends from destroying himself in the same sea.   At last, with the returning tide and a favouring gale, the shattered ships returned, almost all destitute or with garments spread for sails."

The wreck of the Roman fleet in the North Sea made a deep impression on the Roman capital, and many a garbled story of the "extreme parts of the world" was circulated throughout the Empire.

Here was new land outside the boundaries of the Empire-country great with possibilities.   Pliny, writer of the *Natural History*, now arises and endeavours to clear the minds of his countrymen by some account of these northern regions.   Strabo had been dead some fifty

years, and the Empire had grown since his days. But
Pliny has news of land beyond the Elbe. He can tell us of
Scandinavia, " an island of unknown extent," of Norway,
another island, " the inhabitants of which sailed as far
as Thule," of the Seamen or Swedes who lived in the
" northern half of the world."

" It is madness to harass the mind with attempts to
measure the world," he asserts, but he proceeds to tell us
the size of the world as accepted by him. " Our part of
the earth, floating as it were in the ocean, which surrounds
it, stretching out to the greatest extent from India to the
Pillars at Cadiz, is eight thousand five hundred and sixty-
eight miles . . . the breadth from south to north is commonly supposed to be half its length."

But how little was known of the north of Europe at
this time is shown by a startling statement that " certain
Indians sailing from India for the purposes of commerce
had been driven by tempests into Germany."

" Thus it appears," concludes Pliny, " that the seas
flow completely round the globe and divide it into two
parts."

How Balbus discovered and claimed for the Empire
some of the African desert is related by Pliny. He tells
us, too, how another Roman general left the west coast
of Africa, marched for ten days, reached Mt. Atlas, and
" in a desert of dark-coloured sand met a river which he
supposed to be the Niger."

The home of the Ethiopians in Africa likewise interested Pliny.

" There can be no doubt that the Ethiopians are
scorched by their vicinity to the sun's heat, and that they
are born like persons who have been burned, with beard
and hair frizzled, while in the opposite and frozen parts
of the earth there are nations with white skins and long
light hair."

Pliny's geography was the basis of much mediæval writing, and his knowledge of the course of the Niger remained unchallenged, till Mungo Park re-discovered it many centuries after.

A ROMAN GALLEY, ABOUT 110 A.D.

From Trajan's Column at Rome.

CHAPTER X

PTOLEMY'S MAPS

AND so we reach the days of Ptolemy — the last geo-grapher of the Pagan World. This famous Greek was born in Egypt, and the great Roman Empire was already showing signs of decay, while Ptolemy was searching the great Alexandrian library for materials for his book. Alexandria was now the first commercial city of the world, second only to Rome. She supplied the great population in the heart of the Empire with Egyptian corn. Ships sailed from Alexandria to every part of the known world. It was, therefore, a suitable place for Ptolemy to listen to the yarns of the merchants, to read the works of Homer, Herodotus, Eratosthenes, Strabo, Pliny, and others, to study and observe, and finally to write.

He begins his great geography with the north-west extremities of the world—the British Isles, Iverna, and Albion as he calls Ireland and England. But he places Ireland much too far north, and the shape of Scotland has little resemblance to the original.[1] He realised that there were lands to the south of Africa, to the east of Africa, and to the north of Europe, all stretching far away beyond his ken. He agrees with Pliny about the four islands in the neighbourhood of Scandinavia, and draws the Volga correctly. He realises, too, that the Caspian is an inland sea, and unconnected with the surrounding ocean.

Perhaps the most remarkable part of Ptolemy's geography is that which tells us of the lands beyond the

[1] If Ptolemy's longitudes are adjusted, he becomes extraordinarily correct.

"THE UNROLLING OF THE CLOUDS"—II.
THE WORLD AS KNOWN TO PTOLEMY AND THE ROMANS.

Ganges. He knows something of the " Golden Cher-
sonese " or Malay Peninsula, something of China, where
" far away towards the north, and bordering on the eastern
ocean, there is a land containing a great city from which
silk is exported, both raw and spun and woven into
textures."

The wonder is that Ptolemy did not know more of
China, for that land had one of the oldest civilisations in
the world, as wondrous as those of Assyria and Egypt.
But China had had little or no direct intercourse with the
West till after the death of Ptolemy. Merchants had
passed between China and India for long centuries, and
" the Indians had made journeys in the golden deserts
in troops of one or two thousand, and it is said that they
do not return from these journeys till the third or fourth
year." This was the Desert of Gobi, called golden because
it opened the way to wealth.

But perhaps the most interesting part of this great
geography, which was to inform the world for centuries
yet to come, was the construction of a series of twenty-
six maps and a general map of the known world.

This was one of the most important maps ever constructed, and forms our frontispiece from mediæval copies
of the original. The twelve heads blowing sundry winds
on to the world's surface are characteristic of the age.
The twenty-six maps are in sections. They are the first
maps to be drawn with lines of latitude and longitude.
The measurements are very vague. The lines are never
ruled ; they are drawn uncertainly in red ; they are
neither straight nor regular, though the spaces between
the lines indicate degrees of fifty miles. The maps are
crowded with towns, each carefully walled in by little
red squares and drawn by hand. The water is all coloured
a sombre, greeny blue, and the land is washed in a rich
yellow brown. A copy can be seen at the British Museum.

It is only by looking back that we can realise the progress made in earth-knowledge. Ptolemy wrote just a thousand years after Homer, when the little world round the Mediterranean had become a great Empire stretching from the British Isles to China.

Already the barbaric hordes which haunted the frontiers of the Roman Empire were breaking across the ill-defended boundaries, desolating streams were bursting over the civilised world, until at last the storm broke, the unity of the Empire was ended, commerce broken up, and the darkness of ignorance spread over the earth.

During this time little in the way of progress was made, and for the next few centuries our only interest lies in filling up some of the shadowy places of the earth, without extending its known bounds.

CHAPTER XI

PILGRIM TRAVELLERS

MEANWHILE a new inspiration had been given to the world, which affected travelling to no small extent.

In far-off Roman province of Syria, the Christ had lived, the Christ had died. And His words were ringing through the land: " Go ye and make disciples of all the nations, preach the gospel to every creature." Here at once was a new incentive to travel, a definite reason for men to venture forth into the unknown, to brave dangers, to endure hardship. They must carry their Master's words " unto the ends of the world." The Roman Empire had brought men under one rule; they must now be brought to serve one God. So men passed out of Syria; they landed on the islands in the Mediterranean, they made their way to Asia Minor and across to Greece, until in the year 60 A.D. we get the graphic account of Paul the traveller, one of the first and most famous of the missionaries of the first century.

Jerusalem now became, indeed, the world centre. A very stream of pilgrim travellers tramped to the Holy City from far-away lands to see for themselves the land where the Christ had lived and died.

The pilgrim age begins with the journey of a woman— the beautiful and learned daughter of the King of Britain, Helena, mother of the Emperor Constantine. She was a student of divinity and a devoted Christian. In the year 326 she undertook the difficult journey to Jerusalem,

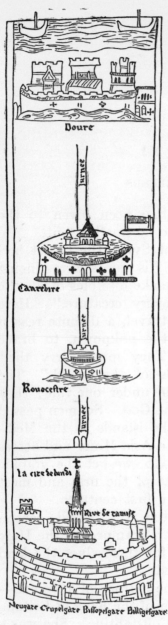

Doure

Iurnee

Cantrebire

Iurnee

Rouocestre

Iurnee

la cize de lundi

Rive de tamise

Neugate Crupelgate Biffopefgate Billigefgate

THE FIRST STAGES OF A MEDIÆVAL PILGRIMAGE : LONDON TO DOVER. From Matthew of Paris's *Itinerary*, thirteenth century.

where she is reported to have discovered the "true cross," which had been buried, with Pilate's inscription in "Hebrew and Greek and Latin." When the news of her discovery was noised abroad a very rush of pilgrims took place from every part of the world. Indeed, one pilgrim—his name is unknown—thought it worth while to write a guide-book for the benefit of his fellow-travellers. His *Itinerary from Bordeaux to Jerusalem* is very interesting, being the first Christian guide-book and one of the earliest travel-documents ever written for the use of travellers. This ancient "Bradshaw" has been translated into English and throws light on fourth-century travelling. Enthusiastic indeed must these early pilgrims have been to undertake the long and toilsome journey.

The guide-book takes them, save for crossing the Bosphorus, entirely by land. It leads them from the "city of Bordeaux, where is the river Garonne in which the ocean ebbs and flows for one hundred leagues more or less," to Arles, with thirty changes and eleven halts in three hundred and seventy-two miles. There were mile-stones along the Roman roads to guide them, and houses at regular intervals where horses were kept for posting. From Arles the pilgrim goes north to Avignon, crosses the Alps, and halts at the Italian frontier. Skirting the north of Italy by Turin, Milan, and Padua, he reaches the Danube at Belgrade, passes through Servia and Bulgaria and so reaches Constantinople—the great new city of Constantine. "Grand total from Bordeaux to Constantinople, two thousand two hundred and twenty-one miles, with two hundred and thirty changes and one hundred and twelve halts."

"From Constantinople," continues the guide-book, "you cross the strait and walk on through Asia Minor, passing the spot where lies King Hannibal, once King of the Africans." Thus onward through the long dreary miles to Tarsus, where "was born the Apostle Paul," till Syria is reached at last.

Then the "Bradshaw" becomes a "Baedeker." Long and detailed accounts are given of the country through which the pilgrim has to pass. From Cæsarea he is led to Jezreel by the spot "where David slew Goliath," by "Job's country house" to Sichem, "where Joseph is laid," and thence to Jerusalem. Full accounts follow of the Holy City and Mount Sion, "the little hill of Golgotha where the Lord was crucified," the Mount of Olives, Jericho, Jordan, Bethlehem, and Hebron. "Here is a monument of square form built of stone of wondrous beauty," in which lie Abraham, Isaac, Jacob, Sara, Rebecca, and Leah.

"From Constantinople to Jerusalem is one thousand one hundred and fifty-nine miles, with sixty-nine changes and fifty-eight halts."

Here the guide-book ends abruptly with a brief summary of distances. Thither then flocked the pilgrims, some by land and some by sea, men and women from all parts of the world.

"Even the Briton, separated from our world, leaves the setting sun and seeks a place known to him only by fame and the narrative of the Scriptures."

One of the earliest was Paula of Rome—a weak, fragile woman accustomed to a life of luxury and ease, but, fired with the enthusiasm of her religion, she resolved to brave the dangers and hardships of a journey to the East. Her travels were written by St. Jerome.

"When the winter was spent and the sea was open," he writes, " she longed and prayed to sail. . . . She went down to the harbour, accompanied by her brother, her relatives, her connections and, more than these, by her children, who strove to surpass the affection of the kindest of mothers. Soon the sails were swelling in the breeze, and the ship, guided by the oars, gained the open sea. Little Lexotinus piteously stretched forth his hands from the shore. Rufina, a grown-up girl, by her tears silently besought her mother to stay until she was married. Yet she herself, without a tear, turned her eyes heavenward, overcoming her love for her children by her love for God. . . . Meanwhile the ship was ploughing the sea—the winds were sluggish and all speed slow." But the ship passed between Scylla and Charybdis and reached Antioch in safety. From this spot she followed the guide-book directions until she arrived at Jerusalem. How Paula and one of her young daughters walked over the rough ground, endured the hardships of desert-life, and finally lived twenty years at Bethlehem, would take too long to tell. And she was but one of many.

Sylvia of Aquitaine, travelling at the same time, wrote a strangely interesting account of her travels. The early part of her manuscript is lost, and we find her first in Arabia. All was new and strange.

"Meanwhile as we walked we arrived at a certain place, where the mountains between which we were passing opened themselves out and formed a great valley, very flat and extremely beautiful; and beyond the valley appeared Sinai, the holy mount of God. . . . This is the same great and flat valley in which the children of Israel waited during the days when holy Moses went up into the Mount

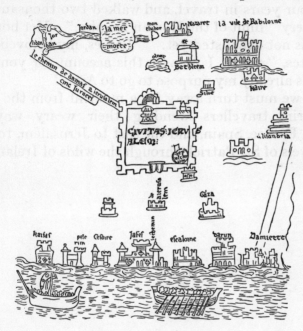

JERUSALEM AND THE EAST.

From Matthew of Paris's *Itinerary*, thirteenth century.

of God. . . . It was late on the Sabbath when we came to the mountain, and, arriving at a certain monastery, the kindly monks who lived there entertained us, showing us all kindliness." Sylvia had to ascend the mountain on foot " because the ascent could not be made in a chair," but the view over " Egypt and Palestine and the Red Sea and the Mediterranean which leads to Alexandria,

6

also the boundless territory of the Saracens, we saw below us, hard though it is to believe, all of which things these holy men pointed out to us."

But we must not follow her to Jerusalem, or to Mesopotamia, where she saw " the great river Euphrates, rushing down in a torrent like the Rhine, but greater." She reached Constantinople by the guide-book route, having spent four years in travel, and walked two thousand miles to the very " limit of the Roman Empire." Her boundless energy is not exhausted yet. " Ladies, my beloved ones," she writes, " whilst I prepare this account for your pious zeal, it is already my purpose to go to Asia."

But we must turn away for a moment from the stream of pilgrim travellers wending their weary way from Britain, France, Spain, and the east to Jerusalem, to follow the travels of St. Patrick through the wilds of Ireland.

CHAPTER XII

IRISH EXPLORERS

PATRICK had been a pilgrim to Rome from the banks of the Clyde, where he lived, and, having seen the Pope, he had returned to Ireland by sea, landing on the Wicklow coast in the year 432. Hungry and tired after the long voyage, he tried to get some fish from the fishermen, but they replied by throwing stones at him, and he put out to sea again and headed north. Past Bray Head, past the Bay of Malahide he sailed, but he could get neither fish nor food till he reached a spot between the Liffey and the Boyne, where he built his first Christian church.

Now in the fifth century, when light first breaks over Ireland, it breaks over a land torn by perpetual tribal strife, a land in the chaos of wild heathendom. It was reserved for St. Patrick to save her from increasing gloom.

Patrick and his companions now sailed on past Louth, by the low-lying shore with long stretches of sandy flats, on under the shadow of great peaks frowning over the sea. He landed near Downpatrick, founded another church, and spent the winter in these parts, for the autumn was far advanced. Spring found him sailing back to the Boyne and attacking the fierce heathen king at Tara, the capital of Ireland. From Tara five great roads led to different parts of the island. St. Patrick now made his way through Meath to the very heart of the country, building churches as he went. Thence he crossed the Shannon, entered the great plain of Roscommon, passed by Mayo, and at length reached the western sea. He had now been eight years in Ireland, eight laborious years, climbing hills, wading through waters, camping out by night, building, organising, preaching. He loved the land on the western sea, little known as yet.

> " I would choose
> To remain here on a little land,
> After faring around churches and waters.
> Since I am weary, I wish not to go further."

St. Patrick climbed the great peak, afterwards called Croaghpatrick, and on the summit, exposed to wind and rain, he spent the forty days of Lent. From here he could look down on to one of the most beautiful bays in Ireland, down on to the hundred little islands in the glancing waters below, while away to the north and south stretched the rugged coast-line. And he tells us how the great white birds came and sang to him there. It would take too long to tell how he returned to Tara and started again with a train of thirteen chariots by the great north-western road to the spot afterwards known as Downpatrick Head; he passed along the broken coast to the extreme north where the great ocean surf breaks on the rugged shore, returning again to the Irish capital. He travelled over a great part of Ireland, founded three hundred and fifty churches, converted heathen tribes to Christianity and civilisation, and finally died at Armagh in 493. His work was carried on by St. Columba, a native of Ireland, who, " deciding to go abroad for Christ," sailed away with twelve disciples to a low rocky island off the west coast of Scotland, where he founded the famous monastery of Iona, about 563. Thence he journeyed away to the Highlands, making his way through rugged and mountainous country that had stayed the warlike Romans long years before. He even sailed across the stormy northern sea to the Orkney Islands.

Let us picture the Scotland of the sixth century in order to realise those long lonely tramps of St. Columba and his disciples across the rough mountains, through the dense forests, across bleak moors and wet bogs, till after dreary wanderings they reached the coast, and in frail ships boldly faced the wild seas that raged round the northern islands.

" We can see Columba and his disciples journeying on foot, as poor and as barely provided as were Christ and His disciples, with neither silver nor gold nor brass in their purses, and over a wilder country and among a wilder people."

IRELAND AND
ST. BRANDON'S ISLE

From the Catalan map,
1375.

These pilgrims tramped to and fro clad in simple tunics over a monkish dress of undyed wool, bound round the waist by a strong cord, all their worldly goods on their backs and a staff in their hands. The hermit instinct was growing, and men were sailing away to lonely islands where God might be better served apart from the haunts of men. Perhaps it was this instinct that inspired St. Brandon to sail away across the trackless ocean in search of the Island of Saints reported in the western seas. His voyage suggests the old expedition of Ulysses. A good deal of it is mythical, some is added at a later date, but it is interesting as being an attempt to cross the wide Atlantic Ocean across which no man had yet sailed. For seven years St. Brandon sailed on the unknown sea, discovering unknown islands, until he reached the Island of Saints—the goal of his desires.

And the fact remains that for ten centuries after this an island, known as Brandon's Isle, was marked on maps somewhere to the west of Ireland, though to the end it remained as mysterious as the island of Thule.

Here is the old story. Brandon, abbot of a large Irish monastery containing one thousand monks, sailed off in an " osier boat covered with tanned hides and carefully greased," provisioned for seven years. After forty days at sea they reached an island with steep sides, where they took in fresh supplies. Thence the winds carried the ship to another island, where they found sheep— " every sheep was as great as an ox."

" This is the island of sheep, and here it is ever summer," they were informed by an old islander.

This may have been Madeira. They found other islands in the neighbourhood, one of which was full of singing-birds, and the passing years found them still tossing to and fro on the unknown sea, until at last the end came. " And St. Brandon sailed forty days south in full great tempest," and another forty days brought the ship right into a bank of fog. But when the fog lifted " they saw the fairest country eastward that any man might see, it was so clear and bright that it was a heavenly sight to behold ; and all the trees were charged with ripe fruit." And they walked about the island for forty days and could not find the end. And there was no night there, and the climate was neither hot nor cold.

" Be ye joyful now," said a voice, " for this is the land ye have sought, and our Lord wills that you laden your ship with the fruit of this land and hie you hence, for ye may no longer abide here, but thou shalt sail again into thine own country."

So the monks took all the fruit they could carry, and, weeping that they might stay no longer in this happy land, they sailed back to Ireland. Hazy, indeed, was the

geography of the Atlantic in the sixth century. Nor
can we leave St. Brandon's story without quoting a

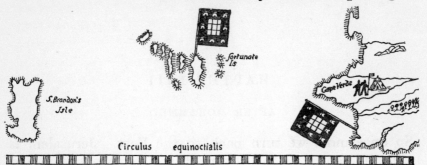

THE MYSTERIOUS ISLE OF ST. BRANDON IN MARTIN BEHAIM'S MAP, 1492.

As geographical knowledge increased, map-makers were compelled to put Brandon's Isle
farther and farther away from Ireland, until here we find it off the coast of Africa
and near the Equator.

modern poet, who believed that the voyage was to the
Arctic regions and not in the Atlantic.

> "Saint Brandon sails the Northern Main,
> The brotherhood of saints are glad.
> He greets them once, he sails again:
> So late! Such storms! The saint is mad.
> He heard across the howling seas
> Chime convent bells on wintry nights;
> He saw, on spray-swept Hebrides,
> Twinkle the monastery lights:
> But north, still north, Saint Brandon steered,
> And now no bells, no convents more,
> The hurtling Polar lights are reached,
> The sea without a human shore."

Some three hundred years were to pass away before
further discoveries in these quarters revealed new lands,
three hundred years before the great energy of the Vikings
brought to light Iceland, Greenland, and even the coast
of America.

CHAPTER XIII

AFTER MOHAMMED

So once more we turn back to the East. Jerusalem is still the centre of the earth. But a change has passed over the world, which influenced not a little the progress of geography. Mohammed in the seventh century lived and died in Arabia. "There is but one God, and Mohammed is His prophet," proclaimed his followers, the Arabs or Saracens as they were called. And just as men had travelled abroad to preach Christianity to those who knew it not, so now the Mohammedans set forth to teach the faith of their Lord and Master. But whereas Christianity was taught by peaceful means, Mohammedanism was carried by the sword. The Roman provinces of Syria and Egypt had been conquered by the Arabs, and the famous cities of Jerusalem and Alexandria were filled with teachers of the new faith. The Mohammedans had conquered Spain and were pressing by Persia towards India.

What deep root their preaching took in these parts is still evident. Still the weary fight between the two religions continues.

The first traveller of note through this distracted Europe was a Frenchman named Arculf, a Christian bishop. When he had visited the Holy Land and Egypt his ship was caught in a violent storm and driven on to the west coast of Scotland. After many adventures Arculf found himself at the famous convent of Iona,

made welcome by an Irish monk Adamnan, who was
deeply interested in Arculf's account of his wanderings,
and wrote them down at his dictation, first on waxed
tablets, copied later on to parchment. How tenderly
the two monks dwell on all the glories of Jerusalem. " But
in that beautiful place where once the Temple had been,
the Saracens now frequent a four-sided house of prayer,
which they have built, rudely constructing it by raising

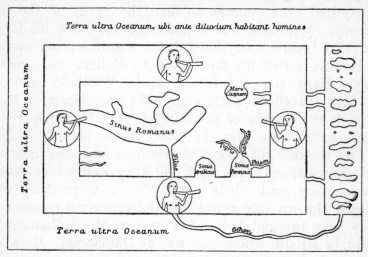

Terra ultra Oceanum, ubi ante diluvium habitant homines

Terra ultra Oceanum

Sinus Romanus

Mare Caspium

Nilus

Tigris

Euphrates

Sinus Arabicus

Sinus Persicus

Phison

Terra ultra Oceanum

Gihon

THE WORLD-MAP OF COSMAS, SIXTH CENTURY.

This is the oldest Christian map. It shows the flat world surrounded by the ocean, with
the four winds and the four sacred rivers running out of the terrestrial Paradise;
beyond all is the "terra ultra oceanum," "the world beyond the ocean, where men
dwelt before the flood."

boards and great beams on some remains of ruins, which
house can hold three thousand men at once." And Arculf
draws on the waxed tablet the picture of some church
or tomb to make his narrative clearer to his friend
Adamnan.

Perhaps the most interesting part of all the travels is
the account of the lofty column that Arculf describes in
the midst of Jerusalem.

" This column," he says, "as it stands in the centre

of the heaven, shining straight down from above, proves
that the city of Jerusalem is situated in the middle of
the earth."

Arculf's journey aroused great interest among the
newly converted Christians of the north, and Willibald,
a high-born Englishman, started off in 721 to explore
farther. But the road through Europe was now full of
danger. The followers of Mohammed were strong, and
it required true courage to face the perils of the long
journey. Willibald was undaunted, and with his father
and two brothers he sailed from Southampton, crossed
to France, sailed up the Seine to Rouen, and reached
Italy. Here the old father died. Willibald and his
brothers travelled on through " the vast lands of Italy,
through the depths of the valleys, over the steep brows
of the mountains, over the levels of the plains, climbing
on foot the difficult passes of the Alps, over the icebound
and snow-capped summits," till they arrived at Rome.
Thence they made their way to Syria, where they were
at once thrown into prison by Mohammedan conquerors.
They were brought before the ruler of the Mohammedan
world, or Khalif, whose seat was at Damascus. He asked
whence they came.

" These men come from the western shore, where the
sun sets : and we know not of any land beyond them,
but water only," was the answer.

Such was Britain to the Mohammedans. They never
got a footing in that country : their Empire lay to the
east, and their capital was even now shifting to Bagdad.

But before turning to their geographical discoveries
we must see how Cosmas, the Egyptian merchant-monk,
set the clock back by his quaint theories of the world in
the sixth century. Cosmas hailed from " Alexander's
great city." His calling carried him into seas and countries
remote from home. He knew the Mediterranean Sea,

the Persian Gulf, and the Red Sea. He had narrowly escaped shipwreck in the Indian Ocean, which in those days was regarded with terror on account of its violent currents and dense fogs. As the ship carrying the merchant approached this dread region, a storm gathered overhead, and flocks of albatross, like birds of ill-omen, hovered about the masts.

"We were all in alarm," relates Cosmas, "for all the men of experience on board, whether passengers or sailors, began to say that we were near the ocean and called out to the pilot: 'Steer the ship to port and make for the

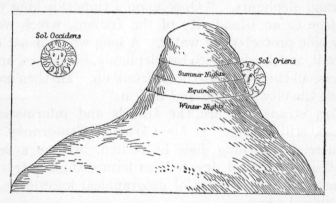

THE MOUNTAIN OF COSMAS, CAUSING NIGHT AND DAY AND THE SEASONS.

gulf, or we shall be swept along by the currents and carried into the ocean and lost.' For the ocean rushing into the gulf was swelling with billows of portentous size, while the currents from the gulf were driving the ship into the ocean, and the outlook was altogether so dismal that we were kept in a state of great alarm."

That he eventually reached India is clear, for he relates strange things concerning Ceylon. "There is a large oceanic island lying in the Indian Sea," he tells us. "It has a length of nine hundred miles and it is of the like extent in breadth. There are two kings in the island, and they are at feud the one with the other. The island, being as it is in a central position, is much frequented by ships from all parts of India, and from Persia and Ethiopia, and from the remotest countries, it receives silk, aloes, cloves, and other products . . . farther away is the clove country, then Tzinista (China), which produces silk. Beyond this there is no other country, for the ocean surrounds it on the east."

Cosmas was the first to realise that China was bounded on the east by the ocean. He tells us a good story about the " Lord of India," who always went to war with two thousand elephants. " Once upon a time this king would lay siege to an island city of the Indians, which was on every side protected by water. A long while he sat down before it, until, what with his elephants, his horses, and his soldiers, all the water had been drunk up. He then crossed over to the city dryshod and took it."

But, strange as are the travels and information of Cosmas, still stranger is his *Christian Topography.* His commercial travelling done he retired, became a devout Christian monk, and devoted his leisure time in trying to reconcile all the progress of geographical knowledge with old Biblical ideas.

He assures us that the world is flat and not round, and that it is surrounded by an immense wall supporting the firmament. Indeed, if we compare the maps of Cosmas in the sixth century with those of the Babylonians thousands of years before, there is mighty little difference. With amazing courage he refutes all the old theories and draws the most astounding maps, which, nevertheless, are the oldest Christian maps which survive.

CHAPTER XIV

THE VIKINGS SAIL THE NORTHERN SEAS

A MORE interesting force than the pilgrim travellers now claims our attention, and we turn to the frozen north, to the wild region at the back of the north wind, for new activity and discovery. Out of this land of fable and myth, legend and poetry, the fierce inhabitants of Scandinavia begin to take shape. Tacitus speaks of them as " mighty in fame," Ptolemy as " savage and clothed in the skins of wild beasts."

From time to time we have glimpses of these folk sailing about in the Baltic Sea. They were known to the Finns of the north as " sea-rovers." " The sea is their school of war and the storm their friend; they are sea-wolves that live on the pillage of the world," sang an old Roman long years ago. The daring spirit of their race had already attracted the attention of Britons across the seas. The careless glee with which they seized either sword or oar and waged war with the stormy seas for a scanty livelihood, raiding all the neighbouring coasts, had earned them the name of Vikings or creek men. Their black-sailed ships stood high out of the water, prow and stern ending in the head and tail of some strange animal, while their long beards, their loose shirts, and battleaxe made them conspicuous. " From the fury of the North-men save us, Lord," prayed those who had come in contact with these Vikings.

In the ninth century they spring into fame as explorers by the discovery of Iceland. It was in this wise. The chief of a band of pirates, one Naddod, during a voyage to the Faroe Islands was driven by a storm upon the eastern coast of an unknown land. Not a soul was to be seen. He climbed a high mountain covered with snow and took a look round, but though he could see far and wide, not a human being could he detect. So he named it Snow-land and sailed home to relate his adventures.

A few years later another Viking, Gardar, bound for the west coast of Scotland, was likewise blown by a storm on to the coast of Snow-land. He sailed right round and found it to be an island. Considering that it was unsafe to navigate the icy northern seas in winter, he built himself a hut on the island, lived there till the spring, and returned home. His account of the island fired the enthusiasm of an old Viking called Floki, who sailed away, meaning to take possession of the newly discovered country. At the Faroe Islands he let fly three ravens. The first returned, the second came back to the ship, the third guided the navigator to the island which he sought. He met a quantity of drift ice about the northern part of the island and called it Ice-land, the name it has borne ever since. But amid the Arctic ice he spent a desolate winter ; the island seemed full of lofty mountains covered with eternal snow. His companions, however, were delighted with the climate and the soil.

" Milk drops from every plant and butter from every twig," they said ; " this was a land where men might live free from the tyranny of kings." Free, indeed, for the island was totally uninhabited.

Iceland soon became a refuge for pirates and other lawless characters. Among these was a young Viking called Erik the Red. He was too lawless even for Iceland,

and, being banished for three years, he sailed away in 985 in search of new lands. At the end of his three years he returned and reported that he had discovered land with rich meadows, fine woods, and good fishing, which he had named Green-land. So glowing was his description that soon a party of men and women, with household goods and cattle, started forth in twenty-five ships to colonise the new land. Still the passion for discovery continued, and Erik's son Lief fitted out a vessel to carry

A VIKING SHIP.

A reconstruction (from Prof. Montelius's book on Scandinavian archæology) of an actual Viking ship found, almost complete, at Gokstad, Norway.

thirty-five men in quest of land already sighted to the west.

It was in the year 1000 that they reached the coast of North America. It was a barren and rocky shore to which Lief gave the name of Rock-land. Sailing farther, they found a low coast wooded to its edge, to which they gave the simple name of Woody-land. Two days later an island appeared, and on the mainland they discovered a river up which they sailed. On low bushes by the banks of the river they found sweet berries or wild grapes from which a sort of wine was made, so Lief called the land Vin-land. It is now supposed that Vinland and Woodyland are really Newfoundland and Labrador on the shores of North America. After this, shipload followed shipload from Iceland to colonise Vinland. But without success.

So the Viking discoveries in these cold and inhospitable regions were but transitory. The clouds lifted but for a moment to settle down again over America, till it was rediscovered some five hundred years later.

Before leaving these northern explorers let us remind ourselves of the old saga so graphic in its description of their ocean lives—

> " Down the fiord sweep wind and rain ;
> Our sails and tackle sway and strain ;
> Wet to the skin
> We're sound within.
> Our sea-steed through the foam goes prancing,
> While shields and spears and helms are glancing
> From fiord to sea,
> Our ships ride free,
> And down the wind with swelling sail
> We scud before the gathering gale."

Now, while these fierce old Vikings were navigating unknown seas, Alfred the Great was reigning over England. Among his many and varied interests he was deeply thrilled in the geography of the world. He was always ready to listen to those who had been on voyages of discovery, and in his account of the geography of Europe he tells us of a famous old sea captain called Othere, who had navigated the unknown seas to the north of Europe.

" Othere told his lord, King Alfred, that he dwelt northmost of all Northmen, on the land by the western sea. He said that the land is very long thence to the north; but it is all waste save that in a few places here and there Finns reside. He said that he wished to find out how far the land lay right north, or whether any man dwelt to the north of the waste. Then he went right north near the land, and he left all the way the waste land on the right and the wide sea on the left for three days. There was he as far north as the whale-hunters ever go. He then went yet right north, as far as he could sail in the next three days. After sailing for another nine days he came to a great river; they turned up into the river, but they durst not sail beyond it on account of hostility, for the land was all inhabited on the other side. He had not before met with any inhabited land since he came from his own home, for the land was un-inhabited all the way on his right save by fishermen, hunters, and fowlers, and they were all Finns, and there was always a wide sea on his left."

And as a trophy of distant lands and a proof of his having reached farthest north, Othere presented the King with a " snow-white walrus tooth."

But King Alfred wanted his subjects to know more of the world around them, and even in the midst of his busy life he managed to write a book in Anglo-Saxon, which sums up for us the world's knowledge some nine hundred years after Ptolemy—nine hundred barren years as far as much geographical progress was concerned. Alfred does not even allude to Iceland, Greenland, or Vinland. The news of these discoveries had evidently not reached him. He repeats the old legend of Thule to the north-west of Ireland, " which is known to few, on account of its very great distance."

So ends the brief but thrilling discoveries of the Northmen, who knew not fear, and we turn again to lands-men and the east.

CHAPTER XV

ARAB WAYFARERS

AND now we leave the fierce energy of the Northmen westwards and turn to another energy, which was leading men toward the east, to the lands beyond the Euphrates, to India, across central Asia, even into far Cathay.

These early travellers to the east were for the most part Arabs. Mohammed had bidden his followers to spread his teaching far and wide; this teaching had always appealed more to the eastern than to the western mind. So farther and farther to the east travelled the Arabs, converting the uncivilised tribes that Christianity had not reached.

What a contrast are these Arabs to the explorers of the vigorous north. They always travelled by land and not by that sea which was life to the Viking folk. To the Arabs the encircling ocean was a very "Sea of Darkness"; indeed, the unknown ocean beyond China was called the "Sea of Pitchy Darkness." Their creed taught that the ocean was boundless, so that ships dared not venture out of sight of land, for there was no inhabited country beyond, and mariners would assuredly be lost in mists and fogs. So, while the Vikings tossed fearlessly about the wild northern seas, the Arab wayfarers rode eastward by well-known caravan tracks, trading and teaching the ways of Mohammed. Arabic enterprise had pushed on far beyond Ptolemy's world. The Arab centre lay in the city of Bagdad, the headquarters of the ruler or Khalif of the Mohammedan world. They had already opened up a considerable trade with the rapidly rising Mongol Empire, which no European had yet reached.

But as this country was to play a large part in the travels of the near future, it will be interesting to hear the account given by two Mohammedan friends who journeyed thither in the year 831, just four hundred years before Marco Polo's famous account. The early part of their story is missing, and we raise the curtain when they have arrived in the land of China itself, then a very small empire compared with what it is now.

"The Emperor of China reckons himself next after the King of the Arabs, who they all allow to be the first and beyond all dispute the most powerful of kings, because he is the head of a great religion. In this great kingdom of China they tell us there are over two hundred cities; each city has four

A KHALIF ON HIS THRONE.
From the Ancona map, 1497.

gates, at each of which are five trumpets, which the Chinese sound at certain hours of the day and of the night. There are also within each city ten drums, which they beat at the same time as a public token of their obedience to the Emperor, as also to signify the hour of the day and of the night, to which end they also have dials and clocks with weights.

"China is a pleasant and fruitful country; the air is much better than the Indian provinces : much rain falls in both these countries. In India are many desert tracts, but China is inhabited and peopled throughout its whole extent. The Chinese are handsomer than the Indians, and come nearer the Arabs, not only in countenance, but in dress, in their way of riding, in their manners, and in their ceremonies. They wear long garments and girdles in form of belts. The Chinese are dressed in silk both winter and summer, and this kind of dress is common to the prince and the peasant. Their food is rice, which they often eat with a broth which they pour upon the rice. They have several sorts of fruits, apples, lemons, quinces, figs, grapes, cucumbers, walnuts, almonds, plums, apricots, and cocoanuts."

A CHINESE EMPEROR GIVING AUDIENCE, NINTH CENTURY.

From an old Chinese MS. at Paris, showing an Emperor of the dynasty that was ruling when the two Mohammedans visited China in 831.

Here, too, we get the first mention of tea, which was not introduced into Europe for another seven hundred years, but which formed a Chinese drink in the ninth century. This Chinese drink "is a herb or shrub, more bushy than the pomegranate tree and of a more pleasant scent, but somewhat bitter to the taste. The Chinese boil water and pour it in scalding hot upon this leaf, and this infusion keeps them from all distempers."

Here, too, we get the first mention of china ware. "They have an excellent kind of earth, wherewith they make a ware of equal fineness with glass and equally transparent."

There is no time here to tell of all the curious manners and customs related by these two Mohammedans. One thing struck them as indeed it must strike us to-day.

" The Chinese, poor and rich, great and small, learn to read and write. There are schools in every town for teaching the poor children, and the masters are maintained at public charge. . . . The Chinese have a stone ten cubits high erected in the public squares of their cities, and on this stone are engraved the names of all the medicines, with the exact price of each ; and when the poor stand in need of physic they go to the treasury where they receive the price each medicine is rated at."

It was out of such travels as these that the famous romance of "Sindbad the Sailor" took shape—a true story of Arab adventures of the ninth and tenth centuries in a romantic setting. As in the case of Ulysses, the adventures of many voyages are ascribed to one man and related in a collection of tales which bears the title of *The Arabian Nights*.

Of course, Sindbad was a native of Bagdad, the Arab centre of everything at this time, and of course he journeyed eastwards as did most Mohammedans.

"It occurred to my mind," says Sindbad, "to travel to the countries of other people ; then I arose and collected what I had of effects and apparel and sold them, after which I sold my buildings and all that my hand possessed and amassed three thousand pieces of silver. So I embarked in a ship, and with a company of merchants we traversed the sea for many days and nights. We had passed by island after island and from sea to sea and land to land, and in every place we sold and bought and exchanged merchandise. We continued our voyage until we arrived at an island like one of the gardens of Paradise."

Here they anchored and lit fires, when suddenly the master of the ship cried aloud in great distress : "Oh, ye passengers, come up quickly into the ship, leave your merchandise and flee for your lives, for this apparent island, upon which ye are, is not really an island, but it is a great fish that hath become stationary in the midst of the sea, and the sand hath accumulated upon it and trees have grown upon it, and when ye lighted a fire it felt the heat, and now it will descend with you into the sea and ye will all be drowned." As he spoke the island moved and " descended to the bottom of the sea with all that were upon it, and the roaring sea, agitated with waves, closed over it."

Let Sindbad continue his own story : " I sank in the sea with the rest. But God delivered me and saved me from drowning and supplied me with a great wooden bowl, and I laid hold upon it and gat into it and beat the water with my feet as with oars, while the waves sported with me. I remained so a day and a night, until the bowl came to a stoppage under a high island whereupon were trees overhanging the sea. So I laid hold upon the branch of a lofty tree and clung to it until I landed on the island. Then I threw myself upon the island like one dead."

After wandering about he found servants of the King of Borneo, and all sailed together to an island beyond the Malay Peninsula. And the King of Borneo sent for Sindbad and heaped him with honours. He gave him costly dress and made him superintendent of the seaport and adviser of affairs of state. And Sindbad saw many wonders in this far-distant sea. At last " one day I stood upon the shore of the sea, with a staff in my hand, as was my custom, and lo ! a great vessel approached wherein were many merchants." They unloaded their wares, telling Sindbad that the owner of their goods, a man from Bagdad, had been drowned and they were selling his things.

" What was the name of the owner of the goods ? " asked Sindbad.

" His name was Sindbad of the Sea."

Then Sindbad cried: " Oh, master, know that I am the owner of the goods and I am Sindbad of the Sea."

Then there was great rejoicing and Sindbad took leave of this King of Borneo and set sail for Bagdad—the Abode of Peace.

But the spirit of unrest was upon him and soon he was off again. Indeed, he made seven voyages in all, but there

The romance of " Sindbad the Sailor" is really a true story of Arab adventures at sea during the ninth and tenth centuries, put into a romantic setting and ascribed to one man. In the above map, which is a portion of the map of the world made by the famous Arab geographer, Edrisi, in 1154 A.D., many of the places to which Sindbad's story relates have been identified. Their modern names are as follows :—

Kotroba is (probably) Socotra.
Koulam Meli is Coulan, near Cape Comorin.
HIND is INDIA.
Serendib is Ceylon.
Murphili (or Monsul), the " Valley of Diamonds," is Masulipatam.
Roibahat, the "Clove Islands," are the Maldive Islands.

Rami, the "Island of Apes," is Sumatra.
Maid Dzaba, the "island with the volcano," is Banca.
Senf is Tsiampa, S. Cochin-China.
Mudza (or Mehrage) is Borneo.
Kamrun is Java.
Maid, the Camphor Island, is Formosa.

Edrisi's names are those which are used in the *Arabian Nights.*

is only room here to note a few of the most important points in each. This time he sailed to the coast of Zanzibar, East Africa, and, anchoring on the beautiful island of Madagascar, amid sweet-smelling flowers, pure rivers, and warbling birds, Sindbad fell asleep. He awoke to find the ship had sailed away, leaving him without food or drink, and not a human being was to be seen on the island.

" Then I climbed up into a lofty tree and began to look from it to the right and left, but saw nothing save sky and water and trees and birds and islands and sands."

At last he found an enormous bird. Unwinding his turban, he twisted it into a rope and, tying one end round his wrist, tied the other to one of the bird's great feet. Up flew the giant bird high into the sky and Sindbad with it, descending somewhere in India in the Valley of Diamonds. This bird was afterwards identified as an enormous eagle.

" And I arose and walked in that valley," says Sindbad, " and I beheld its ground to be composed of diamonds, with which they perforate minerals and jewels, porcelain, and the onyx, and it is a stone so hard that neither iron nor rock have any effect upon it. All that valley was likewise occupied by serpents and venomous snakes."

Here Sindbad found the camphor trees, "under each of which trees a hundred men might shade themselves." From these trees flowed liquid camphor. " In this island, too, is a kind of wild beast, called rhinoceros— it is a huge beast with a single horn, thick, in the middle of its head, and it lifteth the great elephant upon its horn."

Thus, after collecting heaps of diamonds, Sindbad returned to Bagdad—a rich man.

Again his soul yearns for travel. This time he starts for China, but his ship is driven out of its course and cast on the Island of Apes, probably Sumatra. These apes, " the most hideous of beasts, covered with hair like black felt," surrounded the ship. They climbed up the cables and severed them with their teeth to Sindbad's great alarm. He escaped to the neighbouring islands known as the Clove Islands, and again reached Bagdad safely. Again and yet again he starts forth on fresh adventures. Now he is sailing on the seas beyond

Ceylon, now his ship is being pursued by a giant roc whose young have been killed and eaten by Sindbad. Sindbad as usual escapes upon a plank, and sails to an island, where he meets the "Old Man of the Sea," probably a huge ape from Borneo. On he passed to the "Island of Apes," where, every night, the people who reside in it go forth from the doors of the city that open upon the sea in their fear of the apes lest they should come down upon them in the night from the mountains. After this we find Sindbad trading in pepper on the Coromandel coast of modern India and discovering a wealth of pearls by the seashore of Ceylon. But at last he grew tired of seafaring, which was never congenial to Arabs.

SINDBAD'S GIANT ROC.
From an Oriental miniature painting.

> "Hateful was the dark blue sky,
> Vaulted o'er the dark blue sea;
> Sore task to heart, worn out by many wars;
> And eyes grown dim with gazing on the pilot stars."

So he leaves private adventuring alone and is appointed by the Khalif of Bagdad to convey a letter and present to the Indian prince of Ceylon—an expedition that lasts him twenty-seven years. The presents were magnificent. They included a horse worth ten thousand pieces of gold, with its saddle adorned with gold set with jewels, a book, a splendid dress, and some beautiful white Egyptian cloth, Greek carpets, and a crystal cup. Having duly delivered these gifts, he took his leave, meaning to return to his own country. But the usual adventures befell him. This time his ship was surrounded by a number of boats on board of which were men like little devils with swords and daggers. These attacked the ship, captured Sindbad, and sold him to a rich man as a slave. He set him to shoot elephants from a tree with bows and arrows. At last, after many other adventures and having made seven long voyages, poor Sindbad reached his home.

CHAPTER XVI

TRAVELLERS TO THE EAST

But if the Sindbad saga is based on the stories of Mohammedan travellers and sum up Arab adventure by sea in the tenth century, we must turn to another Arab —Massoudy by name—for land travel of the same period. Massoudy left his home at Bagdad very young and seems to have penetrated into every Mohammedan country from Spain to farther India. In his famous *Meadows of Gold*, with its one hundred and thirty-two chapters, dedicated to " the most illustrious Kings," he describes the various lands through which he has travelled, giving us at the same time a good deal of incorrect information about lands he has never seen.

> " I have gone so far towards the setting sun
> That I have lost all remembrance of the east,
> And my course has taken me so far towards the rising sun
> That I have forgotten the very name of west."

One cannot but look with admiration on the energetic Arab traveller, when one remembers the labour of travel even in the tenth century. There were the long, hot rides through central Asia, under a burning sun, the ascent of unknown mountains, the crossing of unbridged rivers. From his lengthy work we will only extract a few details. Though he had " gone so far toward the setting sun," his knowledge of the West was very limited, and while Vikings tossed on the Atlantic westwards, Massoudy tells us that it is "impossible to navigate beyond the Pillars of Hercules, for no vessel sails on that sea; it is without cultivation or inhabitant, and its end, like its depth, is unknown." Such was the "Green Sea of Darkness" as it was called by the Arabs. Massoudy is more at home when he journeys towards the rising sun to the East, but his descriptions of China, the "Flowery Land," the "Celestial Country," were to be excelled by others.

We must pass over Edrisi, who in 1153 wrote on "The going abroad of a curious Man to explore all the Wonders of the World," which wonders he explored very imperfectly, though he has left us a map of the world, which may be seen to-day at the Bodleian Library at Oxford.

But we cannot pass over Benjamin of Tudela in so few words. "Our Benjamin" he is called by Pinkerton, who in the eighteenth century made a wonderful collection of voyages and travels of all ages. "Our Benjamin" was a Jew hailing from Tudela in Spain, and he started forth on his travels with a view to ascertaining the condition and numbers of Jews living in the midst of the great Mohammedan Empire. Benjamin made his way in the year 1160 to the "exceeding great city" of Constantinople, which "hath none to compare with it except Bagdad— the mighty city of the Arabs." With the great temple of St. Sophia and its pillars of gold and silver, he was immensely struck. In wrapt admiration he gazed at the Emperor's palace with its walls of beaten gold, its hanging crown suspended over the Imperial throne, blazing with precious stones, so splendid that the hall needed no other light. No less striking were the crimson embroidered garments worn by the Greeks, who rode to and from the city like princes on horseback. Benjamin turns sadly to the Jewish quarter. No Jew might ride on horseback here. All were treated as objects of contempt; they were herded together, often beaten in the streets.

From the wealth and luxury of Constantinople Benjamin makes his way to Syria. At Jerusalem he finds some two hundred Jews commanding the dyeing trade. And here we must remind ourselves that the second crusade was over and the third had not yet taken place, that Jerusalem, the City of Peace, had been in the hands of the Mohammedans or Saracens till 1099, when it fell into the hands of the Crusaders. From Jerusalem, by way of Damascus, Benjamin entered Persia, and he gives us an interesting account of Bagdad and its Khalifs. The Khalif was the head of the Mohammedans in the same way that the Pope was the head of the Christians. "He was," says "Our Benjamin," "a very dignified personage, friendly towards the Jews, a kind-hearted man, but never to be seen." Pilgrims from distant lands, passing through Bagdad on their way to Mecca, prayed to

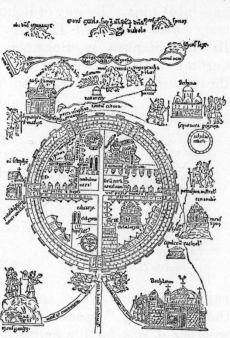

JERUSALEM AND THE PILGRIMS' WAYS TO IT
IN THE TWELFTH CENTURY.

From a map of the twelfth century at Brussels.

be allowed to see "the brightness of his face," but they were only allowed to kiss one end of his garment. Now, although Benjamin describes the journey from Bagdad to China, it is very doubtful if he ever got to China himself, so we will leave him delighting in the glories of Bagdad, with its palm trees, its gardens and orchards, rejoicing in the statistics of Jews, and turn to the adventures of one, Carpini, who really did reach Tartary.

This Carpini, or Friar John, was a Franciscan who was chosen by the Pope to go to the Great Khan of the Mongol Empire, which was threatening to overrun Christendom.   On 16th April 1245, Friar John left the cloister for the unknown tract of country by which he had to pass into China.   By way of Bohemia he passed into Russia, and, having annexed Brother Benedict in Poland and Brother Stephen in Bohemia, together with a guide, Carpini made his way eastwards.   It was mid-winter; the travellers had to ride on Tartar horses, "for they alone could find grass under the snow, or live, as animals must in Tartary, without hay or straw.   Sometimes Friar John fell so ill that he had to be placed in a cart and carried through the deep snow.

TWO EMPERORS OF TARTARY.
From the Catalan map, 1375.

It was Easter 1246, just a year after their start, that Friar John and his companions began the last section of their journey beyond the Volga, and "most tearfully we set out," not knowing whether it was for life or for death."   So thin had they all become that not one of them could ride.   Still they toiled on, till one July day they entered Mongolia and found the headquarters of the Great Khan about half a day's journey from Karakorum.   They arrived in time to witness the enthronement of the new Khan in August. Here were crowds of ambassadors from Russia and Persia as well as from outlying parts of the growing Mongol Empire.   These were laden with gifts—indeed, there were no less than five hundred crates full of silks, satins, brocades, fur, gold embroidery. Friar John and his companions had no gifts to offer save the letter from the Pope.

Impressive, indeed, in the eyes of the once cloistered friar must have been this first sight of Eastern splendour. High on a neighbouring hill stood the Khan's tent, resting on pillars plated with gold, top and sides covered with silk brocades, while the great ceremony took place. But the men of the West were not welcomed by the new Emperor of the East. It was supposed that he intended shortly to unfurl his Standard against the whole of the Western world, and in November Friar John and his companions found themselves formally dismissed with a missive from the Great Khan to the Pope, signed and sealed by the Khan himself.

A TARTAR CAMP.
From the Borgian map, 1453.

The return journey was even more trying; winter was coming on, and for nearly seven months the Pope's faithful envoys struggled on across the endless open plains of Asia towards Russia, resting their eyes on vast expanses of snow. At last they reached home, and Friar John wrote his *Book of the Tartars*, in which he informs us that Mongolia is in the east part of the world and that Cathay is "a country in the east of Asia." To the south-west of Mongolia he heard of a vast desert, where lived certain wild men unable to speak and with no joints in their legs. These occupy themselves in making felt out of camel's hair for garments to protect them from the weather.

Again Carpini tells us about that mythical character figuring in the travel books of this time—Prester John. "The Mongol army," he says, "marched against the

Christians dwelling in the greater India, and the king of that country, known by the name of Prester John, came forth with his army to meet them. This Prester John caused a number of hollow copper figures to be made, resembling men which were stuffed with combustibles and set upon horses, each having a man behind on the horse, with a pair of bellows to stir up the fire. At the first onset of the battle these mounted figures were sent forward to the charge; the men who rode behind them set fire to the combustibles and then strongly blew with the bellows; immediately the Mongol horses and men were burnt with wild-fire and the air was darkened with smoke."

We shall hear of Prester John again. For within a few years of the return of Friar John, another Franciscan friar, William de Rubruquis, was sent forth, this time by the French king, Louis, to carry letters to the Great Khan begging him to embrace Christianity and acknowledge the supremacy of the Pope. William and his chosen companions had a painful and difficult journey of some months before they reached the camps on the Volga of one of the great Mongol lords. Indeed, " if it had not been for the grace of God and the biscuit which we brought with us, we had surely perished," remarks the pious friar in the history of his adventures. Never once did they enjoy the shelter of a house or tent, but passed the nights in the open air in a cart. At last they were ordered to appear at the Court of the great ruler with all their books and vestments.

" We were commanded to array ourselves in our sacred vestments to appear before the prince. Putting on, therefore, our most precious ornaments, I took a cushion in my arms, together with the Bible I had from the King of France and the beautiful Psalter which the Queen bestowed upon me : my companion at the

same time carried the missal and a crucifix; and the
clerk, clothed in his surplice, bore a censer in his hand.
In this order we presented ourselves . . . singing the
Salve Regina." It is a strange picture this—the European
friars, in all the vestments of their religion, standing before
the Eastern prince of this far-off country. They would
fain have carried home news of his conversion, but they
were told in angry tones that the prince was "not a Christian, but a Mongol."

They were dismissed with orders to visit the Great
Khan at Karakorum. Re-
suming their journey early in
August, the messengers did not
arrive at the Court of the Great
Khan till the day after Christmas. They were miserably
housed in a tiny hut with
scarcely room for their beds
and baggage. The cold was
intense. The bare feet of the
friars caused great astonishment
to the crowds of onlookers, who
stared at the strange figures as
though they had been monsters.
However, they could not keep
their feet bare long, for very soon Rubruquis found that
his toes were frozen.

INITIAL LETTER FROM THE MS.
OF RUBRUQUIS AT CAMBRIDGE.

Probably representing the friars starting
on their journey.

Chanting in Latin the hymn of the Nativity, the
visitors were at last admitted to the Imperial tent, hung
about with cloth of gold, where they found the Khan.
He was seated on a couch—a "little man of moderate
height, aged about forty-five, and dressed in a skin spotted
and glossy like a seal." The Mongol Emperor asked
numerous questions about the kingdom of France and
the possibility of conquering it, to the righteous indigna-

8

tion of the friars. They stayed in the country till the end of May, when they were dismissed, having failed in their mission, but having gained a good deal of information about the great Mongol Empire and its somewhat mysterious ruler.

But while the kingdoms in Europe trembled before the growing expansion of the Mongol Empire and the dangers of Tartar hordes, the merchants of Venice rejoiced in the new markets which were opening for them in the East.

CHAPTER XVII

MARCO POLO

Now Venice at this time was full of enterprising merchants —merchants such as we hear of in Shakspere's *Merchant of Venice.* Among these were two Venetians, the brothers Polo. Rumours had reached them of the wealth of the mysterious land of Cathay, of the Great Khan, of Europeans making their way, as we have seen, through barren wildernesses, across burning deserts in the face of hardships indescribable, to open up a highway to the Far East.

So off started Maffio and Niccolo Polo on a trading enterprise, and, having crossed the Mediterranean, came " with a fair wind and the blessing of God " to Constantinople, where they disposed of a large quantity of their merchandise. Having made some money, they directed their way to Bokhara, where they fell in with a Tartar nobleman, who persuaded them to accompany him to the Court of the Great Khan himself. Ready for adventure, they agreed, and he led them in a north-easterly direction ; now they were delayed by heavy snows, now by the swelling of unbridged rivers, so that it was a year before they reached Pekin, which they considered was the extremity of the East. They were courteously received by the Great Khan, who questioned them closely about their own land, to which they replied in the Tartar language which they had learnt on the way.

Now since the days of Friar John there was a new Khan named Kublai, who wished to send messengers to

the Pope to beg him to send a hundred wise men to teach
the Chinese Christianity. He chose the Polo brothers as
his envoys to the Pope, and accordingly they started off

HOW THE BROTHERS POLO SET OUT FROM CONSTANTINOPLE WITH
THEIR NEPHEW MARCO FOR CHINA.

From a miniature painting in the fourteenth century *Livre des Merveilles.*

to fulfil his behests. After an absence of fifteen years
they again reached Venice. The very year they had left
home Niccolo's wife had died, and his boy, afterwards to

become the famous traveller, Marco Polo, had been born. The boy was now fifteen.

The stories told by his father and uncle of the Far East and the Court of the greatest Emperor on earth filled the boy with enthusiasm, and when in 1271 the brothers Polo set out for their second journey to China, not only were they accompanied by the young Marco, but also by

MARCO POLO LANDS AT ORMUZ.

From a miniature in the *Livre des Merveilles.*

two preaching friars to teach the Christian faith to Kublai Khan.

Their journey lay through Armenia, through the old city of Nineveh to Bagdad, where the last Khalif had been butchered by the Tartars. Entering Persia as traders, the Polo family passed on to Ormuz, hoping to take ship from here to China. But, for some unknown reason, this was impossible, and the travellers made their way north-eastwards to the country about the sources of the river Oxus. Here young Marco fell sick of a low fever, and for a whole year they could not proceed. Resuming their journey at last "in high spirits," they crossed the great highlands of the Pamirs, known as the "roof of the world," and, descending on Khotan, found themselves face to face with the great Gobi Desert. For thirty days they journeyed over the sandy wastes of the silent wilderness, till they came to a city in the province of Tangut, where they were met by messengers from the Khan, who had heard of their approach. But it was not till May 1275 that they actually reached the Court of Kublai Khan after their tremendous journey of "one thousand days." The preaching friars had long since turned homewards, alarmed at the dangers of the way, so only the three stout-hearted Polos were left to deliver the Pope's message to the ruler of the Mongol Empire.

"The lord of all the earth," as he was called by his people, received them very warmly. He inquired at once who was the young man with them.

"My lord," replied Niccolo, "he is my son and your servant."

"Then," said the Khan, "he is welcome. I am much pleased with him."

So the three Venetians abode at the Court of Kublai Khan. His summer palace was at Shang-tu, called Xanadu by the poet Coleridge—

> "In Xanadu did Kublai Khan
> A stately pleasure dome decree,
> Where Alph, the sacred river, ran
> Through caverns measureless to man
> Down to a sacred sea.
> So twice five miles of fertile ground,
> With walls and towers were girdled round:
> And there were gardens bright with sinuous rills,
> Where blossom'd many an incense-bearing tree;
> And here were forests ancient as the hills,
> Enfolding sunny spots of greenery."

So the three Venetians abode at the Court of the

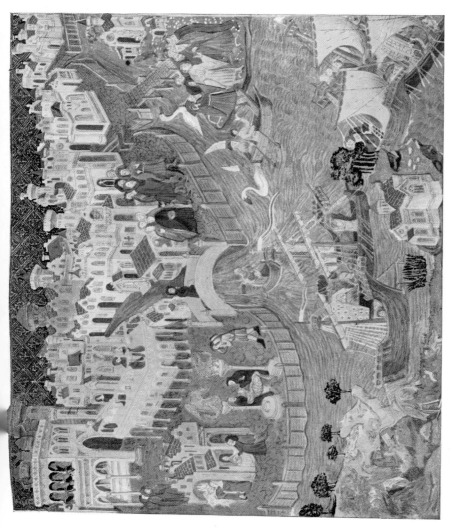

THE POLOS LEAVING VENICE FOR THEIR TRAVELS TO THE FAR EAST.

From a miniature which stands at the head of a late 14th century MS. of the *Travels of Marco Polo* (or the *Book of the Grand Khan*) in the Bodleian Library, Oxford. The drawing shows the Piazzetta at Venice, with the Polos embarking, and in the foreground indications of the strange lands they visited.

Chinese Emperor for no less than seventeen years. Young Marco displayed so great intelligence that he was sent on a mission for the Khan some six months' journey distant; and so well did he describe the things he had seen and the lands through which he had passed, that the Khan heaped on him honours and riches. Let us hear what Marco says of his lord and master.

"The Great Khan, lord of lords, named Kublai, is of middle stature, neither too full nor too short: he has a beautiful fresh complexion, his colour is fair, his eyes dark."

The capital of the Empire, Pekin, two days' journey from the sea, and the residence of the Court during the months of December, January, and February, called out the unbounded enthusiasm of the Polos. The city, two days' journey from the ocean, in the extreme north-east of Cathay, had

KUBLAI KHAN.
From an old Chinese Encyclopædia at Paris.

been newly rebuilt in a regular square, six miles on each side, surrounded by walls of earth and having twelve gates.

"The streets are so broad and so straight," says Marco, "that from one gate another is visible. It contains many beautiful houses and palaces, and a very large one in the midst, containing a steeple with a large bell which at night sounds three times, after which no man must leave the city. At each gate a thousand men keep guard, not from dread of any enemy, but in reverence of the monarch who dwells within it, and to prevent injury by robbers."

This square form of Pekin, the great breadth of the straight streets, the closing of the gates by sound of a bell—the largest in the world—is noted by all travellers to this far-eastern city of Cathay.

But greater even than Pekin was the city of Kin-sai (Hang-tcheou-fou), the City of Heaven, in the south of China. It had but lately fallen into the hands of Kublai Khan.

"And now I will tell you all its nobleness," says Marco, "for without doubt it is the largest city in the world. The city is one hundred miles in circumference and has twelve thousand stone bridges, and beneath the greater part of these a large ship might pass. And you need not wonder there are so many bridges, because the city is wholly on the water and surrounded by it like Venice. The merchants are so numerous and so rich that their wealth can neither be told nor believed. They and their ladies do nothing with their own hands, but live as delicately as if they were kings. These females also are of most angelic beauty, and live in the most elegant manner. The people are idolaters, subject to the Great Khan, and use paper money. They eat the flesh of dogs and other beasts, such as no Christian would touch for the world. In this city, too, are four thousand baths, in which the citizens, both men and women, take great delight and frequently resort thither, because they keep their persons very cleanly. They are the largest and most beautiful baths in the world, insomuch that one hundred of either sex may bathe in them at once. Twenty-five miles from thence is the ocean, and there is a city (Ning-po) which has a very fine port, with large ships and much merchandise of immense value from India and other quarters."

But though Marco revels in the description of wonderful cities, he is continually leading us back to the Great Khan himself. His festivals were splendid. The tables were

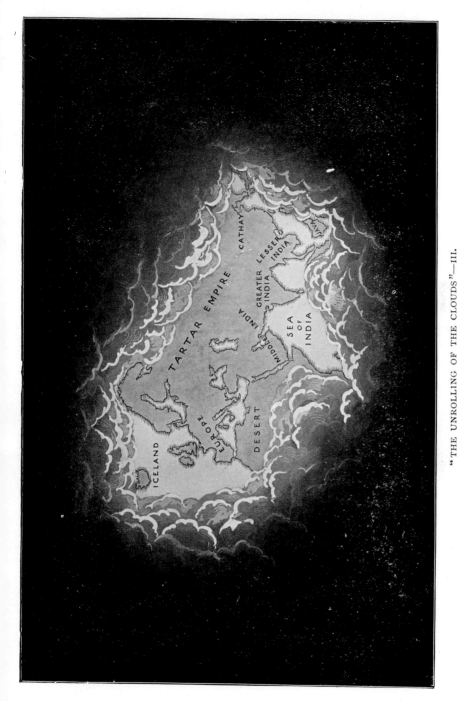

"THE UNROLLING OF THE CLOUDS"—III.

The world as known at the end of the thirteenth century after the travels of Marco Polo and his contemporaries.

arranged so that the Emperor sat higher than all the others, always with his face to the south. His sons and daughters were placed so that their heads were on a level with his feet. Some forty thousand people feast on these occasions, but the Khan himself is served only by his great barons, their mouths wrapped in rich towels embroidered in gold and silver, that their breath might not blow upon the plates. His presents were on a colossal scale; it was no rare occurrence for him to receive five thousand camels, one hundred thousand beautiful horses, and five thousand elephants covered with cloth of gold and silver.

" And now I will relate a wonderful thing," says Marco. " A large lion is led into his presence, which, as soon as it sees him, drops down and makes a sign of deep humility, owning him its lord and moving about without any chain."

His kingdom was ruled by twelve barons all living at Pekin. His provinces numbered thirty-four, hence their method of communication was very complete.

" Messengers are sent to divers provinces," says Marco, " and on all the roads they find at every twenty-five miles a post, where the messengers are received. At each is a large edifice containing a bed covered with silk and everything useful and convenient for a traveller . . . here, too, they find full four hundred horses, whom the prince has ordered to be always in waiting to convey them along the principal roads. . . . Thus they go through the provinces, finding everywhere inns and horses for their reception. Moreover, in the intervals between these stations, at every three miles are erected villages of about forty houses inhabited by foot-runners also employed on these dispatches. They wear large girdles set round with bells, which are heard at a great distance. Receiving a letter or packet, one runs full speed to the next village, when his approach being announced by bells, another is ready to start and proceed to the next, and so on. By these pedestrian messengers the Khan receives news in one day and night from places ten days' journey distant; in two days from those twenty off, and in ten from those a hundred days' journey distant. Thus he sends his messengers through all his kingdoms and provinces to know if any of his subjects have had their crops injured through bad weather; and, if any such injury has happened, he does not exact from them any tribute for that season —nay, he gives them corn out of his own stores to subsist on."

This first European account of China is all so delightful that it is difficult to know where to stop. The mention of coal is interesting. " Throughout the whole province of Cathay," says Marco, " are a kind of black stones cut from the mountains in veins, which burn like logs. They maintain the fire better than wood. If you put them on in the evening they will preserve it the whole night, and it will be found burning in the morning. Throughout the whole of Cathay this fuel is used. They have also wood, but the stones are much less expensive."

Neither can we pass over Marco's account of the wonderful stone bridge with its twenty-four arches of pure marble across the broad river, " the most magnificent object in the whole world," across which ten horsemen could ride abreast, or the Yellow River (Hoang-ho), " so large and broad that it cannot be crossed by a bridge, and flows on even to the ocean," or the wealth of mulberry trees throughout the land, on which lived the silkworms that have made China so famous for her silk.

Then there are the people famous for their manufacture of fine porcelain ware. " Great quantities of porcelain earth were here collected into heaps and in this way exposed to the action of the atmosphere for some forty years, during which time it was never disturbed. By this

process it became refined and fitted for manufacture."
Such is Marco's only allusion to china ware. With regard
to tea he is entirely silent.

But he is the first European to tell us about the
islands of Japan, fifteen hundred miles from the coast
of China, now first discovered to
the geographers of the West.

"Zipangu," says Marco, "is an
island situated at a distance from
the mainland. The people are fair
and civilised in their manners—they
possess precious metals in extraordinary abundance. The people
are white, of gentle manners, idolaters in religion under a king of their
own. These folk were attacked by
the fleet of Kublai Khan in 1264 for
their gold, for the King's house,
windows, and floors were covered
with it, but the King allowed no
exportation of it."

Thus Marco Polo records in dim
outline the existence of land beyond
that ever dreamed of by Europeans
—indeed, denied by Ptolemy and
other geographers of the West. In

MARCO POLO.

From a woodcut in the first printed
edition of Marco Polo's *Travels*,
Nuremburg, 1477.

the course of his service under
Kublai Khan he opened up the eight
provinces of Tibet, the whole of
south-east Asia from Canton to Bengal, and the archipelago of farther India. He tells us, too, of Tibet, that
wide country "vanquished and wasted by the Khan
for the space of twenty days' journey"—a great wilderness
wanting people, but overrun by wild beasts. Here were
great Tibetan dogs as large as asses. Still on duty for

Kublai Khan, Marco reached Bengal, "which borders upon India." But he was glad enough to return to his adopted Chinese home, "the richest and most famous country of all the East."

At last the Polo family wearied of Court honours, and they were anxious to return to their own people at Venice. However, the Khan was very unwilling to let them go. One day their chance came. The Persian ruler was anxious to marry a princess of the house of Kublai Khan, and it was decided to send the lady by sea under the protection of the trusted Polos, rather than to allow her to undergo the hardships of an overland journey from China to Persia.

So in the year 1292 they bade farewell to the great Kublai Khan, and with the little princess of seventeen and her suite they set sail with an escort of fourteen ships for India. Passing many islands "with gold and much trade," after three months at sea they reached Java, at this time supposed to be the greatest island in the world, above three thousand miles round. At Sumatra they were detained five months by stress of weather, till at last they reached the Bay of Bengal. Sailing on a thousand miles westwards, they reached Ceylon—"the finest island in the world," remarks Marco. It was not till two years after their start and the loss of six hundred sailors that they arrived at their destination, only to find that the ruler of Persia was dead. However, they gave the little bride to his son and passed on by Constantinople to Venice, where they arrived in 1295.

And now follows a strange sequel to the story. After their long absence, and in their travel-stained garments, their friends and relations could not recognise them, and in vain did they declare that they were indeed the Polos— father, son, and uncle—who had left Venice twenty-four long years ago. It was no use; no one believed their story. So this is what they did. They arranged for a great banquet to be held, to which they invited all their relations and friends. This they attended in robes of crimson satin. Then suddenly Marco rose from the table and, going out of the room, returned with the three coarse, travel-stained garments. They ripped open seams, tore out the lining, and a quantity of precious stones, rubies, sapphires, diamonds, and emeralds poured forth.

A JAPANESE FIGHT AGAINST THE CHINESE AT THE TIME WHEN
MARCO POLO FIRST SAW JAPANESE.
From an ancient Japanese painting.

The company were filled with wonder, and when the story spread all the people of Venice came forth to do honour to their famous fellow-countrymen.

Marco was surnamed Marco of the Millions, and never tired of telling the wonderful stories of Kublai Khan, the great Emperor who combined the " rude magnificence of the desert with the pomp and elegance of the most civilised empire in the Old World."

CHAPTER XVIII

THE END OF MEDIÆVAL EXPLORATION

THE two names of Ibn Batuta and Sir John Mandeville now conclude our mediæval period of travel to the Eastward. Both the Arab and the Englishman date their travels between the years 1325 and 1355; but while Ibn Batuta, the traveller from Tangiers, adds very valuable information to our geographical knowledge, we have to lay the travel volumes of Sir John Mandeville aside and acknowledge sadly that his book is made up of borrowed experiences, that he has wantonly added fiction to fact, and distorted even the travel stories told by other travellers. And yet, strange to say, while the work of Ibn Batuta remains entirely disregarded, the delightful work of the Englishman is still read vigorously to-day and translated into nearly every European language. In it we read strange stories of Prester John, " the great Emperor of India, who is served by seven kings, seventy-two dukes, and three hundred and sixty earls"; he speaks of the " isle of Cathay " : he repeats the legend of the island near Java on which Adam and Eve wept for one hundred years after they had been driven from Paradise; he speaks of giants thirty feet high, and of Pigmies who came dancing to see him.

We turn to the Arab traveller for a solid document, which rings more true, and we cannot doubt his accounts of shipwreck and hardships encountered by the way. Ibn Batuta left Tangiers in the year 1324 at the early age of twenty-one on a pilgrimage to Mecca. He made his way across the north of Africa to Alexandria. Here history relates he met a learned and pious man named Imam.

" I perceive," said Imam, " that you are fond of visiting distant countries ? "

" That is so," answered Ibn Batuta.

" Then you must visit my brother in India, my brother in Persia, and my brother in China, and when you see them present my compliments to them."

Ibn Batuta left Alexandria with a resolve to visit these three persons, and indeed, wonderful to say, he found them all three and presented to them their brother's compliments.

SIR JOHN MANDEVILLE ON HIS TRAVELS.
From a MS. in the British Museum.

He reached Mecca and remained there for three years, after which he voyaged down the Red Sea to Aden, a port of much trade. Coasting along the east coast of Africa, he reached Mombasa, from which port, so soon to fall into the hands of the Portuguese, he sailed to Ormuz, a " city on the seashore," at the entrance to the Persian Gulf. Here he tells us of the head of a fish " that might be compared to a hill : its eyes were like two doors, so that people could go in at one eye and out at the other." Crossing central Arabia and the Black Sea, he found himself for the first time in a Christian city, and was much dismayed at all the bells ringing. He was anxious to go north through Russia to the Land of Darkness, of which he had heard such wonderful tales. It was a land where there were neither trees, nor stones, nor houses, where dogs with nails in their feet drew little sledges across the ice. Instead he went to Constantinople, arriving at sunset when the bells were ringing so loud "that the very horizon shook with the noise." Ibn was presented to the Emperor as a remarkable traveller, and a letter of safe conduct was given to him.

He then made his way through Bokhara and Herat, Kandahar and Kabul, over the Hindu Koosh and across the Indus to Delhi, "the greatest city in the world." But at this time it was a howling wilderness, as the inhabitants had fled from the cruelty of the Turkish Emperor. Into his presence our traveller was now called and graciously received.

"The lord of the world appoints you to the office of judge in Delhi," said the Emperor; "he gives you a dress of honour with a saddled horse and a large yearly salary."

Ibn held this office for eight years, till one day the Emperor called him and said: "I wish to send you as ambassador to the Emperor of China, for I know you are fond of travelling in foreign countries."

The Emperor of China had sent presents of great value to the Emperor of India, who was now anxious to return the compliment. Quaint, indeed, were the gifts from India to China. There were one hundred high-bred horses, one hundred dancing girls, one hundred pieces of cotton stuff, also silk and wool, some black, some white, blue-green or blue. There were swords of state and golden candlesticks, silver basins, brocade dresses, and gloves embroidered with pearls. But so many adventures did Ibn Batuta have on his way to China that it is certain that none of

these things ever reached that country, for eighty miles
from Delhi the cavalcade was attacked and Ibn was
robbed of all he had.   For days he wandered alone in a
forest, living on leaves, till he was rescued more dead than
alive, and carried back to Delhi.   The second start was
also unfortunate.   By a circuitous route he made his
way to Calicut on the Malabar coast, where he made
a stay of three months till the monsoons should permit
him to take ship for China.   The harbour of Calicut was
full of great Chinese ships called
junks.   These junks struck him
as unlike anything he had seen
before.   "The sails are made of
cane reed woven together like a
mat, which, when they put into
port, they leave standing in the
wind.   In some of these vessels
there will be a thousand men,
sailors and soldiers.   Built in
the ports of China only, they
are rowed with large oars, which
may be compared to great masts.
On board are wooden houses in
which the higher officials reside
with their wives."

AN EMPEROR OF TARTARY.

From the map ascribed to Sebastian
Cabot, 1544.

The time of the voyage came ; thirteen huge junks were
taken, and the imperial presents were embarked.   All
was ready for a start on the morrow.   Ibn stayed on
shore praying in the mosque till starting-time.   That night
a violent hurricane arose and most of the ships in the
harbour were destroyed.   Treasure, crew, and officers
all perished, and Ibn was left alone and almost penniless.
He feared to return to Delhi, so he took ship, which landed
him on one of a group of a thousand islands, which Ibn
calls "one of the wonders of the world."   The chief

9

island was governed by a woman. Here he was made a judge, and soon became a great personage. But after a time he grew restless and set sail for Sumatra. Here at the court of the king, who was a zealous disciple of Mohammed, Ibn met with a kind reception, and after a fortnight, provided with provisions, the " restless Mohammedan " again voyaged northwards into the " Calm Sea," or the Pacific as we call it now. It was so still, " disturbed by neither wind nor waves," that the ship had to be towed by a smaller ship till they reached China.

" This is a vast country," writes Ibn, " and it abounds in all sorts of good things—fruit, corn, gold, and silver. It is traversed by a great river—the Waters of Life—which runs through the heart of China for a distance of six months' journey. It is bordered with villages, cultivated plains, orchards, and markets, just like the Nile in Egypt."

Ibn gives an amusing account of the Chinese poultry. " The cocks and hens are bigger than our geese. I one day bought a hen," he says, " which I wanted to boil, but one pot would not hold it and I was obliged to take two. As for the cocks in China, they are as big as ostriches."

" ' Pooh,' cried an owner of Chinese fowls, ' there are cocks in China much bigger than that,' and I found he had said no more than the truth."

" Silk is very plentiful, for the worms which produce it require little attention. They have silk in such abundance that it is used for clothing even by poor monks and beggars. The people of China do not use gold and silver coin in their commercial dealings. Their buying and selling is carried on by means of pieces of paper about the size of the palm of the hand, carrying the seal of the Emperor." The Arab traveller has much to say about the superb painting of China. They study and paint every stranger that visits their country, and the portrait thus taken is exposed on the city wall. Thus, should a stranger do anything to make flight necessary, his portrait would be sent out into every province and he would soon be discovered.

" China is the safest as well as the pleasantest of all the regions on the earth for a traveller. You may travel the whole nine months' journey to which the Empire extends without the slightest cause to fear, even if you have treasure in your charge. But it afforded me no pleasure. On the contrary, my spirit was sorely troubled within me to see how Paganism had the upper hand."

Troubles now broke out among the Khan's family,

A CARAVAN IN CATHAY.

From the Catalan map, 1375.

which led to civil wars and the death of the Great Khan. He was buried with great pomp. A deep chamber was dug in the earth, into which a beautiful couch was placed, on which was laid the dead Khan with his arms and all his rich apparel, the earth over him being heaped to the height of a large hill.

Batuta now hurried from the country, took a junk to Sumatra, thence to Calicut and by Ormuz home to Tangier, where he arrived in 1348. He had done what he set forth to do. He had visited the three brothers of Imam in Persia, India, and China. In addition he had travelled for twenty-four years and accomplished in all about seventy-five thousand miles.

With him the history of mediæval exploration would seem to end, for within eighty years of his death the modern epoch opens with the energies and enthusiasm of Prince Henry of Portugal.

For the last few centuries we have found all travel undertaken more or less as a religious crusade.

So far during the last centuries, travel had been for the most part by land. Few discoveries had been made by sea. Voyages were too difficult and dangerous. The Phœnicians had ventured far with intrepid courage. The Vikings had tossed fearlessly over their stormy northern seas to the yet unknown land of America, but this was long ago. Throughout the Middle Ages hardly a sail was to be seen on the vast Atlantic and Pacific Oceans, no ships ventured on what was held to be the Sea of Darkness, no man was emboldened to risk life and money on the unknown waters beyond his own safe home.

CHAPTER XIX

MEDIÆVAL MAPS

WE cannot pass from the subject of mediæval exploration without a word on the really delightful, if ignorant,
maps of the period, for they illustrate better than any
description the state of geography at this time. The
Ptolemy map, summing up all the Greek and Roman
learning, with its longitudes and latitudes, with its
shaped continents and its many towns and rivers, " indi-
cates the high-water mark of a tide that was soon to
ebb."

With the decline of the Roman Empire and the
coming of Christianity we get a new spirit inspiring
our mediæval maps, in which Jerusalem, hitherto totally
obscure, dominates the whole situation.

The *Christian Topography* of Cosmas in the sixth
century sets a new model. Figures blowing trumpets
representing the winds still blow on to the world, as
they did in the days of Ptolemy, but the earth is once
more flat and it is again surrounded by the ocean stream.
Round this ocean stream, according to Cosmas, is an
outer earth, the seat of Paradise, " the earth beyond the
ocean where men dwelt before the Flood."

Although these maps of Cosmas were but the expres-
sion of one man's ideas, they served as a model for others.

There is, at Turin, a delightful map of the eighth
century with the four winds and the ocean stream as
usual. The world is divided into three—Asia, Africa,

and Europe. Adam and Eve stand at the top; to the
right of Adam lies Armenia and the Caucasus; to the
left of Eve are Mount Lebanon, the river Jordan, Sidon,
and Mesopotamia. At their feet lie Mount Carmel,
Jerusalem, and Babylon.

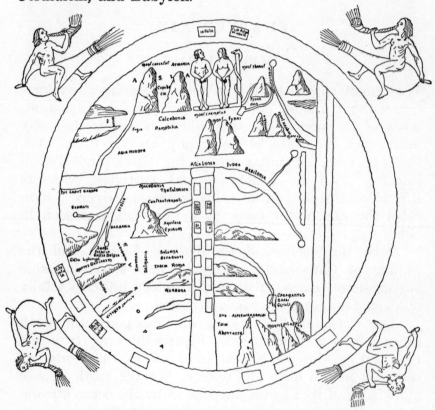

THE TURIN MAP OF THE WORLD, EIGHTH CENTURY.

In Europe we find a few names such as Constantinople, Italy, France. Britannia and Scotland are islands
in the encircling sea. Africa is suitably represented by
the Nile.

Of much the same date is another map known as
the Albi, preserved in the library at Albi in Languedoc.

The world is square, with rounded corners; Britain is an island off the coast of Spain, and a beautiful green sea flows round the whole.

An example of tenth-century map-making, known as the Cottoniana or Anglo-Saxon map, is in the British Museum. Here is a mixture of Biblical and classical knowledge. Jerusalem and Bethlehem are in their place and the Pillars of Hercules stand at the entrance of the Mediterranean Sea. The British Isles are still distorted, and quantities of little unnamed islands lie about the north of Scotland. In the extreme

A T-MAP, TENTH CENTURY.

east lies an enormous Ceylon; in the north-east corner of Asia is drawn a magnificent lion with mane and curling tail, with the words around him: "Here lions abound."

Africa as usual is made up of the Nile, Alexandria at its mouth, and its source in a lake.

There is another form of these early maps. They are quite small and round. They are known as T-maps, being divided into three parts— Europe, Asia, and Africa. Jerusalem is always in the centre, and the ocean stream flows round.

A T-MAP, THIRTEENTH CENTURY.

After the manner of these, only on a very large scale, is the famous *Mappa Mondi*, by Richard of Haldingham, on the walls of the Hereford Cathedral of the thirteenth century. Jerusalem is in the centre, and the Crucifixion is there depicted. At the top is the Last Judgment, with the good and bad folk divided on either side. Adam and Eve are there, so are the Pillars of Hercules, Scylla and Charybdis, the Red Sea coloured red, the Nile and the Mountains of the Moon, strange beasts and stranger men.

With the Hereford map came in that pictorial geography that makes the maps of the later Middle Ages so delightful.

THE KAISER HOLDING THE WORLD.
From a twelfth-century MS.

"This is indeed the true way to make a map," says a modern writer. "If these old maps erred in the course of their rivers and the lines of their mountains and space, they are not so misleading as your modern atlas with its too accurate measurements. For even your most primitive map, with Paradise in the east—a gigantic Jerusalem in the centre—gives a less distorted impression than that which we obtain from the most scientific chart on Mercator's projection."

THE "ANGLO-SAXON" MAP OF THE WORLD, DRAWN ABOUT 990 A.D.

This map, which is found in one of the Cotton MSS. in the British Museum, is a geographical achievement remarkable in the age which produced it. It may perhaps be the work of an Irish scholar-monk. It shows real knowledge and scientific insight in one of the gloomiest of the "dark ages" of Europe.

CHAPTER XX

PRINCE HENRY OF PORTUGAL

BUT now a new era was about to begin—a new age was dawning—and we open a wonderful chapter in the history of discovery, perhaps the most wonderful in all the world. In Portugal a man had arisen who was to awaken the slumbering world of travel and direct it to the high seas.

And the name of this man was Henry, a son of King John of Portugal. His mother was an Englishwoman, daughter of " John of Gaunt, time-honoured Lancaster." The Prince was, therefore, a nephew of Henry IV. and great-grandson of Edward III. of England. But if English blood flowed in his veins he, too, was the son of the " greatest King that ever sat on the throne of Portugal," and at the age of twenty he had already learned something of the sea that lay between his father's kingdom and the northern coast of Africa. Thus, when in the year 1415 King John planned a great expedition across the narrow seas to Ceuta, an important Moorish city in North Africa, it fell to Prince Henry himself to equip seven triremes, six biremes, twenty-six ships of burden, and a number of small craft. These he had ready at Lisbon when news reached him that the Queen, his mother, was stricken ill. The King and three sons were soon at her bedside. It was evident that she was dying.

" What wind blows so strongly against the side of the house ? " she asked suddenly.

" The wind blows from the north," replied her sons.

" It is the wind most favourable for your departure," replied Philippa. And with these words the English Queen died.

This is not the place to tell how the expedition started at once as the dead Queen had wished, how Ceuta was triumphantly taken, and how Prince Henry distinguished himself till all Europe rang with his fame. Henry v. of England begged him to come over and take command of his forces. The Emperor of Germany sent the same request. But he had other schemes for his life. He would not fight the foes of England or of Germany, rather would he fight the great ocean whose waves dashed high against the coast of Portugal. He had learned something of inland Africa, of the distant coast of Guinea, and he was fired with the idea of exploring along this west coast of Africa and possibly reaching India by sea.

Let us recall what was known of the Atlantic only six centuries ago. " It was," says an old writer, " a vast and boundless ocean, on which ships dared not venture out of sight of land. For even if the sailors knew the direction of the winds they would not know whither those winds would carry them, and, as there is no inhabited country beyond, they would run great risk of being lost in mist and vapour. The limit of the West is the Atlantic Ocean."

The ocean was a new and formidable foe, hitherto unconquered and unexplored. At last one had arisen to attempt its conquest. As men had lifted the veil from the unknown land of China, so now the mists were to be cleared from the Sea of Darkness.

On the inhospitable shores of southern Portugal, amid the " sadness of a waste of shifting sand, in a neighbourhood so barren that only a few stunted trees struggled for existence, on one of the coldest, dreariest spots of sunny Portugal," Prince Henry built his naval arsenal.

In this secluded spot, far from the gaieties of Court life, with the vast Atlantic rolling measureless and mysterious before him, Prince Henry took up the study of astronomy and mathematics. Here he gathered round him men of science; he built ships and trained Portuguese sailors in the art of navigation, so far as it was known in those days.

Then he urged them seawards. In 1418 two gentlemen of his household, Zarco and Vaz, volunteered to sail to Cape Bojador towards the south. They started off and as usual hugged the coast for some way, but a violent storm arose and soon they were driven out to sea. They had lost sight of land and given themselves up for lost when, at break of day, they saw an island not far off. Delighted at their escape, they named it Porto Santo and, overjoyed at their discovery, hastened back to Portugal to relate their adventures to Prince Henry. They described the fertile soil and delicious climate of the newly found island, the simplicity of its inhabitants, and they requested leave to return and make a Portuguese settlement there. To reward them, Prince Henry gave them three ships and everything to ensure success in their new enterprise. But unfortunately he added a rabbit and her family. These were turned out and multiplied with such astonishing rapidity that in two years' time they were numerous enough to destroy all the vegetation of the island.

So Porto Santo was colonised by the Portuguese, and one Perestrello was made Governor of the island; and it is interesting to note that his daughter became the wife of Christopher Columbus. But the original founders, Zarco and Vaz, had observed from time to time a dark spot on the horizon which aroused their curiosity. Sailing towards it, they found an island of considerable size, uninhabited and very attractive, but so covered with woods that they named it Madeira, the Island of Woods.

But although these two islands belong to Portugal

to-day, and although Portugal claimed their discovery, there is a legend that already an Englishman and his wife had been there, and the names of the islands appear on an Italian map of 1351.

The story of this first discovery is very romantic. In the reign of Edward III. a young man named Robert Machin sailed away from Bristol with a very wealthy lady. A north-east wind carried them out of their course, and after thirteen days' driving before a storm they were cast on to an island. It was uninhabited and well wooded and watered. But the sufferings and privations proved too much for the poor English lady, who died after three days, and Machin died a few days later of grief and exposure. The crew of the ship sailed away to the coast of Africa, there to be im-

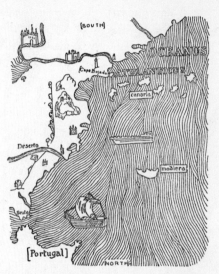

AFRICA—FROM CEUTA TO MADEIRA, THE CANARIES, AND CAPE BOJADOR.

From Fra Mauro's map, 1457.

prisoned by the Moors. Upon their escape in 1416 they made known their discovery.

So Zarco and Vaz divided the island of Madeira, calling half of it Funchal (the Portuguese for fennel, which grew here in great quantities) and the other half Machico after the poor English discoverer Machin. The first two Portuguese children born in the island of Madeira were called Adam and Eve.

Year after year Prince Henry launched his little ships on the yet unknown, uncharted seas, urging his captains to venture farther and ever farther. He longed for them to reach Cape Bojador, and bitter was his disappointment when one of his squires, dismayed by travellers' tales, turned back from the Canary Islands.

"Go out again," urged the enthusiastic Prince, "and give no heed to their opinions, for, by the grace of God, you cannot fail to derive from your voyage both honour and profit."

THE VOYAGE TO CAPE BLANCO FROM CAPE BOJADOR.
From Fra Mauro's map, 1457.

And the squire went forth from the commanding presence of the Prince resolved to double the Cape, which he successfully accomplished in 1434. Seven years passed away, till in 1441 two men— Gonsalves, master of the wardrobe (a strange qualification for difficult navigation), and Nuno Tristam, a young knight—started forth on the Prince's service, with orders to pass Cape Bojador where a dangerous surf, breaking on the shore, had terrified other navigators. There was a story, too, that any man who passed Cape Bojador would be changed from white into black, that there were sea-monsters, sheets of burning flame, and boiling waters beyond. The young knight Tristam discovered the white headland beyond Cape Bojador, named it Cape Blanco, and took home some Moors of high rank to the Prince. A large sum was offered for their ransom, so Gonsalves conveyed them back to Cape Blanco and coasted along to the south, discovering the island of Arguin of the Cape Verde group and reaching the neighbourhood of Sierra Leone, reached by Hanno many centuries before this.

Here he received some gold dust, and with this and some thirty negroes he returned to Lisbon, where the strange black negroes " caused the most lively astonishment among the people." The small quantity of gold dust created a sensation among the Portuguese explorers, and the spirit of adventure grew. No longer had the Prince to urge his navigators forth to new lands and new seas; they were ready and willing to go, for the reward was now obvious. The news was soon noised abroad, and Italians, then reckoned among the most skilful seamen of the time, flocked to Portugal, anxious to take service under the Prince.

" Love of gain was the magic wand that drew them on and on, into unknown leagues of waters, into wild adventures and desperate affrays."

The " Navigator " himself looked beyond these things. He would find a way to India; he would teach the heathen to be Christians. He was always ready to welcome those with superior knowledge of navigation; so in 1454 he sent an Italian, known to history as Cadamosto, to sail the African seas. The young Venetian was but twenty-one, and he tells his story simply.

" Now I—Luigi Ca da Mosto—had sailed nearly all the Mediterranean coasts, but, being caught by a storm off Cape St. Vincent, had to take refuge in the Prince's town, and was there told of the glorious and boundless conquests of the Prince, the which did exceedingly stir my soul—eager as it was for gain above all things else. My age, my vigour, my skill are equal to any toil; above all, my passionate desire to see the world and explore the unknown set me all on fire with eagerness."

In 1455 Cadamosto sailed from Portugal for Madeira, now "thickly peopled with Portuguese." From Madeira to the Canaries, from the Canaries to Cape Blanco, "natives black as moles were dressed in white flowing robes with turbans wound round their heads." Here was a great market of Arab traders from the interior, here were camels laden with brass, silver, and gold, as well as slaves innumerable.

But Cadamosto pushed on for some four hundred miles by the low, sandy shore to the Senegal River. The Portuguese had already sailed by this part of the coast, and the negroes had thought their ships to be great birds from afar cleaving the air with their white wings. When the crews furled their sails and drew into shore the natives changed their minds and thought they were fishes, and all stood on the shore gazing stupidly at this new wonder.

Cadamosto landed and pushed some two hundred and fifty miles up the Senegal River, where he set up a market, exchanging cotton and cloth for gold, while " the negroes came stupidly crowding round me, wondering at our white colour, which they tried to wash off, our dress, our garments of black silk and robes of blue cloth."

Joined by two other ships from Portugal, the Italian explorer now sailed on to Cape Verde, so called from its green grass.

"The land here," he tells us, "is all low and full of fine, large trees, which are continually green. The trees never wither like those in Europe; they grow so near the shore that they seem to drink, as it were, the water of the sea. The coast is most beautiful. Many countries have I been in, to East and West, but never did I see a prettier sight."

But the negroes here—big, comely men—were lawless and impossible to approach, shooting at the Portuguese explorers with poisoned arrows. They discovered that

the capital of the country was called Gambra, where lived
a king, but the negroes of the Gambra were unfriendly;
there was little gold to be had; his crews fell sick and
ill, and Cadamosto turned home again. But he had

A PORTION OF AFRICA FROM FRA MAURO'S MAP ILLUSTRATING
CADAMOSTO'S VOYAGE BEYOND CAPE BLANCO.

reached a point beyond all other explorers of the time,
a point where " only once did we see the North Star,
which was so low that it seemed almost to touch the
sea." We know that he must have been to within eleven
degrees of the Equator, and it is disappointing to find the

promising young Italian disappearing from the pages of history.

And now we come to the last voyage planned by Prince Henry, that of Diego Gomez, his own faithful servant. It followed close on Cadamosto's return.

No long time after, the Prince equipped a ship called the *Wren* and set over it Diego Gomez, with two other ships, of which he was commander-in-chief. Their orders were to go as far as they could. Gomez wrote his own travels, and his adventures are best told in his own words. We take up his story from the far side of Cape Blanco.

"After passing a great river beyond Rio Grande we met such strong currents in the sea that no anchor could hold. The other captains and their men were much alarmed, thinking we were at the end of the ocean, and begged me to put back. In the mid-current the sea was very clear, and the natives came off from the shore and brought us their merchandise. As the current grew even stronger we put back and came to a land, where were groves of palms near the shore, with their branches broken. There we found a plain covered with hay and more than five thousand animals like stags, but larger, who showed no fear of us. Five elephants with two young ones came out of a small river that was fringed by trees. We went back to the ships, and next day made our way from Cape Verde and saw the broad mouth of a great river, which we entered and guessed to be the Gambia. We went up the river as far as Cantor (some five hundred miles). Farther than this the ships could not go, because of the thick growth of trees and underwood. When the news spread through the country that the Christians were in Cantor, they came from Timbuktu in the north, from Mount Gelu in the south. Here I was told there is gold in plenty, and caravans of camels cross over there with goods from Carthage, Tunis, Fez, Cairo, and all the land

of the Saracens.   I asked the natives of Cantor about the
road to the gold country.   They told me the King lived
in Kukia and was lord of all the mines on the right side
of the river of Cantor, and that he had before the door of

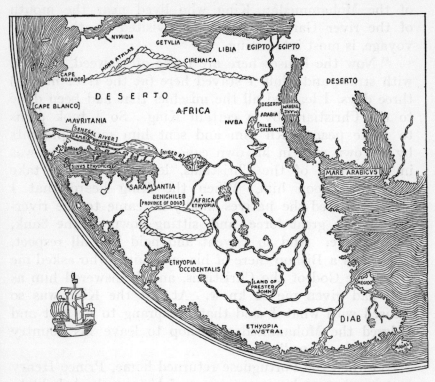

SKETCH OF AFRICA FROM FRA MAURO'S GREAT MAP OF THE WORLD, 1457.

In the African portions of Fra Mauro's map which have already been given they are
shown exactly as Fra Mauro drew them, with the north at the *bottom* and the south
at the *top*, as is nearly always the case in mediæval maps.   In this outline of Africa,
which is generally supposed to show the results of Prince Henry's labours, the map
has been put the right way up.   It was prepared between 1457 and 1459.

this palace a mass of gold just as it was taken from the
earth, so large that twenty men could hardly move it, and
that the King always fastened his horse to it.   While I was
thus trafficking with these negroes, my men became worn
out with the heat, and so we returned towards the ocean."

But Diego Gomez had succeeded in making friends with the hostile natives of this part. He left behind him a better idea of Christian men than some of the other explorers had done. His own account of the conversion of the Mohammedan King who lived near the mouth of the river Gambia, which was visited on the return voyage, is most interesting.

" Now the houses here are made of seaweed, covered with straw, and while I stayed here (at the river mouth) three days, I learned all the mischief that had been done to the Christians by a certain King. So I took pains to make peace with him and sent him many presents by his own men in his own canoes. Now the King was in great fear of the Christians, lest they should take vengeance upon him. When the King heard that I always treated the natives kindly he came to the riverside with a great force, and, sitting down on the bank, sent for me. And so I went and paid him all respect. There was a Bishop there of his own faith, who asked me about the God of the Christians, and I answered him as God had given me to know. At last the King was so pleased with what I said that he sprang to his feet and ordered the Mohammedan Bishop to leave his country within three days."

So when the Portuguese returned home, Prince Henry sent a priest and a young man of his own household to the black King at the mouth of the Gambia. This was in 1458.

" In the year of our Lord 1460, Prince Henry fell ill in his town on Cape St. Vincent," says his faithful explorer and servant, Diego Gomez, " and of that sickness he died."

Such was the end of the man who has been called the " originator of modern discovery." What had he done ? He had inspired and financed the Portuguese navigators to sail for some two thousand miles down the West African coast. "From his wave-washed home he inspired the courage of his men and planned their voyages, and by the purity of his actions and the devotion of his life really lived up to his inspiring motto, 'Talent de bien faire.'" And more than this. For each successive discovery had been carefully noted at the famous Sagres settlement, and these had been worked up by an Italian monk named Fra Mauro into an enormous wall-map over six feet across, crammed with detail—the work of three years' incessant labour.

CHAPTER XXI

BARTHOLOMEW DIAZ REACHES THE STORMY CAPE

But though Prince Henry was dead, the enthusiasm he had aroused among Portuguese navigators was not dead, and Portuguese ships still stole forth by twos and threes to search for treasure down the West African coast. In 1462 they reached Sierra Leone, the farthest point attained by Hanno of olden days. Each new headland was now taken in the name of Portugal : wooden crosses already marked each successive discovery, and many a tree near the coast bore the motto of Prince Henry carved roughly on its bark. Portugal had officially claimed this " Kingdom of the Seas " as it was called, and henceforth stone crosses some six feet high, inscribed with the arms of Portugal, the name of the navigator, and the date of discovery, marked each newly found spot.

It was not until 1471 that the navigators unconsciously crossed the Equator, " into a new heaven and a new earth." They saw stars unknown in the Northern Hemisphere, and the Northern Pole star sank nearly out of sight. Another thirteen years and Diego Cam, a knight of the King's household, found the mouth of the Congo and erected a great Portuguese pillar on the famous spot. It was in the year 1484 that Diego Cam was ordered to go " as far to the south as he could." He crossed the Equator, which for past years had been the limit of knowledge, and, continuing southwards he reached the mouth of the mighty river Congo, now known as the second of all the African rivers for size. The explorer ascended the river, falling in with peacefully inclined natives. But they could not make themselves understood, so Cam took back four of them to Portugal, where they learned enough Portuguese to talk a little. They were much struck with Portugal and the kind treatment they received from the King, who sent them back to their country laden with presents for their black King at home. So with Diego Cam they all sailed back to the Congo River. They were received by the King in royal state. Seated on a throne of ivory raised on a lofty wooden platform, he could be seen from all sides, his " black and glittering skin " shining out above a piece of damask given to him to wear by the Portuguese explorer. From his shoulder hung a dressed horse's tail, a symbol of royalty; on his head was a cap of palm leaves.

NEGRO BOYS, FROM
CABOT'S MAP, 1544.

It was here in this Congo district that the first negro was baptized in the presence of some twenty-five thousand heathen comrades. The ceremony was performed by Portuguese priests, and the negro King ordered all idols to be destroyed throughout his dominions. Here, too, a little Christian church was built, and the King and Queen became such earnest Christians that they sent their children to Portugal to be taught.

But even the discoveries of Diego Cam pale before the great achievement of Bartholomew Diaz, who was now to accomplish the great task which Prince Henry the Navigator had yearned to see fulfilled—the rounding of the Cape of Storms.

The expedition set sail for the south in August 1486. Passing the spot where Diego Cam had erected his farthest pillar, Diaz reached a headland, now known as Diaz Point, where he, too, placed a Portuguese pillar that remained unbroken till about a hundred years ago. Still to the south he sailed, struggling with wind and weather, to Cape Voltas, close to the mouth of the Orange River. Then for another fortnight the little ships were driven before the wind, south and ever south, with half-reefed sails and no land in sight. Long days and longer nights passed to find them still drifting in an unknown sea, knowing not what an hour might bring forth. At last the great wind ceased to blow and it became icy cold. They had sailed to the south of South Africa. Steering north, Diaz now fell in with land—land with cattle near the shore and cowherds tending them, but the black cowherds were so alarmed at the sight of the Portuguese that they fled away inland.

We know now, what neither Diaz nor his crew even suspected, that he had actually rounded, without seeing, the Cape of Good Hope. The coast now turned eastward till a small island was reached in a bay we now call Algoa Bay. Here Bartholomew Diaz set up another pillar with its cross and inscription, naming the rock Santa Cruz. This was the first land beyond the Cape ever trodden by European feet. Unfortunately the natives —Kafirs—threw stones at them, and it was impossible to make friends and to land. The crews, too, began to complain. They were worn out with continual work, weary for fresh food, terrified at the heavy seas that broke on these southern shores. With one voice they protested against proceeding any farther. But the explorer could not bear to turn back; he must sail onwards now, just three days more, and then if they found nothing he would turn back. They sailed on and came to the mouth of a large river—the Great Fish River. Again the keen explorer would sail on and add to his already momentous discoveries. But the crews again began their complaints and, deeply disappointed, Diaz had to turn. "When he reached the little island of Santa Cruz and bade farewell to the cross which he had there erected, it was with grief as intense as if he were leaving his child in the wilderness with no hope of ever seeing him again." To him it seemed as though he had endured all his hardships in vain. He knew not what he had really accomplished as yet. But his eyes were soon to be opened. Sailing westward, Diaz at last came in sight of "that remarkable Cape which had been hidden from the eyes of man for so many centuries."

Remembering their perils past, he called it "the Stormy Cape" and hastened home to the

THE WEST COAST OF AFRICA.

From Martin Behaim's map, 1492.

King of Portugal with his great news. The King was over-joyed, but he refused to name it the Cape of Storms. Would not such a name deter the seamen of the future?

Was not this the long-sought passage to India? Rather it should be called the Cape of Good Hope, the name which it has held throughout the centuries. In the course of one voyage, Diaz had accomplished the great task which for the past seventy years Prince Henry had set before his people. He had lifted for the first time in the history of the world the veil that had hung over the mysterious extremity of the great African continent. The Phœnicians may have discovered it some seventeen hundred years before Diaz, but the record of tradition alone exists.

Now with the new art of printing, which was transforming the whole aspect of life, the brilliant achievement of Bartholomew Diaz was made known far and wide.

It was shortly to be followed by a yet more brilliant feat by a yet more brilliant navigator, " the most illustrious that the world has seen." The very name of Christopher Columbus calls up the vision of a resolute man beating right out into the westward unknown seas and finding as his great reward a whole new continent— a New World of whose existence mankind had hardly dreamt.

CHAPTER XXII

CHRISTOPHER COLUMBUS

EVERY event in the eventful life of Christopher Columbus is of supreme interest. We linger over all that leads up to the momentous start westwards: we recall his birth and early life at Genoa towards the middle of the fifteenth century, his apprenticeship to his father as a weaver of cloth, his devotion to the sea, his love of the little sailing ships that passed in and out of the busy Genoese harbour from all parts of the known world. At the age of fourteen the little Christoforo went to sea—a red-haired, sunburnt boy with bright blue eyes. He learnt the art of navigation, he saw foreign countries, he learnt to chart the seas, to draw maps, and possibly worked with some of the noted Italian draughtsmen. At the age of twenty-eight, in 1474, he left Genoa for Portugal, famous throughout the world for her recent discoveries, though as yet the Stormy Cape lay veiled in mystery. Columbus wanted to learn all he could about these discoveries; he made voyages to Guinea, Madeira, and Porto Santo. He also went to England and " sailed a hundred leagues to the island of Thule in 1477."

He was now a recognised seaman of distinction, with courteous manners and fine appearance. He set himself to study maps and charts at Lisbon, giving special attention to instruments for making observations at sea. For many long years he had been revolving a scheme for reaching India by sailing westward instead of the route by Africa. The more he studied these things the more convinced he became that he was right.

THE PARTING OF COLUMBUS WITH FERDINAND AND ISABELLA,
3RD AUGUST 1492.

From De Bry's account of the *Voyages to India*, 1601.

"What if wise men had, as far back as Ptolemy,
  Judged that the earth like an orange was round.
  None of them ever said, 'Come along, follow me,
  Sail to the West and the East will be found.'"

It was not till the year 1480 that Columbus proposed
to the King of Portugal his idea of sailing westwards.   He
explained his reasons : how there were grounds for thinking
there was an unknown land to the west, how artistically
sculptured pieces of wood had been driven across the
ocean by the west wind, suggesting islands not yet discovered, how once the corpses of two men with broad faces,
unlike Europeans, had been washed ashore, how on the
west coast of Ireland seeds of tropical plants had been
discovered.

The King listened and was inclined to believe Columbus.
But his councillors persuaded him to get from the Genoese
navigator his plans, and while they kept Columbus waiting
for the King's answer they sent off some ships privately
to investigate the whole matter.   The ships started westward, encountered a great storm, and returned to Lisbon,
scoffing at the scheme of the stranger.   When this news
reached his ears, Columbus was very angry.   He would
have nothing more to do with Portugal, but left that
country at once for Spain to appeal to the King and Queen
of that land.

Ferdinand and Isabella were busy with affairs of state
and could not give audience to the man who was to
discover a New World.   It was not till 1491 that he was
summoned before the King and Queen.   Once more
his wild scheme was laughed at, and he was dismissed the
Court.   Not only was he again indignant, but his friends
were indignant too.   They believed in him, and would not
rest till they had persuaded the Queen to take up his
cause.   He demanded a good deal.   He must be made
Admiral and Viceroy of all the new seas and lands he

might discover, as well as receiving a large portion of his gains. The Queen was prevailed on to provide means for the expedition, and she became so enthusiastic over it that she declared she would sell her own jewels to provide the necessary supplies. Columbus was created Admiral of the Ocean in all the islands and continents he might discover; two little ships were made ready, and it seemed as though the dream of his life might be fulfilled. The explorer was now forty-six; his red hair had become grey with waiting and watching for the possibility of realising his great scheme.

COLUMBUS'S SHIP, THE
SANTA MARIA.

From a woodcut of 1493 supposed to be after a drawing by Columbus himself.

At last the preparations were complete. The *Santa Maria* was to lead the way with the Admiral on board; she was but one hundred tons' burden, with a high poop and a fore-castle. It had been difficult enough to find a crew; men were shy about venturing with this stranger from Genoa on unknown seas, and it was a motley party that finally took service under Columbus. The second ship, the *Pinta*, was but half the size of the flagship; she had a crew of eighteen and was the fastest sailer of the little squadron, while the third, the *Nina* of forty tons, also carried eighteen men.

On 3rd August 1492 the little fleet sailed forth from Spain on a quest more perilous perhaps than any yet on record. No longer could they sail along with a coast always in sight; day after day and night after night they must sail on an unknown sea in search of an unknown

THE BEST PORTRAIT OF COLUMBUS.

From the original painting (by an unknown artist) in the Naval Museum at Madrid.

land. No one ever expected to see them again. It has well been said that, " looking back at all that has grown out of it in the four centuries that have elapsed, we now know that the sailing of those three little boats over the bar was, since the Fall of Rome, the most momentous event in the world's history." The ships steered for the Canary Islands, and it was not till 9th September that the last land faded from the eyes of that daring little company.

Something of a panic among the sailors ensued when they realised their helpless position; some even burst into tears, begging to be taken home. The days passed on. By the 16th they had come within the influence of the trade winds.

"The weather was like April," says Columbus in his journal. Still westward they sailed, eagerly looking for signs of land. Now they see two pelicans, "an indication that land was near," now a large dark cloud to the north, another "sign that land is near."

As the days pass on, their hopes die away and "the temper of the crews was getting uglier and uglier as the three little vessels forged westward through the blue weed-strewn waters." On 9th October hope revives; all night they hear birds passing through the still air.

On the evening of the 11th a light was seen glimmering in the distance; from the high stern deck of the *Santa Maria* it could be plainly seen, and when the sun rose on that memorable morning the low shores of land a few miles distant could be plainly seen. "Seabirds are wheeling overhead heedless of the intruders, but on the shore human beings are assembling to watch the strange birds which now spread their wings and sail towards the island.

"The *Pinta* leads and her crew are raising the 'Te Deum.' The crews of the *Santa Maria* and the *Nina* join in the solemn chant and many rough men brush away tears. Columbus, the two Pinzons, and some of the men step into the cutter and row to the shore." Columbus, fully armed under his scarlet cloak, sprang ashore, the unclothed natives fleeing away at sight of the first white man who had ever stepped on their shores. Then, unfurling the royal standard of Spain and setting up a large cross, the great navigator fell on his knees and gave thanks to God for this triumphant ending to his perilous voyage. He named the island San Salvador and formally took possession of it for Spain. It was one of the Bahama group, and is now known as Watling Island (British).

COLUMBUS LANDING ON HISPANIOLA.
From a woodcut of 1494.

"Thus was the mighty enterprise achieved, mighty in its conception, still more important in its results."

But Columbus thought he had discovered the Indies, a new route to the east and the Cathay of Marco Polo. He had done more than this; he had discovered another continent. He had sailed over three thousand miles without seeing land, a feat unparalleled in the former history of discovery.

He made friends with the natives, who resembled those of the Canary Islands. "I believe they would easily become Christians," wrote Columbus. "If it please our Lord at the time of my departure, I will take six from here that they may learn to speak." He also notes that they will make good slaves.

From island to island he now made his way, guided by natives. He hoped to find gold; he hoped to find Cathay, for he had a letter from Ferdinand and Isabella to deliver to the Great Khan. The charm and beauty of these enchanted islands were a source of joy to the explorer : "The singing of the little birds is such that it appears a man would wish never to leave here, and the flocks of parrots obscure the sun." The island of Cuba "seemed like heaven itself," but Columbus could not forget that he was searching for gold, for Oriental spices, for the land of Marco Polo, as he hastened from point to point, from island to island. Already the *Pinta* under Martin Pinzon had gone off independently in search of a vague land of gold, to the vexation of the Admiral. A worse disaster was now to befall him. On Christmas Day, off the island of Hayti, the *Santa Maria* struck upon a reef and went over. Columbus and his crew escaped on board the little *Nina*. But she was too small to carry home the double crew, and Columbus made a little fortress on the island where the native King was friendly, and left there a little colony of Spaniards.

He now prepared for the homeward voyage, and one January day in 1493 he left the newly discovered islands and set his face for home in company with the *Pinta*, which by this time had returned to him. For some weeks they got on fairly well. Then the wind rose. A violent storm came on; the sea was terrible, the waves breaking right over the little homeward-bound ships, which tossed about helplessly for long days and nights. Suddenly the *Pinta* disappeared. The wind and sea increased. The little forty-ton *Nina* was in extreme peril, and the crew gave themselves up for lost; their provisions were nearly finished. Columbus was agonised lest he should perish

II

and the news of his great discovery should never reach Spain. Taking a piece of parchment, he noted down as best he could amid the tossing of the ship a brief account of his work, and, wrapping it in a waxed cloth, he put it into an empty cask and threw it overboard. Then, while the mountainous seas threatened momentary destruction, he waited and prayed.

Slowly the storm abated, and on 18th February they reached the Azores. A few days for refreshment and on he sailed again, feverishly anxious to reach Spain and proclaim his great news. But on 3rd March the wind again rose to a hurricane and death stared the crew in the face. Still, "under bare poles and in a heavy cross-sea," they scudded on, until they reached the mouth of the Tagus. The news of his arrival soon spread, and excited crowds hurried to see the little ship that had crossed the fierce Atlantic. Bartholomew Diaz came aboard the *Nina*, and for a short time the two greatest explorers of their century were together. An enthusiastic welcome awaited him in Spain. Was he not the "Admiral of the Ocean Sea, Viceroy of the Western Indies," the only man who had crossed the unknown for the sake of a cherished dream ?

"Seven months had passed since Columbus had sailed from Spain in the dim light of that summer morning. Now he was back. Through tempestuous seas and raging winter gales he had guided his ship well, and Spain knew how to do him honour. His journey from the coast to the Court was like a royal progress. The roads were lined with excited people ; the air was rent with shouts of joy."

On Palm Sunday, 1493, he passed through the streets of Seville. A procession preceded him in which walked the six natives, or Indians as they were called, brought home by Columbus ; parrots and other birds with strange

and radiant colouring were also borne before the triumphant explorer, who himself rode on horseback among
the mounted chivalry of Spain. From windows and
roofs a dense throng watched Christopher Columbus
as he rode through the streets of Seville. From here

THE FIRST REPRESENTATION OF THE PEOPLE OF THE NEW WORLD.

From a woodcut published at Augsburg between 1497 and 1504. The only copy known
is in the British Museum. The inscription states that the Americans "eat each
other," "become a hundred and fifty years of age, and have no government."

he passed on to Barcelona, to be received by the King
and Queen.

> " The city decked herself
> To meet me, roar'd my name : the king, the queen,
> Bad me be seated, speak, and tell them all
> The story of my voyage, and while I spoke
> The crowd's roar fell as at the ' Peace be still.'
> And when I ceased to speak, the king, the queen,
> Sank from their thrones, and melted into tears,
> And knelt, and lifted hand and heart and voice
> In praise to God who led me thro' the waste.
> And then the great ' Laudamus ' rose to heaven." (

It is curious to think what a strange mistake caused all their rejoicing. Not only Spain, but the whole civilised world firmly believed that Columbus had discovered some islands off the coast of Asia, not far from the land of the Great Khan, in the Indian seas. Hence the islands were called the West Indies, which name they have kept to this day.

CHAPTER XXIII

A GREAT NEW WORLD

THE departure of Columbus six months later on his second voyage was a great contrast to the uncertain start of a year ago. The new fleet was ready by September 1493. The three largest ships were some four hundred tons' burden, with fourteen smaller craft and crews of fifteen thousand men. There was no dearth of volunteers this time. High-born Spaniards, thirsting for the wealth of the Indies, offered their services, while Columbus took his brother James and a Benedictine monk chosen by the Pope. They took orange and lemon seeds for planting in the new islands, horses, pigs, bulls, cows, sheep, and goats, besides fruit and vegetables.

So, full of hope and joyful expectation, they set sail; and so well had Columbus calculated his distance and direction with but imperfect instruments at his disposal, that he arrived at the islands again on 3rd November. It was another new island, which he named Domenica, as the day was Sunday. Making for the island of Hayti, where he had left his little Spanish colony, he passed many islands, naming Guadeloupe, San Martin, Santa Cruz, and others. Porto Rico was also found, but they arrived at Hayti to find no trace of Spaniards. Disaster had overtaken the colony, and the deserted men had been killed by the natives who had apparently been so friendly. Another spot was selected by Columbus, and a town was soon built to which he gave the name of Isabella.

This is not the place to tell of the miserable disputes and squabbles that befell the little Spanish colony. We are here concerned with the fuller exploration of the West Indies by Columbus. Taking three ships provisioned for six months, with a crew of fifty-two, he set out for the coast of Cathay. Instead of this, he found the island of Jamaica, with its low, hazy, blue coast of extreme beauty. Still convinced that he was near the territory of the Great Khan, he explored the coast of Cuba, not realising that it was an island. He sailed about among the islands, till he became very ill, fever seized him, and at last his men carried him ashore at Isabella, thinking that he must die. He recovered to find a discontented colony, members of which had already sent back stories to Spain of the misdeeds of their founder. Columbus made up his mind to return to Spain to carry a true report of the difficulties of colonisation in the Indies.

THE TOWN OF ISABELLA AND THE COLONY FOUNDED BY COLUMBUS.
From a woodcut of 1494.

" It was June 1496 before he found himself again in the harbour of Cadiz. People had crowded down to greet the great discoverer, but instead of a joyous crew, flushed with new success and rich with the spoils of the golden Indies, a feeble train of wretched men crawled on shore—thin, miserable, and ill. Columbus himself was dressed as a monk, in a long gown girded with a cord. His beard was long and unshaven. The whole

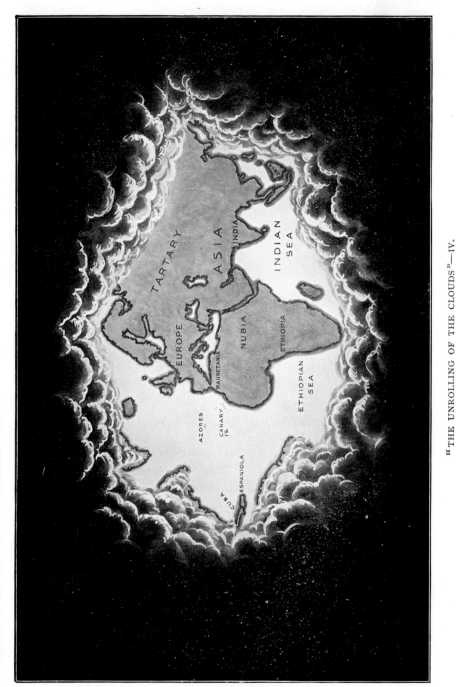

"THE UNROLLING OF THE CLOUDS"—IV.

The world as known at the end of the fifteenth century after the discoveries of Columbus and his age.

man was utterly broken down with all he had been through."

But after a stay of two years in Spain, Columbus again started off on his third voyage. With six ships he now took a more southerly direction, hoping to find land to the south of the West Indies. And this he did, but he never lived to know that it was the great continent of South America. Through scorching heat, which melted the tar of their rigging, they sailed onwards till they were rewarded by the sight of land at last. Columbus had promised to dedicate the first land he saw to the Holy Trinity. What, then, was his surprise when land appeared from which arose three distinct peaks, which he at once named La Trinidad. The luxuriance of the island pleased the Spaniards, and as they made their way slowly along the shore their eyes rested for the first time, and unconsciously, on the mainland of South America. It appeared to the explorer as a large island which he called Isla Santa. Here oysters abounded and " very large fish, and parrots as large as hens." Between the island and the mainland lay a narrow channel through which flowed a mighty current. While the ships were anchoring here a great flood of fresh water came down with a great roar, nearly destroying the little Spanish ships and greatly alarming both Columbus and his men. It was one of the mouths of the river Orinoco, to which they gave the name of the Dragon's Mouth. The danger over, they sailed on, charmed with the beautiful shores, the sight of the distant mountains, and the sweetness of the air.

Columbus decided that this must be the centre of the earth's surface, and with its mighty rivers surely it was none other than the earthly Paradise with the rivers of the Garden of Eden, that " some of the Fathers had declared to be situated in the extreme east of the Old World, and in a region so high that the flood had not overwhelmed it." The world then, said Columbus, could not be a perfect round, but pear-shaped. With these conclusions he hastened across to Hayti where his brother was ruling over the little colony in his absence. But treachery and mutiny had been at work. Matters had gone ill with the colony, and Columbus did not improve the situation by his presence. He was a brilliant navigator, but no statesman. Complaints reached Spain, and a Spaniard was sent out to replace Columbus. This high-handed official at once put the poor navigator in chains and placed him on board a ship bound for Spain. Queen Isabella was overwhelmed with grief when the snowy-haired explorer once again stood before her, his face lined with suffering. He was restored to royal favour and provided with ships to sail forth on his fourth and last voyage. But his hardships and perils had told upon him, and he was not really fit to undertake the long voyage to the Indies. However, he arrived safely off the coast of Honduras and searched for the straits that he felt sure existed, but which were not to be found till some eighteen years later by Magellan. The natives brought him cocoanuts, which the Spaniards now tasted for the first time; they also brought merchandise from a far land denoting some high civilisation. Columbus believed that he had reached the golden east, whence the gold had been obtained for Solomon's temple.

Had Columbus only sailed west he might have discovered Mexico with all its wealth, and "a succession of splendid discoveries would have shed fresh glory on his declining age, instead of his sinking amidst gloom, neglect, and disappointment." At the isthmus of Darien, Columbus gave up the search. He was weary of the bad weather. Incessant downpours of rain, storms of thunder and lightning with terrific seas—these discouraged him. Disaster followed disaster. The food was nearly finished:

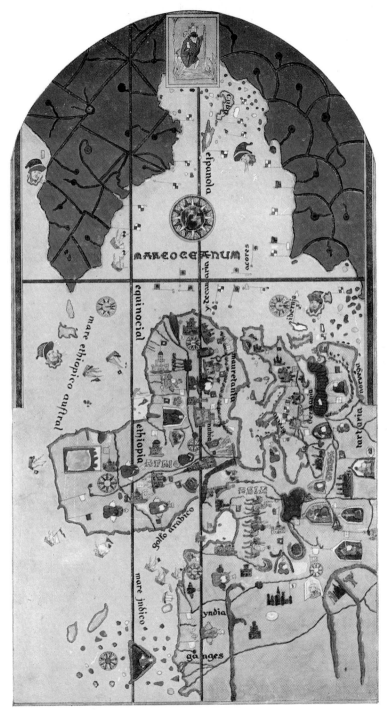

MAP OF THE WORLD, DRAWN IN 1500, THE FIRST TO SHOW AMERICA.

By Juan de la Cosa, who is supposed to have been the pilot of Columbus. At the top,
between the two green masses representing America, La Cosa has drawn Columbus
as St. Christopher carrying the infant Christ, according to the legend.

the biscuit " was so full of maggots that the people could only eat it in the dark, when they were not visible." Columbus himself seemed to be at the point of death. " Never," he wrote, " was the sea seen so high, so terrific, so covered with foam; the waters from heaven never ceased—it was like a repetition of the deluge."

He reached Spain in 1504 to be carried ashore on a litter, and to learn that the Queen of Spain was dead. He was friendless, penniless, and sick unto death.

" After twenty years of toil and peril," he says pitifully, " I do not own a roof in Spain."

> " I, lying here, bedridden and alone,
> Cast off, put by, scouted by count and king,
> The first discoverer starves."

And so the brilliant navigator, Christopher Columbus, passed away, all unconscious of the great New World he had reached. Four centuries have passed away, but—

> " When shall the world forget
> The glory and the debt,
> Indomitable soul,
>   Immortal Genoese?
> Not while the shrewd salt gale
> Whines amid shroud and sail,
> Above the rhythmic roll
> And thunder of the seas."

It has been well said, " injustice was not buried with Columbus," and soon after his death an attempt was made, and made successfully, to name the New World after another—a Florentine pilot, Amerigo Vespucci.

It was but natural that when the first discoveries by Columbus of land to westward had been made known, that others should follow in the track of the great navigator. Among these was a handsome young Spaniard— one Hojeda—who had accompanied Columbus on his second voyage. Soon after, he fitted out an expedi-

tion, 1499, reaching the mainland of the yet unknown
continent near the Trinidad of Columbus. With him was
Amerigo Vespucci. Here they found a native village
with houses built on tree trunks and connected by bridges.
It was so like a bit of old Venice that the explorers
named it Little Venice or Venezuela, which name it bears
to-day.

Nothing was publicly known of this voyage till a year
after the death of Columbus, when men had coasted
farther to the south of Venezuela and discovered that
this land was neither Asia nor Africa, that it was not
the land of Marco Polo, but a new continent indeed.

" It is proper to call it a New World," says Amerigo
Vespucci. " Men of old said over and over again that
there was no land south of the Equator. But this last
voyage of mine has proved them wrong, since in southern
regions I have found a country more thickly inhabited by
people and animals than our Europe or Asia or Africa."

These words among others, and an account of his
voyages published in Paris, 1507, created a deep impression.
A letter from Columbus announcing his discoveries had
been published in 1493, but he said nothing, because he
knew nothing, of a New World. Men therefore said that
Amerigo Vespucci had discovered a new continent, " wherefore the new continent ought to be called America from its
discoverer Amerigo, a man of rare ability, inasmuch as
Europe and Asia derived their names from women."

AMERIGO VESPUCCI

From the sculpture by Grazzini in the Uffizi Gallery, Florence.

CHAPTER XXIV

VASCO DA GAMA REACHES INDIA

THUS the name of America was gradually adopted for the New World, though the honour and glory of its first discovery must always belong to Christopher Columbus.

But while all this wonderful development westwards was thrilling the minds of men, other great discoveries were being made to the East, whither the eyes of the Portuguese were still straining. Portugal had lost Columbus; she could lay no claim to the shores of America discovered by Spaniards, but the sea-route to India by the East was yet to be found by one of her explorers, Vasco da Gama. His achievement stands out brilliantly at this time; for, within a few years of the discovery of the New World, he had been able to tell the world that India and the East could be reached by the Cape of Good Hope !

The dream of Prince Henry the Navigator was fulfilled !

How Vasco da Gama was chosen for the great command has been graphically described by a Portuguese historian, whose words are received with caution by modern authorities. The King of Portugal—Dom Manuel—having set his kingdom in order, " being inspired by the Lord, took the resolution to inform himself about the affairs of India." He knew that the province of India was very far away, inhabited by dark people who had great riches and merchandise, and there was much risk in crossing the wide seas and land to reach it. But he felt it a sacred duty to try and reach it. He ordered ships to be built according to a design of Bartholomew Diaz, the Hero of the Cape, " low amidships, with high castles towering fore and aft; they rode the water like ducks." The ships ready, the King prayed the Lord " to show him the man whom it would please Him to send upon this voyage. Days passed. One day the King was sitting in his hall with his officers when he raised his eyes and saw a gentleman of his household crossing the hall. It suddenly occurred to the King that this was the man for his command, and, calling Vasco da Gama, he offered him the command at once. He was courageous, resolute, and firm of purpose. On his knees he accepted the great honour. A silken banner blazing with the Cross of the Order of Christ was bestowed upon him; he chose the *S. Gabriel* for his flagship, appointed his brother to the *S. Raphael*, and prepared for his departure. Books and charts were supplied, Ptolemy's geography was on board, as well as the *Book of Marco Polo*. All being ready, Vasco da Gama and his captains spent the night in the little chapel by the sea at Belem, built for the mariners of Henry the Navigator.

Next morning—it was July—they walked in solemn procession to the shore, lighted candles in their hands, priests chanting a solemn litany as they walked. The beach was crowded with people. Under the blazing summer sun they knelt once more before taking leave of the weeping multitudes. Listen to the Portuguese poet, Camoens, who makes Vasco da Gama the hero of his " Lusiad "—

> " The neighbouring mountains murmur'd back the sound,
>   As if to pity moved for human woe;
>   Uncounted as the grains of golden sand,
>   The tears of thousands fell on Belem's strand."

So the Portuguese embarked, weighed anchor, and unfurled the sails that bore the red cross of the Order of Christ. The four little ships started on what was to be the longest and most momentous voyage on record, while crowds stood on the shore straining their eyes till the fleet, under full sail, vanished from their sight.

After passing Cape Verde, in order to escape the currents of the Gulf of Guinea, Vasco da Gama steered south-west into an unknown part of the South Atlantic. He did not know that at one time he was within six hundred miles of the coast of South America. Day after day, week after week passed in dreary monotony as they sailed the wide ocean that surrounds St. Helena, "a lonely, dreary waste of seas and boundless sky." Everything ends at last, and, having spent ninety-six days out of sight of land and sailed some four thousand five hundred

VASCO DA GAMA.
From a contemporary portrait.

miles, they drifted on to the south-west coast of Africa. It was a record voyage, for even Columbus had only been two thousand six hundred miles without seeing land. November found them in a broad bay, " and," says the old log of the voyage, " we named it St. Helena," which name it still retains. After a skirmish with some tawny-coloured Hottentots the explorers sailed on, putting " their trust in the Lord to double the Cape."

But the sea was all broken with storm, high rolled the waves, and so short were the days that darkness prevailed. The crews grew sick with fear and hardship, and all clamoured to put back to Portugal.

With angry words Vasco da Gama bade them be silent, though " he well saw how much reason they had at every moment to despair of their lives " ; the ships were now letting in much water, and cold rains soaked them all to the skin.

" All cried out to God for mercy upon their souls, for now they no longer took heed of their lives." At last the storm ceased, the seas grew calm, and they knew that, without seeing it, they had doubled the dreaded Cape, " on which great joy fell upon them and they gave great praise to the Lord."

But their troubles were not yet over. The sea was still very rough, " for the winter of that country was setting in," and even the pilot suggested turning back to take refuge for a time. When Vasco da Gama heard of turning backward he cried that they should not speak such words, because as he was going out of the bar of Lisbon he had promised God in his heart not to turn back a single span's breadth of the way, and he would throw into the sea whosoever spoke such things. None could withstand such an iron will, and they struggled on to Mossel Bay, already discovered by Diaz. Here they landed " and bought a fat ox for three bracelets. This ox we dined off on Sunday ; we found him very fat, and his meat nearly as toothsome as the beef of Portugal "—a pleasant meal, indeed, after three months of salted food. Here, too, they found " penguins as large as ducks, which had no feathers on their wings and which bray like asses."

But there was no time to linger here. They sailed onwards till they had passed and left behind the last

pillar erected by Diaz, near the mouth of the Great Fish
River. All was new now. No European had sailed these
seas, no European had passed this part of the African
coast. On Christmas Day they found land to which,
in commemoration of Christ's Nativity, they gave the

AFRICA AS IT WAS KNOWN AFTER DA GAMA'S EXPEDITIONS.

From Juan de la Cosa's map of 1500.

name of Natal. Passing Delagoa Bay and Sofala without
sighting them, Vasco da Gama at last reached the mouth
of a broad river, now known as Quilimane River, but
called by the weary mariners the River of Mercy or Good
Tokens. Here they spent a month cleaning and repairing,

and here for the first time in the history of discovery
the fell disease of scurvy broke out. The hands and
feet of the men swelled, their gums grew over their teeth,
which fell out so that they could not eat. This proved
to be one of the scourges of early navigation—the result
of too much salted food on the high seas, and no cure
was found till the days of Captain Cook. Arrived at
Mozambique—a low-lying coral island—they found no
less than four ocean-going ships belonging to Arab traders
laden with gold, silver, cloves, pepper, ginger, rubies, and
pearls from the East.

There were rumours, too, of a land belonging to Prester
John where precious stones and spices were so plentiful
that they could be collected in baskets. His land could
only be reached by camels. " This information rendered
us so happy that we cried with joy, and prayed God
to grant us health that we might behold what we so
desired," relates the faithful journal. But difficulties
and delays prevented their reaching the ever-mythical
land of Prester John. Their next landing-place was
Mombasa. Here they were nearly killed by some
treacherous Mohammedans, who hated these " dogs of
Christians " as they called them. And the Portuguese
were glad to sail on to Melindi, where the tall, white-
washed houses standing round the bay, with their coco-
palms, maize fields, and hop gardens, reminded them
of one of their own cities on the Tagus. Here all was
friendly. The King of Melindi sent three sheep and
free leave for the strangers to enter the port. Vasco,
in return, sent the King a cassock, two strings of coral,
three washhand basins, a hat, and some bells. Whereupon the King, splendidly dressed in a damask robe
with green satin and an embroidered turban, allowed
himself to be rowed out to the flagship. He was protected from the sun by a crimson satin umbrella.

Nine days were pleasantly passed in the port at Melindi, and then, with a Christian pilot provided by the King, the most thrilling part of the voyage began with a start across the Arabian Gulf to the west coast of India. For twenty-three days the ships sailed to the north-east, with no land visible. Suddenly the dim outline of land was sighted and the whole crew rushed on deck to catch the first glimpse of the unknown coast

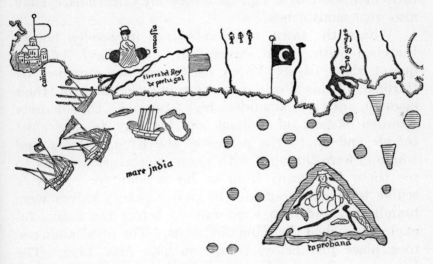

CALICUT AND THE SOUTHERN INDIAN COAST.

From Juan de la Cosa's map, 1500.

of India. They had just discerned the outline of lofty mountains, when a thunderstorm burst over the land and a downpour of heavy rain blotted out the view.

At last on 21st May—nearly eleven months after the start from Portugal—the little Portuguese ships anchored off Calicut.

"What has brought you hither?" cried the natives, probably surprised at their foreign dress; "and what seek ye so far from home?"

12

" We are in search of Christians and spice," was the ready answer.

" A lucky venture. Plenty of emeralds. You owe great thanks to God for having brought you to a country holding such riches," was the Mohammedan answer.

"The city of Calicut," runs the diary, " is inhabited by Christians. They are of a tawny complexion. Some of them have big beards and long hair, whilst others clip their hair short as a sign that they are Christians. They also wear moustaches."

Within the town, merchants lived in wooden houses thatched with palm leaves. It must have been a quaint sight to see Vasco da Gama, accompanied by thirteen of his Portuguese, waving the flag of their country, carried shoulder high through the densely crowded streets of Calicut on his way to the chief temple and on to the palace of the King. Roofs and windows were thronged with eager spectators anxious to see these Europeans from so far a country. Many a scuffle took place outside the palace gates; knives were brandished, and men were injured before the successful explorer reached the King of Calicut. The royal audience took place just before sunset on 28th May 1498. The King lay on a couch covered with green velvet under a gilt canopy, while Vasco da Gama related an account of Portugal and his King, the " lord of many countries and the possessor of great wealth exceeding that of any King of these parts, adding that for sixty years the Portuguese had been trying to find the sea-route to India. The King gave leave for the foreigners to barter their goods, but the Indians scoffed at their offer of hats, scarlet hoods, coral, sugar, and oil.

" That which I ask of you is gold, silver, corals, and scarlet cloth," said the King, " for my country is rich in cinnamon, cloves, ginger, pepper, and precious stones."

Vasco da Gama left India with a scant supply of Christians and spices, but with his great news he now hurried back to Portugal. What if he had lost his brother Paul and over one hundred of his men after his two years' absence, he had discovered the ocean-route to India—a discovery more far-reaching than he had any idea of at this time.

" And the King," relates the old historian, " overjoyed at his coming, sent a Nobleman and several Gentlemen to bring him to Court; where, being arrived through Crowds of Spectators, he was received with extraordinary honour. For this Glorious Price of Service, the Privilege of being called Don was annexed to his Family : To his Arms was added Part of the King's. He had a Pension of three thousand Ducats yearly, and he was afterwards presented to greater Honours for his Services in the Indies, where he will soon appear again."

CHAPTER XXV

DISCOVERY OF THE SPICE ISLANDS

IT was but natural that the Portuguese, flushed with victory, should at once dispatch another expedition to India.

Was there some vexation in the heart of the " Admiral of India " when the command of the new fleet was given to Pedro Cabral ? History is silent. Anyhow, in the March of 1500 we find this " Gentleman of Great Merit " starting off with thirteen powerfully armed ships and some fifteen hundred men, among them the veteran explorer Bartholomew Diaz, a party of eight Franciscan friars to convert the Mohammedans, eight chaplains, skilled gunners, and merchants to buy and sell in the King's name at Calicut. The King himself accompanied Cabral to the waterside. He had already adopted the magnificent title, " King, by the Grace of God, of Portugal, and of the Algarves, both on this side the sea and beyond it in Africa, Lord of Guinea and of the Conquest, Navigation, and Commerce of Ethiopia, Arabia, Persia, and India."

Then Cabral, flying a banner with the royal arms of Portugal, started on a voyage which was to secure for Portugal " an empire destined to be richer and greater than all her dominions in Asia." Sailing far to the west, he fell in with the South American continent and was carried to a new land. The men went on shore and brought word that " it was a fruitful country, full of trees and well inhabited. The people were swarthy and used bows and arrows." That night a storm arose and they ran along the coast to seek a port. Here Mass was said and parrots exchanged for paper and cloth. Then Cabral erected a cross (which was still shown when Lindley visited Brazil three hundred years later) and named the country the "Land of the Holy Cross." This name was, however, discarded later when the new-found land was identified with Brazil already sighted by Pinzon in one of the ships of Christopher Columbus.

Meanwhile, unconscious of the importance of this discovery, Cabral sailed on towards the Cape of Good Hope. There is no time to tell of the great comet that appeared, heralding a terrific storm that suddenly burst upon the little fleet. In the darkness and tempest four ships went down with all hands—amongst them old Bartholomew Diaz, the discoverer of the Cape of Good Hope, who thus perished in the waters he had been the first to navigate.

September found Cabral at last at anchor off Calicut. He found the King yet more resplendent than Vasco da Gama the year before. The old historians revel in their descriptions of him. "On his Head was a Cap of Cloth of Gold, at his Ears hung Jewels, composed of Diamonds, Sapphires, and Pearls, two of which were larger than Walnuts. His Arms, from the Elbow to the Wrist and from the knees downwards, were loaded with bracelets set with infinite Precious Stones of great Value. His Fingers and Toes were covered with Rings. In that on his great Toe was a large Rubie of a surprising Lustre. Among the rest there was a Diamond bigger than a large Bean. But all this was nothing, in comparison to the Richness of his Girdle, made with precious stones set in Gold, which cast a Lustre that dazzled every Body's Eyes."

He allowed Cabral to establish a dépôt at Calicut for European goods, so a house was selected by the water-side and a flag bearing the arms of Portugal erected on the top. For a time all went well, but the Mohammedans proved to be difficult customers, and disputes soon arose. A riot took place; the infuriated native traders stormed the dépôt and killed the Portuguese within. Cabral in revenge bombarded the city, and, leaving the wooden houses in flames, he sailed away to Cochin and Cananor on the coast of Malabar. Soon after this he returned home with only six out of the thirteen ships, and from this time he disappears from the pages of history.

Just before his return, the King of Portugal, thinking trade was well established between India and his own country, dispatched a "valiant gentleman" in command of four ships to carry merchandise to the newly discovered country. But his voyage and adventures are only important inasmuch as he discovered the island of Ascension when outward bound and the island of St. Helena on the way home. So favourable was the account of this island that all Portugal admirals were ordered for the future to touch there for refreshments.

The news of Cabral's adventures at Calicut inspired a yet larger expedition to the East, and Vasco da Gama, now Admiral of the Eastern seas, was given command of some fifteen ships which sailed from the Tagus in February 1502. The expedition, though avowedly Christian, was characterised by injustice and cruelty. Near the coast of Malabar the Portuguese fleet met with a large ship full of Mohammedan pilgrims from Mecca. The wealth on board was known to be enormous, and Don Vasco commanded the owners to yield up their riches to the King of Portugal. This they somewhat naturally refused to do. Whereupon the Portuguese fired, standing calmly to watch the blazing ships with their human freight of men, women, and children. True, one historian declares that all the children were removed to the Portuguese ship to be converted into good little Catholics. Another is more nearly concerned with the money. " We took a Mecca ship on board of which were three hundred and eighty men and many women and children, and we took from it fully twelve thousand ducats, with goods worth at least another ten thousand. And we burned the ship and all the people on board with gunpowder on the first day of October."

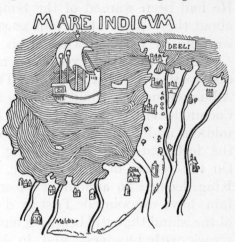

THE MALABAR COAST.

From Fra Mauro's map.

Their instructions to banish every Mohammedan in Calicut was faithfully obeyed. Don Vasco seized and hanged a number of helpless merchants quietly trading in the harbour. Cutting off their heads, hands, and feet, he had them flung into a boat, which was allowed to drift ashore, with a cruel suggestion that the severed limbs would make an Indian curry. Once more Calicut was bombarded and Don Vasco sailed on to other ports on the Malabar coast, where he loaded his ships with spices taken from poor folk who dared not refuse. He then sailed home again, reaching Portugal " safe and sound, *Deo gratias*," but leaving behind him hatred and terror and a very quaint idea of these Christians who felt it their duty to exterminate all followers of Mohammed.

Conquest usually succeeds discovery, and the Portuguese, having discovered the entire coast of West, South, and a good deal of East Africa and western coast of India, now proceeded to conquer it for their own. It was a far cry from Portugal to India in these days, and the isolated dépôts on the coast of Malabar were obviously in danger, when the foreign ships laden with spoil left their shores. True, Vasco da Gama had left six little ships this time under Sodrez to cruise about the Indian seas, but Sodrez wanted treasure, so he cruised northwards and found the southern coasts of Arabia as well as the island of Socotra. He had been warned of the tempestuous seas that raged about these parts at certain seasons, but, heeding not the warning, he perished with all his knowledge and treasure.

Expedition after expedition now left Portugal for the east coast of Africa and India. There were the two cousins Albuquerque, who built a strong fort of wood and mud at Cochin, leaving a garrison of one hundred and fifty trained soldiers under the command of one Pacheco, who saved the fort and kept things going under great difficulties. On the return of Albuquerque, the hero of Cochin, the King decided to appoint a Viceroy of India. He would fain have appointed Tristan d'Acunha,—the discoverer of the island that still bears his name,—but he was suddenly struck with blindness, and in his stead Dom Francisco Almeida, " a nobleman of courage and experience," sailed off with the title of Viceroy. Not only was he to conquer, but to command, not only to sustain the sea-power of Portugal, but to form a government.

There is a story told of the ignorance of the men sent to man the ships under Almeida. So raw were they that they hardly knew their right hand from their left, still less the difference between starboard and larboard, till their captain hit on the happy notion of tying a bundle of garlic over one side of the ship and a handful of onions over the other, so the pilot gave orders to the helmsman thus : " Onion your helm ! " or " Garlic your helm ! "

On the way out, Almeida built a strong fortress near Zanzibar, organised a regular Portuguese Indian pilot service, and established his seat of government at Cochin. Then he sent his son, a daring youth of eighteen, to bom-

A SHIP OF ALBUQUERQUE'S FLEET.

From a very fine woodcut, published about 1516, of Albuquerque's siege and capture of Aden.   In the British Museum.

bard the city of Quilon, whose people were constantly intriguing against the Portuguese. Having carried out his orders, young Lorenzo, ordered to explore the Maldive Islands, was driven by a storm to an "island opposite

Cape Comorin, called Ceylon, and separated from thence by a narrow sea," where he was warmly received by the native King, whose dress sparkled with diamonds. Lorenzo erected here a marble pillar with the arms of Portugal carved thereon and took possession of the island. He also sent back to Portugal the first elephant ever sent thither.

Ceylon was now the farthest point which flew the flag of Portugal toward the east. Doubtless young Lorenzo would have carried it farther, but he was killed at the early age of twenty-one, his legs being shattered by a cannon-ball during a sea-fight. He sat by the mainmast and continued to direct the fighting till a second shot ended his short but brilliant career. The Viceroy, " whose whole being was centred in his devotion to his only son, received the tidings with outward stoicism." " Regrets," he merely remarked, " regrets are for women."

Nevertheless he revenged the death of his son by winning a victory over the opposing fleet and bidding his captains rejoice over " the good vengeance our Lord has been pleased, of His mercy, to grant us."

But the days of Almeida were numbered. He had subdued the Indian coast, he had extended Portuguese possessions in various directions, his term of office was over, and he was succeeded by the famous Albuquerque, who had already distinguished himself in the service of Portugal by his efforts to obtain Ormuz for the Portuguese. Now Viceroy of India, he found full scope for his boundless energy and vast ambition. He first attacked Calicut and reduced it to ashes. Then he turned his attention to Goa, which he conquered, and which became the commercial capital of the Portuguese in India for the next hundred years. Not only this, but it was soon the wealthiest city on the face of the earth and the seat of the government. Albuquerque's next exploit was yet more brilliant and yet more important.

In 1509 he had sent a Portuguese explorer Sequira with a small squadron to make discoveries in the East. He was to cross the Bay of Bengal and explore the coast of Malacca. Sequira reached the coast and found it a centre for trade from east and west, " most rich and populous." But he had reason to suspect the demonstra-

A SHIP OF JAVA AND THE CHINA SEAS IN THE SIXTEENTH CENTURY.

From Linschoten's *Navigatio ac Itinerarium*, 1598.

tions of friendship by the king of these parts, and refused to attend a festival prepared in his honour. This was fortunate, for some of his companions who landed for trade were killed. He sailed about the island of Sumatra, " the first land in which we knew of men's flesh being eaten by certain people in the mountains who gild their teeth. In their opinion the flesh of the blacks is sweeter than that of whites." Many were the strange tales brought back to Cochin by Sequira from the new lands—

rivers of oil—hens with flesh as black as ink—people with tails like sheep.

Anyhow, Albuquerque resolved that Malacca should belong to the Portuguese, and with nineteen ships and fourteen hundred fighting men he arrived off the coast of Sumatra, spreading terror and dismay among the multitudes that covered the shore. The work of destruction was short, though the King of Pahang and King Mahomet came out in person on huge elephants to help in the defence of their city. At last every inhabitant of the city was driven out or slain, and the Portuguese plundered the city to their hearts' content. The old historian waxes eloquent on the wealth of the city, and the laden ships started back, leaving a fort and a church under the care of Portuguese conquerors. The amount of booty mattered little, as a violent storm off the coast of Sumatra disposed of several ships and a good deal of treasure.

The fall of Malacca was one of vast importance to the Portuguese. Was it not the key to the Eastern gate of the Indian Ocean—the " gate through which the whole commerce of the Spice Islands, the Philippines, Japan, and far Cathay passed on its road to the Mediterranean ? Was it not one of the largest trade markets in Asia, where rode the strange ships of many a distant shore ? The fame of Albuquerque spread throughout the Eastern world. But he was not content with Malacca. The Spice Islands lay beyond—the Spice Islands with all their cloves and nutmegs and their countless riches must yet be won for Portugal.

Up to this year, 1511, they had not been reached by the Portuguese. But now Francisco Serrano was sent off from Malacca to explore farther. Skirting the north of Java, he found island after island rich in cloves and nutmeg. So struck was he with his new discoveries that he wrote to his friend Magellan: " I have discovered yet another new world larger and richer than that found by Vasco da Gama."

It is curious to remember how vastly important was this little group of islands—now part of the Malay Archipelago and belonging to the Dutch—to the explorers of the sixteenth century. Strange tales as usual reached Portugal about these newly found lands. Here lived men with " spurs on their ankles like cocks," hogs with horns, hens that laid their eggs nine feet under ground, rivers with living fish, yet so hot that they took the skin off any man that bathed in their waters, poisonous crabs, oysters with shells so large that they served as fonts for baptizing children.

Truly these mysterious Spice Islands held more attractions for the Portuguese explorers than did the New World of Columbus and Vespucci. Their possession meant riches and wealth and—this was not the end. Was there not land beyond ? Indeed, before the Spice Islands were conquered by Portugal, trade had already been opened up with China and, before the century was half over, three Portuguese seamen had visited Japan.

CHAPTER XXVI

BALBOA SEES THE PACIFIC OCEAN

IT is said that Ferdinand Magellan, the hero of all geographical discovery, with his circumnavigation of the whole round world, had cruised about the Spice Islands, but what he really knew of them from personal experience no one knows. He had served under Almeida, and with Albuquerque had helped in the conquest of Malacca. After seven years of a " vivid life of adventure by sea and land, a life of siege and shipwreck, of war and wandering," inaction became impossible. He busied himself with charts and the art of navigation. He dreamt of reaching the Spice Islands by sailing *west*, and after a time he laid his schemes before the King of Portugal. Whether he was laughed at as a dreamer or a fool we know not. His plans were received with cold refusal. History repeats itself. Like Christopher Columbus twenty years before, Magellan now said good-bye to Portugal and made his way to Spain.

Since the first discovery of the New World by Spain, that country had been busy sending out explorer after explorer to discover and annex new portions of America. Bold navigators, Pinzon, Mendoza, Bastidas, Juan de la Cosa, and Solis—these and others had almost completed the discovery of the east coast, indeed, Solis might have been the first to see the great Pacific Ocean had he not been killed and eaten at the mouth of the river La Plata. This great discovery was left to Vasco Nunez de Balboa, who first saw beyond the strange New World from the Peak of Darien. Now his discovery threw a lurid light on to the limitation of land that made up the new country and illuminated the scheme of Magellan.

Balboa was " a gentleman of good family, great parts, liberal education, of a fine person, and in the flower of his age." He had emigrated to the new Spanish colony of Hayti, where he had got into debt. No debtor was allowed to leave the island, but Balboa, the gentleman of good family, yearned for further exploration ; he " yearned beyond the sky-line where the strange roads go down." And one day the yearning grew so great that he concealed himself in a bread cask on board a ship leaving the shores of Hayti. For some days he remained hidden. When the ship was well out to sea he made his appearance. Angry, indeed, was the captain— so angry that he threatened to land the stowaway on a desert island. He was, however, touched by the entreaties of the crew, and Balboa was allowed to sail on in the ship. It was a fortunate decision, for when, soon after, the ship ran heavily upon a rock, it was the Spanish stowaway Balboa who saved the party from destruction. He led the shipwrecked crew to a river of which he knew, named Darien by the Indians. He did *not* know that they stood on the narrow neck of land—the isthmus of Panama—which connects North and South America. The account of the Spanish intrusion is typical : " After having performed their devotions, the Spaniards fell resolutely on the Indians, whom they soon routed, and then went to the town, which they found full of provisions to their wish. Next day they marched up the country among the neighbouring mountains, where they found houses replenished with a great deal of cotton, both spun and unspun, plates of gold in all to the value of ten thousand pieces of fine gold."

A trade in gold was set up by Balboa, who became governor of the new colony formed by the Spaniards; but the greed of these foreigners quite disgusted the native prince of these parts.

" What is this, Christians ? Is it for such a little thing that you quarrel ? If you have such a love of gold, I will show you a country where you may fulfil your desires. You will have to fight your way with great kings whose country is distant from our country six suns."

So saying, he pointed away to the south, where he said lay a great sea. Balboa resolved to find this great sea. It might be the ocean sought by Columbus in vain, beyond which was the land of great riches where people drank out of golden cups. So he collected some two hundred men and started forth on an expedition full of doubt and danger. He had to lead his troops, worn with fatigue and disease, through deep marshes rendered impassable with heavy rains, over mountains covered with trackless forest, and through defiles from which the Indians showered down poisoned arrows.

At last, led by native guides, Balboa and his men struggled up the side of a high mountain. When near the top he bade his men stop. He alone must be the first to see the great sight that no European had yet beheld. With " transports of delight " he gained the top and, "silent upon a peak in Darien," he looked down on the boundless ocean, bathed in tropical sunshine. Falling on his knees, he thanked God for his discovery of the Southern Sea. Then he called up his men. " You see here, gentlemen and children mine, the end of our labours."

The notes of the " Te Deum " then rang out on the still summer air, and, having made a cross of stones, the little party hurried to the shore. Finding two canoes, they sprang in, crying aloud joyously that they were the first

Europeans to sail on the new sea, whilst Balboa himself plunged in, sword in hand, and claimed possession of the Southern Ocean for the King of Spain. The natives told him that the land to the south was *without end,* and that it was possessed by powerful nations who had abundance of gold. And Balboa thought this referred to the Indies, knowing nothing as yet of the riches of Peru.

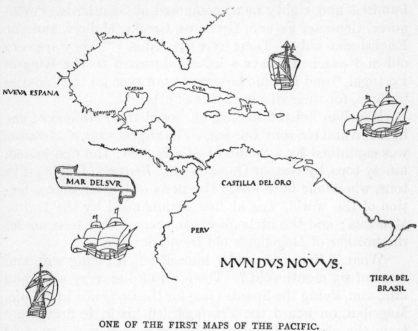

NVEVA ESPANA

VCATAN

CVBA

HAITI

MAR DELSVR

CASTILLA DEL ORO

PERV

MVNDVS NOVVS.

TIERA DEL BRASIL

ONE OF THE FIRST MAPS OF THE PACIFIC.
From Diego Ribero's map, 1529.

It is melancholy to learn that the man who made this really great discovery was publicly hanged four years later in Darien. But his news had reached Magellan. There was then a great Southern Ocean beyond the New World. He was more certain than ever now that by this sea he could reach the Spice Islands. Moreover, he persuaded the young King of Spain that his country had a right to these valuable islands, and promised that he

13

would conduct a fleet round the south of the great new continent westward to these islands. His proposal was accepted by Charles v., and the youthful Spanish monarch provided Spanish ships for the great enterprise. The voyage was not popular, the pay was low, the way unknown, and in the streets of Seville the public crier called for volunteers. Hence it was a motley crew of some two hundred and eighty men, composed of Spaniards, Portuguese, Genoese, French, Germans, Greeks, Malays, and one Englishman only. There were five ships. " They are very old and patched," says a letter addressed to the King of Portugal, " and I would be sorry to sail even for the Canaries in them, for their ribs are soft as butter."

Magellan hoisted his flag on board the *Trinidad* of one hundred and ten tons' burden. The largest ship, *S. Antonio*, was captained by a Spaniard—Cartagena; the *Conception*, ninety tons, by Gaspar Quesada; the *Victoria* of eighty-five tons, who alone bore home the news of the circumnavigation of the world, was at first commanded by the traitor Mendoza; and the little *Santiago*, seventy-five tons, under the brother of Magellan's old friend Serrano.

What if the commander himself left a young wife and a son of six months old ? The fever of discovery was upon him, and, flying the Spanish flag for the first time in his life, Magellan, on board the *Trinidad*, led his little fleet away from the shores of Spain. He never saw wife or child again. Before three years had passed all three were dead.

Carrying a torch or faggot of burning wood on the poop, so that the ships should never lose sight of it, the *Trinidad* sailed onwards.

" Follow the flagship and ask no questions."

Such were his instructions to his not too loyal captains.

CHAPTER XXVII

MAGELLAN SAILS ROUND THE WORLD

THEY had left Seville on 20th September 1519. A week later they were at the Canaries. Then past Cape Verde, and land faded from their sight as they made for the south-west. For some time they had a good run in fine weather. Then "the upper air burst into life" and a month of heavy gales followed. The Italian count, who accompanied the fleet, writes long accounts of the sufferings of the crew during these terrific Atlantic storms.

"During these storms," he says, "the body of St. Anselm appeared to us several times; one night that it was very dark on account of the bad weather the saint appeared in the form of a fire lighted at the summit of the mainmast and remained there near two hours and a half, which comforted us greatly, for we were in tears only expecting the hour of perishing; and, when that holy light was going away from us, it gave out so great a brilliancy in the eyes of each, that we were like people blinded and calling out for mercy. For without any doubt nobody hoped to escape from that storm."

Two months of incessant rain and diminished rations added to their miseries. The spirit of mutiny now began to show itself. Already the Spanish captains had murmured against the Portuguese commander.

"Be they false men or true, I will fear them not; I will do my appointed work," said the commander firmly.

It was not till November that they made the coast of Brazil in South America, already sighted by Cabral and explored by Pinzon. But the disloyal captains were not satisfied, and one day the captain of the *S. Antonio* boarded the flagship and openly insulted Magellan. He must have been a little astonished when the Portuguese commander seized him by the collar, exclaiming: "You are my prisoner!" giving him into custody and appointing another in his place.

Food was now procurable, and a quantity of sweet pine-apples must have had a soothing effect on the discontented crews. The natives traded on easy terms. For a knife they produced four or five fowls; for a comb, fish for ten men; for a little bell, a basket full of sweet potatoes. A long drought had preceded Magellan's visit to these parts, but rain now began with the advent of the strangers, and the natives made sure that they had brought it with them. Such an impression once made there was little difficulty in converting them to the Christian faith. The natives joined in prayer with the Spaniards, "remaining on their knees with their hands joined in great reverence so that it was a pleasure to see them," writes one of the party.

The day after Christmas again found them sailing south by the coast, and early in the New Year they anchored at the mouth of the Rio de la Plata, where Solis had lost his life at the hands of the cannibals some five years before. He had succeeded Vespucci in the service of Spain, and was exploring the coast when a body of Indians, "with a terrible cry and most horrible aspect," suddenly rushed out upon them, killed, roasted, and devoured them.

Through February and March, Magellan led his ships along the shores of bleak Patagonia seeking for an outlet for the Spice Islands. Winter was coming on and no straits had yet been found. Storm after storm now burst over the little ships, often accompanied by thunder and lightning; poops and forecastles were carried away, and all expected destruction, when " the holy body of St. Anselm appeared and immediately the storm ceased."

It was quite impossible to proceed farther to the unknown south, so, finding a safe and roomy harbour, Magellan decided to winter there. Port St. Julian he named it, and he knew full well that there they must remain some four or five months. He put the crew on diminished

AN ATLANTIC FLEET OF MAGELLAN'S TIME.
From Mercator's *Mappe Monde*, 1569, where the drawing is spoken of as " Magellan's ships."

rations for fear the food should run short before they achieved their goal. This was the last straw. Mutiny had long been smouldering. The hardships of the voyage, the terrific Atlantic storms, the prospect of a long Antarctic winter of inaction on that wild Patagonian coast—these alone caused officers and men to grumble and to demand an immediate return to Spain.

But the " stout heart of Magellan " was undaunted.

On Easter Day the mutiny began. Two of the Spanish captains boarded the *S. Antonio*, seized the Portuguese captain thereof, and put him in chains. Then stores were broken open, bread and wine generously handed round, and a plot hatched to capture the flagship, kill Magellan, seize his faithful Serrano, and sail home to Spain.

The news reached Magellan's ears. He at once sent a messenger with five men bearing hidden arms to summon the traitor captain on board the flagship. Of course he stoutly refused. As he did so, the messenger sprang upon him and stabbed him dead. As the rebellious captain fell dead on the deck of his ship, the dazed crew at once surrendered. Thus Magellan by his prompt measures quelled a mutiny that might have lost him the whole expedition. No man ever tried to mutiny again while he lived and commanded.

The fleet had been two whole months in the Port S. Julian without seeing a single native.

" However, one day, without any one expecting it, we saw a giant, who was on the shore of the sea, dancing and leaping and singing. He was so tall that the tallest of us only came up to his waist; he was well built; he had a large face, painted red all round, and his eyes also were painted yellow around them, and he had two hearts painted on his cheeks; he had but little hair on his head and it was painted white."

The great Patagonian giant pointed to the sky to know whether these Spaniards had descended from above. He was soon joined by others evidently greatly surprised to see such large ships and such little men. Indeed, the heads of the Spaniards hardly reached the giants' waists, and they must have been greatly astonished when two of them ate a large basketful of biscuits and rats without skinning them and drank half a bucket of water at each sitting.

With the return of spring weather in October 1520, Magellan led the little fleet upon its way. He was rewarded a few days later by finding the straits for which he and others had been so long searching.

FERDIN·MAGALLANUS·
SUPERATIS·ANTARCTICI·FRETI·
ANGUSTIIS·CLARISSIMUS·

FERDINAND MAGELLAN, THE FIRST CIRCUMNAVIGATOR OF THE WORLD.
After the engraving by Selma in Navarrete's *Coleccion de los Viages*.

" It was the straight," says the historian simply, " now cauled the straight of Magellans."

A struggle was before them. For more than five weeks the Spanish mariners fought their way through the winding channels of the unknown straits. On one side rose high mountains covered with snow. The weather was bad, the way unknown. Do we wonder to read that " one of the ships stole away privily and returned into Spain," and the remaining men begged piteously to be taken home ? Magellan spoke " in measured and quiet tones " : "If I have to eat the leather of the ships' yards, yet will I go on and do my work." His words came truer than he knew. On the southern side of the strait constant fires were seen, which led Magellan to give the land the name it bears to-day —Tierra del Fuego. It was not visited again for a hundred years.

A SHIP OF THE SIXTEENTH CENTURY.

From Amoretti's translation of *Magellan's Voyage round the World.*

At last the ships fought their way to the open sea—Balboa's Southern Ocean — and " when the Captain Magellan was past the strait and saw the way open to the other main sea he was so glad thereof that for joy the tears fell from his eyes."

The expanse of calm waters seemed so pleasant after the heavy tiring storms that he called the still waters before him the Pacific Ocean. Before following him across the unknown waters, let us recall the quaint lines of Camoens—

" Along these regions, from the burning zone
   To deepest south, he dares the course unknown.

A land of giants shall his eyes behold,
Of camel strength, surpassing human mould ;
And, onward still, thy fame his proud heart's guide,
Beneath the southern stars' cold gleam he braves
And stems the whirls of land-surrounded waves,
For ever sacred to the hero's fame,
These foaming straits shall bear his deathless name.
Through these dread jaws of rock he presses on
Another ocean's breast, immense, unknown,
Beneath the south's cold wings, unmeasur'd, wide,
Received his vessels, through the dreary tide,
In darkling shades, where never man before
Heard the waves howl, he dares the nameless shore."

Three little ships had now emerged, battered and worn, manned by crews gaunt and thin and shivering. Magellan took a northerly course to avoid the intense cold, before turning to cross the strange obscure ocean, which no European had yet realised. Just before Christmas the course was altered and the ships were turned to the north-west, in which direction they expected soon to find the Spice Islands. No one had any idea of the vastness of the Pacific Ocean.

" Well was it named the Pacific," remarks the historian, " for during three months and twenty days we met with no storm."

Two months passed away, and still they sailed peacefully on, day after day, week after week, across a waste of desolate waters.

" Alone, alone, all, all alone,
Alone on a wide, wide sea."

At last one January day they sighted a small wooded island, but it was uninhabited ; they named it S. Paul's Island and passed on their way. They had expected to find the shores of Asia close by those of America. The size of the world was astounding. Another island was passed. Again no people, no consolation, only many sharks. There was bitter disappointment on board. They had little food left. " We ate biscuit, but in truth it was biscuit no longer, but a powder full of worms. So great was the want of food that we were forced to eat the hides with which the main yard was covered to prevent the chafing against the rigging. These hides we exposed to the sun first to soften them by putting them overboard for four or five days, after which we

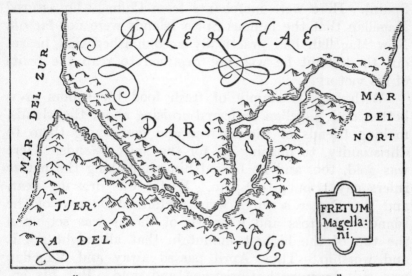

"HONDIUS HIS MAP OF THE MAGELLAN STREIGHT."

From a map by Jodocus Hondius, about 1590. It gives a particularly clear picture of the ideas held by the age following Magellan's discovery of the land which, it was supposed, enveloped the southern point of South America.

put them on the embers and ate them thus. We had also to make use of sawdust for food, and rats became a great delicacy." No wonder scurvy broke out in its worst form—nineteen died and thirteen lay too ill to work.

For ninety-eight days they sailed across the unknown sea, " a sea so vast that the human mind can scarcely grasp it," till at last they came on a little group of islands peopled with savages of the lowest type—such expert thieves that Magellan called the new islands the Ladrones or isle of robbers. Still, there was fresh food here, and the crews were greatly refreshed before they sailed away. The food came just too late to save the one Englishman of the party—Master Andrew of Bristol—who died just as they moved away. Then they found the group afterwards known as the Philippines (after Philip II. of Spain). Here were merchants from China, who assured Magellan that the famous Spice Islands were not far off. Now Magellan had practically accomplished that he set out to do, but he was not destined to reap the fruits of his victory.

With a good supply of fresh food the sailors grew better, and Magellan preferred cruising about the islands, making friends of the natives and converting them to Christianity, to pushing on for the Spice Islands. Here was gold, too, and he busied himself making the native rulers pay tribute to Spain. Easter was drawing near, and the Easter services were performed on one of the islands. A cross and a crown of thorns was set upon the top of the highest mountain that all might see it and worship. Thus April passed away and Magellan was still busy with Christians and gold. But his enthusiasm carried him too far. A quarrel arose with one of the native kings. Magellan landed with armed men, only to be met by thousands of defiant natives. A desperate fight ensued. Again and again the explorer was wounded, till " at last the Indians threw themselves upon him with iron-pointed bamboo spears and every weapon they had and ran him through—our mirror, our light, our comforter, our true guide—until they killed him."

Such was the tragic fate of Ferdinand Magellan, " the greatest of ancient and modern navigators," tragic because, after dauntless resolution and unwearied courage, he died in a miserable skirmish at the last on the very eve of victory.

With grief and despair in their hearts, the remaining members of the crew, now only one hundred and fifteen, crowded on to the *Trinidad* and *Victoria* for the homeward

THE FIRST SHIP THAT SAILED ROUND THE WORLD.
Magellan's *Victoria*, from Hulsius's *Collection of Voyages*, 1602.

voyage. It was September 1522 when they reached the Spice Islands—the goal of all their hopes. Here they took on board some precious cloves and birds of Paradise, spent some pleasant months, and, laden with spices, resumed their journey. But the *Trinidad* was too overladen with cloves and too rotten to undertake so long a voyage till she had undergone repair, so the little *Victoria* alone sailed for Spain with sixty men aboard to carry home their great and wonderful news. Who shall describe the terrors of that homeward voyage, the suffering, starvation, and misery of the weary crew? Man after man drooped and died, till by the time they reached the Cape Verde Islands there were but eighteen left.

When the welcome shores of Spain at length appeared, eighteen gaunt, famine-stricken survivors, with their captain, staggered ashore to tell their proud story of the first circumnavigation of the world by their lost commander, Ferdinand Magellan.

We miss the triumphal return of the conqueror, the audience with the King of Spain, the heaped honours, the crowded streets, the titles, and the riches. The proudest crest ever granted by a sovereign—the world, with the words: "Thou hast encompassed me"—fell to the lot of Del Cano, the captain who brought home the little *Victoria*. For Magellan's son was dead, and his wife Beatrix, "grievously sorrowing," had passed away on hearing the news of her husband's tragic end.

CHAPTER XXVIII

CORTES EXPLORES AND CONQUERS MEXICO

ONE would have thought that the revelation of this immense sheet of water on the far side of America would have drawn other explorers to follow, but news was slowly assimilated in those days, and it was not till fifty-three years later that the Pacific was crossed a second time by Sir Francis Drake.

In the maps of the day, Newfoundland and Florida were both placed in Asia, while Mexico was identified with the Quinsay of Marco Polo. For even while Magellan was fighting the gales of the Atlantic *en route* for his long-sought strait, another strange and wonderful country was being unveiled and its unsurpassed wealth laid at the feet of Spain. The starting-place for further Spanish exploration had been, from the days of Columbus, the West Indies. From this centre, the coast of Florida had been discovered in 1513; from here, the same year, Balboa had discovered the Pacific Ocean; from here in 1517 a little fleet was fitted out under Francisco Hernando de Cordova, " a man very prudent and courageous and strongly disposed to kill and kidnap Indians." As pilot he had been with Columbus on his fourth voyage some fourteen years before. He suggested that his master had heard rumours of land to the West, and sure enough, after sailing past the peninsula of Yucatan, they found signs of the Eastern civilisation so long sought in vain.

"Strange-looking towers or pyramids, ascended by stone steps, greeted their eyes, and the people who came out in canoes to watch the ships were clad in quilted cotton doublets and wore cloaks and brilliant plumes."

They had heard of the Spaniards. Indeed, only one hundred miles of sea divided Yucatan from Cuba, and they were anything but pleased to see these strangers off their coast.

"Couez cotoche" (Come to my house), they cried, for which reason Cordova called the place Cape Catoche, as it is marked in our maps to-day. Along the coast sailed the Spaniards to a place called by the Indians Quimpeche, now known as Campechy Bay. They were astonished to find how civilised were these natives, and how unlike any others they had met in these parts. But the inhabitants resented the landing of Cordova and his men, and with arrows and stones and darts they killed or wounded a great number of Spaniards, including the commander himself, who sent an account of his voyage to the Governor of Cuba and died a few days later.

His information was interesting and inspiring, and soon young Juan Grijalva was on his way to the same land, accompanied by "two hundred and fifty stout soldiers" and the old pilot, Alvarado, who had led both Columbus and Cordova. Grijalva explored for the first time the coast of this great new country.

"Mexico, Mexico," repeated the Indians with whom they conversed. Gold, too, was produced, gold ornaments, gold workmanship, until the young and handsome Grijalva was fitted out completely with a complete suit of gold armour. He returned enthusiastic over the new land where lived a powerful ruler over many cities. Surely this was none other than the Great Khan of Marco Polo fame, with the riches and magnificence of an Eastern potentate— a land worthy of further exploration.

The conqueror of Mexico now comes upon the scene—
young, bold, devout, unscrupulous, " a respectable gentleman of good birth "—Hernando Cortes. Great was the
enthusiasm in Cuba to join the new expedition to the long-
lost lands of the Great Khan; men sold their lands to buy
horses and arms, pork was
salted, armour was made,
and at last Cortes, a plume
of feathers and a gold medal
in his cap, erected on board
his ship a velvet flag with
the royal arms embroidered
in gold and the words:
"Brothers, follow the cross
in faith, for under its guid-
ance we shall conquer."

His address to his men
called forth their devotion:
"I hold out to you a glorious
prize, but it is to be won by
incessant toil. Great things
are achieved only by great
exertions, and glory was
never the reward of sloth.
If I have laboured hard and
staked my all on this undertaking, it is for the love of
that renown, which is the
noblest recompense of man.

HERNANDO CORTES,
CONQUEROR OF MEXICO.

After the original portrait at Mexico.

But if any among you covet riches more, be but true to
me, as I will make you masters of such as our countrymen have never dreamed of. You are few in number,
but strong in resolution; doubt not but that the
Almighty, who has never deserted the Spaniard in his
contest with the infidel, will shield you, for your cause is

a just cause, and you are to fight under the banner of the Cross."

In this spirit of enthusiasm the fleet sailed from the shores of Cuba on 18th February 1519, and was soon on its way to the land of Mexico. The pilot Alvarado was with this expedition also. Rounding Cape Catoche and coasting along the southern shores of Campechy Bay, with a pleasant breeze blowing off the shore, Cortes landed with all his force—some five hundred soldiers—on the very spot where now stands the city of Vera Cruz. " Little did the conqueror imagine that the desolate beach on which he first planted his foot was one day to be covered by a flourishing city, the great mart of European and Oriental trade—the commercial capital of New Spain."

On a wide, level plain Cortes encamped, his soldiers driving in stakes and covering them with boughs to protect themselves from the scorching rays of the fierce, tropical sun. Natives came down to the shore, bringing their beautiful featherwork cloaks and golden ornaments. Cortes had brought presents for the great King—the Khan as he thought—and these he sent with a message that he had come from the King of Spain and greatly desired an audience with the Great Khan. The Indians were greatly surprised to hear that there was another King in the world as powerful as their Montezuma, who was more god than king, who ate from dishes of gold, on whose face none dared look, in whose presence none dared speak without leave.

To impress the messengers of the King, Cortes ordered his soldiers to go through some of their military exercises on the wet sands. The bold and rapid movement of the troops, the glancing of the weapons, and the shrill cry of the trumpet filled the spectators with astonishment; but when they heard the thunder of the cannon and witnessed the volumes of smoke and flame issuing from these terrible engines, the rushing of the balls as they hissed through the trees of the neighbouring forest shivering their branches, they were filled with consternation.

To the intense surprise of the Spaniards, these messengers sketched the whole scene on canvas with their pencils, not forgetting the Spanish ships or " water-houses " as they called them, with their dark hulls and snow-white sails reflected in the water as they swung lazily at anchor.

Then they returned to the King and related the strange doings of the white strangers who had landed on their shores; they showed him their picture-writing, and Montezuma, king of the great Mexican empire which stretched from sea to sea, was " sore troubled." He refused to see the Spaniards—the distance of his capital was too great, since the journey was beset with difficulties. But the presents he sent were so gorgeous, so wonderful, that Cortes resolved to see for himself the city which produced such wealth, whatever its ruler might decree. Here was a plate of gold as large as a coach wheel representing the sun, one in silver even larger, representing the moon; there were numbers of golden toys representing dogs, lions, tigers, apes, ducks, and wonderful plumes of green feathers.

The man who had sailed across two thousand leagues of ocean held lightly the idea of a short land journey, however difficult, and Cortes began his preparations for the march to Mexico. He built the little settlement at Vera Cruz, " The Rich Town of the True Cross," on the seashore as a basis for operations. Although the wealth allured them, there were many who viewed with dismay the idea of the long and dangerous march into the heart of a hostile land. After all they were but a handful of men pitted against a powerful nation. Murmurs arose which

14

reached the ears of Cortes. He was equal to the occasion and resolutely burnt all the ships in the harbour save one. Then panic ensued. Mutiny threatened.

" I have chosen my part ! " cried Cortes. " I will remain here while there is one to bear me company. If there be any so craven as to shrink from sharing the dangers of our glorious enterprise, let them go home. There is still one vessel left. Let them take that and return to Cuba. They can tell there how they have deserted their commander and their comrades, and patiently wait till we return loaded with the spoils of Mexico."

He touched the right chord. Visions of future wealth and glory rose again before them, confidence in their leader revived, and, shouting bravely, " To Mexico ! to Mexico ! " the party started off on their perilous march. It was 16th August 1519 when the little army, " buoyant with high hopes and lofty plans of conquest," set forth. The first part of the way lay through beautiful country rich in cochineal and vanilla, with groves of many-coloured birds and " insects whose enamelled wings glistened like diamonds in the blazing sun of the tropics."

Then came the long and tedious ascent of the Cordilleras leading to the tableland of Mexico. Higher and higher grew the mountains. Heavy falls of sleet and hail, icy winds, and driving rain drenched the little Spanish party as they made their way bravely upwards, till at last they reached the level of seven thousand feet to find the great tableland rolling out along the crest of the Cordilleras.

Hitherto they had met with no opposition among the natives they had met. Indeed, as the little army advanced, it was often found that the inhabitants of the country fled awestruck from before them. Now the reason was this. The Mexicans believed in a god called the Bird-Serpent, around whom many a legend had grown up. Temples had been built in his honour and horrible human sacrifices offered to appease him, for was he not the Ruler of the Winds, the Lord of the Lightning, the Gatherer of the Clouds ?   But the bright god had sailed away one day, saying he would return with fair-skinned men to possess the land in the fulness of time.   Surely, then, the time had come and their god had come again.   Here were the fair-skinned men in shining armour marching back to their own again, and Cortes at their head—was he not the god himself ?   The cross, too, was a Mexican symbol, so Cortes was allowed to put it up in the heathen temples without opposition.

The inhabitants of Tlascala—fierce republicans who refused to own the sway of Montezuma—alone offered resistance, and how Cortes fought and defeated them with his handful of men is truly a marvel.

It was three months before they reached the goal of all their hopes—even the golden city of Mexico.   The hardships and horrors of the march had been unsurpassed, but as the beautiful valley of Mexico unfolded itself before them in the early light of a July morning, the Spaniards shouted with joy : " It is the promised land !   Mexico !   Mexico ! "

" Many of us were disposed to doubt the reality of the scene before us and to suspect we were in a dream," says one of the party.   " I thought we had been transported by magic to the terrestrial paradise."

Water, cultivated plains, shining cities with shadowy hills beyond lay like some gorgeous fairyland before and below them.   At every step some new beauty appeared in sight, and the wonderful City of the Waters with its towers and shining palaces arose out of the surrounding mists.

The city was approached by three solid causeways some five miles long.   It was crowded with spectators " eager to behold such men and animals as had never been seen in that part of the world."

At any moment the little army of four hundred and fifty Spaniards might have been destroyed, surrounded as they were by overwhelming numbers of hostile Indian foes. It was a great day in the history of European discovery, when the Spaniard first set foot in the capital of the Western world. Everywhere was evidence of a crowded and thriving population and a high civilisation. At the walls of the city they were met by Montezuma himself. Amid a crowd of Indian nobles, preceded by officers of state bearing golden wands, was the royal palanquin blazing with burnished gold. It was borne on the shoulders of the nobles, who, barefooted, walked slowly with eyes cast to the ground. Descending from his litter, Montezuma then advanced under a canopy of gaudy featherwork powdered with jewels and fringed with silver. His cloak and sandals were studded with pearls and precious stones among which emeralds were conspicuous. Cortes dismounted, greeted the King, and spoke of his mission to the heathen and of his master, the mighty ruler of Spain. Everywhere Cortes and his men were received with friendship and reverence, for was he not the long-lost Child of the Sun ? The Spanish explorer begged Montezuma to give up his idols and to stop his terrible human sacrifices. The King somewhat naturally refused. Cortes grew angry. He was also very anxious. He felt the weakness of his position, the little handful of men in this great populous city, which he had sworn to win for Spain. The King must go. " Why do we waste time on this barbarian ? Let us seize him and, if he resists, plunge our swords into his body ! " cried the exasperated commander.

This is no place for the pathetic story of Montezuma's downfall. Prescott's *Conquest of Mexico* is within the reach of all. It tells of the Spanish treachery, of the refusal of the Mexican ruler to accept the new faith, of his final appeal

to his subjects, of chains, degradation, and death.   It tells
of the three great heaps of gold, pearls, and precious stones
taken by Cortes, of the final siege and conquest.

The news of this immense Mexican Empire, discovered

THE BATTLES OF THE SPANIARDS IN MEXICO.

From an ancient Aztec drawing, showing a leader of the Spaniards with his native
allies defeating the Mexicans.

and conquered for Spain, brought honours from the King,
Charles v., to the triumphant conqueror.

Nor did Cortes stop even after this achievement.
As Governor and Captain-General of Mexico, he sent off
ships to explore the neighbouring coasts.   Hearing that
Honduras possessed rich mines and that a strait into the

Pacific Ocean might be found, Cortes led an expedition by land. Arrived at Tabasco, he was provided with an Indian map of cotton cloth, whereon were painted all the towns, rivers, mountains, as far as Nicaragua. With this map and the mariner's compass, he led his army through gloomy woods so thick that no sun ever penetrated, and after a march of one thousand miles reached the sea-coast of Honduras, took over the country for Spain to be governed with Mexico by himself.

This enormous tract of country was known to the world as " New Spain."

CHAPTER XXIX

EXPLORERS IN SOUTH AMERICA

THE success of Cortes and his brilliant conquest of Mexico gave a new impulse to discovery in the New World. The spirit of exploration dominated every adventurous young Spaniard, and among those living in the West Indies there were many ready to give up all for the golden countries in the West, rumours of which were always reaching their ears.

No sooner had these rich lands been realised than the news of Magellan's great voyage revealed the breadth of the ocean between America and Asia, and destroyed for ever the idea that the Spice Islands were near. Spanish enterprise, therefore, lay in the same direction as heretofore, and we must relate the story of how Pizarro discovered Peru for the King of Spain. He had accompanied Balboa to Darien, and had with him gazed out on to the unknown waters of the Pacific Ocean below. With Balboa after crossing the isthmus of Darien he had reached Panama on the South Sea, where he heard of a great nation far to the south. Like Mexico, it was spoken of as highly civilised and rich in mines of gold and silver. Many an explorer would have started off straightway for this new country, but there was a vast tract of dark forest and tangled underwood between Panama and Peru, which had damped the ardour of even the most ardent of Spanish explorers.

But Pizarro was a man of courage and dauntless resolution, and he was ready to do and dare the impossible.

He made a bad start. A single ship with some hundred men aboard left Panama under the command of Pizarro in 1526. He was ignorant of southern navigation, the Indians along the shore were hostile, his men died one by one, the rich land of Peru was more distant than they had thought, and, having at length reached the island of Gallo near the Equator, they awaited reinforcements from Panama. Great, then, was the disappointment of Pizarro when only one ship arrived and no soldiers. News of hardships and privations had spread through Panama, and none would volunteer to explore Peru. By this time the handful of wretched men who had remained with Pizarro, living on crabs picked up on the shore, begged to be taken home—they could endure no longer. Then came one of those tremendous moments that lifts the born leader of men above his fellows. Drawing his sword, Pizarro traced a line on the sand from east to west. "Friends," he cried, turning to the south, "on that side are toil, hunger, nakedness, the drenching storm, desertion, and death, and on this side ease and pleasure. There lies Peru with its riches, here Panama and its poverty. For my part, I go south."

So saying, he stepped across the line. Twelve stout-hearted men followed him. The rest turned wearily homewards. The reduced but resolute little party then sailed south, and a voyage of two days brought them within sight of the long-sought land of Peru. Communication with the natives assured them that here was wealth and fortune to be made, and they hurried back to Panama, whence Pizarro sailed for Spain, for permission to conquer the empire of Peru. It is interesting to find Cortes contributing some of his immense wealth from Mexico towards this new quest.

In February 1531 three small ships with one hundred and eighty soldiers and thirty-six horses sailed south under

Pizarro.   It was not till the autumn of 1532 that he was
ready to start on the great march to the interior.   A city
called Cuzco was the capital—the Holy City with its great
Temple of the Sun, the most magnificent building in the
New World, had never yet been seen by Europeans.   But
the residence of the King was at Caxamalea, and this
was the goal of the Spaniards for the present.

Already the news was spreading through the land that
" white and bearded strangers were coming up from the
sea, clad in shining panoply,
riding upon unearthly monsters, and wielding deadly
thunderbolts."

Pizarro's march to the
heart of Peru with a mere
handful of men was not
unlike that of Cortes' expedition to Mexico. Both coveted
the rich empire of unknown
monarchs and dared all—to
possess.   Between Pizarro
and his goal lay the stu-
pendous mountain range of
the Andes or South American
Cordilleras, rock piled upon

PIZARRO.
From the portrait at Cuzco.

rock, their crests of everlasting snow glittering high in
the heavens. Across these and over narrow mountain
passes the troops had now to pass. So steep were the
sides that the horsemen had to dismount and scramble
up, leading their horses as best they might. Frightful
chasms yawned below them, terrific peaks rose above,
and at any moment they might be utterly destroyed by
bodies of Peruvians in overwhelming numbers. It was
bitterly cold as they mounted higher and higher up the
dreary heights, till at last they reached the crest. Then

began the descent—precipitous and dangerous—until after seven days of this the valley of Caxamalea unrolled before their delighted eyes, and the little ancient city with its white houses lay glittering in the sun. But dismay filled the stoutest heart when, spread out below for the space of several miles, tents as thick as snowflakes covered the ground. It was the Peruvian army. And it was too late to turn back. " So, with as bold a countenance as we could, we prepared for our entrance into Caxamalea."

The Peruvians must already have seen the cavalcade of Spaniards, as with banners streaming and armour glistening in the rays of the evening sun Pizarro led them towards the city. As they drew near, the King, Atahualpa, covered with plumes of feathers and ornaments of gold and silver blazing in the sun, was carried forth on a throne followed by thirty thousand men to meet the strangers. It seemed to the Spanish leader that only one course was open. He must seize the person of this great ruler at once. He waved his white scarf. Immediately the cavalry charged and a terrible fight took place around the person of the ruler of Peru until he was captured and taken prisoner. Atahualpa tried to regain his liberty by the offer of gold, for he had discovered—amid all their outward show of religious zeal—a greed for wealth among these strange white men from over the stormy seas. He suggested that he should fill with gold the room in which he was confined as high as he could reach. Standing on tiptoe, he marked the wall with his hand. Pizarro accepted the offer, and the Spaniards greedily watched the arrival of their treasure from the roofs of palace and temple. They gained a sum of something like three million sterling and then put the King to death. Pizarro was the conqueror of Peru, and he had no difficulty in controlling the awestruck Peruvians, who regarded the relentless

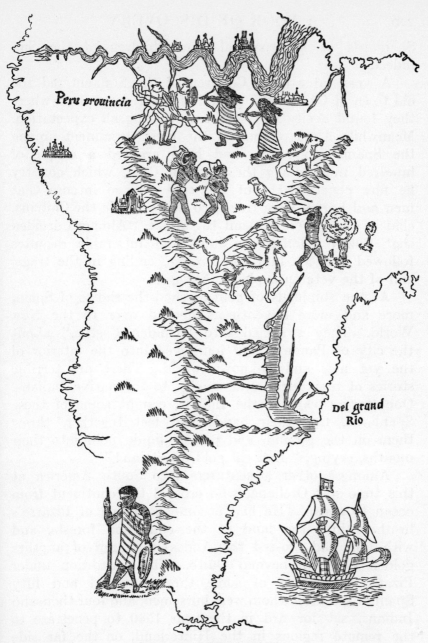

Peru prouincia

Del grand
Rio

PERU AND SOUTH AMERICA.

From the Map of the World of 1544, usually ascribed to Sebastian Cabot. At the top is
shown the river Amazon, discovered by Orellana in 1541.

219

Spaniards as supernatural—the Children of the Sun indeed.

A year later these Children of the Sun entered the old town of Cuzco—the capital of this rich empire—where they found a city of treasure surpassing all expectation. Meanwhile Almagro, one of the most prominent among the Spanish explorers, had been granted a couple of hundred miles along the coast of Chili, which country he now penetrated; but the cold was so intense that men and horses were frozen to death, while the Chilians, clad in skins, were difficult to subdue. Almagro decided that Cuzco belonged to him, and miserable disputes followed between him and Pizarro, ending in the tragic end of the veteran explorer, Almagro.

As the shiploads of gold reached the shores of Spain, more and more adventurers flocked over to the New World. They swarmed into "Golden Castile," about the city of Panama, and journeyed into the interior of the yet new and unknown world. There are terrible stories of their greed and cruelty to the native Indians. One story says that the Indians caught some of these Spaniards, tied their hands and feet together, threw them on the ground, and poured liquid gold into their mouths, crying, "Eat, eat gold, Christian!"

Amongst other adventurers into South America at this time was Orellana, who crossed the continent from ocean to ocean. He had accompanied one of Pizarro's brothers into the land of the cinnamon forests, and with him had crossed the Andes in search of another golden kingdom beyond Quito. The expedition under Pizarro, consisting of some three hundred and fifty Spaniards, half of whom were horsemen, and four thousand Indians, set forward in the year 1540 to penetrate to the remote regions in the Hinterland, on the far side of the Andes. Their sufferings were intense. Violent thunderstorms and earthquakes terrified man and beast; the earth opened and swallowed up five hundred houses; rain fell in such torrents as to flood the land and cut off all communication between the explorers and cultivated regions; while crossing the lofty ridge of the Andes the cold was so intense that numbers of the party were literally frozen to death. At length they reached the land of the cinnamon trees, and, still pushing on, came to a river which must be crossed to reach the land of gold. They had finished their provisions, and had nothing to subsist on now save the wild fruit of the country. After following the course of the river for some way, Pizarro decided to build a little vessel to search for food along the river. All set to work, Pizarro and Orellana, one of his chief captains, working as hard as the men. They set up a forge for making nails, and burnt charcoal with endless trouble owing to the heavy rains which prevented the tinder from taking fire. They made nails from the shoes of the horses which had been killed to feed the sick. For tar they used the resin from the trees, for oakum they used blankets and old shirts. Then they launched the little home-made boat, thinking their troubles would be at an end. For some four hundred miles they followed the course of the river, but the supply of roots and berries grew scarcer and men perished daily from starvation. So Pizarro ordered Orellana to go quickly down the river with fifty men to some inhabited land of which they had heard, to fill the boat with provisions, and return.

Off started Orellana down the river, but no villages or cultivated lands appeared; nothing was to be seen save flooded plains and gloomy, impenetrable forests. The river turned out to be a tributary of a much larger river. It was, indeed, the great river Amazon. Orellana now decided to go on down this great river and to desert

Pizarro. True, his men were utterly weary, the current was too strong for them to row against, and they had no food to bring to their unhappy companions. There was likewise the possibility of reaching the kingdom of gold for which they were searching. There were some among his party who objected strongly to the course proposed by Orellana, to whom he responded by landing them on the edge of the dense forest and there leaving them to perish of hunger.

It was the last day of 1540 that, having eaten their shoes and saddles boiled with a few wild herbs, they set out to reach the kingdom of gold. It was truly one of the greatest adventures of the age, and historic, for here we get the word El Dorado, used for the first time in the history of discovery—the legendary land of gold which was never found, but which attracted all the Elizabethan sailors to this romantic country. It would take too long to tell how they had to fight Indian tribes in their progress down the fast-flowing river, how they had to build a new boat, making bellows of their leather buskins and manufacturing two thousand nails in twenty days, how they found women on the banks of the river fighting as valiantly as men, and named the new country the Amazon land, and how at long last, after incredible hardship, they reached the sea in August 1541. They had navigated some two thousand miles. They now made their rigging and ropes of grass and sails of blankets, and so sailed out into the open sea, reaching one of the West India islands a few days later.

And the deserted Pizarro? Tired of waiting for Orellana, he made his way sorrowfully home, arriving after two years' absence in Peru, with eighty men left out of four thousand three hundred and fifty, all the rest having perished in the disastrous expedition. And so we must leave the Spanish conquerors for the present, still exploring, still conquering, in these parts, ever adding glory and riches to Spain. Indeed, Spain and Portugal, as we have seen, entirely monopolise the horizon of geographical discovery till the middle of the sixteenth century, when other nations enter the arena.

PERUVIAN WARRIORS OF THE INCA PERIOD.

From an ancient Peruvian painting.

CHAPTER XXX

CABOT SAILS TO NEWFOUNDLAND

IT was no longer possible for the Old World to keep secret the wealth of the New World. English eyes were already straining across the seas, English hands were ready to grasp the treasure that had been Spain's for the last fifty years. While Spain was sending Christopher Columbus to and fro across the Atlantic to the West Indies, while Portugal was rejoicing in the success of Vasco da Gama, John Cabot, in the service of England, was making his way from Bristol to the New World. News of the first voyage of Columbus had been received by the Cabots—John and his son Sebastian—with infinite admiration. They believed with the rest of the world that the coast of China had been reached by sailing westward. Bristol was at this time the chief seaport in England, and the centre of trade for the Iceland fisheries. The merchants of the city had already ventured far on to the Atlantic, and various little expeditions had been fitted out by the merchants for possible discovery westward, but one after another failed, including the " most scientific mariner in all England," who started forth to find the island of Brazil to the west of Ireland, but, after nine miserable weeks at sea, was driven back to Ireland again by foul weather.

Now Columbus had crossed the Atlantic, Cabot got leave from the English King, Henry VII., " to sail to the east, west, or north, with five ships carrying the English flag, to seek and discover all the islands, countries, regions, or provinces of pagans in whatever part of the world."

Further, the King was to have one-fifth of the profits, and at all risks any conflict with Spain must be avoided. Nothing daunted, Cabot started off to fulfil his lord's

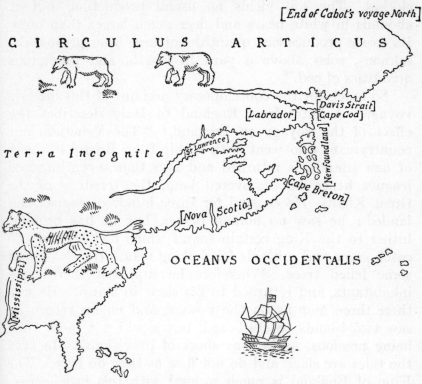

PART OF NORTH AMERICA, SHOWING SEBASTIAN CABOT'S
VOYAGE TO NEWFOUNDLAND.

From the Map of 1544, usually ascribed to Cabot. The names in brackets are inserted
in order to make this extract and its reference to Cabot's discoveries clear.

commands in a tiny ship with eighteen men. We have the barest outlines of his proceedings. Practically all is contained in this one paragraph. "In the year 1497 John Cabot, a Venetian, and his son Sebastian discovered on the 24th of June, about five in the morning, that land

15

to which no person had before ventured to sail, which they named Prima Vista or first seen, because, as I believe, it was the first part seen by them from the sea. The inhabitants use the skins and furs of wild beasts for garments, which they hold in as high estimation as we do our finest clothes. The soil yields no useful production, but it abounds in white bears and deer much larger than ours. Its coasts produce vast quantities of large fish—great seals, salmons, soles above a yard in length, and prodigious quantities of cod."

So much for the contemporary account of this historic voyage. A letter from England to Italy describes the effect of the voyage on England. "The Venetian, our countryman, who went with a ship from Bristol in quest of new islands, is returned and says that seven hundred leagues hence he discovered land, the territory of the Great Khan. He coasted for three hundred leagues and landed; he saw no human beings, but he has brought hither to the King certain snares which had been set to catch game and a needle for making nets. He also found some felled trees. Wherefore he supposed there were inhabitants, and returned to his ships in alarm. He was there three months on the voyage, and on his return he saw two islands to starboard, but would not land, time being precious, as he was short of provisions. He says the tides are slack and do not flow as they do here. The King of England is much pleased with this intelligence. The King has promised that in the spring our countryman shall have ten ships to his order, and at his request has conceded to him all the prisoners to man his fleet. The King has also given him money wherewith to amuse himself till then, and he is now at Bristol with his wife and sons. His name is Cabot, and he is styled the great Admiral. Vast honour is paid to him; he dresses in silk, and the English run after him like mad people."

Yet another letter of the time tells how " Master John Cabot has won a part of Asia without a stroke of the sword." This Master John, too, " has the description of the world in a chart and also in a solid globe which he has made, and he shows where he landed. And they say that it is a good and temperate country, and they think that Brazil wood and silks grow there, and they affirm that that sea is covered with fishes."

But " Master John " had set his heart on something greater. Constantly hugging the shore of America, he expected to find the island of Cipango (Japan) in the equinoctial region, where he should find all the spices of the world and any amount of precious stones.

But after all this great promise Master John disappears from the pages of history and his son Sebastian continues to sail across the Atlantic, not always in the service of England, though in 1502 we find him bringing to the King of England three men taken in the Newfoundland, clothed in beasts' skins and eating raw flesh, and speaking a language which no man could understand. They must have been kindly dealt with by the King, for two years later the poor savages are " clothed like Englishmen."

Though England claimed the discovery of this New-foundland, the Portuguese declared that one of their countrymen, Cortereal—a gentleman of the royal household —had already discovered the " land of the cod-fish " in 1463. But then had not the Vikings already discovered this country five hundred years before ?

CHAPTER XXXI

JACQUES CARTIER EXPLORES CANADA

ALL the nations of Europe were now straining westward for new lands to conquer. French sailors had fished in the seas washing the western coast of North America; Verazzano, a Florentine, in the service of France, had explored the coast of the United States, and a good deal was known when Jacques Cartier, a Frenchman, steps upon the scene and wins for his country a large tract of land about the river St. Lawrence. His object was to find a way across America to Cathay. With two little ships of sixty tons and sixty-one " chosen men," Cartier left St. Malo on 20th April 1534. With prosperous weather he tells us he made the coast of Newfoundland in three weeks, which would mean sailing over one hundred miles a day. He was a little too early in the season, for the easterly winds which had helped him on his way had blocked the east coast of the island with Arctic ice. Having named the point at which he first touched land Cape Bona Vista, he cruised about till, the ice having melted, he could sail down the straits of Belle Isle between the mainland of Labrador and Newfoundland, already discovered by Breton fishermen. Then he explored the now familiar Gulf of St. Lawrence—the first European to report on it. All through June the little French ships sailed about the Gulf, darting across from island to island and cape to cape. Prince Edward Island appealed to him strongly. " It is very pleasant to behold," he tells

us. " We found sweet-smelling trees as cedars, yews,
pines, ash, willow. Where the ground was bare of trees
it seemed very fertile and was full of wild corn, red and
white gooseberries, strawberries, and blackberries, as if it
had been cultivated on purpose." It now grew hotter,
and Cartier must have been glad of a little heat. He
sighted Nova Scotia and sailed by the coast of New Bruns-
wick, without naming or sur-
veying them. He describes
accurately the bay still called
Chaleur Bay : " We named
this the Warm Bay, for the
country is warmer even than
Spain and exceedingly pleasant." They sailed up as far
as they could, filled with hope
that this might be the long-
sought passage to the Pacific
Ocean. Hope Cape they
named the southern point,
but they were disappointed
by finding only a deep bay,
and to-day, by a strange coincidence, the point opposite
the northern shore is known
as Cape Despair—the Cap
d'Espoir of the early French

JACQUES CARTIER.
From an old pen drawing at the
Bibliothèque Nationale, Paris.

mariners. Sailing on to the north amid strong currents
and a heavy sea, Cartier at last put into a shelter (Gaspé
Bay). Here, "on the 24th of July, we made a great
cross thirty feet high, on which we hung up a shield with
three fleurs-de-lis, and inscribed the cross with this motto :
' Vive le roi de France.' When this was finished, in
presence of all the natives, we all knelt down before the
cross, holding up our hands to heaven and praising God."

Storms and strong tides now decided Cartier to return to France. He knew nothing of the Cabot Strait between Newfoundland and the land afterwards called Nova Scotia, so he guided his little ships right through the Straits of Belle Isle, and after being " much tossed by a heavy tempest from the east, which we weathered by the blessing of God," he arrived safely home on 5th September, after his six months' adventure. He was soon commissioned to continue the navigation of these new lands, and in May 1535 he safely led three ships slightly larger than the last across the stormy Atlantic. Contrary winds, heavy gales, and thick fogs turned the voyage of three weeks into five—the ships losing one another not to meet again till the coast of Labrador was reached. Coasting along the southern coast, Cartier now entered a " very fine and large bay, full of islands, and with channels of entrance and exit in all winds." Cartier named it " Baye Saint Laurens," because he entered it on 10th August—the feast of St. Lawrence.

Do any of the English men and women who steam up the Gulf of St. Lawrence in the great ocean steamers to-day, on their way to Canada, ever give a thought to the little pioneer French ships that four hundred years ago thought they were sailing toward Cathay ?

" Savages," as Cartier calls the Indians, told him that he was near the mouth of the great river Hochelaga (now the St. Lawrence), which became narrower " as we approach towards Canada, where the water is fresh."

" On the first day of September," says Cartier, " we set sail from the said harbour for Canada." Canada was just a native word for a town or village. It seems strange to read of the " lord of Canada " coming down the river with twelve canoes and many people to greet the first white men he had ever seen; strange, too, to find Cartier arriving at " the place called Hochelaga—twenty-five leagues above Canada," where the river becomes very narrow, with a rapid current and very dangerous on account of rocks. For another week the French explorers sailed on up the unknown river. The country was pleasant, well-wooded, with " vines as full of grapes as they would hang." On 2nd October, Cartier arrived at the native town of Hochelaga. He was welcomed by hundreds of natives,—men, women, and children,—who gave the travellers as " friendly a welcome as if we had been of their own nation come home after

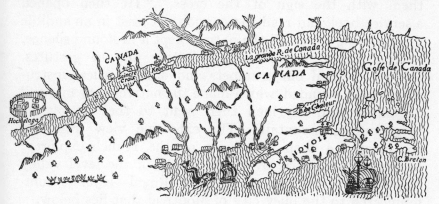

CANADA AND THE RIVER ST. LAWRENCE, SHOWING QUEBEC (KEBEC).
From Lescarbot's *Histoire de la Nouvelle France*, 1609.

a long and perilous absence." The women carried their children to him to touch them, for they evidently thought that some supernatural being had come up from the sea. All night they danced to the light of fires lit upon the shore.

The next morning Cartier, " having dressed himself splendidly," went ashore with some of his men. All were well armed, though the natives seemed peacefully disposed. They marched along a well-beaten track to the Indian city, which stood in the midst of cultivated fields of Indian corn and maize. Again the inhabitants met them with signs of joy and gladness, and the King was carried shoulder high, seated on a large deer-skin with a red wreath round his head made of the skins of hedgehogs instead of a crown.

A curious scene then took place. The King placed his crown on the head of the French explorer, before whom he humbled himself as before a god. Thus evidently did the people regard him, for they brought to him their blind, their lame, and their diseased folk that he might cure them. Touched with pity at the groundless confidence of these poor people, Cartier signed them with the sign of the cross. "He then opened a service book and read the passion of Christ in an audible voice, during which all the natives kept a profound silence, looking up to heaven and imitating all our gestures. He then caused our trumpets and other musical instruments to be sounded, which made the natives very merry."

Cartier and his men then went to the top of the neighbouring mountain. The extensive view from the top created a deep impression on the French explorer; he grew enthusiastic over the beauty of the level valley below and called the place Mont Royal—a name communicated to the busy city of Montreal that lies below.

Winter was now coming on, and Cartier decided against attempting the homeward voyage so late in the year; but to winter in the country he chose a spot between Montreal and Quebec, little thinking what the long winter months would bring forth. The little handful of Frenchmen had no idea of the severity of the Canadian climate; they little dreamt of the interminable months of ice and snow when no navigation was possible. Before Christmas had come round the men were down with scurvy; by the middle of February, " out of one hundred and ten persons composing the companies of our three ships, there were not ten in perfect health. Eight were dead already. The sickness increased

to such a pitch that there were not above three sound
men in the whole company; we were obliged to bury
such as died under the snow, as the ground was frozen
quite hard, and we were all reduced to extreme weakness,
and we lost all hope of ever returning to France." From

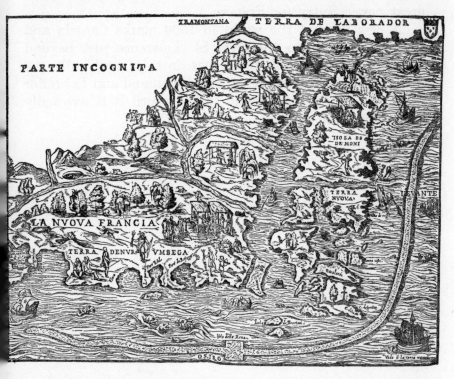

NEW FRANCE, SHOWING NEWFOUNDLAND, LABRADOR, AND THE ST. LAWRENCE.

From Jocomo di Gastaldi's Map, about 1550. The "Isola de Demoni" is Labrador, and
"Terra Nuova" and the islands south of it make up Newfoundland. The snaky-
like line represents a sandbank, which was then thought, and agreed, to be the limit
of fishing. Montreal (Port Real) will be noticed on the coast.

November to March four feet of snow lay upon the
decks of their little ships. And yet, shut up as they
were in the heart of a strange and unknown land, with
their ships icebound and nought but savages around,
there is no sound of murmur or complaint. "It must

be allowed that the winter that year was uncommonly long " is all we hear.

May found them free once more and making for home with the great news that, though they had not found the way to Cathay, they had discovered and taken a great new country for France.

A new map of the world in 1536 marks Canada and Labrador, and gives the river St. Lawrence just beyond Montreal. A map of 1550 goes further, and calls the sea that washes the shores of Newfoundland and Labrador the " Sea of France," while to the south it is avowedly the " Sea of Spain."

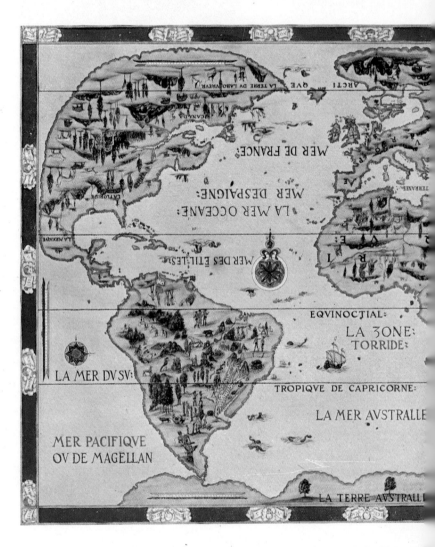

MAP OF THE WO

This map gives a remarkably clear and
sixteenth century. (It is to be note

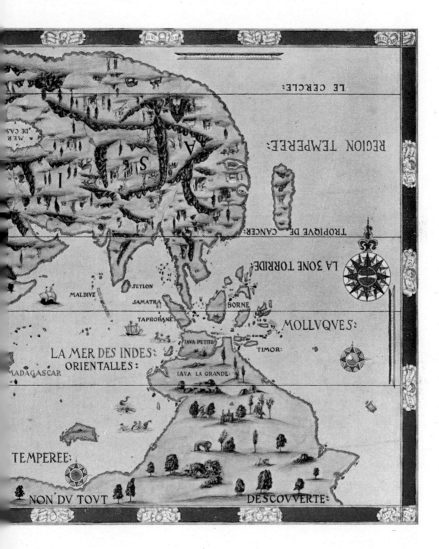

DESCELIERS, 1546.

...hical knowledge in the first half of the
...de of the Equinoctial are reversed.)

CHAPTER XXXII

SEARCH FOR A NORTH-EAST PASSAGE

ENGLAND was now awaking from her sleep—too late to possess the Spice Islands—too late for India and the Cape of Good Hope—too late, it would seem, for the New World. The Portuguese held the eastern route, the Spaniards the western route to the Spice Islands. But what if there were a northern route? All ways apparently led to Cathay. Why should England not find a way to that glorious land by taking a northern course?

"If the seas toward the north be navigable we may go to these Spice Islands by a shorter way than Spain and Portugal," said Master Thorne of Bristol—a friend of the Cabots.

"But the northern seas are blocked with ice and the northern lands are too cold for man to dwell in," objected some.

"*There is no land uninhabitable, nor sea unnavigable,*" was the heroic reply.

"It was in this belief, and in this heroic temper, that England set herself to take possession of her heritage, the north. But it was not till the reign of Edward VI. that a Company of Merchant Adventurers was formed for the discovery of Regions, Dominions, Islands, and places unknown," with old Sebastian Cabot as its first governor, and not till the year 1553 that three little ships under Sir Hugh Willoughby and Richard Chancellor were fitted out for a northern cruise. They carried letters of introduction from the boy-king of England to "all Kings, Princes, Rulers, Judges, and Governors of the Earth in all places under the universal heaven," including those "inhabiting the north-east parts of the world toward the mighty Empire of Cathay."

Sir Hugh Willoughby, "a most valiant gentleman," hoisted the English flag on the *Bona Esperanza*, a good little ship of one hundred and twenty tons. The next in command was Richard Chancellor, "a man of great estimation for many good parts of wit in him," who sailed the *Edward Bonadventure*, which though not so fast as the flag-ship, was slightly larger. So certain were the promoters that the ships would reach the hot climates beyond Cathay that they had them sheathed with lead to protect them from worms which had proved so destructive in the tropics before.

The account of the start of these first English Arctic explorers is too quaint to be passed in silence. "It was thought best that by the 20th of May the Captains and Mariners should take shipping and depart if it pleased God. They, having saluted their acquaintance, one his wife, another his children, another his kinsfolk, and another his friends dearer than his kinsfolk, were ready at the day appointed. The greater ships are towed down with boats and oars, and the mariners, being all apparelled in sky-coloured cloth, made way with diligence. And being come near to Greenwich (where the Court then lay), the Courtiers came running out and the common people flocked together, standing very thick upon the shore : the Privy Council, they looked out of the windows of the Court, and the rest ran up to the tops of the towers, and the mariners shouted in such sort that the sky rang again with the noise thereof. But, alas! the good King

Edward—he only by reason of his sickness was absent from this show."

The ships dropped down to Woolwich with the tide and coasted along the east coast of England till " at the last with a good wind they hoisted up sail and committed themselves to the sea, giving their last adieu to their native country—many of them could not refrain from tears." Richard Chancellor himself had left behind two little sons, and his poor mind was tormented with sorrow and care.

By the middle of July the North Sea had been crossed, and the three small ships were off the shores of Norway, coasting among the islands and fiords that line that indented kingdom. Coasting still northward, Willoughby led his ships to the Lofoten Islands, " plentifully inhabited by very gentle people " under the King of Denmark. They sailed on—

> " To the west of them was the ocean,
>   To the right the desolate shore."

till they had passed the North Cape, already discovered by Othere, the old sea-captain who dwelt in Helgoland.

A terrible storm now arose, and " the sea was so outrageous that the ships could not keep their intended course, but some were driven one way and some another way to their great peril and hazard." Then Sir Hugh Willoughby shouted across the roaring seas to Richard Chancellor, begging him not to go far from him. But the little ships got separated and never met again. Willoughby was blown across the sea to Nova Zembla.

> " The sea was rough and stormy,
>   The tempest howled and wailed,
>   And the sea-fog like a ghost
>   Haunted that dreary coast,
>   But onward still I sailed."

The weather grew more and more Arctic, and he made his way over to a haven in Lapland where he decided to winter. He sent men to explore the country, but no signs of mankind could be found; there were bears and foxes and all manner of strange beasts, but never a human being. It must have been desperately dreary as the winter advanced, with ice and snow and freezing winds from the north. What this little handful of Englishmen did, how they endured the bitter winter on the desolate shores of Lapland, no man knows. Willoughby was alive in January 1554—then all is silent.

And what of Richard Chancellor on board the *Bonadventure* ? " Pensive, heavy, and sorrowful," but resolute to carry out his orders, " Master Chancellor held on his course towards that unknown part of the world, and sailed so far that he came at last to the place where he found no night at all, but a continual light and brightness of the Sun, shining clearly upon the huge and mighty Sea." After a time he found and entered a large bay where he anchored, making friends with the fisher folk on the shores of the White Sea to the north of Russia. So frightened were the natives at the greatness of the English ships that at first they ran away, half-dead with fear. Soon, however, they regained confidence and, throwing themselves down, they began to kiss the explorer's feet, " but he (according to his great and singular courtesy) looked pleasantly upon them." By signs and gestures he comforted them until they brought food to the " new-come guests," and went to tell their king of the arrival of " a strange nation of singular gentleness and courtesy."

Then the King of Russia or Muscovie—Ivan Vasiliwich —sent for Master Chancellor to go to Moscow. The journey had to be made in sledges over the ice and snow. A long and weary journey it must have been, for his guide lost the way, and they had travelled nearly one thousand five hundred miles before Master Chancellor came at last to Moscow, the chief city of the kingdom, " as great as the city of London with all its suburbs," remarks Chancellor. Arrived at the King's palace, Master Chancellor was received by one hundred Russian courtiers dressed in cloth of gold to the very ankles. The King sat aloft on a high throne, with a crown of gold on his head, holding in his hand a glittering sceptre studded with precious stones. The Englishman and his companions saluted the King, who received them graciously and read the letter from Edward VI. with interest. They did not know that the boy-king was dead, and that his sister Mary was on the throne of England. The King was much interested in the long beards grown by the Englishmen. That of one of the company was five foot two inches in

IVAN VASILIWICH, KING OF MUSCOVIE.

From a sixteenth century woodcut.

length, "thick, broad, and yellow coloured." "This is God's gift," said the Russians.

To Edward VI. of England the King sent a letter by the hands of Richard Chancellor, giving leave readily for England to trade with Russia.

Master Chancellor seems to have arrived home again safely with his account of Russia, which encouraged the Merchant Adventurers to send forth more ships to develop

trade with this great new country of which they knew
so little.

To this end Anthony Jenkinson, " a resolute and in-
telligent gentleman," was selected, and " with four tall,
well-appointed ships he sailed on 12th May 1557 toward
the land of Russia."   He reached Cape North on 2nd
July, and a few days later he passed the spot where Sir
Hugh Willoughby and all his company had perished.
Anchoring in the Bay of St. Nicholas, he took a sledge for
Moscow, where he delivered his letters safely to the King.
So icebound was the country that it was April 1558
before he was able to leave Moscow for the south, to accomplish, if possible, the orders of the Merchant Adventurers
to find an overland route to Cathay.   With letters of
introduction from the Russian King to the princes and
kings through whose dominions he was to pass, Master
Jenkinson made his way to the Volga, whence he continued his voyage with a Russian captain who was
travelling south in great style to take up a command at
Astrakan with five hundred boats laden with soldiers,
stores, food, and merchandise.

After three months' travelling, and having passed over
some one thousand two hundred miles, the Englishman
reached the south.   The city of Astrakan offered no attractions and no hope of trade, so Jenkinson boldly took
upon himself to navigate the mouth of the Volga and to
reach the Caspian Sea.   He was the first Englishman to
cross Russia from the White Sea to the Caspian.   Never
before on the Caspian had the red cross of St. George been
seen flying from the masthead of a ship sailed by Englishmen.   After three weeks' buffeting by contrary winds, they
found themselves on the eastern shores, and, getting together a caravan of one thousand camels, they went forward.
No sooner had they landed than they found themselves
in a land of thieves and robbers.   Jenkinson hastened to

the Sultan of these parts, a noted robber himself, to be kindly received by the Tartar Prince, who set before him the flesh of a wild horse and some mare's milk. Then the little English party travelled on for three weeks through desolate land with no rivers, no houses, no inhabitants, till they reached the banks of the Oxus. "Here we refreshed ourselves," says the explorer, "having been three days without water and drink, and tarried there all the next day making merry with our slain horses and camels." For a hundred miles they followed the course of this great river until they reached another desert, where they were again attacked by bands of thieves and robbers.

It was Christmas Eve when they at last reached Bokhara, only to find that the merchants were so poor that there was no hope of any trade worth following, though the city was full of caravans from India and the Far East. And here they heard that the way to Cathay was barred by reason of grievous wars which were going on. Winter was coming on; so Jenkinson remained for a couple of months before starting on his long journey home. With a caravan of six hundred camels he made his way back to the Caspian, and on 2nd September he had reached Moscow safely with presents of " a white cow's tail of Cathay and a drum of Tartary " for the King, which seemed to give that monarch the greatest pleasure. He evidently stayed for a time in Russia, for it is not till the year 1560 that we find him writing to the Merchant Adventurers that " at the next shipping I embark myself for England."

While Jenkinson was endeavouring to reach the Far East by land, a Portuguese named Pinto had succeeded in reaching it by sea. The discovery of Japan is claimed by three people. Antonio de Mota had been thrown by a storm on to the island of Nison, called by the Chinese Jepwen—Japan—in the year 1542. Pinto claims to have

16

ANTHONY JENKINSON'S MA[P]

MOL:
GOM:
ZAIA.

BAIDA.

COLMACK.

OYEDA

KITAIA
LACVS.

CAS

SAC

KI
A
RI.

K

IA

A

BO:

GHA:
R.

SHA:
MAR:
GHAN.

Taskent

TASKENT.

KIR:

GES.

MHOGOL

SIA.

Paraponifi montes.

640	720	800
480	540	600
160	180	200

discovered it the same year. It seems that the Japanese were expecting the return of a god, and as the white men hove in sight they exclaimed : " These are certainly the Chinchi cogies spoken of in our records, who, flying over the waters, shall come to be lords of the lands where God has placed the greatest riches of the world. It will be fortunate for us if they come as friends."

Now men of the time refused to believe in the travels of Mendex Pinto. " He should be called Mendax Pinto," said one, " whose book is one continued chain of monstrous fiction which deserves no credit," while a hundred and fifty years later Congreve wrote—

> " Ferdinando Mendez Pinto was but a type of thee,
> Thou liar of the first magnitude."

CHAPTER XXXIII

MARTIN FROBISHER SEARCHES FOR A NORTH-WEST PASSAGE

So far the expeditions of Willoughby, Chancellor, and Jenkinson had all failed to reach the Far East. The Spanish had a way thither by Magellan's Strait, the Portuguese by the Cape of Good Hope. England in the middle of the sixteenth century had no way. What about a North-West Passage leading round Labrador from the Atlantic to the Pacific? England was waking up to possibilities of future exploration. She was also ready and anxious to annoy Spain for having monopolised the riches and wealth of the New World. And so it was that Queen Elizabeth turned with interest to the suggestions of one of her subjects—Martin Frobisher— "a mariner of great experience and ability," when he enthusiastically consulted her on the navigation of the North-West Passage. For the last fifteen years he had been trying to collect ships and men for the enterprise. "It is the only thing in the world left undone whereby a notable mind might be made famous and fortunate," he affirmed.

But it was not till the year 1576 that he got a chance of fitting out two small ships—two very small ships—the *Gabriel* of twenty tons, the *Michael* of twenty-five tons, to explore the icy regions of the north. A wave of the Queen's hand gladdened his heart as he sailed past the palace of Greenwich, where the Court resided, and he was soon sailing northward harassed and battered by many storms.

His little ten-ton pinnace was lost, and the same storm that overtook the little fleet to the north of Scotland so terrified the captain of the *Michael* that he deserted and turned home with the news that Frobisher had perished with all hands.

Meanwhile Frobisher, resolute in his undertaking, was nearing the coast of Greenland—alone in the little *Gabriel* with a mere handful of men all inexperienced in the art of navigating the Polar seas.

> " And now there came both mist and snow,
>   And it grew wondrous cold "

as Frobisher sailed his storm - beaten ship across the wintry seas. But " I will sacrifice my life to God rather than return home without discovering a north-west passage to Cathay," he told his eighteen men with sublime courage. Passing Cape Farewell, he sailed north-west with the Greenland current, which brought him to the icebound shores near Hudson's Bay. He did not see the straits afterwards discovered by Hudson, but, finding an inlet farther north, he sailed some hundred miles, in the firm belief that this was the passage for which he was searching, that America lay on his left and Asia on his right. Magellan had discovered straits in the extreme south; Frobisher made sure that he had found corresponding straits to the extreme north, and Frobisher's Straits they were accordingly named, and as such they appeared on the maps of the day till they had to be re-named Lumley's Inlet. The snow and ice made further navigation impossible for this year, and full of their great news they returned home accompanied by an Eskimo. These natives had been taken for porpoises by our English explorers, but later they were reported to be " strange infidels whose like was never seen, read, or heard of before."

Martin Frobisher was received with enthusiasm and "highly commended of all men for his great and notable attempt, but specially famous for the great hope he brought of the passage to Cathay." Besides the Eskimo the explorers carried home a black stone, which, when thrown on the fire by one of the sailor's wives, glittered like gold.

GREENLANDERS AS SEEN BY MARTIN FROBISHER.
From Captain Beste's account of Frobisher's voyages, 1578.

The gold refiners of London were hastily called in, and they reported that it contained a quantity of gold.

A new incentive was now given to Polar exploration. The Queen herself contributed a tall ship of some two hundred tons to the new expedition that was eagerly fitted out, and the High Admiral of all seas and waters, countries, lands, and isles, as Frobisher was now called, sailed away again for the icy north, more to search for gold than to discover the North-West Passage. He added nothing more to the knowledge of the world, and though he sailed through the strait afterwards known as Hudson's Strait, he never realised his discovery. His work was hampered by the quest for gold, for which England was eagerly clamouring, and he disappears from our history of discovery.

The triumphant return of Francis Drake in 1580 laden with treasure from the Spice Islands put into the shade all schemes for a north-west passage for the moment.

Nevertheless, this voyage of Martin Frobisher is important in the history of exploration. It was the first attempt of an Englishman to make search amid the ice of the Arctic regions—a search in which so many were yet to lay down their lives.

CHAPTER XXXIV

DRAKE'S FAMOUS VOYAGE ROUND THE WORLD

" Call him on the deep sea, call him up the sound,
   Call him when ye sail to meet the foe;
   Where the old trade's plyin' and the old flag flyin',
   They shall find him ware an' wakin', as they found him long ago!"
                                                                    HENRY NEWBOLT.

DRAKE'S famous voyage, as it is known to history
(1577–1580), was indeed fa-
mous, for although Magel-
lan's ship had sailed round
the world fifty years before,
Drake was the first Englishman to do so, and, further,
he discovered for us land
to the south of Magellan's
Strait round which washed
the waters of Atlantic and
Pacific Oceans, showing that
the mysterious land marked
on contemporary maps as
Terra Australis and joined
to South America was a
separate land altogether.
He also explored the coast
of America as far north as

SIR FRANCIS DRAKE.
From Holland's *Heroologia*, 1620.

Vancouver Island, and disclosed to England the secret of

the Spice Islands. The very name of Drake calls up a vision of thrilling adventure on the high seas. He had been at sea since he was a boy of fifteen, when he had been apprenticed to the master of a small ship trading between England and the Netherlands, and many a time he had sailed on the grey North Sea. " But the narrow seas were a prison for so large a spirit born for greater undertakings," and in 1567 we find Drake sailing forth on board the *Judith* in an expedition over to the Spanish settlements in America under his kinsman, John Hawkins. Having crossed the Atlantic and filled his ships with Spanish treasure from " the Spanish Main," and having narrowly escaped death from the hands of the Spaniards, Drake had hurried home to tell of the riches of this new country still closed to all other nations. Two years later Drake was off again, this time in command himself of two ships with crews of seventy-three young men, their modest aim being nothing less than to seize one of the Spanish ports and empty into their holds the " Treasure House of the World." What if this act of reckless daring was unsuccessful ? The undertaking was crowned with a higher success than that of riches, for Drake was the first Englishman to see the waters of the Pacific Ocean. His expedition was not unlike that of Balboa some sixty years before, as with eighteen chosen companions he climbed the forest-clad spurs of the ridge dividing the two great oceans. Arrived at the top, he climbed up a giant tree, and the Golden Sea of which he had so often heard—the Pacific Ocean of Magellan, the waters washing the golden shores of Mexico and Peru—all lay below him. Descending from the heights, he sank upon his knees and " humbly besought Almighty God of His goodness to give him life and leave to sail once in an English ship in that sea."

Jealously had the Spanish guarded this beautiful Southern Sea, now her secrets were laid bare, for an

Englishman had gazed upon it and he was not likely to remain satisfied with this alone.

In 1573 Drake came home with his wonderful news, and it was not long before he was eagerly talking over with the Queen a project for a raid into this very Golden Sea guarded by the Spaniards. Elizabeth promised help on condition that the object of the expedition should remain a secret. Ships were bought for " a voyage to Egypt "; there was the *Pelican* of one hundred tons, the *Marygold* of thirty tons, and a provision ship of fifty tons. A fine new ship of eighty tons, named the *Elizabeth*, mysteriously added itself to the little fleet, and the crews numbered in all some one hundred and fifty men. No expense was spared in the equipment of the ships. Musicians were engaged for the voyage, the arms and ammunition were of the latest pattern. The flagship was lavishly furnished : there were silver bowls and mugs and dishes richly gilt and engraved with the family arms, while the commander's cabin was full of sweet-smelling perfumes presented by the Queen herself. Thus, complete at last, Drake led his gay little squadron out of Plymouth harbour on 15th November 1577, bound for Alexandria—so the crews thought.

Little did Drake know what was before him, as, dressed in his seaman's shirt, his scarlet cap with its gold band on his head, he waved farewell to England. Who could foresee the terrible beginning, with treachery and mutiny at work, or the glorious ending when the young Englishman sailed triumphantly home after his three years' voyage—the world encompassed ?

Having reached the Cape de Verde Islands in safety, the object of the expedition could no longer remain a secret, and Drake led his squadron boldly across the Atlantic Ocean.

On 5th April the coast of Brazil appeared, but fogs and heavy weather scattered the ships and they had to run into the mouth of the La Plata for shelter. Then for six weary weeks the ships struggled southward, battered by gales and squalls during which nothing but the daring seamanship of the English navigators saved the little vessels from destruction. It was not till 20th June that they reached Port St. Julian of Magellan fame, on the desolate shores of Patagonia. As they entered the harbour, a grim sight met their eyes. On that windswept shore was the skeleton of the man hung by Magellan years before.

THE SILVER MAP OF THE WORLD.

From the medallion in the British Museum, probably struck in 1581, showing the line of Drake's voyage from England in 1577 westwards through the Magellan Strait to California and New Albion.

History was to repeat itself, and the same fate was now to befall an unhappy Englishman guilty of the same conduct.

Drake had long had reason to suspect the second in command, Doughty, though he was his dear friend. He had been guilty of worse than disobedience, and the very success of the voyage was threatened. So Drake called a council together and Doughty was tried according to English law. After two days' trial he was found guilty and condemned to die. One of the most touching scenes in the history of exploration now took place. One sees the little English crews far away on that desolate shore, the ships lying at anchor in the harbour, the block prepared, the altar raised beside it, the two old friends, Drake and Doughty, kneeling side by side, then the flash of the sword and Drake holding up the head of his friend with the words, " Lo, this is the end of traitors."

SIR FRANCIS DRAKE,
THE FIRST ENGLISHMAN TO SAIL ROUND THE WORLD.

After the engraving attributed to Hondius.

It was now midwinter, and for six weeks they remained in harbour till August came, and with three ships they emerged to continue their way to the Straits of Magellan. At last it was found and boldly they entered.   From the towering mountains that guarded the entry, tempests of wind and snow swept down upon the " daring intruders." As they made their way through the rough and winding waters, they imagined with all the other geographers of their time that the un-known land to the south was one great continent leading beyond the boun-daries of the world.   Fires lit by the natives on this southern coast added terror to the wild scene. But at the end of sixteen days they found them-selves once more in the open sea.   They were at last on the Pacific Ocean. But it was anything but pacific.   A terrible tem-pest arose, followed by other storms no less violent, and the ships

THE SILVER MAP OF THE WORLD.

The reverse half, showing the route of Drake's voyage home from California in 1579-1580, through the Spice Islands and the Indian Ocean. The end of the homeward track, round the Azores, will be seen on the opposite page.

were driven helplessly southward and westward far beyond Cape Horn.   When they once more reached the coast they found in the place of the great southern continent an in-dented wind-swept shore washed by waves terrific in their height and strength.   In the ceaseless gale the *Marygold* foundered with all hands and was never heard of again.   A week later the captain of the *Elizabeth* turned home, leaving the *Pelican*, now called the *Golden Hind*, to struggle on alone.   After nearly two months of storm, Drake anchored among the islands southward of anything yet known to the geographers, where Atlantic and Pacific rolled together in one boisterous flood. Walking alone to the farthest end of the island, Drake is said to have laid himself down and with his arms embraced the southernmost point of the known world.

He showed that the Tierra del Fuego, instead of being part of a great continent—the Terra Australis—was a group of islands with open sea to east, south, and west. This discovery was first shown on a Dutch silver medallion struck in Holland about 1581, known as The Silver Map of the world, and may be seen to-day in the British Museum.

Remarking that the ocean he was now entering would have been better called " Mare Furiosum " than " Mare Pacificum," Drake now directed his course along the western coast of South America. He found the coast of Chili, but not as the general maps had described it, " wherefore it appeareth that this part of Chili hath not been truly hitherto discovered," remarked one on board the *Golden Hind*. Bristling with guns, the little English ship sailed along the unknown coast, till they reached Valparaiso. Here they found a great Spanish ship laden with treasure from Peru. Quickly boarding her, the English sailors bound the Spaniards, stowed them under the hatches, and hastily transferred the cargo on to the *Golden Hind*. They sailed on northwards to Lima and Panama, chasing the ships of Spain, plundering as they went, till they were deeply laden with stolen Spanish treasure and knew that they had made it impossible to return home by that coast. So Drake resolved to go on northward and discover, if possible, a way home by the north. He had probably heard of Frobisher's Strait, and hoped to find a western entrance.

As they approached the Arctic regions the weather grew

bitterly cold, and "vile, thick, stinking fogs" determined them to sail southward. They had reached a point near what we now know as Vancouver Island when contrary winds drove them back and they put in at a harbour, now known as San Francisco, to repair the ship for the great voyage across the Pacific and home by the Cape of Good Hope. Drake had sailed past seven hundred miles of new coast-line in twelve days, and he now turned to explore the new country, to which he gave the name of New Albion. The Indians soon began to gather in large quantities on the shore, and the King himself, tall and comely, advanced in a friendly manner. Indeed, he took off his crown and set it on the head of Drake and, hanging chains about his neck, the Indians made him understand that the land was now his and that they were his vassals.

THE *GOLDEN HIND* AT NEW ALBION.

From the Chart of Drake's Voyages, 1589.

Little did King Drake dream, as he named his country New Albion, that Californian gold was so near. His subjects were loving and peaceable, evidently regarding the English as gods and reverencing them as such. The chronicler is eloquent in his detailed description of all the royal doings.

"Before we left," he says, "our General caused to be set up a monument of our being there, as also of Her Majesty's right and title to that kingdom, namely, a plate of brass, fast nailed to a great and firm post, whereon is engraved Her Grace's name and the day and year of our arrival here, and of the free giving up of the province, both by the people and king, into Her Majesty's hands, together with Her Highness' picture and arms in a piece of sixpence current money. The Spanish never so much as set foot in this country—the utmost of their discoveries reaching only to many degrees southward of this place.

"And now, as the time of our departure was perceived by the people, so did the sorrows and miseries seem to increase upon them—not only did they lose on a sudden all mirth, joy, glad countenance, pleasant speeches, agility of body, but with signs and sorrowings, with heavy hearts and grieved minds, they poured out woeful complaints and moans, with bitter tears and wringing of their hands, tormenting themselves. And, as men refusing all comfort, they only accounted themselves as those whom the gods were about to forsake."

Indeed, the poor Indians looked on these Englishmen as gods, and, when the day came for them to leave, they ran to the top of the hills to keep the little ship in sight as long as possible, after which they burnt fires and made sacrifices at their departure.

Drake left New Albion on 23rd July 1579, to follow the lead of Magellan and to pass home by the southern seas and the Atlantic Ocean. After sixty-eight days of quick and straight sailing, with no sight of land, they fell in with the Philippine Islands, and on 3rd November with the famous Spice Islands. Here they were well received by the King — a magnificent person attired in cloth of gold, with bare legs and shoes of Cordova skins, rings of gold in his hair, and a chain " of perfect gold " about his neck. The Englishmen were glad enough to get fresh food after their long crossing, and fared sumptuously on rice, hens, "imperfect and liquid sugar," sugar-canes, and a fruit they call figo, with plenty of cloves. On a little island near Celebes the *Golden Hind* was thoroughly repaired for her long voyage home. But the little treasure-laden ship was nearly wrecked before she got away from the dangerous shoals and currents of these islands.

"Upon the 9th of January we ran suddenly upon a rock, where we stuck fast from eight of the clock at night till four of the clock in the afternoon the next day, being, indeed, out of all hope to escape the danger; but our General, as he had always hitherto showed himself courageous, so now he and we did our best endeavours to save ourselves, which it pleased God so to bless, that in the end we cleared our-selves most happily of the danger."

THE *GOLDEN HIND* AT JAVA.
From the Chart of Drake's Voyages.

Then they ran across the Indian Ocean, rounded the Cape of Good Hope in calm weather, abusing the Portuguese for calling it the most dangerous Cape in the world for intolerable storms, for "This Cape," said the English, "is a most stately thing and the finest Cape we saw in the whole circumference of the earth."

And so they came home. After nearly three years' absence Drake triumphantly sailed his little *Golden Hind* into Plymouth harbour, where he had long ago been given up as lost. Shouts of applause rang through the land at the news that an Englishman had circumnavigated the world. The Queen sent for Drake to tell his wonderful story, to which she listened spellbound. A great banquet was held on board the little ship, at which Elizabeth was present and knighted Drake, while she ordered that the *Golden Hind* should be preserved "as a worthy rival of Magellan's *Victoria*" and as "a monument to all posterity of that famous and worthy exploit of Sir Francis

17

Drake." It was afterwards taken to pieces, and the best parts of wood were made into a chair at Oxford, commemorated by Cowley's lines—

> "To this great ship, which round the world has run
> And matched in race the chariot of the sun;
>
> Drake and his ship could ne'er have wished from fate
> A happier station or more blest estate;
> For lo, a seat of endless rest is given
> To her in Oxford and to him in Heaven."

Sir Francis Drake died at sea in 1596.

> "The waves became his winding sheet, the waters were his tomb,
> But for his fame the ocean sea was not sufficient room."

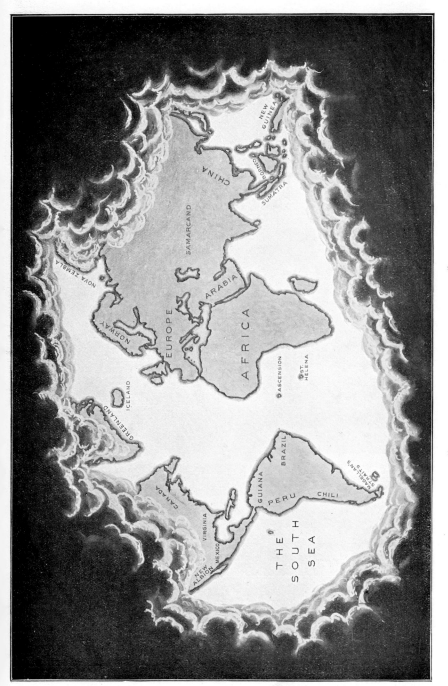

"THE UNROLLING OF THE CLOUDS"—V.

The world as known after its circumnavigation by Sir Francis Drake in the years 1577–1580.

CHAPTER XXXV

DAVIS STRAIT

BUT even while Drake was sailing round the world, and Frobisher's search for a north-west passage had been diverted into a quest for gold, men's minds were still bent on the achievement of reaching Cathay by some northern route. A discourse by Sir Humphrey Gilbert to prove the existence of a passage by the north-west to Cathay and the East Indies, in ten chapters, was much discussed, and the Elizabethan seamen were still bent on its discovery.

"When I gave myself to the study of geography," said Sir Humphrey, "and came to the fourth part of the world, commonly called America, which by all descriptions I found to be an island environed round by sea, having on the south side of it the Strait of Magellan, on the west side the Sea of the South, which sea runneth toward the north, separating it from the east parts of Asia, and on the north side the sea that severeth it from Greenland, through which Northern Seas the Passage lieth which I take now in hand to discover."

The arguments of Sir Humphrey seemed conclusive, and in 1585 they chose John Davis, " a man well grounded in the principles of the art of navigation," to search for the North-West Passage to China. They gave him two little ships, the *Sunshine* of fifty tons, with a crew of seventeen seamen, four musicians, and a boy, and the *Moonshine* of thirty-five tons. It was a daring venture, but the expedition was ill-equipped to battle with the icebound

seas of the frozen north. The ships left Dartmouth on
7th June, and by July they were well out on the Atlantic
with porpoises and whales playing round them. Then
came a time of fog and mist, "with a mighty great
roaring of the sea." On 20th July they sailed out of
the fog and beheld the snow-covered mountains of Greenland, beyond a wide stream of pack-ice—so gloomy, so
"waste, and void of any creatures," so bleak and inhospitable that the Englishmen named it the Land of Desolation
and passed on to the north. Rounding the point, afterwards named by Davis Cape Farewell, and sailing by the
western coast of Greenland, they hoped to find the passage
to Cathay. Landing amid the fiords and the " green and
pleasant isles " about the coast, they anchored a while
to refresh, and named their bay Gilbert Sound, after Sir
Humphrey and Davis' own little boy, Gilbert, left at home.

" The people of the country," says Davis, " having
espied our ships, came down unto us in their canoes,
holding up their right hand toward the sun. We doing
the like, the people came aboard our ships, men of good
stature, unbearded, small-eyed, and of tractable conditions.
We bought the clothes from their backs, which were all
made of seals' skins and birds' skins, their buskins, their
hose, their gloves, all being commonly sewed and well
dressed."

These simple Greenlanders who worshipped the sun
gave Davis to understand that there was a great and open
sea to the north-west, and full of hope he sailed on. But
he soon abandoned the search, for the season was advancing, and, crossing the open sea, he entered the broad
channel named after him Davis Strait, crossed the
Arctic Circle, and anchored under a promontory, "the cliffs
whereof were orient as gold," naming it Mount Raleigh.
Here they found four white bears of " a monstrous bigness," which they took to be goats or wolves, till on nearer

acquaintance they were discovered to be great Polar
bears. There were no signs of human life, no wood, no
grass, no earth, nothing but rock, so they coasted southwards, and to their joy they found an open strait to the
west free from ice. Eagerly they sailed the little *Moonshine* and *Sunshine* up the opening, which they called
Cumberland Sound, till thick
fogs and adverse winds drove
them back. Winter was now
advancing, the six months'
provisions were ended, and,
satisfied with having found
an open passage westward,
Davis sailed home in triumph
to fit out another expedition
as soon as spring came round.
His news was received with
delight. " The North-West
Passage is a matter nothing
doubtful," he affirmed, " but
at any time almost to be
passed, the sea navigable,
void of ice, the air tolerable,
and the waters very deep."

With this certainty of
success the merchants readily
fitted out another expedition, and Davis sailed early
in May 1586 with four ships.

AN ESKIMO.

From a water-colour drawing by John White,
about 1585, who may have seen Eskimo
either in Frobisher's or Davis's voyages.

The little *Moonshine* and *Sunshine* were included in
the new fleet, but Davis himself commanded the *Mermaid*
of one hundred and twenty tons. The middle of June
found him on the west coast of Greenland, battling his
way with great blocks of ice to his old quarters at
Gilbert Sound. What a warm welcome they received

from their old Eskimo friends; "they rowed to the
boat and took hold on the oars and hung about with
such comfortable joy as would require a long discourse
to be uttered." Followed by a wondering crowd of
natives eager to help him up and down the rocks,
Davis made his way inland to find an inviting country,
"with earth and grass such as our moory and waste
grounds of England are"; he found, too, mosses and wild
flowers in the sheltered places. But his business lay in
the icy waters, and he boldly pushed forward. But ice and
snow and fog made further progress impossible; shrouds,
ropes, and sails were turned into a frozen mass, and the
crew was filled with despair. "Our men began to grow
sick and feeble and hopeless of good success, and they
advised me that in conscience I ought to regard the safety
of mine own life with the preservation of theirs, and that I
should not through my over-boldness leave their widows
and fatherless children to give me bitter curses."

So Davis rearranged his crews and provisions, and with
the *Moonshine* and a selection of his best men he determined to voyage on "as God should direct him," while
the *Mermaid* should carry the sick and feeble and faint-
hearted home. Davis then crossed over the strait called
by his name and explored the coast about Cumberland
Sound. Again he tried here to discover the long-sought
passage, but the brief summer season was almost past
and he had to content himself with exploring the shores
of Labrador, unconsciously following the track made by
John Cabot eighty-nine years before.

But on his return home the merchants of London
were disappointed. Davis had indeed explored an immense
extent of coast-line, and he had brought back a cargo of
cod-fish and five hundred seal skins, but Cathay seemed as
far off as ever. One merchant prince, Sanderson by name,
was still very keen, and he helped Davis to fit out yet

another expedition. With three ships, the *Sunshine*, the *Elizabeth*, and the *Helen*, the undaunted Arctic explorer now found himself for the third summer in succession at his old halting-place, Gilbert's Sound, on the west coast of Greenland.

Leaving his somewhat discontented crews to go fishing off the coast of Labrador, he took the little twenty-ton pinnace, with a small party of brave spirits like his own, and made his way northwards in a free and open sea. The weather was hot, land was visible on both sides, and the English mariners were under the impression that they were sailing up a gulf. But the passage grew wider and wider, till Davis found himself with the sea all open to west and north. He had crossed the Arctic Circle and reached the most northerly point ever yet reached by an explorer. Seeing on his right a lofty cliff, he named it " Sanderson his Hope," for it seemed to give hope of the long-sought passage to Cathay.

It was a memorable day in the annals of discovery, 30th June 1587, when Davis reached this famous point on the coast of Greenland. " A bright blue sea extended to the horizon on the north and west, obstructed by no ice, but here and there a few majestic icebergs with peaks snowy shooting up into the sky. To the eastward were the granite mountains of Greenland, and beyond them the white line of the mightiest glacier in the world. Rising immediately above the tiny vessel was the beetling wall of Hope Sanderson, with its summit eight hundred and fifty feet above sea-level. At its base the sea was a sheet of foam and spray. It must have been a scene like fairyland, for, as Davis remarked, there was " no ice towards the north, but a great sea, free, large, very salt and blue, and of an unsearchable depth."

But again disappointment awaited him. That night a wind from the north barred further advance as a mighty bank of ice some eight feet thick came drifting down toward the Atlantic. Again and again he attempted to get on, but it was impossible, and reluctantly enough he turned the little ship southwards.

"This Davis hath been three times employed; why hath he not found the passage?" said the folk at home when he returned and reported his doings. How little they realised the difficulties of the way. The commander of the twenty-ton *Ellen* had done more than any man had done before him in the way of Arctic exploration. He had discovered seven hundred and thirty-two miles of coast from Cape Farewell to Sanderson's Hope; he had examined the whole coast of Labrador; he had "converted the Arctic regions from a confused myth into a defined area." "He lighted Baffin into his bay. He lighted Hudson into his strait. He lighted Hans Egede to the scene of his Greenland labour." And more than this, says his enthusiastic biographer: "His true-hearted devotion to the cause of Arctic discovery, his patient scientific research, his loyalty to his employers, his dauntless gallantry and enthusiasm form an example which will be a beacon-light to maritime explorers for all time to come."

> "And Davis three times forth for the north-west made,
> Still striving by that course t'enrich the English trade;
> And as he well deserved, to his eternal fame,
> There, by a mighty sea, immortalised his name."

CHAPTER XXXVI

BARENTS SAILS TO SPITZBERGEN

With the third failure of John Davis to find the North-West Passage the English search for Cathay came to an end for the present. But the merchants of Amsterdam took up the search, and in 1594 they fitted out an expedition under William Barents, a burgher of Amsterdam and a practical seaman of much experience. The three voyages of Barents form some of the most romantic reading in the history of geographical discovery, and the preface to the old book compiled for the Dutch after the death of Barents sums up in pathetic language the tragic story of the " three Voyages, so strange and wonderful that the like hath never been heard of before." They were " done and performed three years," says the old preface, " one after the other, by the ships of Holland, on the North sides of Norway, Muscovy, and Tartary, towards the kingdoms of Cathay and China, showing discoveries of the Country lying under 80 degrees : which is thought to be Greenland ; where never any man had been before, with the cruel Bears and other Monsters of the sea and the unsupportable and extreme cold that is found to be in these places. And how that in the last Voyage the Ship was enclosed by the Ice, that it was left there, whereby the men were forced to build a house in the cold and desert country of Nova Zembla, wherein they continued ten months together and never saw nor heard of any man, in most great cold and extreme misery ; and how after that, to save their lives, they were constrained to sail about one thousand miles in little open boats, along and over the main Seas in most great danger and with extreme labour, unspeakable troubles, and great hunger."

Surely no more graphic summary of disaster has ever appeared than these words penned three hundred and fourteen years ago, which cry to us down the long, intervening ages of privation and suffering endured in the cause of science.

A SHIP OF THE LATE
SIXTEENTH CENTURY.

From Ortelius, 1598.

In the year 1594, then, four ships were sent forth from Amsterdam with orders to the wise and skilful pilot, William Barents, that he was to sail into the North Seas and " discover the kingdoms of Cathay and China." In the month of July the Dutch pilot found himself off the south coast of Nova Zembla, whence he sailed as the wind pleased to take him, ever making for the north and hugging the coast as close as possible. On 9th July they found a creek very far north to which they gave the name of Bear Creek, because here they suddenly discovered their first Polar bear. It tried to get into their boat, so they shot it with a musket, " but the bear showed most wonderful strength, for, notwithstanding that she was shot into the body, yet she leapt up and swam in the water; the men that were in the boat, rowing after her, cast a rope about her neck and drew her at the stern of the boat, for, not having seen the like bear before, they thought to have carried her alive in the ship and to have showed her for a strange wonder in Holland ; but she used such force that they were glad they were rid of her, and contented themselves with her skin only." This they brought back to Amsterdam in great triumph—their first white Polar bear. But they went farther north than this, until they came to a plain field of ice and encountered very misty weather. Still they kept sailing on, as best they might, round about the ice till they found the land of Nova

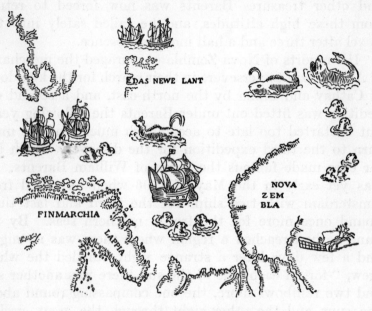

EDAS NEWE LANT

NOVA ZEM BLA

FINMARCHIA

LAPPIA

NOVA ZEMBLA AND THE ARCTIC REGIONS.

From a map in De Bry's *Grands Voyages,* 1598.

Zembla was covered with snow. From " Ice Point " they made their way to islands which they named Orange Islands after the Dutch Prince. Here they found two hundred walrus or sea-horses lying on the shore and basking in the sun.

" The sea-horse is a wonderful strong monster of the sea," they brought back word, " much bigger than an ox, having a skin like a seal, with very short hair, mouthed like a lion ; it hath four feet, but no ears." The little party of Dutchmen advanced boldly with hatchets and pikes to kill a few of these monsters to take home, but it was harder work than they thought. The wind suddenly rose, too, and rent the ice into great pieces, so they had to content themselves by getting a few of their ivory teeth, which they reported to be half an ell long. With these and other treasures Barents was now forced to return from these high altitudes, and he sailed safely into the Texel after three and a half months' absence.

His reports of Nova Zembla encouraged the merchants of Amsterdam to persevere in their search for the kingdoms of Cathay and China by the north-east, and a second expedition was fitted out under Barents the following year; but it started too late to accomplish much, and we must turn to the third expedition for the discovery which has for ever made famous the name of William Barents. It was yet early in the May of 1596 when he sailed from Amsterdam with two ships for the third and last time, bound once more for the frozen northern seas. By 1st June he had reached a region where there was no night, and a few days later a strange sight startled the whole crew, " for on each side of the sun there was another sun and two rainbows more, the one compassing round about the suns and the other right through the great circle," and they found they were " under 71 degrees of the height of the Pole."

Sighting the North Cape of Lapland, they held on a north-westerly course till on 9th June they came upon a little island which they named Bear Island. Here they nearly met their end, for, having ascended a steep snow mountain on the island to look around them, they found it too slippery to descend. "We thought we should all have broken our necks, it was so slippery, but we sat up on the snow and slid down, which was very dangerous for us, and break both our arms and legs for that at the foot of the hill there were many rocks." Barents himself seems to have sat in the boat and watched them with intense anxiety. They were once more amid ice and Polar bears. In hazy weather they made their way north till on the

BARENTS IN THE ARCTIC: "HUT WHEREIN WE WINTERED."

From De Veer's account of the voyages of Barents, 1598.

19th they saw land, and the "land was very great." They thought it was Greenland, but it was really Spitzbergen, of which he was thus the discoverer.

Many things astonished the navigators here. Although they were in such high latitudes, they saw grass and leafy trees and such animals as bucks and harts, while several degrees to the south "there groweth neither leaves nor grass nor any beasts that eat grass or leaves, but only such beasts as eat flesh, as bears and foxes."

By 1st July he had explored the western shore and was sailing south to Bear Island. He never landed on the coast of Spitzbergen : so we have no further account of this Arctic discovery. Sailing across the wide northern sea now known as Barents Sea, he made land again in the north of Nova Zembla, and, hugging the western shore, came to Ice Point. Here they were sorely harassed by Polar bears and floating ice and bitter gales of wind. Still they coasted on till they had rounded the northern end of Nova Zembla and unexpectedly sailed into a good harbour where they could anchor. The wind now blew with redoubled vigour, the " ice came mightily driving in " until the little ship was nearly surrounded, " and withal the wind began more and more to rise and the ice still drave harder and harder, so that our boat was broken in pieces between the ship and the ice, and it seemed as if the ship would be crushed in pieces too."

As the August days passed on, they tried to get out of their prison, but it was impossible, and there was nothing for it but to winter " in great cold, poverty, misery, and grief " in this bleak and barren spot. The successful pilot was to explore no more, but the rest of the tragic tale must be shortly told. With the ice heaping high, " as the salt hills that are in Spain," and the ship in danger of going to pieces, they collected trees and roots driven on to the desolate shores from Tartary, " wherewith as if God had purposely sent them unto us we were much comforted." Through the September days they drew wood across the ice and snow to build a house for the winter. Only sixteen men could work and they were none too strong and well.

Throughout October and November they were snowed up in their winter hut, with " foul stormie weather " outside, the wind blowing ceaselessly out of the north and snow lying deep around. They trapped a few foxes from

BARENTS'S SHIP AMONG THE ARCTIC ICE.

From a coloured woodcut in the account of Barents's three voyages by Gerard de Veer, published in 1598.

day to day to eat, making warm caps out of their fur; they heated stones and took them into their cabin beds, but their sheets froze as they washed them and at last their clock froze too.

"They looked pitifully upon one another, being in great fear that if the extremity of the cold grew to be more and more we should all die there with the cold." Christmas came and went and they comforted one another by remembering that the sun was as low as it could go, and that it must begin to come to them again; but "as the day lengthens, so the cold strengthens," and the snow now lay deeper until it covered the roof of their house.

The New Year found them still imprisoned, "with great cold, danger, and disease." January, February, March, April passed and still the little ship was stuck fast in the ice. But as the sun began to gain power, hope revived, and they began to repair their boats, to make new sails, and repair tackle. They were too weak and ill to do much work, but by the middle of June the boats were fairly ready and they could cut a way through the ice to the open sea. This was their only hope of escape, to leave the ship behind and embark in two little open boats for the open sea.

"Then William Barents wrote a letter, which he put into a musket's charge and hanged it up in the chimney, showing how we came out of Holland to sail to the kingdom of China, and how we had been forced in our extremity to make that house and had dwelt ten months therein, and how we were forced to put to sea in two small open boats, for that the ship lay fast in the ice."

Barents himself was now too ill to walk, so they carried him to one of the little boats, and on 14th June 1597 the little party put off from their winter quarters and sailed round to Ice Point. But the pilot was dying. "Are we about Ice Point?" he asked feebly. "If we be, then I pray you lift me up, for I must view it once again."

Then suddenly the wind began to rise, driving the ice so fast upon them " that it made our hair stand upright upon our heads, it was so fearful to behold, so that we thought verily that it was a foreshadowing of our last end."

They drew the boats up on to the ice and lifted the sick commander out and laid him on the icy ground, where a few days later he died—" our chief guide and only pilot on whom we reposed ourselves next under God." The rest of the story is soon told.

On 1st November 1597 some twelve gaunt and haggard men, still wearing caps of white fox and coats of bear-skin, having guided their little open boats all the way from Nova Zembla, arrived at Amsterdam and told the story of their exploration to the astonished merchants, who had long since given them up as dead.

It was not till 1871 that Barents' old winter quarters on Nova Zembla were discovered. " There stood the cooking-pans over the fireplace, the old clocks against the wall, the arms, the tools, the drinking vessels, the instruments and the books that had beguiled the weary hours of that long night, two hundred and seventy-eight years ago." Among the relics were a pair of small shoes and a flute which had belonged to a little cabin-boy who had died during the winter.

CHAPTER XXXVII

HUDSON FINDS HIS BAY

HENRY HUDSON was another victim to perish in the hopeless search for a passage to China by the north. John Davis had been dead two years, but not till after he had piloted the first expedition undertaken by the newly formed East India Company for commerce with India and the East. It was now more important than ever to find a short way to these countries other than round by the Cape of Good Hope. So Henry Hudson was employed by the Muscovy Company " to discover a shorter route to Cathay *by sailing over the North Pole*." He knew the hardships of the way; he must have realised the fate of Willoughby, the failure of Frobisher, the sufferings of Barents and his men, the difficulties of Davis—indeed, it is more than probable that he had listened to Davis speaking on the subject of Arctic exploration to the merchants of London at his uncle's house at Mortlake.

Never did man start on a bolder or more perilous enterprise than did this man, when he started for the North Pole in a little boat of eighty tons, with his little son Jack, two mates, and a crew of eight men.

" Led by Hudson with the fire of a great faith in his eyes, the men solemnly marched to St. Ethelburga Church, off Bishopsgate Street, London, to partake of Holy Communion and ask God's aid. Back to the muddy water

18   273

front, opposite the Tower, a hearty God-speed from the gentlemen of the Muscovy Company, pompous in self-importance and lace ruffles—and the little crew steps into a clumsy river-boat with brick-red sails."

After a six weeks' tumble over a waste of waters, Hudson arrived off the coast of Greenland, the decks of the little *Hopewell* coated with ice, her rigging and sails hard as boards, and a north-east gale of wind and snow against her. A barrier of ice forbade further advance; but, sailing along the edge of this barrier—the first navigator to do so—he made for the coast of Spitzbergen, already roughly charted by Barents. Tacking up the west coast to the north, Hudson now explored further the fiords, islands, and harbours, naming some of them—notably Whale Bay and Hakluyt Headland, which may be seen on our maps of to-day. By 13th July he had reached his Farthest North, farther than any explorer had been before him, farther than any to be reached again for over one hundred and fifty years. It was a land of walrus, seal, and Polar bear; but, as usual, ice shut off all further attempts to penetrate the mysteries of the Pole, thick fog hung around the little ship, and with a fair wind Hudson turned southward. " It pleased God to give us a gale and away we steered," says the old ship log. Hudson would fain have steered Greenland way and had another try for the north. But his men wanted to go home, and home they went, through " slabbie " weather.

But the voice of the North was still calling Hudson, and he persuaded the Muscovy Company to let him go off again. This he did in the following year. Only three of his former crew volunteered for service, and one of these was his son. But this expedition was devoid of result. The icy seas about Nova Zembla gave no hope of a passage in this direction, and, " being void of hope, the wind stormy and against us, much ice driving, we weighed and set sail westward."

Hudson's voyages for the Muscovy Company had already come under the notice of the Dutch, who were vying with the English for the discovery of this short route to the East. Hudson was now invited to undertake an expedition for the Dutch East India Company, and he sailed from Amsterdam in the early spring of 1609 in a Dutch ship called the *Half-Moon*, with a mixed crew of Dutch and English, including once more his own son. Summer found the enthusiastic explorer off the coast of

HUDSON'S MAP OF HIS VOYAGES IN THE ARCTIC.
From his book published in 1612.

Newfoundland, where some cod-fishing refreshed the crews before they sailed on south, partly seeking an opening to the west, partly looking for the colony of Virginia, under Hudson's friend, Captain John Smith. In hot, misty weather they cruised along the coast. They passed what is now Massachusetts, " an Indian country of great hills—a very sweet land." On 7th August, Hudson was near the modern town of New York, so long known as New Amsterdam, but mist hid the low-lying hills and the *Half-Moon* drifted on to James River; then, driven back by a heat hurricane, he made for the inlet on the old charts, which might lead yet east.

It was 2nd September when he came to the great mouth of the river that now bears his name. He had been beating about all day in gales and fogs, when " the sun arose and we saw the land all like broken islands. From the land which we had first sight of, we came to a large lake of water, like drowned land, which made it to rise like islands. The mouth hath many shores and the sea breaketh on them. This is a very good land to fall in with, and a pleasant land to see. At three of the clock in the afternoon we came to three great rivers. We found a very good harbour and went in with our ship. Then we took our nets to fish and caught ten great mullets of a foot and a half long each, and a ray as great as four men could haul into the ship. The people of the country came aboard of us, seeming very glad of our coming, and brought green tobacco—they go in deer skins, well-dressed, they desire clothes and are very civil—they have great store of maize, whereof they make good bread. The country is full of great and tall oaks." To this he adds that the women had red copper tobacco pipes, many of them being dressed in mantles of feathers or furs, but the natives proved treacherous. Sailing up the river, Hudson found it a mile broad, with high land on both sides. By the night of 19th September the little *Half-Moon* had reached the spot where the river widens near the modern town of Albany. He had sailed for the first time the distance covered to-day by magnificent steamers which ply daily between Albany and New York city. Hudson now went ashore with an old chief of the country. " Two men were dispatched in quest of game," so records Hudson's manuscript, " who brought in a pair of pigeons. They likewise killed a fat dog and skinned it with great haste with shells. The land is the finest for cultivation that ever I in my life set foot upon."

Hudson had not found a way to China, but he had

found the great and important river that now bears his name. Yet he was to do greater things than these, and to lose his life in the doing. The following year, 1610, found him once more bound for the north, continuing the endless search for a north-west passage—this time for the English, and not for the Dutch. On board the little *Discovery* of fifty-five tons, with his young son, Jack, still his faithful companion, with a treacherous old man as mate, who had accompanied him before, with a good-for-nothing young spendthrift taken at the last moment "because he wrote a good hand," and a mixed crew, Hudson crossed the wide Atlantic for the last time. He sailed by way of Iceland, where "fresh fish and dainty fowl, part-ridges, curlew, plover, teale, and goose" much refreshed the already discontented crews, and the hot baths of Iceland de-lighted them. The

A SHIP OF HUDSON'S FLEET.
From his *Voyages*, 1612.

men wanted to return to the pleasant land discovered in the last expedition, but the mysteries of the frozen North still called the old explorer, and he steered for Greenland. He was soon battling with ice upon the southern end of "Desolation," whence he crossed to the snowy shores of Labrador, sailing into the great straits that bear his name to-day. For three months they sailed aimlessly about that "labyrinth without end" as it was called by Abacuk Prickett who wrote the account of this fourth and last voyage of Henry Hudson. But they could find no opening to the west, no way of escape.

Winter was coming on, "the nights were long and cold, and the earth was covered with snow." They were several hundred miles south of the straits, and no way had been found to the Pacific; they had followed the south shore "to the westernmost bay of all," James Bay, but lo! there was no South Sea. Hudson recognised the fact that he was land-bound and winter-bound in a desolate region, with a discontented crew, and that the discontent was amounting to mutiny. On 1st November they hauled up the ship and selected a wintering place. Ten days later they were frozen in, and snow was falling continuously every day. "We were victualled for six months, and of that which was good," runs the record. For the first three months they shot "partridges as white as milk," but these left with the advent of spring, and hunger seized on the handful of Englishmen wintering in this unknown land. "Then we went into the woods, hills, and valleys—and the moss and the frog were not spared." Not till the month of May did the ice begin to melt and the men could fish. The first day this was possible they caught "five hundred fish as big as good herrings and some trout," which revived their hopes and their health. Hudson made a last despairing effort to find a westward passage. But now the men rose in mutiny. "We would rather be hanged at home than starved abroad!" they cried miserably.

So Hudson "fitted all things for his return, and first delivered all the bread out of the bread room (which came to a pound apiece for every man's share), and he wept when he gave it unto them." It was barely sufficient for fourteen days, and even with the fourscore small fish they had caught it was "a poor relief for so many hungry bellies."

With a fair wind in the month of June, the little *Discovery* was headed for home. A few days later she

was stopped by ice. Mutiny now burst forth. The
" master " and his men had lost confidence in each other.
There were ruffians on board, rendered almost wild by
hunger and privation. There is nothing more tragic in
the history of exploration than the desertion of Henry
Hudson and his boy in their newly discovered bay.
Every detail of the conspiracy is given by Prickett. We
know how the rumour spread, how the crew resolved to
turn the " master " and the sick men adrift and to share
the remaining provisions among themselves. And how
in the early morning Hudson was seized and his arms
bound behind him.

" What does this mean ? " he cried.

" You will know soon enough when you are in the
shallop," they replied.

The boat was lowered and into it Hudson was put
with his son, while the " poor, sick, and lame men were
called upon to get them out of their cabins into the
shallop." Then the mutineers lowered some powder and
shot, some pikes, an iron pot, and some meal into her, and
the little boat was soon adrift with her living freight of
suffering, starving men—adrift in that icebound sea, far
from home and friends and all human help. At the last
moment the carpenter sprang into the drifting boat,
resolved to die with the captain sooner than desert him.
Then the *Discovery* flew away with all sail up as from an
enemy.

And " the master " perished—how and when we know
not.

Fortunately the mutineers took home Hudson's
journals and charts. Ships were sent out to search for
the lost explorer, but the silence has never been broken
since that summer's day three hundred years ago, when he
was deserted in the waters of his own bay.

CHAPTER XXXVIII

BAFFIN FINDS HIS BAY

Two years only after the tragedy of Henry Hudson, another Arctic explorer appears upon the scene. William Baffin was already an experienced seaman in the prime of life ; he had made four voyages to the icy north, when he was called on by the new Company of Merchants of London —"discoverers of the North-West Passage"—formed in 1612, to prepare for another voyage of discovery. Distressed beyond measure at the desertion of Henry Hudson, the Muscovy Company had dispatched Sir Thomas Button with our old friend Abacuk Prickett to show him the way. Button had reached the western side of Hudson's Bay, and after wintering there returned fully convinced that a north-west passage existed in this direction. Baffin returned from an expedition to Greenland the same year. The fiords and islets of west Greenland, the ice-floes and glaciers of Spitzbergen, the tidal phenomena of Hudson's Strait, and the geographical secrets of the far-northern bay were all familiar to him. "He was, therefore, chosen as mate and associate " to Bylot, one of the men who had deserted Hudson, but who had sailed three times with him previously and knew well the western seas. So in " the good ship called the *Discovery*," of fifty-five tons, with a crew of fourteen men and two boys, William Baffin sailed for the northern seas. May found the expedition on the coast of Greenland, with a gale of wind and great islands of ice. However, Baffin crossed

Davis Strait, and after a struggle with ice at the entrance to Hudson's Strait he sailed along the northern side till he reached a group of islands which he named Savage Islands. For here were Eskimos again—very shy and fearful of the white strangers. "Among their tents," relates Baffin, " all covered with seal skins, were running up and down about forty dogs, most of them muzzled, about the bigness of our mongrel mastiffs, being a brindled black colour, looking almost like wolves. These dogs they used instead of horses, or rather as the Lapps do their deer, to draw their sledges from place to place over the ice, their sledges being shod or lined with bones of great fishes to keep them from wearing out, and the dogs have furniture and collars very fitting."

The explorers went on bravely till they were stopped by masses of ice. They thought they must be at the mouth of a large bay, and, seeing no prospect of a passage to the west, they turned back. When, two hundred years later, Parry sailed in Baffin's track he named this place Baffin Land " out of respect to the memory of that able and enterprising navigator."

The *Discovery* arrived in Plymouth Sound by September, *without the loss of one man*—a great achievement in these days of salt junk and scurvy.

" And now it may be," adds Baffin, " that some expect I should give my opinion concerning the Passage. To these my answer must be that doubtless there *is* a Passage. But within this Strait, which is called Hudson Strait, I am doubtful, supposing to the contrary."

Baffin further suggested that if there was a Passage it must now be sought by Davis Strait.

Accordingly another expedition was fitted out and Baffin had his instructions : " For your course, you must make all possible haste to Cape Desolation ; and from hence you, William Baffin, as pilot, keep along the coast of

Greenland and up Davis Strait, until you come toward the height of 80 degrees, if the land will give you leave. Then shape your course west and southerly, so far as you shall think it convenient, till you come to the latitude of 60 degrees, then direct your course to fall in with the land of *Yedzo*, leaving your further sailing southward to your own discretion : although our desires be if your voyage prove so prosperous that you may have the year before you that you go far south as that you may touch the north part of Japan from whence we would have you bring home one of the men of the country and so, God blessing you, with all expedition to make your return home again."

The *Discovery* had proved a good little ship for exploration, so she was again selected by Baffin for this new attempt in the far north. Upon 26th March 1616 she sailed from Gravesend, arriving off the coast of Greenland in the neighbourhood of Gilbert Sound about the middle of May. Working against terrible winds, they plied to the northward, the old ship making but slow progress, till at last they sighted " Sanderson his Hope," the farthest point of Master Davis. Once more English voices broke the silence of thirty years. The people who appeared on the shore were wretchedly poor. They lived on seals' flesh, which they ate raw, and clothed themselves in the skins. Still northwards they sailed, cruising along the western coast. Though the ice was beginning to disappear the weather kept bitterly cold, and on Midsummer Day the sails and ropes were frozen too hard to be handled. Stormy weather now forced them into a sound which they named Whale Sound from the number of whales they discovered here. It was declared by Baffin to be the " greatest and largest bay in these parts."

But beyond this they could not go ; so they sailed across the end of what we now know as Baffin's Bay and explored the opposite coast of America, naming one of the greater openings Lancaster Sound, after Sir James Lancaster of East India Company fame.

"Here," says Baffin pitifully, "our hope of Passage began to grow less every day."

It was the old story of ice, advancing season, and hasty conclusions.

"There is no hope of Passage to the north of Davis' Straits," the explorer further asserts; but he asserts

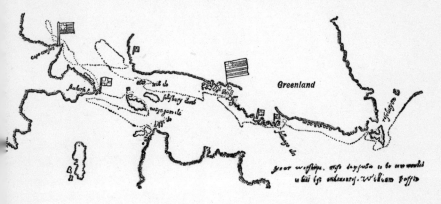

BAFFIN'S MAP OF HIS VOYAGES TO THE NORTH.
From the original MS., drawn by Baffin, in the British Museum.

wrongly, for Lancaster Sound was to prove an open channel to the West.

So he returned home. He had not found the Passage, but he had discovered the great northern sea that now bears his name. The size of it was for long plunged in obscurity, and the wildest ideas centred round the extent of this northern sea. A map of 1706 gives it an indefinite amount of space, adding vaguely: "Some will have Baffin's Bay to run as far as this faint Shadow," while a map of 1818 marks the bay, but adds that "it is not now believed."

For the next two hundred years the icebound regions

of the north were practically left free from invasion, silent, inhospitable, unapproachable.

But while these Arctic explorers were busy battling with the northern seas to find a passage which should lead them to the wealth of the East, others were exploring the New World and endeavouring by land and river to attain the same end.

CHAPTER XXXIX

SIR WALTER RALEIGH SEARCHES FOR EL DORADO

IT is pleasant to turn from the icy regions of North America to the sunny South, and to follow the fortunes of that fine Elizabethan gentleman, Sir Walter Raleigh, to " the large, rich, and beautiful Empire of Guiana and the Great and Golden City of Manoa (which the Spaniards call El Dorado)." Ever since the conquest of Peru, sixty years before, there had floated about rumours of a great kingdom abounding in gold. The King of this Golden Land was sprinkled daily with gold dust, till he shone as the sun, while Manoa was full of golden houses and golden temples with golden furniture. The kingdom was wealthier than Peru ; it was richer than Mexico. Expedition after expedition had left Spain in search of this El Dorado, but the region was still plunged in romantic mists. Raleigh had just failed to establish an English colony in Virginia. To gain a rich kingdom for his Queen, to extend her power and enrich her treasury was now his greatest object in life. What about El Dorado ?

" Oh, unwearied feet, travelling ye know not whither ! Soon, soon, it seems to you, you must come forth on some conspicuous hilltop, and but a little way further, against the setting sun, descry the spires of El Dorado."

February 1595 found him ready and leaving England with five ships and, after a good passage of forty-six days, landing on the island of Trinidad, and thence making his way to the mouth of the Orinoco. Here Raleigh soon found that it was impossible to enter the Orinoco with his English ships, but, nothing daunted, he took a hundred men and provisions for a month in three little open boats, and started forward to navigate this most difficult labyrinth of channels, out of which they were guided by an old Indian pilot named Ferdinando. They had much to observe. The natives, living along the river-banks, dwelt in houses all the summer, but in the winter months they constructed small huts to which they ascended by means of ladders.

These folk were cannibals, but cannibals of a refined sort, who " beat the bones of their lords into powder " and mixed the powder with their drinks. The stream was very strong and rapid, and the men rowed against it in great discomfort, " the weather being extreme hot, the river bordered with very high trees that kept away the air, and the current against us every day stronger than the other," until they became, as Raleigh tells us, " wearied and scorched and doubtful."

The heat increased as they advanced, and the crews grew weaker as the river " ran more violently against them." But Raleigh refused to return yet, lest " the world would laugh us to scorn."

Fortunately delicious fruits hung over the banks of the Orinoco, and, having no bread and for water only the thick and troubled water of the river, they refreshed themselves gladly. So they rowed on up the great river, through province after province of the Indians, but no El Dorado appeared. Suddenly the scene changed as if by magic, the high banks giving way to low-lying plains ; green grass grew close to the water's edge, and deer came down to feed.

" I never saw a more beautiful country," says Raleigh, " nor more lively prospects, hills raised here and there over the valleys, the river winding into different branches,

plains without bush or stubble, all fair green grass, deer
crossing our path, the birds towards evening singing on
every tree with a thousand several tunes, herons of white,
crimson, and carnation perching on the riverside, the air
fresh with a gentle wind, and every stone we stooped to
pick up promised either gold or silver." His account of
the great cataract at the junction of the tributary Caroni
is very graphic. They had already heard the roar, so
they ran to the tops of
some neighbouring hills,
discovering the wonder-
ful "breach of waters"
which ran down Caroli,
and from that "moun-
tain see the river how it
ran in three parts, about
twenty miles off, and
there appeared some ten
or twelve overfalls in
sight, every one as high
over the other as a
church tower, which fell
with that fury that the
rebound of waters made
it seem as if it had been

SIR WALTER RALEIGH.

all covered over with a great shower of rain; and in some
places we took it at the first for a smoke that had risen
over some great town."

The country was the province of Guiana, but it was not
El Dorado, the object of their quest. And though it was
very beautiful, it was inhabited by cannibals; moreover,
winter was advancing, and they were already some four
hundred miles from their ships in little open boats and
in the heart of a strange country.

Suddenly, too, the river began to rise, to "rage and overflow very fearfully," rain came down in torrents accompanied by great gusts of wind, and the crews with no change of clothes got wet through, sometimes ten times a day. " Whosoever had seen the fury of that river after it began to rise would perchance have turned his back somewhat sooner than we did if all the mountains had been gold or precious stones," remarked Raleigh, who indeed was no coward. So they turned the boats for home, and at a tremendous rate they spun down the stream, sometimes doing as much as one hundred miles a day, till after sundry adventures they safely reached their ships at anchor off Trinidad. Raleigh had not reached the golden city of Manoa, but he gave a very glowing account of this country to his Queen.

" Guiana," he tells her, " is a country that hath yet her maidenhood. The face of the earth hath not been torn, the graves have not been opened for gold. It hath never been entered by any army of strength, and never conquered by any Christian prince. Men shall find here more rich and beautiful cities, more temples adorned with gold, than either Cortes found in Mexico or Pizarro in Peru, and the shining glory of this conquest will eclipse all those of the Spanish nation."

But Raleigh had brought back no gold, and his schemes for a conquest of Guiana were received coldly by the Queen. She could not share his enthusiasm for the land—

> " Where Orinoco, in his pride,
>   Rolls to the main no tribute tide,
>   But 'gainst broad Ocean wages far
>   A rival sea of roaring war;
>   While in ten thousand eddies driven
>   The billows fling their foam to heaven;
>   And the pale pilot seeks in vain
>   Where rolls the river, where the main."

But, besides the Orinoco in South America, there was

the St. Lawrence in North America, still very imperfectly known. Since Jacques Cartier had penetrated the hitherto undisturbed regions lying about the " river of Canada," little had been explored farther west, till Samuel Champlain, one of the most remarkable men of his day, comes upon the scene, and was still discovering land to the west when Raleigh was making his second expedition to Guiana in the year 1617.

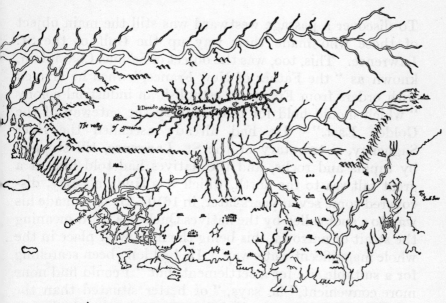

RALEIGH'S MAP OF GUIANA, EL DORADO, AND THE ORINOCO COAST.

From the original map, drawn by Raleigh, in the British Museum. This map, like so many of the older charts, is drawn upside down, the South being at the top and the East on the left, while the Panama Isthmus is at the bottom on the right. The river above the " Lake of Manoa " is the Amazon.

CHAPTER XL

CHAMPLAIN DISCOVERS LAKE ONTARIO

To discover a passage westward was still the main object of those who made their way up the Gulf of the St. Lawrence. This, too, was the object of Samuel Champlain, known as " the Father of New France," when he arrived with orders from France to establish an industrial colony " which should hold for that country the gateway of the Golden East." He had already ascended the river Saguenay, a tributary of the St. Lawrence, till stopped by rapids and rocks, and the natives had told him of a great salt sea to the north, which was Hudson's Bay, discovered some seven years later, in 1610. He now made his way to a spot called by the natives Quebec, a word meaning the strait or narrows, this being the narrowest place in the whole magnificent waterway. He had long been searching for a suitable site for a settlement, but " I could find none more convenient," he says, " or better situated than the point of Quebec, so called by the savages, which was covered with nut trees." Accordingly here, close to the present Champlain market, arose the nucleus of the city of Quebec—the great warehouse of New France.

Having passed the winter of 1608 at Quebec, the passion of exploration still on him, in a little two-masted boat piloted by Indians, he went up the St. Lawrence, towards Cartier's Mont Royal. From out the thick forest land that lined its banks, Indians discovered the steel-clad strangers and gazed at them from the river-banks in speechless wonder. The river soon became alive with Indian canoes, but the Frenchmen made their way to the mouth of the Richelieu River, where they encamped for a couple of days' hunting and fishing. Then Champlain sailed on, his little two-masted boat outstripping the native canoes, till the unwelcome sound of rapids fell on the silent air, and through the dark foliage of the islet of St. John he could see " the gleam of snowy foam and the flash of hurrying waters." The Indians had assured him that his boat could pass unobstructed through the whole journey. " It afflicted me and troubled me exceedingly," he tells us, " to be obliged to return without having seen so great a lake, full of fair islands and bordered with the fine countries which they had described to me." He could not bear to give up the ex-

THE FIRST SETTLEMENT AT QUEBEC.

From Champlain's *Voyages*, 1613. The bigger house in front is Champlain's own residence.

ploration into the heart of a land unvisited by white men. So, sending back his party, accompanied only by two Frenchmen as brave as himself, he stepped into an Indian canoe to be carried round the rapids and so continue his perilous journey—perilous, indeed, for bands of hostile natives lurked in the primeval forests that clothed the river-banks in dense masses.

As they advanced the river widened out ; the Indian canoes carried them safely over the broad stream shimmer·

ing in the summer sun till they came to a great silent lake over one hundred miles long, hitherto unexplored. The beauty of the new country is described with enthusiasm by the delighted explorer, but they were now in the Mohawk country and progress was fraught with danger. They travelled only by night and lay hidden by day in the depth of the forest, till they had reached the far end of the lake, named Lake Champlain after its discoverer. They were near the rocky promontory where Fort Ticonderoga was afterwards built, when they met a party of Iroquois ; war-cries pealed across the waters of the lake, and by daybreak battle could no longer be averted. Champlain and his two companions, in doublet and hose, buckled on their breastplates, cuisses of steel and plumed helmets, and with sword and arquebus advanced. Their firearms won the day, but all hope of further advance was at an end, and Champlain returned to Quebec with his great story of new lands to the south. It was not till the spring of 1611 that he was again free to start on another exploring expedition into the heart of Canada.

His journey to the rapids of the St. Louis has been well described : " Like specks on the broad bosom of the waters, two pigmy vessels held their course up the lonely St. Lawrence. They passed abandoned Tadoussac, the channel of Orleans, the tenantless rock of Quebec, the wide Lake of St. Peter with its crowded archipelago, and the forest plain of Montreal. All was solitude. Hochelaga had vanished, and of the savage population that Cartier had found sixty-eight years before, no trace remained."

In a skiff with a few Indians, Champlain tried to pass the rapids of St. Louis ; but oars, paddles, and poles alike proved vain against the foaming surges, and he was forced to return, but not till the Indians had drawn for him rude plans of the river above, with its chain of rapids and its lakes and its cataracts. They were quite impassable, said the natives, though, indeed, to these white strangers everything seemed possible.

"These white men must have fallen from the clouds," they said. "How else could they have reached us through the woods and rapids which even we find it hard to pass?" Champlain wanted to get to the upper waters of the Ottawa River, to the land of the cannibal Nipissings, who

THE DEFEAT OF THE IROQUOIS BY CHAMPLAIN AND HIS PARTY
ON LAKE CHAMPLAIN.

From a drawing in Champlain's *Voyages*, 1613.

dwelt on the lake that bears their name; but they were enemies, and the natives refused to advance into their country.

Two years later he accomplished his desire, and found himself at last in the land of the Nipissings. He crossed their lake and steered his canoes down the French river. Days passed and no signs of human life appeared amid the rocky desolation, till suddenly three hundred savages, tattooed, painted, and armed, rushed out on them. Fortunately they were friendly, and it was from them that Champlain learned the good news that the great freshwater lake of the Hurons was close at hand.

What if the Friar Le Caron, one of Champlain's party, had preceded him by a few days, Champlain was the first white man to give an account of it, if not the first to sail on its beautiful waters. For over one hundred miles he made his way along its eastern shores, until he reached a broad opening with fields of maize and bright patches of sunflower, from the seeds of which the Indians made their hair-oil. After staying a few days at a little Huron village where he was feasted by friendly natives, Champlain pushed on by Indian trails, passing village after village till he reached the narrow end of Lake Simcoe. A " shrill clamour of rejoicing and the screaming flight of terrified children " hailed his approach. The little fleet of canoes pursued their course along the lake and then down the chain of lakes leading to the river Trent. The inhabited country of the Hurons had now given place to a desolate region with no sign of human life, till from the mouth of the Trent, " like a flock of venturous wild fowl," they found themselves floating on the waters of Lake Ontario, across which they made their way safely.

It was a great day in the life of Champlain when he found himself in the very heart of a hostile land, having discovered the chain of inland lakes of which he had heard so much. But they were now in the land of the Iroquois— deadly foes of the Hurons. There was nothing for it but to fight, and a great battle now took place between the rival tribes, every warrior yelling at the top of his voice. Champlain himself was wounded in the fray, and all further exploration had to be abandoned. He was packed up in a basket and carried away on the back of a Huron warrior. "Bundled in a heap," wrote the explorer, "doubled and strapped together after such a fashion that one could move no more than an infant in swaddling clothes, I never was in such torment in my life, for the pain of the wound was nothing to that of being bound and pinioned on the back of one of our savages. As soon as I could bear my weight, I got out of this prison." How Champlain wintered with the Hurons, who would not allow him to return to Quebec, how he got lost while hunting in one of the great forests in his eagerness to shoot a strange-looking bird, how the lakes and streams froze, and how his courage and endurance were sorely tried over the toilsome marches to Lake Simcoe, but how finally he reached Montreal by way of Nipissing and the Ottawa River, must be read elsewhere. Champlain's work as an explorer was done. Truly has he been called the Father of New France. He had founded Quebec and Montreal; he had explored Canada as no man has ever done before or since. Faithful to the passion of his life, he died in 1635 at Quebec—the city he had founded and loved.

CHAPTER XLI

EARLY DISCOVERERS OF AUSTRALIA

WHILE the French and English were feverishly seeking a way to the East, either by the North Pole or by way of America, the Dutch were busy discovering a new land in the Southern Seas.

And as we have seen America emerging from the mist of ages in the sixteenth century, so now in the seventeenth we have the great Island Continent of Australia mysteriously appearing bit by bit out of the yet little-known Sea of the South. There is little doubt that both Portuguese and Spanish had touched on the western coast early in the sixteenth century, but gave no information about it beyond sketching certain rough and undefined patches of land and calling it Terra Australis in their early maps; no one seems to have thought this mysterious land of much importance. The maritime nations of that period carefully concealed their knowledge from one another. The proud Spaniard hated his Portuguese neighbour as a formidable rival in the race for wealth and fame, and the Dutchman, who now comes on the scene, was regarded by both as a natural enemy by land or sea.

Magellan in 1520 discovered that the Terra Australis was not joined to South America, as the old maps had laid down; and we find Frobisher remarking in 1578 that " Terra Australis seemeth to be a great, firm land, lying

under and about the South Pole, not thoroughly discovered. It is known at the south side of the Strait of
Magellan and is called Terra del Fuego. It is thought
this south land about the pole Antarctic is far bigger than
the north land about the pole Arctic; but whether it be

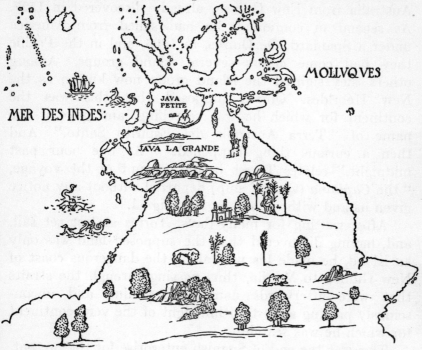

MOLLVQVES

MER DES INDES:

JAVA PETITE

JAVA LA GRANDE

AN EARLY MAP OF "TERRA AUSTRALIS," CALLED "JAVA LA GRANDE"
IN ITS SUPPOSED EASTERN PART.

From the "Dauphin" map of 1546. There was then supposed to be a great mainland of Java,
separated from the island of "Java Minor" by a narrow strait. See the copy of the whole of
this map in colour, where it will be seen that the "Terra Australis" was supposed to
stretch from east to west.

so or not, we have no certain knowledge, for we have
no particular description thereof, as we have of the land
about the North Pole."

And even one hundred years later the mystery was
not cleared up. "This land about the straits is not
perfectly discovered whether it be continent or islands.

Some take it for continent, esteeming that Terra Australis or the Southern Continent may for the largeness thereof take a first place in the division of the whole world."

The Spaniards were still masters of the sea, when one Lieutenant Torres first sailed through the strait dividing Australia from New Guinea, already discovered in 1527. As second in command, he had sailed from America under a Spaniard, De Quiros, in 1605, and in the Pacific they had come across several island groups. Among others they sighted the island group now known as the New Hebrides. Quiros supposed that this was the continent for which he was searching, and gave it the name of " Terra Australis del Espirito Santo." And then a curious thing happened. " At one hour past midnight," relates Torres in his account of the voyage, " the *Capitana* (Quiros' ship) departed without any notice given us and without making any signal."

After waiting for many days, Torres at last set sail, and, having discovered that the supposed land was only an island, he made his way along the dangerous coast of New Guinea to Manila, thus passing through the straits that were afterwards named after him, and unconsciously passing almost within sight of the very continent for which he was searching.

This was the end of Spanish enterprise for the present. The rivals for sea-power in the seventeenth century were England and Holland. Both had recently started East India Companies, both were keen to take a large part in East Indian trade and to command the sea. For a time the Dutch had it all their own way ; they devoted themselves to founding settlements in the East Indies, ever hoping to discover new islands in the South Seas as possible trade centres. Scientific discovery held little interest for them.

As early as 1606 a Dutch ship—the little *Sun*—had

been dispatched from the Moluccas to discover more about the land called by the Spaniards New Guinea, because of its resemblance to the West African coast of Guinea. But the crews were greeted with a shower of arrows as they attempted a landing, and with nine of their party killed, they returned disheartened.

A more ambitious expedition was fitted out in 1617 by private adventurers, and two ships—the *Unity* and the *Horn*—sailed from the Texel under the command of a rich Amsterdam merchant named Isaac Le Maire and a clever navigator, Cornelius Schouten of Horn. Having been provided with an English gunner and carpenter, the ships were steered boldly across the Atlantic. Hitherto the object of the expedition had been kept a secret, but on crossing the line the crews were informed that they were bound for the Terra Australis del Espirito Santo of Quiros. The men had never heard of the country before, and we are told they wrote the name in their caps in order to remember it. By midwinter they had reached the eastern entrance of the Straits of Magellan, through which many a ship had passed since the days of Magellan, some hundred years before this. Unfortunately, while undergoing some necessary repairs here, the little *Horn* caught fire and was burnt out, the crews all having to crowd on to the *Unity*. Instead of going through the strait they sailed south and discovered Staaten Land, which they thought might be a part of the southern continent for which they were seeking. We now know it to be an island, whose heights are covered with perpetual snow. It was named by Schouten after the Staaten or States-General of Holland. Passing through the strait which divided the newly discovered land from the Terra del Fuego (called later the Straits of Le Maire after its discoverer), the Dutchmen found a great sea full of whales and monsters innumerable. Sea-mews larger than swans, with wings stretching six feet across, fled screaming round the ship. The wind was against them, but after endless tacking they reached the southern extremity of land, which Schouten named after his native town and the little burnt ship—*Horn*—and as Cape Horn it is known to-day.

But the explorers never reached the Terra Australis. Their little ship could do no more, and they sailed to Java to repair.

Many a name on the Australian map to-day testifies to Dutch enterprise about this time. In 1616, Captain Dirck Hartog of Amsterdam discovered the island that bears his name off the coast of Western Australia. A few years later the captain of a Dutch ship called the *Lewin* or *Lioness* touched the south-west extremity of the continent, calling that point Cape Lewin. Again a few years and we find Captain Nuyts giving his name to a part of the southern coast, though the discovery seems to have been accidental. In 1628, Carpentaria received its name from Carpenter, a governor of the East India Company. Now, one day a ship from Carpenter's Land returned laden with gold and spice; and though certain men had their suspicions that these riches had been fished out of some large ship wrecked upon the inhospitable coast, yet a little fleet of eleven ships was at once dispatched to reconnoitre further. Captain Pelsart commanded the *Batavia*, which in a great storm was separated from the other ships and driven alone on to the shoals marked as the Abrolhos (a Portuguese word meaning " Open your eyes," implying a sharp look-out for dangerous reefs) on the west coast of Australia. It was night when the ship struck, and Captain Pelsart was sick in bed. He ran hastily on to the deck. The moon shone bright. The sails were up. The sea appeared to be covered with white foam. Captain Pelsart charged the master with the loss of the ship, and asked him " in what part of the world he thought they were."

" God only knows that," replied the master, adding that the ship was fast on a bank hitherto undiscovered. Suddenly a dreadful storm of wind and rain arose, and, being surrounded with rocks and shoals, the ship was constantly striking. " The women, children, and sick people were out of their wits with fear," so they decided to land these on an island for " their cries and noise served only to disturb them." The landing was extremely

THE WRECK OF CAPTAIN PELSART'S SHIP THE *BATAVIA* ON
THE COAST OF NEW HOLLAND, 1644.
From the Dutch account of Pelsart's *Voyages*, 1647.

difficult owing to the rocky coast, where the waves were dashing high. When the weather had moderated a bit, Captain Pelsart took the ship and went in search of water, thereby exploring a good deal of coast, which, he remarked, " resembled the country near Dover." But his exploration amounted to little, and the account of his adventures is mostly taken up with an account of the disasters that befell the miserable party left on the rock-bound islands of Abrolhos—conspiracies, mutinies, and plots. His was only one of many adventures on this unknown and inhospitable coast, which about this time, 1644, began to take the name of New Holland.

CHAPTER XLII

TASMAN FINDS TASMANIA

AT this time Anthony Van Diemen was governor at Batavia, and one of his most trusted commanders was Abel Tasman. In 1642, Tasman was given command of two ships " for making discoveries of the Unknown South Land," and, hoisting his flag on board the *Sea-Hen*, he sailed south from Batavia without sighting the coast of Australia. Despite foggy weather, " hard gales, and a rolling sea," he made his way steadily south. It was three months before land was sighted, and high mountains were seen to the south-east. The ship stood in to shore. " As the land has not been known before to any European, we called it Anthony Van Diemen's Land in honour of our Governor-General, who sent us out to make discoveries. I anchored in a bay and heard the sound of people upon the shore, but I saw nobody. I perceived in the sand the marks of wild beasts' feet, resembling those of a tiger."

Setting up a post with the Dutch East India Company's mark, and leaving the Dutch flag flying, Tasman left Van Diemen's Land, which was not to be visited again for over one hundred years, when it was called after its first discoverer. He had no idea that he was on an island. Tasman now sailed east, and after about a week at sea he discovered a high mountainous country, which he named " Staaten Land." " We found here abundance of inhabitants : they had very hoarse voices and were very large-made people ; they were of a colour between brown and yellow, their hair long and thick, combed up and fixed on the top of their heads with a quill in the very same manner that Japanese fastened their hair behind their heads."

Tasman anchored on the north coast of the south island of New Zealand, but canoes of warlike Maoris surrounded the ships, a conflict took place in which several Dutch seamen were killed, the weather grew stormy, and Tasman sailed away from the bay he named Murderer's Bay— rediscovered by Captain Cook about a hundred years later.

" This is the second country discovered by us," says Tasman. " We named it Staaten Land in honour of the States-General. It is possible that it may join the other Staaten Land (of Schouten and Le Maire to the south of Terra del Fuego), but it is uncertain ; it is a very fine country, and we hope it is part of the unknown south continent." Is it necessary to add that this Staaten Land was really New Zealand, and the bay where the ships anchored is now known as Tasman Bay ? When the news of Tasman's discoveries was noised abroad, all the geographers, explorers, and discoverers at once jumped to the conclusion that this was the same land on whose coast Pelsart had been wrecked. " It is most evident," they said, " that New Guinea, Carpentaria, New Holland, Van Diemen's Land make all one continent, from which New Zealand seems to be separated by a strait, and perhaps is part of another continent answering to Africa as this plainly does to America, making indeed a very large country."

After a ten months' cruise Tasman returned to Batavia. He had found Van Diemen's Land and New Zealand, without sighting Australia.

A second expedition was now fitted out. The instructions for the commodore, Captain Abel Jansen Tasman, make interesting reading. The orders are detailed and clear. He will start the end of January 1644, and "we shall expect you in July following attended with good success."

"Of all the lands, countries, islands, capes, inlets, bays, rivers, shoals, reefs, sands, cliffs, and rocks which you pass in this discovery you are to make accurate maps —be particularly careful about longitude and latitude. But be circumspect and prudent in landing with small craft, because at several times New Guinea has been found to be inhabited by cruel, wild savages. When you converse with any of these savages behave well and friendly to them, and try by all means to engage their affection to you. You are to show the samples of the goods which you carry along with you, and inquire what materials and goods they possess. To

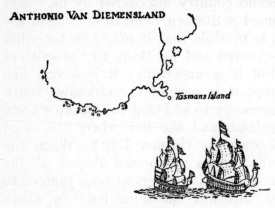

VAN DIEMAN'S LAND AND TWO OF
TASMAN'S SHIPS.

From the map drawn by Tasman in his "Journal."

prevent any other European nation from reaping the fruits of our labour in these discoveries, you are everywhere to take possession in the name of the Dutch East India Company, to put up some sign, erect a stone or post, and carve on them the arms of the Netherlands. The yachts are manned with one hundred and eleven persons, and for eight months plentifully victualled. Manage everything well and orderly, take notice you see the ordinary portion of two meat and two pork days, and a quarter of vinegar and a half-quarter of sweet oil per week."

He was to coast along New Guinea to the farthest-known spot, and to follow the coast *despite adverse winds,* in order that the Dutch might be sure " whether this land is not divided from the great known South Continent or not."

What he accomplished on this voyage is best seen in " The complete map of the Southern Continent surveyed by Captain Abel Tasman," which was inlaid on the floor of the large hall in the Stadthouse at Amsterdam. The Great South Land was henceforth known as New Holland.

CHAPTER XLIII

DAMPIER DISCOVERS HIS STRAIT

IT was not long before the great stretch of coast-line carefully charted by Tasman became known to the English, and while the Dutch were yet busy exploring farther, Dampier—the first Englishman to visit the country—had already set foot on its shores.

" We lie entirely at the mercy of the Dutch East India Company's geography for the outline of this part of the coast of New Holland : for it does not appear that the ships of any other nation have ever approached it," says an old history of the period.

Some such information as this became known in South America, in which country the English had long been harassing the Spaniards. It reached the ears of one William Dampier, a Somersetshire man, who had lived a life of romance and adventure with the buccaneers, pillaging and plundering foreign ships in these remote regions of the earth. He had run across the Southern Pacific carrying his life in his hand. He had marched across the isthmus of Panama—one hundred and ten miles in twenty-three days—through deep and swiftly flowing rivers, dense growths of tropical vegetation full of snakes, his only food being the flesh of monkeys. Such was the man who now took part in a privateering cruise under Captain Swan, bound for the East Indies.

On 1st March 1686, Swan and Dampier sailed away from the coast of Mexico on the voyage that led to Dampier's circumnavigation of the globe. For fifty days they sailed without sighting land, and when at last they found themselves off the island of Guam, they had only three days' food left, and the crews were busy plotting to kill Captain Swan and eat him, the other commanders sharing the same fate in turn.

" Ah, Dampier," said Captain Swan, when he and all the men had refreshed themselves with food, " you would have made but a poor meal," for Dampier was as lean as the Captain was " fat and fleshy." Soon, however, fresh trouble arose among the men. Captain Swan lost his life, and Dampier on board the little *Cygnet* sailed hurriedly for the Spice Islands.

He was now on the Australian parallels, " in the shadow of a world lying dark upon the face of the ocean." It was January 1688 when Dampier sighted the coast of New Holland and anchored in a bay, which they named Cygnet Bay after their ship, somewhere off the northern coast of eastern Australia. Here, while the ship was undergoing repairs, Dampier makes his observations.

" New Holland," he tells us, " is a very large tract of land. It is not yet determined whether it is an island or a main continent, but I am certain that it joins neither to Africa, Asia, or America."

" The inhabitants of this country," he tells us, " are the miserablest people in the world. They have no houses, but lie in the open air without any covering, the earth being their bed and the heaven their canopy. Their food is a small sort of fish, which they catch at low tide, while the old people that are not able to stir abroad by reason of their age and the tender infants wait their return, and what Providence has bestowed on them they presently broil on the coals and eat it in common. They are tall and thin, and of a very unpleasing aspect; their hair is black, short, and curled, like that of the negroes of Guinea."

This Englishman's first description of the Australian natives cannot fail to be interesting. " After we had been here a little while, we clothed some of the men, designing to have some service from them for it ; for we found some wells of water here, and intended to carry two or three barrels of it aboard. But it being somewhat troublesome to carry to the canoes, we thought to have made these men to have carry'd it for us, and therefore we gave them some clothes ; to one an old pair of breeches, to another a ragged shirt, to a third a jacket that was scarce worth owning. We put them on, thinking that this finery would have brought them to work heartily for us ; and our water being filled in small, long barrels, about six gallons in each, we brought these our new servants to the wells and put a barrel on each of their shoulders. But they stood like statues, without motion, but grinn'd like so many monkeys staring one upon another. So we were forced to carry the water ourselves."

They had soon had enough of the new country, weighed anchor, and steered away to the north. Dampier returned to England even a poorer man than he had left it twelve years before. After countless adventures and hairbreadth escapes, after having sailed entirely round the world, he brought back with him nothing but one unhappy black man, " Prince Jeoly," whom he had bought for sixty dollars. He had hoped to recoup himself by showing the poor native with his rings and bracelets and painted skin, but he was in such need of money on land- ing that he gladly sold the poor black man on his arrival in the Thames.

But Dampier had made himself a name as a successful traveller, and in 1699 he was appointed by the King, William III., to command the *Roebuck*, two hundred and ninety tons, with a crew of fifty men and provisions for twenty months. Leaving England in the middle of January

1699, he sighted the west coast of New Holland toward the end of July, and anchored in a bay they called Sharks Bay, not far from the rocks where the *Batavia* was wrecked with Captain Pelsart in 1629. He gives us a graphic picture of this place, with its sweet-scented trees, its shrubs gay as the rainbow with blossoms and berries, its many-coloured vegetation, its fragrant air and delicious soil. The men caught sharks and devoured them with relish, which speaks of scarce provisions. Inside one of the sharks (eleven feet long) they found a hippopotamus. "The flesh of it was divided among my men," says the Captain, "and they took care that no waste should be made of it, but thought it, as things stood, good entertainment."

DAMPIER'S SHIP THE *CYGNET*.
From a drawing in the Dutch edition of his *Voyage Round the World*, 1698.

As it had been with Pelsart, so now with Dampier, fresh water was the difficulty, and they sailed north-east in search of it. They fell in with a group of small rocky islands still known as Dampier's Archipelago, one island of which they named Rosemary Island, because "there grow here two or three sorts of shrubs, one just like rosemary." Once again he comes across natives—"very much the same blinking creatures, also abundance of the same kind of flesh-flies teasing them, with the same black skins and hair frizzled." Indeed, he writes as though the whole country of New Holland was a savage and worthless land inhabited by dreadful monsters.

" If it were not," he writes, " for that sort of pleasure which results from the discovery even of the barrenest spot upon the globe, this coast of New Holland would not have charmed me much." His first sight of the kangaroo— now the emblem of Australia—is interesting. He describes it as " a sort of raccoon, different from that of the West Indies, chiefly as to the legs, for these have very short fore-legs, but go jumping upon them as the others do, and like them are very good meat." This must have been the small kangaroo, for the large kind was not found till later by Captain Cook in New South Wales.

But Dampier and his mates could not find fresh water, and soon wearied of the coast of New Holland ; an outbreak of scurvy, too, decided them to sail away in search of fresh foods. Dampier had spent five weeks cruising off the coast ; he had sailed along some nine hundred miles of the Australian shore without making any startling discoveries. A few months later the *Roebuck* stood off the coast of New Guinea, " a high and mountainous country, green and beautiful with tropical vegetation, and dark with forests and groves of tall and stately trees." Innumerable dusky-faced natives peeped at the ship from behind the rocks, but they were not friendly, and this they showed by climbing the cocoanut trees and throwing down cocoanuts at the English, with passionate signs to them to depart. But with plenty of fresh water, this was unlikely, and the crews rowed ashore, killed and salted a good load of wild hogs, while the savages still peeped at them from afar.

Thus then they sailed on, thinking they were still coasting New Guinea. So doing, they arrived at the straits which still bear the name of the explorer, and discovered a little island which he called New Britain. He had now been over fifteen months at sea and the *Roebuck* was only provisioned for twenty months, so

Dampier, who never had the true spirit of the explorer in him, left his discoveries and turned homewards. The ship was rotten, and it took three months to repair her at Batavia before proceeding farther. With pumps going night and day, they made their way to the Cape of Good Hope; but off the island of Ascension the *Roebuck* went down, carrying with her many of Dampier's books and papers. But though many of the papers were lost, the " Learned and Faithful Dampier " as he is called, the "Prince of Voyagers," has left us accounts of his adventures un-equalled in those strenuous ocean-going days for their picturesque and graphic details.

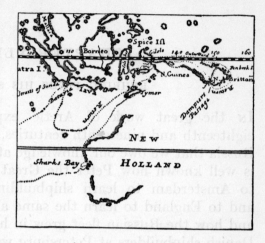

DAMPIER'S STRAITS AND THE ISLAND OF NEW BRITAIN.

From a map in Dampier's *Voyages*, 1697.

CHAPTER XLIV

BEHRING FINDS HIS STRAIT

In the great work of Arctic exploration during the eighteenth and nineteenth centuries, it is to England and Russia that we owe our knowledge at the present day. It is well known how Peter the Great of Russia journeyed to Amsterdam to learn shipbuilding under the Dutch, and to England to learn the same art under the English, and how the Russian fleet grew in his reign. Among the Danish shipbuilders at Petersburg was one Vitus Behring, already a bold and able commander on the high seas.

The life of the great Russian Czar was drawing to its close—he was already within a few weeks of the end—when he planned an expedition under this same Vitus Behring, for which he wrote the instructions with his own hands.

"(1) At Kamtchatka two decked boats are to be built. (2) With these you are to sail northward along the coast and, as the end of the coast is not known, this land is undoubtedly America. (3) For this reason you are to inquire where the American coast begins, and go to some European colony and, when European ships are seen, you are to ask what the coast is called, note it down, make a landing, and after having charted the coast return."

Were Asia and America joined together, or was there a strait between the two ? The question was yet undecided in 1725. Indeed, the east coast of Asia was only known as far as the island of Yezo, while the Pacific coast of America had been explored no farther than New Albion.

Peter the Great died on 28th January 1725. A week later Behring started for Kamtchatka. Right across snow-covered Russia to the boundary of Siberia he led his expedition. March found him at Tobolsk. With rafts and boats they then made their way by the Siberian rivers till they reached Yakutsk, where they spent their first winter. Not till the middle of June 1726 did Behring reach the capital of East Siberia. The rest of the journey was through utterly unknown land. It was some six hundred and eighty-five miles eastwards to Okhotsk through a rough and mountainous country, cut up by deep and bridgeless streams ; the path lay over dangerous swamps and through dense forest.

The party now divided. Behring, with two hundred horses, travelled triumphantly, if painfully, to Okhotsk in forty-five days. The town consisted of eleven huts containing Russian families who lived by fishing. Snow lay deep on the frozen ground, and the horses died one by one for lack of food, but the undaunted explorer had soon got huts ready for the winter, which was to be spent in felling trees and pushing forward the building of his ship, the *Fortuna*, for the coming voyage of discovery. Behring himself had made a successful journey to the coast, but some of the party encountered terrible hardships, and it was midsummer 1727 before they arrived, while others were overtaken by winter in the very heart of Siberia and had to make their way for the last three hundred miles on foot through snow in places six feet deep. Their food was finished, famine became a companion to cold, and they were obliged to gnaw their shoes and straps and leathern bags. Indeed, they must have perished had they not stumbled on Behring's route, where they found his dead horses. But at last all was ready and the little ship *Fortuna* was sailing bravely across the Sea of Okhotsk some six hundred and fifty miles to the coast of Kamtchatka. This she did in sixteen days. The country of Kamtchatka had now to be crossed, and with boats and sledges this took the whole winter. It was a laborious undertaking following the course of the Kamtchatka River; the expedition had to camp in the snow, and few natives were forthcoming for the transport of heavy goods.

It was not till March 1728 that Behring reached his goal, Ostrog, a village near the sea, inhabited by a handful of Cossacks. From this point, on the bleak shores of the Arctic sea, the exploring party were ordered to start. It had taken over three years to reach this starting-point, and even now a seemingly hopeless task lay before them.

After hard months of shipbuilding, the stout little *Gabriel* was launched, her timber had been hauled to Ostrog by dogs, while the rigging, cable, and anchors had been dragged nearly two thousand miles through one of the most desolate regions of the earth. As to the food on which the explorers lived: "Fish oil was their butter and dried fish their beef and pork. Salt they were obliged to get from the sea." Thus supplied with a year's provisions, Behring started on his voyage of discovery along an unknown coast and over an unknown sea. On 13th July 1728 the sails of the *Gabriel* were triumphantly hoisted, and Behring, with a crew of forty-four, started on the great voyage. His course lay close along the coast northwards. The sea was alive with whales, seals, sea-lions, and dolphins as the little party made their way north, past the mouth of the Anadir River. The little *Gabriel* was now in the strait between Asia and America, though Behring knew it not. They had been at sea some three weeks, when eight men came rowing towards them in a leathern boat. They were the

Chukches—a warlike race living on the north-east coast of Siberia, unsubdued and fierce. They pointed out a small island in the north, which Behring named the Isle of St. Lawrence in honour of the day. Then he turned back. He felt he had accomplished his task and obeyed his orders. Moreover, with adverse winds they might never return to Kamtchatka, and to winter among the Chukches was to court disaster. After a cruise of three months they reached their starting-point again. Had he only known that the coast of America was but thirty-nine miles off, the results of his voyage would have been greater. As it was, he ascertained that "there really does exist a north-east passage, and that from the Lena River it is possible, provided one is not prevented by Polar ice, to sail to Kamtchatka and thence to Japan, China, and the East Indies."

The final discovery was left for Captain Cook. As he approached the straits which he called after Behring, the sun broke suddenly through the clouds, and the continents of Asia and America were visible at a glance.

There was dissatisfaction in Russia with the result of Behring's voyage, and though five years of untold hardship in the "extremest corner of the world" had told on the Russian explorer, he was willing and anxious to start off again. He proposed to make Kamtchatka again his headquarters, to explore the western coast of America, and to chart the long Arctic coast of Siberia— a colossal task indeed.

So the Great Northern Expedition was formed, with Behring in command, accompanied by two well-known explorers to help, Spangberg and Chirikoff, and with five hundred and seventy men under him. It would take too long to follow the various expeditions that now left Russia in five different directions to explore the unknown coasts of the Old World. "The world has never witnessed a more heroic geographical enterprise than these Arctic expeditions." Amid obstacles indescribable the north line of Siberia, hitherto charted as a straight line, was explored and surveyed. Never was greater courage and endurance displayed. If the ships got frozen in, they were hauled on shore, the men spent the long winter in miserable huts and started off again with the spring, until the northern coast assumed shape and form.

One branch of the Great Northern Expedition under Behring was composed of professors to make a scientific investigation of Kamtchatka! These thirty learned Russians were luxuriously equipped. They carried a library with several hundred books, including *Robinson Crusoe* and *Gulliver's Travels*, seventy reams of writing-paper, and artists' materials. They had nine wagon-loads of instruments, carrying telescopes fifteen feet long. A surgeon, two landscape painters, one instrument maker, five surveyors accompanied them, and " the convoy grew like an avalanche as it worked its way into Siberia." Behring seems to have moved this " cumbersome machine " safely to Yakutsk, though it took the best part of two years. Having left Russia in 1733, it was 1741 when Behring himself was ready to start from the harbour of Okhotsk for the coast of America with two ships and provisions for some months. He was now nearly sixty, his health was undermined with vexation and worry, and the climate of Okhotsk had nearly killed him.

On 18th July—just six weeks after the start—Behring discovered the continent of North America. The coast was jagged, the land covered with snow, mountains extended inland, and above all rose a peak towering into the clouds—a peak higher than anything they knew in Siberia or Kamtchatka, which Behring named Mount St. Elias, after the patron saint of the day. He made his way with difficulty through the string of islands that skirt

the great peninsula of Alaska. Through the months of
August and September they cruised about the coast in
damp and foggy weather, which now gave way to violent
storms, and Behring's ship was driven along at the mercy
of the wind. He himself was ill, and the greater part
of his crew were disabled by scurvy. At last one day, in
a high-running sea, the ship struck upon a rock and they

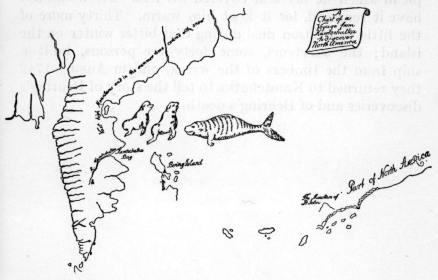

THE CHART OF BEHRING'S VOYAGE FROM KAMTCHATKA TO NORTH AMERICA.

From a chart drawn in 1741 by Lieut. Waxell, a member of Behring's expedition. It is also
interesting for the drawing of the sea-cow, one of the very few authentic drawings of this
curious animal, which has long been extinct, and is only known by these drawings.

found themselves stranded on an unknown island off the
coast of Kamtchatka. Only two men were fit to land;
they found a dead whale on which they fed their sick.
Later on sea-otters, blue and white foxes, and sea-cows
provided food, but the island was desolate and solitary—
not a human being was to be seen.

Here, however, the little party was forced to winter.
With difficulty they built five underground huts on the

sandy shore of the island now known as Behring Island. And each day amid the raging snowstorms and piercing winds one man went forth to hunt for animal food.

Man after man died, and by December, Behring's own condition had become hopeless. Hunger and grief had added to his misery, and in his sand-hut he died. He was almost buried alive, for the sand rolled down from the pit in which he lay and covered his feet. He would not have it removed, for it kept him warm. Thirty more of the little expedition died during that bitter winter on the island; the survivors, some forty-five persons, built a ship from the timbers of the wreck, and in August 1742 they returned to Kamtchatka to tell the story of Behring's discoveries and of Behring's death.

CHAPTER XLV

COOK DISCOVERS NEW ZEALAND

BUT while the names of Torres, Carpenter, Tasman, and Dampier are still to be found on our modern maps of Australia, it is the name of Captain Cook that we must always connect most closely with the discovery of the great island continent—the Great South Land which only became known to Europe one hundred and fifty years ago.

Dampier had returned to England in 1701 from his voyage to New Holland, but nearly seventy years passed before the English were prepared to send another expedition to investigate further the mysterious land in the south.

James Cook had shown himself worthy of the great command that was given to him in 1768, although exploration was not the main object of the expedition. Spending his boyhood in the neighbourhood of Whitby, he was familiar with the North Sea fishermen, with the colliers, even with the smugglers that frequented this eastern coast. In 1755 he entered the Royal Navy, volunteering for service and entering H.M.S. *Eagle* as master's mate. Four years later we find him taking his share on board H.M.S. *Pembroke* in the attack on Quebec by Wolfe, and later transferred to H.M.S. *Northumberland*, selected to survey the river and Gulf of St. Lawrence. So satisfactory was his work that a few years later he was instructed to survey and chart the coasts of Newfoundland and Labrador. While engaged on this work, he observed an eclipse of the sun, which led to the appointment that necessitated a voyage to the Pacific Ocean. It had been calculated that a Transit of Venus would occur in June 1769. A petition to the King set forth : "That, the British nation being justly celebrated in the learned world for their knowledge of astronomy, in which they are inferior to no nation upon earth, ancient or modern, it would cast dishonour upon them should they neglect to have correct observations made of this important phenomenon." The King agreed, and the Royal Society selected James Cook as a fit man for the appointment. A stout, strongly built collier of three hundred and seventy tons was chosen at Whitby, manned with seventy men, and victualled for twelve months. With instructions to observe the Transit of Venus at the island of Georgeland (Otaheite), to make further discoveries in the South Pacific Ocean and to explore New Zealand if possible, Cook hoisted his flag on H.M.S. *Endeavour* and started in May 1768.

It was an interesting party on board, joined at the last moment by Mr. Joseph Banks, a very rich member of the Royal Society and a student of Natural History. He had requested leave to sail in "the ship that carries the English astronomers to the new-discovered country in the South Sea." "No people ever went to sea better fitted out for the purpose of Natural History, nor more elegantly," says a contemporary writer. "They have a fine library, they have all sorts of machines for catching and preserving insects, they have two painters and draughtsmen—in short, this expedition will cost Mr. Banks £10,000."

Their astronomical instruments were of the best, including a portable observatory constructed for sixteen guineas. But most important of all was the careful assortment of provisions, to allay, if possible, that scourge of all navigators, the scurvy. A quantity of malt was shipped to be made into wort, mustard, vinegar, wheat, orange and lemon juice and portable soup was put on board, and Cook received special orders to keep his men with plenty of fresh food whenever this was possible. He carried out these orders strenuously, and at Madeira we find him punishing one of his own seamen with twelve lashes for refusing to eat fresh beef. Hence they left

THE ISLAND OF OTAHEITE, OR ST. GEORGE,

From a painting by William Hodges, who accompanied Captain Cook.

Rio de Janeiro " in as good a condition for prosecuting the voyage as on the day they left England."

Christmas Day was passed near the mouth of the river Plate, and, early in the New Year of 1769, the *Endeavour* sailed through the Strait of Le Maire. The wealthy Mr. Banks landed on Staaten Island and hastily added a hundred new plants to his collection. Then they sailed on to St. George's Island. It had been visited by Captain Wallis in the *Dolphin* the previous year; indeed, some of

Cook's sailors had served on board the *Dolphin* and knew
the native chiefs of the island. All was friendly, tents
were soon pitched, a fort built with mounted guns at
either side, the precious instruments landed, and on 3rd
June, with a cloudless sky and in intolerable heat, they
observed the whole passage of the planet Venus over the
sun's disk.

After a stay of three months they left the island, taking
Tupia, a native, with them. Among other accomplish-
ments this Tupia roasted dogs to perfection, and Cook
declares that dogs' flesh is "next only to English lamb."

They visited other islands in the group—now known
as the Society Islands and belonging to France—and
took possession of all in the name of His Britannic Majesty,
George III.

All through the month of September they sailed south,
till on 7th October land was sighted. It proved to be
the North Island of New Zealand, never before approached
by Europeans from the east. It was one hundred and
twenty-seven years since Tasman had discovered the west
coast and called it Staaten Land, but no European had
ever set foot on its soil. Indeed, it was still held to be part
of the Terra Australis Incognita.

The first to sight land was a boy named Nicholas
Young, hence the point was called "Young Nick's
Head," which may be seen on our maps to-day, covering
Poverty Bay. The natives here were unfriendly, and
Cook was obliged to use firearms to prevent an attack.
The Maoris had never seen a great ship before, and at
first thought it was a very large bird, being struck by the
size and beauty of its wings (sails). When a small boat
was let down from the ship's side they thought it must be
a young unfledged bird, but when the white men in their
bright-coloured clothes rowed off in the boat they concluded these were gods.

Cook found the low sandy coast backed by well-wooded hills rising to mountains on which patches of snow were visible, while smoke could be seen through the trees, speaking of native dwellings. The natives were too treacherous to make it safe landing for the white men, so they sailed out of Poverty Bay and proceeded south. Angry Maoris shook their spears at the Englishmen as

AN IPAH, OR MAORI FORT, ON THE COAST BETWEEN POVERTY BAY
AND CAPE TURNAGAIN.

From an engraving in the Atlas to Cook's first *Voyage*.

they coasted south along the east coast of the North Island. But the face of the country was unpromising, and Cook altered his course for the north at a point he named Cape Turnagain. Unfortunately he missed the only safe port on the east coast between Auckland and Wellington, but he found good anchorage in what is now known as Cook's Bay. Here they got plenty of good fish, wild fowl, and oysters, " as good as ever came out of

Colchester." Taking possession of the land they passed
in the name of King George, Cook continued his northerly
course, passing many a river which seemed to resemble
the Thames at home. A heavy December gale blew them
off the northernmost point of land, which they named
North Cape, and Christmas was celebrated off Tasman's
islands, with goose-pie.

The New Year of 1770 found Cook off Cape Maria van
Diemen, sailing south along the western coast of the North
Island, till the *Endeavour* was anchored in Ship Cove,
Queen Charlotte's Sound, only about seventy miles from
the spot where Tasman first sighted land.

Here the English explorer landed. The country
was thickly wooded, but he climbed a hill, and away to
the eastward he saw that the seas washing both east and
west coasts of the northern island were united. He had
solved one problem. Tasman's Staaten Land was not
part of a great southern continent. He now resolved to
push through his newly discovered straits between the
two islands, and, having done this, he sailed north till he
reached Cape Turnagain. And so he proved beyond a
doubt that this was an island. The men thought they
had done enough. But Cook, with the true instinct
of an explorer, turned a deaf ear to the murmurings of his
crew for roast beef and Old England, and directed his
course again south. From the natives he had learned
of the existence of two islands, and he must needs sail
round the southern as he had sailed round the northern
isle. Storms and gales harassed the navigators through the
month of February as they made their way slowly southwards. Indeed, they had a very narrow escape from death
towards the end of the month, when in a two days' gale,
with heavy squalls of rain, their foresail was split to pieces
and they lost sight of land for seven days, nearly running
on to submerged rocks which Cook named The Traps.

It was nearly dark on 14th March when they entered a bay which they suitably christened Dusky Bay, from which they sailed to Cascade Point, named from the four streams that fell over its face.

" No country upon earth," remarks Cook, " can appear with a more rugged and barren aspect than this does from the sea, for, as far inland as the eye can reach, nothing is to be seen but the summit of these rocky mountains." At last on 24th March they rounded the north point of the South Island. Before them lay the familiar waters of Massacre Bay, Tasman Bay, and Queen Charlotte Sound.

" As we have now circumnavigated the whole of this country, it is time for me to think of quitting it," Cook remarks simply enough.

Running into Admiralty Bay, the *Endeavour* was repaired for her coming voyage home. Her sails, " ill-provided from the first," says Banks, " were now worn and damaged by the rough work they had gone through, particularly on the coast of New Zealand, and they gave no little trouble to get into order again."

While Banks searched for insects and plants, Cook sat writing up his *Journal* of the circumnavigation. He loyally gives Tasman the honour of the first discovery, but clearly shows his error in supposing it to be part of the great southern land.

The natives he describes as " a strong, raw-boned, well-made, active people rather above the common size, of a dark brown colour, with black hair, thin black beards, and white teeth. Both men and women paint their faces and bodies with red ochre mixed with fish oil. They wear ornaments of stone, bone, and shells at their ears and about their necks, and the men generally wear long white feathers stuck upright in their hair. They came off in canoes which will carry a hundred people ; when within a stone's throw of the ship, the chief of the party would brandish a battleaxe, calling out : ' Come ashore with us and we will kill you.' They would certainly have eaten them too, for they were cannibals."

The ship was now ready and, naming the last point of land Cape Farewell, they sailed away to the west, " till we fall in with the east coast of New Holland." They had spent six and a half months sailing about in New Zealand waters, and had coasted some two thousand four hundred miles.

Nineteen days' sail brought them to the eagerly sought coast, and on 28th April, Cook anchored for the first time in the bay known afterwards to history as Botany Bay, so named from the quantity of plants found in the neighbourhood by Mr. Banks. Cutting an inscription on one of the trees, with the date and name of the ship, Cook sailed north early in May, surveying the coast as he passed and giving names to the various bays and capes. Thus Port Jackson, at the entrance of Sydney harbour, undiscovered by Cook, was so named after one of the Secretaries of the Admiralty—Smoky Cape from smoke arising from native dwellings—Point Danger by reason of a narrow escape on some shoals—while Moreton Bay, on which Brisbane, the capital of Queensland, now stands, was named after the President of the Royal Society. As they advanced, the coast became steep, rocky, and unpromising.

" Hitherto," reports Cook, " we had safely navigated this dangerous coast, where the sea in all parts conceals shores that project suddenly from the shore and rocks that rise abruptly like a pyramid from the bottom more than one thousand three hundred miles. But here we became acquainted with misfortune, and we therefore called the point which we had just seen farthest to the northward, Cape Tribulation."

It was the 10th of May. The gentlemen had left the

deck " in great tranquillity " and gone to bed, when suddenly the ship struck and remained immovable except for the heaving of the surge that beat her against the crags of the rock upon which she lay.   Every one rushed to the deck " with countenances which sufficiently expressed the horrors of our situation." Immediately they took in all sails, lowered the boats, and found they were on a reef of coral rocks.   Two days of sickening

CAPTAIN COOK'S VESSEL BEACHED AT THE ENTRANCE OF ENDEAVOUR RIVER, WHERE THE SEAPORT OF COOKTOWN NOW STANDS.

From an engraving in the Atlas to Cook's first *Voyage*.

anxiety followed, the ship sprang a leak, and they were threatened with total destruction.   To their intense relief, however, the ship floated off into deep water with a high tide.   Repairs were now more than ever necessary, and the poor battered collier was taken into the "*Endeavour*" river. Tupia and others were also showing signs of scurvy ; so a hospital tent was erected on shore, and with a supply of fresh fish, pigeons, wild plantains, and turtles they began to improve.   Here stands to-day the seaport of Cooktown, where a monument of Captain Cook looks out over the waters that he discovered.

The prospect of further exploration was not encouraging. " In whatever direction we looked, the sea was covered with shoals as far as the eye could see." As they sailed out of their little river, they could see the surf breaking on the " Great Barrier Reef." Navigation now became very difficult, and, more than once, even Cook himself almost gave up hope. Great, then, was their joy when they found themselves at the northern promontory of the land which " I have named York Cape in honour of His late Royal Highness the Duke of York. We were in great hopes that we had at last found out a passage into the Indian Seas." And he adds an important paragraph : " As I was now about to quit the eastern coast of New Holland, which I am confident no European had ever seen before, I once more hoisted the English colours, and I now took possession of the whole eastern coast in right of His Majesty King George III., by the name of New South Wales, with all the bays, harbours, rivers, and islands situated upon it."

This part of the new land was called by the name of New South Wales.

So the *Endeavour* sailed through the straits that Torres had accidentally passed one hundred and sixty-four years before, and, just sighting New Guinea, Cook made his way to Java, for his crew were sickly and " pretty far gone with longing for home." The ship, too, was in bad condition ; she had to be pumped night and day to keep her free from water, and her sails would hardly stand the least puff of wind. They reached Batavia in safety and were kindly received by the Dutch there.

Since leaving Plymouth two years before, Cook had only lost seven men altogether—three by drowning, two frozen, one from consumption, one from poisoning—none from scurvy—a record without equal in the history of Navigation. But the climate of Batavia now wrought havoc among the men. One after another died, Tupia among others, and so many were weakened with fever that only twenty officers and men were left on duty at one time.

Glad, indeed, they were to leave at Christmas time, and gladder still to anchor in the Downs and to reach London after their three years' absence. The news of his arrival and great discoveries seems to have been taken very quietly by those at home. " Lieutenant Cook of the Navy," says the *Annual Register* for 1771, " who sailed round the globe, was introduced to His Majesty at St. James's, and presented to His Majesty his *Journal* of his voyage, with some curious maps and charts of different places that he had drawn during the voyage ; he was presented with a captain's commission."

CHAPTER XLVI

COOK'S THIRD VOYAGE AND DEATH

ALTHOUGH the importance of his discoveries was not realised at this time, Cook was given command of two new ships, the *Resolution* and *Adventure*, provisioned for a year for "a voyage to remote parts," a few months later. And the old *Endeavour* went back to her collier work in the North Sea.

Perhaps a letter written by Cook to a friend at Whitby on his return from the second voyage is sufficient to serve our purpose here; for, though the voyage was important enough, yet little new was discovered. And after spending many months in high latitudes, Cook decided that there was no great southern continent to the south of New Holland and New Zealand.

"DEAR SIR,"—he writes from London in September 1775—" I now sit down to fulfil the promise I made you to give you some account of my last voyage. I left the Cape of Good Hope on 22nd November 1772 and proceeded to the south, till I met with a vast field of ice and much foggy weather and large islets or floating mountains of ice without number. After some trouble and not a little danger, I got to the south of the field of ice; and after beating about for some time for land, in a sea strewed with ice, I crossed the Antarctic circle and the same evening (17th January 1773) found it unsafe, or rather impossible, to stand farther to the south for ice.

" Seeing no signs of meeting with land in these high latitudes, I stood away to the northward, and, without seeing any signs of land, I thought proper to steer for New Zealand, where I anchored in Dusky Bay on 26th March and then sailed for Queen Charlotte's Sound. Again I put to sea and stood to the south, where I met with nothing but ice and excessive cold, bad weather. Here I spent near four months beating about in high latitudes. Once I got as high as seventy-one degrees, and farther it was not possible to go for ice which lay as firm as land. Here we saw ice mountains, whose summits were lost in clouds. I was now fully satisfied that there was no Southern Continent. I nevertheless resolved to spend some time longer in these seas, and with this resolution I stood away to the north."

In this second voyage Cook proved that there was no great land to the south of Terra Australis or South America, except the land of ice lying about the South Pole.

But he did a greater piece of work than this. He fought, and fought successfully, the great curse of scurvy, which had hitherto carried off scores of sailors and prevented ships on voyages of discovery, or indeed ships of war, from staying long on the high seas without constantly landing for supplies of fresh food. It was no uncommon occurrence for a sea captain to return after even a few months' cruise with half his men suffering from scurvy. Captain Palliser on H.M.S. *Eagle* in 1756 landed in Plymouth Sound with one hundred and thirty sick men out of four hundred, twenty-two having died in a month. Cook had resolved to fight this dreaded scourge, and we have already seen that during his three years' cruise of the *Endeavour* he had only to report five cases of scurvy, so close a watch did he keep on his crews. In his second voyage he was even more particular, with the result that in the course of three years he did not lose a single man from scurvy. He enforced cold bathing, and encouraged it by example. The allowance of salt beef and pork was cut down, and the habit of mixing salt beef fat with the flour was strictly forbidden. Salt butter and cheese were stopped, and raisins were substituted for salt suet; wild celery was collected in Terra del Fuego and breakfast made from this with ground wheat and portable soup. The cleanliness of the men was insisted on. Cook never allowed any one to appear dirty before him. He inspected the men once a week at least, and saw with his own eyes that they changed their clothing; equal care was taken to keep the ship clean and dry between decks, and she was constantly " cured with fires " or " smoked with gunpowder mixed with vinegar."

For a paper on this subject read before the Royal Society in 1776, James Cook was awarded a gold medal (now in the British Museum).

But although the explorer was now forty-eight, he was as eager for active adventure as a youth of twenty. He had settled the question of a southern continent. Now when the question of the North-West Passage came up again, he offered his services to Lord Sandwich, first Lord of the Admiralty, and was at once accepted. It was more than two hundred years since Frobisher had attempted to solve the mystery, which even Cook—the first navigator of his day—with improved ships and better-fed men, did not succeed in solving. He now received his secret instructions, and, choosing the old *Resolution* again, he set sail in company with Captain Clerke on board the *Discovery* in the year 1776 for that voyage from which there was to be no return. He was to touch at New Albion (discovered by Drake) and explore any rivers or inlets that might lead to Hudson's or Baffin's Bay.

After once more visiting Tasmania and New Zealand, he

made a prolonged stay among the Pacific Islands, turning north in December 1777. Soon after they had crossed the line, and a few days before Christmas, a low island was seen on which Cook at once landed, hoping to get a fresh supply of turtle. In this he was not disappointed. Some three hundred, " all of the green kind and perhaps as good as any in the world," were obtained ; the island was named Christmas Island, and the *Resolution* and *Discovery* sailed upon their way. A few days later they came upon a group of islands hitherto unknown. These they named after the Earl of Sandwich, the group forming the kingdom of Hawaii—the chief island. Natives came off in canoes bringing pigs and potatoes, and ready to exchange fish for nails. Some were tempted on board, " the wildness of their looks expressing their astonishment." Anchorage being found, Cook landed, and as he set foot on shore a large crowd of natives pressed forward and, throwing themselves on their faces, remained thus till Cook signed to them to rise.

CAPTAIN JAMES COOK.

From the painting by Dance in the gallery of Greenwich Hospital.

With a goodly supply of fresh provisions, Cook sailed away from the Sandwich Islands, and after some five weeks' sail to the north the " longed-for coast of New Albion was seen." The natives of the country were clad in fur, which they offered for sale. They exacted payment for everything, even for the wood and water that the strangers took from their shores. The weather was cold and stormy, and the progress of the little English ships was slow. By 22nd March they had passed Cape Flattery; a week later they named Hope Bay, " in which we hoped to find a good harbour, and the event proved we were not mistaken." All this part of the coast was called by Cook King George's Sound, but the native name of Nootka has since prevailed. We have an amusing account of these natives. At first they were supposed to be dark coloured, " till after much cleaning they were found to have skins like our people in England." Expert thieves they were. No piece of iron was safe from them. " Before we left the place," says Cook, " hardly a bit of brass was left in the ship. Whole suits of clothes were stripped of every button, copper kettles, tin canisters, candlesticks, all went to wreck, so that these people got a greater variety of things from us than any other people we had visited."

It was not till 26th April that Cook at last managed to start forward again, but a two days' hard gale drove him from the coast and onwards to a wide inlet to which he gave the name of Prince William's Sound. Here the natives were just like the Eskimos in Hudson's Bay. The ships now sailed westward, doubling the promontory of Alaska, and on 9th August they reached the westernmost point of North America, which they named Cape Prince of Wales. They were now in the sea discovered by Behring, 1741, to which they gave his name. Hampered by fog and ice, the ships made their way slowly on to a point named Cape North. Cook decided that the eastern point of Asia was but thirteen leagues from the western point of America. They named the Sound on the American side Norton Sound after the Speaker of the House of Commons. Having passed the Arctic Circle and penetrated into the Northern Seas, which were never free from ice, they met Russian traders who professed to have known Behring.

CAPTAIN COOK, THE DISCOVERER OF THE SANDWICH ISLANDS, WITH HIS SHIPS IN KEALAKEKUA BAY, HAWAII, WHERE HE WAS MURDERED.

From an engraving in the Atlas to *Cook's Voyages*, 1779.

Then having discovered four thousand miles of new coast, and refreshed themselves with walrus or sea - horse, the expedition turned joyfully back to the Sandwich Islands.

On the last day of November, Cook discovered the island of Owhyhee (Hawaii), which he carefully surveyed, till he came to anchor in Karakakooa Bay.

The tragic death of Captain Cook at the hands of these natives is well known to every child. The reason for his murder is not entirely understood to-day, but the natives, who had hitherto proved friendly, suddenly attacked the English explorer and slew him, and " he fell into the water and spoke no more."

Such was the melancholy end of England's first great navigator—James Cook—the foremost sailor of his time, the man who had circumnavigated New Zealand, who had explored the coast of New South Wales, named various unknown islands in the Pacific Ocean, and discovered the Sandwich Islands. He died on 14th February 1779. It was not till 11th January 1780 that the news of his death reached London, to be recorded in the quaint language of the day by the *London Gazette*.

" It is with the utmost concern," runs the announcement, " that we inform the Public, that the celebrated Circumnavigator, Captain Cook, was killed by the inhabitants of a new-discover'd island in the South Seas. The Captain and crew were first treated as deities, but, upon their revisiting that Island, hostilities ensued and the above melancholy scene was the Consequence. This account is come from Kamtchatka by Letters from Captain Clerke and others. But the crews of the Ships were in a very good state of health, and all in the most desirable condition. His successful attempts to preserve the Healths of his Crews are well known, and his Discoveries will be an everlasting Honour to his Country."

Cook's First Voyages were published in 1773, and were widely read, but his account of the new country did not at once attract Europeans to its shores. We hear of "barren sandy shores and wild rocky coast inhabited by naked black people, malicious and cruel," on the one hand, "and low shores all white with sand fringed with foaming surf," with hostile natives on the other.

It was not till eighteen years after Cook's death that Banks—his old friend—appealed to the British Government of the day to make some use of these discoveries. At last the loss of the American colonies in 1776 induced men to turn their eyes toward the new land in the South Pacific. Banks remembered well his visit to Botany Bay with Captain Cook in 1770, and he now urged the dispatch of convicts, hitherto transported to America, to this newly found bay in New South Wales.

So in 1787 a fleet of eleven ships with one thousand people on board left the shores of England under the command of Captain Phillip. After a tedious voyage of thirty-six weeks, they reached Botany Bay in January 1788.

Captain Phillip had been appointed Governor of all New South Wales, that is from Cape York to Van Diemen's Land, still supposed to be part of the mainland. But Phillip at once recognised that Botany Bay was not a suitable place for a settlement. No white man had described these shores since the days of Captain Cook. The green meadows of which Banks spoke were barren swamps and bleak sands, while the bay itself was exposed to the full sweep of violent winds, with a heavy sea breaking with tremendous surf against the shore.

"Warra, warra!" (begone, begone), shouted the natives, brandishing spears at the water's edge as they had done eighteen years before. In an open boat—for it was midsummer in these parts—Phillip surveyed the coast; an

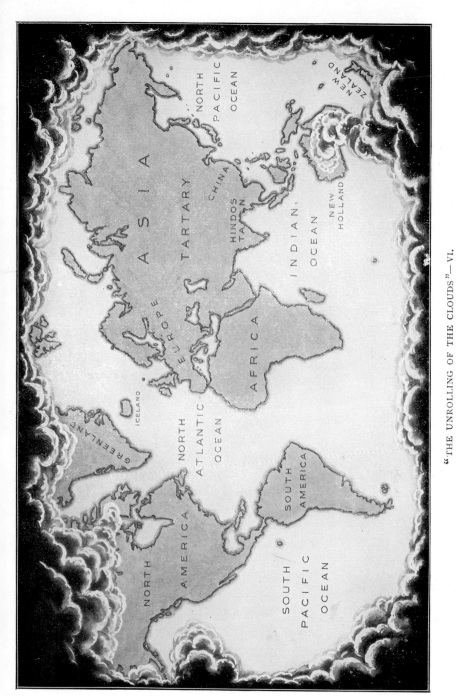

"THE UNROLLING OF THE CLOUDS"— VI.

The world as known after the voyages of Captain Cook (1768–1779).

opening marked Port Jackson on Cook's chart attracted his notice and, sailing between two rocky headlands, the explorer found himself crossing smooth, clear water with a beautiful harbour in front and soft green foliage reaching down to the water's edge. Struck with the loveliness of the scene, and finding both wood and water here, he chose the spot for his new colony, giving it the name of Sydney, after Lord Sydney, who as Home Secretary had appointed him to his command.

"We got into Port Jackson," he wrote to Lord Sydney,

PORT JACKSON AND SYDNEY COVE A FEW YEARS AFTER COOK AND PHILLIP.
From the Atlas to the *Voyage de l'Astrolabe.*

"early in the afternoon, and had the satisfaction of finding the finest harbour in the world, in which a thousand sail of the line may ride in perfect security."

"To us," wrote one of his captains, "it was a great and important day, and I hope will mark the foundation of an empire."

But, interesting as it is, we cannot follow the fortunes of this first little English colony in the South Pacific Ocean.

The English had not arrived a day too soon. A few

22

days later the French explorer, La Perouse, guided hither by Cook's chart, suddenly made his appearance on the shores of Botany Bay. The arrival of two French men-of-war caused the greatest excitement among the white strangers and the black natives.

La Perouse had left France in 1785 in command of two ships with orders to search for the North-West Passage from the Pacific side—a feat attempted by Captain Cook only nine years before—to explore the China seas, the Solomon Islands, and the Terra Australis. He had reached the coast of Alaska in June 1786, but after six weeks of bad weather he had crossed to Asia in the early part of the following year.

Thence he had made his way by the Philippine Islands to the coasts of Japan, Korea, and "Chinese Tartary." Touching at Quelpart, he reached a bay near our modern Vladivostock, and on 2nd August 1787 he discovered the strait that bears his name to-day, between Saghalien and the North Island of Japan. Fortunately, from Kamt-chatka, where he had landed, he had sent home his journals, notes, plans, and maps by Lesseps—uncle of the famous Ferdinand de Lesseps of Suez Canal fame.

On 26th January 1788 he landed at Botany Bay. From here he wrote his last letter to the French Government. After leaving this port he was never seen again. Many years later, in 1826, the wreck of his two ships was found on the reefs of an island near the New Hebrides.

CHAPTER XLVII

BRUCE'S TRAVELS IN ABYSSINIA

PERHAPS one of the strangest facts in the whole history of exploration is that Africa was almost an unknown land a hundred years ago, and stranger still, that there remains to-day nearly one-eleventh of the whole area still unexplored. And yet it is one of the three old continents that appear on every old chart of the world in ancient days, with its many-mouthed Nile rising in weird spots and flowing in sundry impossible directions. Sometimes it joins the mysterious Niger, and together they flow through country labelled "Unknown" or "Desert" or "Negroland," or an enterprising cartographer fills up vacant spaces with wild animals stalking through the land.

The coast tells a different tale. The west shores are studded with trading forts belonging to English, Danes, Dutch, and Portuguese, where slaves from the interior awaited shipment to the various countries that required negro labour. The slave trade was the great, in fact the only, attraction to Africa at the beginning of the eighteenth century. In pursuit of this, men would penetrate quite a long way into the interior, but through the long centuries few explorers had travelled to the Dark Continent.

Towards the end of the century we suddenly get one man—a young Scottish giant, named James Bruce, thirsting for exploration for its own sake. He cared not for slaves or gold or ivory. He just wanted to discover the source of the Nile, over which a great mystery had hung since the days of Herodotus. The Mountains of the Moon figure largely on the Old World maps, but Bruce decided to rediscover these for himself. Herodotus had said the Nile turned west and became the Niger, others said it turned east and somehow joined the Tigris and Euphrates. Indeed, such was the uncertainty regarding its source that to discover the source of the Nile seemed equivalent to performing the impossible.

James Bruce, athletic, daring, standing six feet four, seemed at the age of twenty-four made for a life of travel and adventure. His business took him to Spain and Portugal. He studied Arabic and the ancient language of Abyssinia. He came under the notice of Pitt, and was made consul of Algiers. The idea of the undiscovered sources of the Nile took strong hold of Bruce's imagination.

" It was at this moment," he says, " that I resolved that this great discovery should either be achieved by me or remain—as it has done for three thousand years— a defiance to all travellers."

A violent dispute with the old bey of Algiers ended Bruce's consulate, and in 1765, the spirit of adventure strong upon him, he sailed along the North African coast, landed at Tunis, and made his way to Tripoli. On the frontier he found a tribe of Arabs set apart to destroy the lions which beset the neighbourhood. These people not only killed but ate the lions, and they prevailed on Bruce to share their repast. But one meal was enough for the young explorer.

In burning heat across the desert sands he passed on. Once a great caravan arrived, journeying from Fez to Mecca, consisting of three thousand men with camels laden with merchandise. But this religious pilgrimage was plundered in the desert soon after. Arrived at Bengazi, Bruce found a terrible famine raging, so he embarked on a little Greek ship bound for Crete. It was crowded with Arabs; the captain was ignorant; a violent storm arose and, close to Bengazi, the ship struck upon a rock. Lowering a boat, Bruce and a number of Arabs sprang in and tried to row ashore. But wave after wave broke over them, and at last they had to swim for their lives. The surf was breaking on the shore, and Bruce was washed up breathless and exhausted. Arabs flocking down to plunder the wreck, found Bruce, and with blows and kicks stripped him of all his clothes and left him naked on the barren shore. At last an old Arab came along, threw a dirty rag over him, and led him to a tent, whence he reached Bengazi once more, and soon after crossed to Crete.

It was not till July 1768 that the explorer at last reached Cairo *en route* for Abyssinia, and five months later embarked on board a

A NILE BOAT, OR CANJA.

From Bruce's *Travels to Discover the Source of the Nile.*

Nile boat, or canja. His cabin had close latticed windows made not only to admit fresh air, but to be a defence against a set of robbers on the Nile, who were wont to swim under water in the dark or on goatskins to pilfer any passing boats. Then, unfurling her vast sails, the canja bore Bruce on the first stage of his great journey. The explorer spent some time in trying to find the lost site of old Memphis, but this was difficult. " A man's heart fails him in looking to the south," he says;

" he is lost in the immense expanse of desert, which he sees full of pyramids before him. Struck with terror from the unusual scene of vastness opened all at once upon leaving the palm trees, he becomes dispirited from the effect of the sultry climate."

For some days the canja, with a fair wind, stemmed the strong current of the Nile. " With great velocity" she raced past various villages through the narrow green valley of cultivation, till the scene changed and large plantations of sugar-canes and dates began. " The wind had now become so strong that the canja could scarcely carry her sails ; the current was rapid and the velocity with which she dashed against the water was terrible." Still she flew on day after day, till early in January they reached the spot " where spreading Nile parts hundred-gated Thebes." Solitude and silence reigned over the magnificent old sepulchres ; the hundred gates were gone, robbers swarmed, and the traveller hastened away. So on to Luxor and Karnac to a great encampment of Arabs, who held sway over the desert which Bruce had now to cross. The old sheikh, whose protection was necessary, known as the Tiger from his ferocious disposition, was very ill in his tent. Bruce gave him some lime water, which eased his pain, and, rising from the ground, the old Arab stood upright and cried : " Cursed be those of my people that ever shall lift up their hand against you in the desert."

He strongly advised Bruce to return to Kenne and cross the desert from there instead of going on by the Nile. Reluctantly Bruce turned back, and on 16th February 1769 he joined a caravan setting out to cross the desert to the shores of the Red Sea.

" Our road," he says, " was all the way in an open plain bounded by hillocks of sand and fine gravel—perfectly hard, but without trees, shrubs, or herbs. There

are not even the traces of any living creature, neither
serpent, lizard, antelope, nor ostrich—the usual inhabitants of the most dreary deserts. There is no sort of
water—even the birds seem to avoid the place as
pestilential—the sun was burning hot." In a few days
the scene changed, and Bruce is noting that in four days
he passes more granite, porphyry, marble, and jasper than
would build Rome, Athens, Corinth, Memphis, Alexandria,
and half a dozen more.

At last after a week's
travel they reached Cossier,
the little mud-walled village on the shores of the
Red Sea. Here Bruce em-
barked in a small boat, the
planks of which were sewn
together instead of nailed,
with a "sort of straw mat-
tress as a sail," for the
emerald mines described
by Pliny, but he was
driven back by a tremen-
dous storm. Determined
to survey the Red Sea, he
sailed to the north, and
after landing at Tor at the

AN ARAB SHEIKH.
From Bruce's *Travels*.

foot of Mount Sinai, he sailed down the bleak coast of
Arabia to Jidda, the port of Mecca.

By this time he was shaking with ague and fever,
scorched by the burning sun, and weather-beaten by wind
and storm—moreover, he was still dressed as a Turkish
soldier. He was glad enough to find kindly English at
Jidda, and after two months' rest he sailed on to the
Straits of Babelmandeb. Being now on English ground,
he drank the King's health and sailed across to Masuah,

the main port of Abyssinia. Although he had letters of introduction from Jidda he had some difficulty with the chief of Masuah, but at last, dressed in long white Moorish robes, he broke away, and in November 1769 started forth for Gondar, the capital of Abyssinia.

It was nearly one hundred and fifty years since any European of note had visited the country, and it was hard to get any information.

His way led across mountainous country—rugged and steep. " Far above the top of all towers that stupendous mass, the mountain of Taranta, probably one of the highest in the world, the point of which is buried in the clouds and very rarely seen but in the clearest weather ; at other times abandoned to perpetual mist and darkness, the seat of lightning, thunder, and of storm." Violent storms added to the terrors of the way, trees were torn up by the roots, and swollen streams rushed along in torrents.

Bruce had started with his quadrant carried by four men, but the task of getting his cumbersome instruments up the steep sides of Taranta was intense. However, they reached the top at last to find a huge plain, " perhaps one of the highest in the world," and herds of beautiful cattle feeding. " The cows were completely white, with large dewlaps hanging down to their knees, white horns, and long silky hair." After ninety-five days' journey, on 14th February Bruce reached Gondar, the capital, on the flat summit of a high hill.

Here lived the King of Abyssinia, a supposed descendant of King Solomon ; but at the present time the country was in a lawless and unsettled condition. Moreover, small-pox was raging at the palace, and the royal children were smitten with it. Bruce's knowledge of medicine now stood him again in good stead. He opened all the doors and windows of the palace, washed his little patients with vinegar and warm water, sent away those not already infected, and all recovered. Bruce had sprung into court favour. The ferocious chieftain, Ras Michael, who had killed one king, poisoned another, and was now ruling in the name of a third, sent for him. The old chief was dressed in a coarse, dirty garment wrapped round him like a blanket, his long white hair hung down over his shoulders, while behind him stood soldiers, their lances ornamented with shreds of scarlet cloth, one for every man slain in battle.

Bruce was appointed " Master of the King's horse," a high office and richly paid.

But " I told him this was no kindness," said the explorer. " My only wish was to see the country and find the sources of the Nile."

But time passed on and they would not let him go, until, at last, he persuaded the authorities to make him ruler over the province where the Blue Nile was supposed to rise. Amid great opposition he at last left the palace of Gondar on 28th October 1770, and was soon on his way to the south " to see a river and a bog, no part of which he could take away "—an expedition wholly incomprehensible to the royal folk at Gondar. Two days' march brought him to the shores of the great Lake Tsana, into which, despite the fact that he was tremendously hot and that crocodiles abounded there, the hardy young explorer plunged for a swim. And thus refreshed he proceeded on his way. He had now to encounter a new chieftain named Fasil, who at first refused to give him leave to pass on his way. It was not until Bruce had shown himself an able horseman and exhibited feats of strength and prowess that leave was at last granted. Fasil tested him in this wise. Twelve horses were brought to Bruce, saddled and bridled, to know which he would like to ride. Selecting an apparently quiet beast, the young traveller mounted.

" For the first two minutes," he says, " I do not know whether I was most in the earth or in the air ; he kicked behind, reared before, leaped like a deer all four legs off the ground—he then attempted to gallop, taking the bridle in his teeth; he continued to gallop and ran away as hard as he could, flinging out behind every ten yards, till he had no longer breath or strength and I began to think he would scarce carry me to the camp."

On his return Bruce mounted his own horse, and, taking his double-barrelled gun, he rode about, twisting and turning his horse in every direction, to the admiration of these wild Abyssinian folk. Not only did Fasil now let him go, but he dressed him in a fine, loose muslin garment which reached to his feet, gave him guides and a handsome grey horse.

" Take this horse," he said, " as a present from me. Do not mount it yourself; drive it before you, saddled and bridled as it is; no man will touch you when he sees that horse." Bruce obeyed his orders, and the horse was driven in front of him. The horse was magic; the people gave it handfuls of barley and paid more respect to it than to Bruce himself, though in many cases the people seemed scared by the appearance of the horse and fled away.

On 2nd November the Nile came into sight. It was only two hundred and sixty feet broad; but it was deeply revered by the people who lived on its banks. They refused to allow Bruce to ride across, but insisted on his taking off his shoes and walking through the shallow stream. It now became difficult to get food as they crossed the scorching hot plains. But Bruce was nearing his goal, and at last he stood at the top of the great Abyssinian tableland. " Immediately below us appeared the Nile itself, strangely diminished in size, now only a brook that had scarcely water to turn a mill."

Throwing off his shoes, trampling down the flowers that
grew on the mountain-side, falling twice in his excitement, Bruce ran down in breathless haste till he reached
the "hillock of green sod" which has made his name so
famous.

"It is easier to guess than to describe the situation
of my mind at that moment, standing in that spot
which had baffled the genius, industry, and inquiry of
both ancients and moderns for the course of near three
thousand years. Kings had attempted this discovery at
the heads of their armies—fame, riches, and honour had
been held out for a series of ages without having produced
one man capable of wiping off this stain upon the enterprise and abilities of mankind or adding this desideratum
for the encouragement of geography. Though a mere
private Briton, I triumphed here over kings and their
armies. I was but a few minutes arrived at the source
of the Nile, through numberless dangers and sufferings,
the least of which would have overwhelmed me but for
the continual goodness and protection of Providence.
I was, however, but then half through my journey, and
all those dangers which I had already passed awaited me
again on my return. I found a despondency gaining
ground fast upon me and blasting the crown of laurels
I had too rashly woven for myself."

Bruce then filled a large cocoa-nut shell, which he had
brought from Arabia, full of the Nile water, and drank
to the health of His Majesty King George III.

CHAPTER XLVIII

MUNGO PARK AND THE NIGER

BRUCE died in the spring of 1794. Just a year later another Scotsman, Mungo Park, from Selkirk, started off to explore the great river Niger—whose course was as mysterious as that of the Nile. Most of the early geographers knew something of a great river running through Negroland. Indeed, Herodotus tells of five young men, the Nasamones, who set out to explore the very heart of Africa. Arrived at the edge of the great sandy desert, they collected provisions and supplied themselves with water and plunged courageously into the unknown. For weary days they made their way across to the south, till they were rewarded by finding themselves in a fertile land well watered by lakes and marshes, with fruit trees and a little race of men and women whom they called pigmies.

And a large river was flowing from west to east—probably the Niger. But the days of Herodotus are long since past. It was centuries later when the Arabs, fiery with the faith of Mohammed, swept over the unexplored lands. " With a fiery enthusiasm that nothing could withstand, and inspired by a hope of heaven which nothing could shake, they swept from district to district, from tribe to tribe," everywhere proclaiming to roving multitudes the faith of their master. In this spirit they had faced the terrors of the Sahara Desert, and in the tenth century reached the land of the negroes, found the

Niger, and established schools and mosques westward of Timbuktu.

Portugal had then begun to play her part, and the fifteenth century is full of the wonderful voyages inspired by Prince Henry of Portugal, which culminated in the triumph of Vasco da Gama's great voyage to India by the Cape of Good Hope.

Then the slave trade drew the Elizabethan Englishmen to the shores of West Africa, and the coast was studded with forts and stations in connection with it. Yet in the eighteenth century the Niger and Timbuktu were still a mystery.

In 1778 the African Association was founded, with our old friend Sir Joseph Banks as an active member inquiring for a suitable man to follow up the work of the explorer Houghton, who had just perished in the desert on his way to Timbuktu.

The opportunity produced the man. Mungo Park, a young Scotsman, bitten with the fever of unrest, had just returned from a voyage to the East on board an East India Company's ship. He heard of this new venture, and applied for it. The African Association instantly accepted his services, and on 22nd May 1795, Mungo Park left England on board the *Endeavour*, and after a pleasant voyage of thirty days landed at the mouth of the river Gambia. The river is navigable for four hundred miles from its mouth, and Park sailed up to a native town, where the *Endeavour* was anchored, while he set out on horseback for a little village, Pisania, where a few British subjects traded in slaves, ivory, and gold. Here he stayed a while, to learn the language of the country. Fever delayed him till the end of November, when the rains were over, the native crops had been reaped, and food was cheap and plentiful. On 3rd December he made a start, his sole attendants being a negro servant, Johnson, and a slave boy. Mungo Park was mounted on a strong, spirited little horse, his attendants on donkeys. He had provisions for two days, beads, amber, and tobacco for buying fresh food, an umbrella, a compass, a thermometer and pocket sextant, some pistols and firearms, and " thus attended, thus provided, thus armed, Mungo Park started for the heart of Africa."

Three days' travelling brought him to Medina, where he found the old king sitting on a bullock's hide, warming himself before a large fire. He begged the English explorer to turn back and not to travel into the interior, for the people there had never seen a white man and would most certainly destroy him. Mungo Park was not so easily deterred, and taking farewell of the good old king, he took a guide and proceeded on his way.

A day's journey brought him to a village where a curious custom prevailed. Hanging on a tree, he found a sort of masquerading dress made out of bark. He discovered that it belonged to a strange bugbear known to all the natives of the neighbourhood as Mumbo Jumbo. The natives or Kafirs of this part had many wives, with the result that family quarrels often took place. If a husband was offended by his wife he disappeared into the woods, disguised himself in the dress of Mumbo Jumbo, and, armed with the rod of authority, announced his advent by loud and dismal screams near the town. All hurried to the accepted meeting-place, for none dare disobey. The meeting opened with song and dance till midnight, when Mumbo Jumbo announced the offending wife. The unlucky victim was then seized, stripped, tied to a post, and beaten with Mumbo's rod amid the shouts of the assembled company.

A few days before Christmas, Park entered Fatticonda —the place where Major Houghton had been robbed and badly used. He therefore took some amber, tobacco, and an

MUNGO PARK.

After a portrait in Park's *Travels into the Interior of Africa*, 1799.

umbrella as gifts to the king, taking care to put on his
best blue coat, lest it should be stolen. The king was
delighted with his gifts; he furled and unfurled his umbrella
to the great admiration of his attendants. " The king
then praised my blue coat," says Park, " of which the
yellow buttons seemed particularly to catch his fancy,
and entreated me to give it to him, assuring me that he
would wear it on all public occasions. As it was against
my interests to offend him by a refusal, I very quietly
took off my coat—the only good one in my possession—
and laid it at his feet." Then without his coat and
umbrella, but in peace, Park travelled onward to the
dangerous district which was so invested with robbers
that the little party had to travel by night. The howling
of wild beasts alone broke the awful silence as they crept
forth by moonlight on their way. But the news that a
white man was travelling through their land spread, and he
was surrounded by a party of horsemen, who robbed him
of nearly all his possessions. His attendant Johnson
urged him to return, for certain death awaited him.
But Park was not the man to turn back, and he was soon
rewarded by finding the king's nephew, who conducted
him in safety to the banks of the Senegal River.

Then he travelled on to the next king, who rejoiced in
the name of Daisy Korrabarri. Here Mungo learnt to his
dismay that war was going on in the province that lay
between him and the Niger, and the king could offer no
protection. Still nothing deterred the resolute explorer,
who took another route and continued his journey. Again
he had to travel by night, for robbers haunted his path,
which now lay among Mohammedans. He passed the
very spot where Houghton had been left to die of starvation in the desert. As he advanced through these inhospitable regions, new difficulties met him. His attendants
firmly refused to move farther. Mungo Park was now alone

in the great desert Negroland, between the Senegal and the Niger, as with magnificent resolution he continued his way. Suddenly a clear halloo rang out on the night air. It was his black boy, who had followed him to share his fate. Onward they went together, hoping to get safely through the land where Mohammedans ruled over low-caste negroes. Suddenly a party of Moors surrounded him, bidding him come to Ali, the chief, who wished to see a white man and a Christian. Park now found himself the centre of an admiring crowd. Men, women, and children crowded round him, pulling at his clothes and examining his waist-coat buttons till he could hardly move. Arrived at Ali's tent, Mungo found an old man with a long white beard. "The surrounding attendants, and especially the ladies, were most inquisitive; they asked a thousand questions, inspected every part of my clothes, searched my pockets, and obliged me to unbutton my waistcoat and display the whiteness of my skin—they even counted my toes and fingers, as if they doubted whether I was in truth a human being." He was lodged in a hut made of corn stalks, and a wild hog was tied to a stake as a suitable companion for the hated Christian. He was brutally ill-treated, closely watched, and insulted by " the rudest savages on earth." The desert winds scorched him, the sand choked him, the heavens above were like brass, the earth beneath as the floor of an oven. Fear came on him, and he dreaded death with his work yet unfinished. At last he escaped from this awful captivity amid the wilds of Africa. Early one morning at sunrise, he stepped over the sleeping negroes, seized his bundle, jumped on to his horse, and rode away as hard as he could. Looking back, he saw three Moors in hot pursuit, whooping and brandishing their double-barrelled guns. But he was beyond reach, and he breathed again. Now starvation stared him in the face. To the pangs of hunger were added the agony of

thirst. The sun beat down pitilessly, and at last Mungo fell
on the sand. "Here," he thought—"here after a short but
ineffectual struggle I must end all my hopes of being
useful in my day and generation; here must the short
span of my life come to an end."

But happily a great storm came and Mungo spread out
his clothes to collect the drops of rain, and quenched his
thirst by wringing them out and sucking them. After this
refreshment he led his tired horse, directing his way by

THE CAMP OF ALI, THE MOHAMMEDAN CHIEF, AT BENOWN.
From a sketch by Mungo Park.

the compass, lit up at intervals by vivid flashes of lightning. It was not till the third week of his flight that
his reward came. "I was told I should see the Niger
early next day," he wrote on 20th July 1796. "We
were riding through some marshy ground, when some one
called out 'See the water!' and, looking forwards, I
saw with infinite pleasure the great object of my mission
—the long-sought-for majestic Niger glittering to the
morning sun, as broad as the Thames at Westminster,

and flowing slowly *to the eastward.* I hastened to the brink and, having drunk of the water, lifted up my fervent thanks in prayer to the Great Ruler of all things, for having thus far crowned my endeavours with success. The circumstance of the Niger's flowing towards the east did not excite my surprise, for although I had left Europe in great hesitation on this subject, I had received from the negroes clear assurances that its general course was *towards the rising sun.*"

He was now near Sego—the capital of Bambarra—on the Niger, a city of some thirty thousand inhabitants. "The view of this extensive city, the numerous canoes upon the river, the crowded population, and the cultivated state of the surrounding country, formed altogether a prospect of civilisation and magnificence which I little expected to find in the bosom of Africa." The natives looked at the poor, thin, white stranger with astonishment and fear, and refused to allow him to cross the river. All day he sat without food under the shade of a tree, and was proposing to climb the tree and rest among its branches to find shelter from a coming storm, when a poor negro woman took pity on his deplorable condition. She took him to her hut, lit a lamp, spread a mat upon the floor, broiled him a fish, and allowed him to sleep. While he rested she spun cotton with other women and sang: "The winds roared and the rains fell. The poor white man, faint and weary, came and sat under our tree. He has no mother to bring him milk, no wife to grind his corn"; and all joined in the chorus: "Let us pity the white man, no mother has he."

Mungo Park left in the morning after presenting his landlady with two of his last four brass buttons. But though he made another gallant effort to reach Timbuktu and the Niger, which, he was told, "ran to the world's end," lions and mosquitoes made life impossible. His

horse was too weak to carry him any farther, and on
29th July 1796 he sadly turned back. " Worn down by
sickness, exhausted by hunger and fatigue, half-naked,
and without any article of value by which I might get
provisions, clothes, or lodging, I felt I should sacrifice
my life to no purpose, for my discoveries would perish
with me." Joining a caravan of slaves, he reached the coast

KAMALIA, A NATIVE VILLAGE NEAR THE SOUTHERN COURSE OF THE NIGER.
From a sketch by Mungo Park.

after some nineteen hundred miles, and after an absence
of two years and nine months he found a suit of English
clothes, "disrobed his chin of venerable encumbrance,"
and sailed for home. He published an account of the
journey in 1799, after which he married and settled in
Scotland as a doctor. But his heart was in Africa, and
a few years later he started off again to reach Timbuktu.
He arrived at the Gambia early in April 1805. " If

all goes well," he wrote gaily, "this day six weeks I expect to drink all your healths in the water of the Niger." He started this time with forty-four Europeans, each with donkeys to carry baggage and food, but it was a deplorable little party that reached the great river on 19th August. Thirty men had died on the march, the donkeys had been stolen, the baggage lost. And the joy experienced by the explorer in reaching the waters of the Niger, "rolling its immense stream along the plain," was marred by the reduction of his little party to seven. Leave to pass down the river to Timbuktu was obtained by the gift of two double-barrelled guns to the King, and in their old canoes patched together under the magnificent name of "His Majesty's schooner the *Joliba*" (great water), Mungo Park wrote his last letter home.

A NATIVE WOMAN WASHING GOLD IN SENEGAL.

From a sketch by Mungo Park made on his last expedition.

"I am far from desponding. I have changed a large canoe into a tolerably good schooner, on board of which I shall set sail to the east with a fixed resolution to discover the termination of the Niger or perish in the attempt; and though all the Europeans who are with me should die, and though I myself were half-dead, I would still persevere; and if I could not succeed in the object of my journey, I would at least die on the Niger."

It was in this spirit that the commander of the *Joliba* and a crew of nine set forth to glide down a great river toward the heart of savage Africa, into the darkness of the unexplored.

The rest is silence.

CHAPTER XLIX

WHILE Mungo Park was attempting to find the course of the Niger, the English were busy opening up the great fur-trading country in North America. Although Captain Cook had taken possession of Nootka Sound, thinking it was part of the coast of New Albion, men from other nations had been there to establish with the natives a trade in furs. The Spaniards were specially vigorous in opening up communications on this bleak bit of western coast. Great Britain became alarmed, and decided to send Captain Vancouver with an English ship to enforce her rights to this valuable port.

Vancouver had already sailed with Cook on his second southern voyage ; he had accompanied him on the *Discovery* during his last voyage. He therefore knew something of the coast of North-West America. " On the 15th of December 1790, I had the honour of receiving my commission as commander of His Majesty's sloop the *Discovery*, then lying at Deptford, where I joined her," says Vancouver. " Lieutenant Broughton having been selected as a proper officer to command the *Chatham*, he was accordingly appointed. At day dawn on Friday the 1st of April we took a long farewell of our native shores. Having no particular route to the Pacific Ocean pointed out in my instructions, I did not hesitate to prefer the passage by way of the Cape of Good Hope."

In boisterous weather Vancouver rounded the Cape,

made some discoveries on the southern coast of New Holland, surveyed part of the New Zealand coast, discovered Chatham Island, and on 17th April 1792 he fell in with the coast of New Albion. It was blowing and raining hard when the coast, soon after to be part of the United States of America, was sighted by the captains and crews of the *Discovery* and *Chatham*. Amid gales of wind and torrents of rain they coasted along the rocky and precipitous shores on which the surf broke with a dull roar. It was dangerous enough work coasting along this unsurveyed coast, full of sunken rocks on which the sea broke with great violence. Soon they were at Cape Blanco (discovered by Martin D'Aguilar), and a few days later at Cape Foulweather of Cook fame, close to the so-called straits discovered by the Greek pilot John da Fuca in 1592. Suddenly, relates Vancouver, " a sail was discovered to the westward. This was a very great novelty, not having seen any vessel during the last eight months. She soon hoisted American colours, and proved to be the ship *Columbia*, commanded by Captain Grey, belonging to Boston. He had penetrated about fifty miles into the disputed strait. He spoke of the mouth of a river that was inaccessible owing to breakers." (This was afterwards explored by Vancouver and named the Columbia River on which Washington now stands.)

Having examined two hundred and fifteen miles of coast, Vancouver and his two ships now entered the inlet —Da Fuca Straits—now the boundary between the United States and British Columbia. All day they made their way up the strait, till night came, and Vancouver relates with pride that " we had now advanced farther up this inlet than Mr. Grey or any other person from the civilised world."

" We are on the point of examining an entirely new region," he adds, " and in the most delightfully pleasant weather." Snowy ranges of hills, stately forest trees, vast spaces, and the tracks of deer reminded the explorers of " Old England." The crews were given holiday, and great joy prevailed. Natives soon brought them fish and venison for sale, and were keen to sell their children in exchange for knives, trinkets, and copper. As they advanced through the inlet, the fresh beauty of the country appealed to the English captain : " To describe the beauties of this region will be a very grateful task to the pen of a skilful panegyrist—the serenity of the climate, the pleasing landscapes, and the abundant fertility that unassisted nature puts forth, require only to be enriched by the industry of man with villages, mansions, and cottages to render it the most lovely country that can be imagined."

A fortnight was spent among the islands of this inlet, which " I have distinguished by the name of Admiralty Inlet," and on 4th June 1792 they drank the health of the King, George III., in a double allowance of grog, and on his fifty-fourth birthday took formal possession of the country, naming the wider part of the strait the Gulf of Georgia and the mainland New Georgia. The two ships then made their way through the narrow and intricate channels separating the island of Vancouver from the mainland of British Columbia, till at last, early in August, they emerged into an open channel discovered by an Englishman four years before and named Queen Charlotte's Sound. Numerous rocky islets made navigation very difficult, and one day in foggy weather the *Discovery* suddenly grounded on a bed of sunken rocks. The *Chatham* was near at hand, and at the signal of distress lowered her boats for assistance. For some hours, says Vancouver, " immediate and inevitable destruction presented itself." She grounded at four in the p.m. Till two next morning all hands were working at throwing ballast overboard to lighten her, till, " to our inexpressible joy," the return of the tide floated her once more. Having now satisfied himself that this was an island lying close to the mainland, Vancouver made for Nootka Sound, where he arrived at the end of August.

At the entrance of the Sound he was visited by a Spanish officer with a pilot to lead them to a safe anchorage in Friendly Cove, where the Spanish ship, under one Quadra, was riding at anchor. Civilities were interchanged " with much harmony and festivity. As many officers as could

VANCOUVER'S SHIP, THE *DISCOVERY*, ON THE ROCKS IN
QUEEN CHARLOTTE'S SOUND.
From a drawing in Vancouver's *Voyage*, 1798.

be spared from the vessel and myself dined with Señor Quadra, and were gratified with a repast we had lately been little accustomed to. A dinner of five courses, consisting of a superfluity of the best provisions, was served with great elegance ; a royal salute was fired on drinking health to the sovereigns of England and Spain, and a salute of seventeen guns to the success of the service in which the *Discovery* and *Chatham* were engaged." But when the true nature of Vancouver's mission was disclosed, there was some little difficulty, for the Spaniards had fortified Nootka, built houses, laid out gardens, and evidently intended to stay. Vancouver sent Captain Broughton home to report the conduct of the Spaniards, and spent his time surveying the coast to the south. Finally all was arranged satisfactorily, and Vancouver sailed off to the Sandwich Islands. When he returned home in the autumn of 1794 he had completed the gigantic task of surveying nine thousand miles of unknown coast chiefly in open boats, with only the loss of two men in both crews—a feat that almost rivalled that of Captain Cook.

It has been said that Vancouver " may proudly take his place with Drake, Cook, Baffin, Parry, and other British navigators to whom England looks with pride and geographers with gratitude."

CHAPTER L

MACKENZIE AND HIS RIVER

EVEN while Vancouver was making discoveries on the western coast of North America, Alexander Mackenzie, an enthusiastic young Scotsman, was making discoveries on behalf of the North-Western Company, which was rivalling the old Hudson Bay Company in its work of expansion. His journey right across America from sea to sea is worthy of note, and it has well been said that " by opening intercourse between Atlantic and Pacific Oceans and forming regular establishments through the interior and at both extremes, as well as along the coasts and islands, the entire command of the fur trade of North America might be obtained. To this may be added the fishing in both seas and the markets of the four quarters of the globe."

Mackenzie had already explored the great river flowing through North America to the Arctic seas in 1789. He had brought back news of its great size, its width, its volume of water, only to be mistrusted, till many years later it was found that every word was true, and tributes were paid not only to his general accuracy, but to his general intelligence as an explorer.

In 1792 he started off again, and this time he discovered the immense country that lay hidden behind the Rocky Mountains, known to-day as British Columbia. He ascended the Peace River, which flows from the Rocky Mountains, and in the spring of 1793, having made his way with much difficulty across this rugged chain, he embarked on a river running to the south-west. Through wild mountainous country on either side he paddled on; the cold was still intense and the strong mountain currents nearly dashed the canoes to pieces. His Indian guides were obstinate, ignorant, and timid. Mackenzie relates some of his difficulties in graphic language : " Throughout the whole of this day the men had been in a state of extreme ill-humour, and as they did not choose to vent it openly upon me, they disputed and quarrelled among themselves. About sunset the canoe struck upon the stump of a tree, which broke a large hole in her bottom, a circumstance that gave them an opportunity to let loose their discontents without reserve. I left them as soon as we had landed and ascended an elevated bank. It now remained for us to fix on a proper place for building another canoe, as the old one was become a complete wreck. At a very early hour of the morning every man was employed in making preparations for building another canoe, and different parties went in search of wood and gum." While the boat was building, Mackenzie gave his crew a good lecture on their conduct. " I assured them it was my fixed unalterable determination to proceed in spite of every difficulty and danger."

The result was highly satisfactory. " The conversation dropped and the work went on."

In five days the canoe was ready and they were soon paddling happily onwards towards the sea, where the Indians told him he would find white men building houses. They reached the coast some three weeks later. The Salmon River, as it is called, flows through British Columbia and reaches the sea just north of Vancouver Island, which had been discovered by Vancouver the year before.

Alexander Mackenzie had been successful. Let us hear the end of his tale : " I now mixed up some vermilion in melted grease, and inscribed in large characters, on the south-east face of the rock on which we had slept last night, this brief memorial—' Alexander Mackenzie, from Canada, by land, the twenty-second of July, one thousand seven hundred and ninety three.' "

CHAPTER LI

PARRY DISCOVERS LANCASTER SOUND

THE efforts of Arctic explorers of past years, Frobisher, Davis, Baffin, Behring, and Cook, had all been more or less frustrated by the impenetrable barrier of ice, which seemed to stretch across the Polar regions like a wall, putting an end to all further advance.

Now, early in the nineteenth century, this impenetrable bar of ice had apparently moved and broken up into detached masses and icebergs. The news of a distinct change in the Polar ice was brought home by various traders in the Greenland waters, and soon gave rise to a revival of these voyages for the discovery of the North Pole and a passage round the northern coast of America to the Pacific Ocean. For this coast was totally unknown at this time. Information was collected from casual travellers, whale-fishers, and others, with the result that England equipped two ships for a voyage of discovery to the disputed regions. These were the *Isabella* (385 tons) and the *Alexander* (252 tons), Commander Ross being appointed to one and Lieutenant Parry to the other.

Parry had served on the coast of North America, and had written a little treatise on the stars in the Northern Hemisphere. He was thinking of offering his services for African discovery when he caught sight of a paragraph in a paper about an expedition for the discovery of the North-West Passage. He wrote at once that "he was ready for hot or for cold—Africa or the Polar regions."

And he was at once appointed to the latter. The object of the voyage was clearly set forth. The young explorers were to discover a passage from Davis Strait along the northern coast of America and through the Behring Strait into the Pacific Ocean. Besides this, charts and pictures were to be brought back, and a special artist was to accompany the expedition. Ross himself was an artist, and he has delightfully illustrated his own journals of the expedition. The ships were well supplied with books, and we find the journals of Mackenzie, Hearne, Vancouver, Cook, and other old travelling friends taken for reference—thirty Bibles and sixty Testaments were distributed among the crews. For making friends with the natives, we find a supply of twenty-four brass kettles, one hundred and fifty butchers' knives, three hundred and fifty yards of coloured flannel, one hundred pounds of snuff, one hundred and fifty pounds of soap, forty umbrellas, and much gin and brandy. The expedition left on 18th April 1818, and "I believe," says Ross, "there was not a man who did not indulge after the fashion of a sailor in feeling that its issue was placed in His hands whose power is most visible in the Great Deep."

Before June had set in, the two ships were ploughing their way up the west coast of Greenland in heavy snowstorms. They sailed through Davis Strait, past the island of Disco into Baffin's undefined bay. Icebergs stood high out of the water on all sides, and navigation was very dangerous. Towards the end of July a bay to which Ross gave the name of Melville Bay, after the first Lord of the Admiralty, was passed. " Very high mountains of land and ice were seen to the north side of Melville's Bay, forming an impassable barrier, the precipices next the sea being from one thousand to two thousand feet high."

The ships were sailing slowly past the desolate shores

amid these high icebergs when suddenly several natives appeared on the ice. Now Ross had brought an Eskimo with him named Sacheuse.

" Come on ! " cried Sacheuse to the astonished natives.

" No—no—go away ! " they cried. " Go away ; we can kill you ! "

" What great creatures are these ? " they asked, pointing to the ships. " Do they come from the sun or the moon ? Do they give us light by night or by day ? "

Pointing southwards, Sacheuse told them that the strangers had come from a distant country.

" That cannot be ; there is nothing but ice there," was the answer.

Soon the Englishmen made friends with these people, whom they called Arctic Highlanders, giving the name of the Arctic Highlands to all the land in the north-east corner of Baffin's Bay. Passing Cape York, they followed the almost perpendicular coast, even as Baffin had done. They passed Wolstenholme Sound and Whale Sound; they saw Smith's Sound, and named the capes on either side Isabella and Alexander after their two ships. And then Ross gave up all further discovery for the time being in this direction. " Even if it be imagined that some narrow strait may exist through these mountains, it is evident that it must for ever be unnavigable," he says decidedly. " Being thus satisfied that there could be no further inducement to continue longer in this place, I shaped my course for the next opening which appeared in view to the westward." This was the Sound which was afterwards called " Jones Sound."

" We ran nine miles among very heavy ice, until noon, when, a very thick fog coming on, we were obliged to take shelter under a large iceberg. Sailing south, but some way from land, a wide opening appeared which answered exactly to the Lancaster Sound of Baffin. Lieutenant

Parry and many of his officers felt sure that this was a strait communicating with the open sea to westward, and were both astonished and dismayed when Ross, declaring that he was " perfectly satisfied that there was no passage in this direction," turned back. He brought his expedition back to England after a seven months' trip. But, though he was certain enough on the subject, his officers did not agree with him entirely, and the subject of the North-West Passage was still discussed in geographical circles.

When young Lieutenant Parry, who had commanded the *Alexander* in Ross' expedition, was consulted, he pressed for further exploration of the far north. And two expeditions were soon fitted out, one under Parry and one under Franklin, who had already served with Flinders in Australian exploration. Parry started off first with instructions to explore Lancaster's Sound ; failing to find a passage, to explore Alderman Jones Sound, failing this again, Sir Thomas Smith's Sound. If he succeeded in getting through to the Behring Strait, he was to go to Kamtchatka and on to the Sandwich Islands. " You are to understand," ran the instructions, "that the finding of a passage from the Atlantic to the Pacific is the main object of this expedition."

On board the *Hecla*, a ship of three hundred and seventy-five tons, with a hundred-and-eighty-ton brig, the *Griper*, accompanying, Parry sailed away early in May 1819. The first week in July found him crossing the Arctic Circle amid immense icebergs against which a heavy southerly swell was violently agitated, " dashing the loose ice with tremendous force, sometimes raising a white spray over them to the height of more than a hundred feet, accompanied with a loud noise exactly resembling the roar of distant thunder."

The entrance to Lancaster Sound was reached on 31st

July, and, says Parry: "It is more easy to imagine than to describe the almost breathless anxiety which was now visible in every countenance, while, as the breeze increased to a fresh gale, we ran quickly up the Sound." Officers and men crowded to the masthead as the ships ran on and on till they reached Barrow's Strait, so named by them after the Secretary of the Admiralty.

"We now began to flatter ourselves that we had fairly

PARRY'S SHIPS, THE *HECLA* AND *GRIPER*, IN WINTER HARBOUR, DECEMBER 1819.
From a drawing in Parry's *Voyage for the North-West Passage*, 1821.

entered the Polar Sea, and some of the most sanguine among us had even calculated the bearing and distance of Icy Cape as a matter of no very difficult accomplishment."

Sailing westward, they found a large island, which they named Melville Island after the first Lord of the Admiralty, and a bay which still bears the name of Hecla and Griper Bay. "Here," says Parry, "the ensigns and pendants were hoisted, and it created in us no ordinary feelings of pleasure to see the British flag waving, for the first time, in those

24

regions which had hitherto been considered beyond the limits of the habitable world."

Winter was now quickly advancing, and it was with some difficulty that the ships were forced through the newly formed ice at the head of the Bay of the Hecla and Griper. Over two miles of ice, seven inches thick, had to be sawn through to make a canal for the ships. As soon as they were moored in " Winter Harbour " the men gave three loud and hearty cheers as a preparation for eight or nine months of long and dreary winter. By the end of September all was ready; plenty of grouse and deer remained as food through October, after which there were foxes and wolves. To amuse his men, Parry and his officers got up a play; *Miss in her Teens* was performed on 5th November, the last day of sun for ninety-six days to come. He also started a paper, *The North Georgian Gazette and Winter Chronicle*, which was printed in England on their return. The New Year, 1819, found the winter growing gloomier. Scurvy had made its appearance, and Parry was using every device in his power to arrest it. Amongst other things he grew mustard and cress in boxes of earth near the stove pipe of his cabin to make fresh vegetable food for the afflicted men. Though the sun was beginning to appear again, February was the coldest part of the year, and no one could be long out in the open without being frostbitten. It was not till the middle of April that a slight thaw began, and the thermometer rose to freezing point. On 1st August the ships were able to sail out of Winter Harbour and to struggle westward again. But they could not get beyond Melville Island for the ice, and after the ships had been knocked about by it, Parry decided to return to Lancaster Sound once more. Hugging the western shores of Baffin's Bay, the two ships were turned homewards, arriving in the Thames early in November 1820.

THE SEARCH FOR A NORTH-WEST PASSAGE : THE CREWS OF PARRY'S SHIPS, THE *HECLA* AND *GRIPER*, CUTTING
THROUGH THE ICE FOR A WINTER HARBOUR, 1819.

Drawn by William Westall, A.R.A., after a sketch by Lieut. Beechey, a member of the expedition.

" And," says Parry, " I had the happiness of seeing every officer and man on board both ships—ninety-three persons— return to their native country in as robust health as when they left it, after an absence of nearly eighteen months."

Parry had done more than this. He not only showed the possibility of wintering in these icy regions in good health and good spirits, but he had certainly discovered straits communicating with the Polar sea.

THE NORTH SHORE OF LANCASTER SOUND.

From a drawing in Parry's *Voyage for the North-West Passage*, 1821.

CHAPTER LII

THE FROZEN NORTH

MEANWHILE Franklin and Parry started on another expedition in the same month and year. While Parry's orders were to proceed from east to west, Franklin was to go from west to east, with a chance—if remote—that they might meet. He was to go by Hudson's Bay to the mouth of the Copper Mine River and then make his way by sea eastward along the coast. Franklin had made himself a name by work done in the Spitzbergen waters; he was to succeed in the end where others had failed in finding the North-West Passage. The party selected for this work consisted of Captain Franklin, Dr. Richardson, a naval surgeon, two midshipmen, Back and Hood, one of whom was afterwards knighted, and an English sailor named John Hepburn.

Just a fortnight after Parry's start these five English explorers sailed on board a ship belonging to the Hudson Bay Company, but it was the end of August before they arrived at the headquarters of the Company. They were cordially received by the Governor, and provided with a large boat well stored with food and arms. Amid a salute of many guns and much cheering the little party, with some Canadian rowers, started off for Cumberland House, one of the forts belonging to the Hudson Bay Company. Six weeks' hard travelling by rivers and lakes, now dragging the boats round rapids, now sleeping in " buffalo-robes " on the hard ground, brought the party to the

first stage of their journey. Snow was now beginning
to fall, and ice was thick on the rivers, when Franklin
resolved to push on to Lake Athabasca that he might
have more time to prepare for the coming voyage in the
summer. Leaving Richardson and Hood at the fort, he
started off with Back and the faithful Hepburn on
18th January 1820, in the very heart of the Arctic winter.
Friends at the fort had provided him with Indian snow-
shoes turned up at the toes like the prow of a boat—with
dog sledges, furs, leather trousers, drivers, and food for a
fortnight. The snow was very deep, and the dogs found
great difficulty in dragging their heavy burdens through
the snow. But the record was good. A distance of
eight hundred and fifty-seven miles was accomplished in
sixty-eight days, with the thermometer at fifty degrees
below zero. The hardships endured are very briefly
recorded: "Provisions becoming scarce; dogs without
food, except a little burnt leather; night miserably cold;
tea froze in the tin pots before we could drink it."

Lake Athabasca was reached on the 26th of March
and preparations for the voyage were pushed forward.
Four months later they were joined by Richardson and
Hood. "This morning Mr. Back and I had the sincere
gratification of welcoming our long-separated friends,
Dr. Richardson and Mr. Hood, who arrived in perfect
health with two canoes." This is the simple entry in
Franklin's journal.

Everything was now ready. Spring in these northern
climates was enchanting. "The trees quickly put on their
leaves after the long, hard winter months, and the whole
vegetable world comes forth with a luxuriance no less
astonishing than agreeable." At the same time clouds of
mosquitoes and stinging sand-flies made the nights horrible.
On 18th July the little party in high glee set forward
in canoes rowed by Canadian boatmen, hoping to reach

the Copper Mine River before winter set in. But the difficulties of the way were great, provisions were scarce, the boatmen grew discontented, ice appeared early, and Franklin had to satisfy himself with wintering at a point five hundred and fifty miles from Lake Athabasca, which he called Fort Enterprise. Here there was prospect of plenty, for large herds of reindeer were grazing along the shores of the lake, and from their flesh " pemmican " was made; but the winter was long and cheerless, and Franklin soon realised that there was not enough food to last through it. So he dispatched the midshipman Back to Lake Athabasca for help. Back's journey was truly splendid, and we cannot omit his simple summary : " On the 17th of March," he says, " at an early hour we arrived at Fort Enterprise, having travelled about eighteen miles a day. I had the pleasure of meeting my friends all in good health, after an absence of nearly five months, during which time I had travelled one thousand one hundred and four miles on snow-shoes and had no other covering at night than a blanket and deer skin, with the thermometer frequently at forty degrees below zero, and sometimes two or three days without tasting food." By his courage and endurance he saved the whole party at Fort Enterprise. By June the spring was sufficiently advanced to set out for the Copper Mine River, and on July they reached the mouth after a tedious journey of three hundred and thirty-four miles.

The real work of exploration was now to begin, and the party embarked in two canoes to sail along the southern coast of the Polar sea, with the possibility always of meeting the Parry expedition. But the poor Canadian boatmen were terrified at the sight of the sea on which they had never yet sailed, and they were with difficulty persuaded to embark. Indeed, of the two crews, only the five Englishmen had ever been on the sea, and it has been well

said that this voyage along the shores of the rock-bound
coast of the Arctic sea must always take rank as one of
the most daring and hazardous exploits that have ever
been accomplished in the interest of geographical research.
" The two canoes hugged the icy coast as they made their
way eastward, and Franklin named the bays, headlands,
and islands for a distance of five hundred and fifty-five
miles, where a point he called Cape Turnagain marks his
farthest limit east. Here is George IV. Coronation Gulf

A WINTER VIEW OF FORT ENTERPRISE.
From a drawing, by Wm. Back, in Franklin's *Journey to the Polar Sea*, 1823.

studded with islands, Hood's River, Back's River, Bathurst's
Inlet, named after the Secretary of State, and Parry Bay
after " my friend, Captain Parry, now employed in the
interesting research for a North-West Passage."
    The short season for exploration was now over; rough
weather and want of food turned them home, only half
satisfied with their work. The worst part of their journey
was yet to come. Perhaps never, even in the tragic history
of Arctic exploration, had greater hardships been endured

than Franklin and his handful of men were to endure on their homeward way. On 22nd August the party left Point Turnagain, hoping by means of their newly discovered Hood River to reach Fort Enterprise. The ground was already covered with snow, and their food was reduced to one meal a day when they left the shores of the Arctic sea for their long inland tramp. Needless to say, the journey had to be performed on foot, and the way was stony and barren. For the first few days nothing was to be found save lichen to eat, and the temperature was far below freezing-point. An uncooked cow after six days of lichen " infused spirit into our starving party," relates Franklin. But things grew no better, and as they proceeded sadly on their way, starvation stared them in the face. One day we hear of the pangs of hunger being stilled by " pieces of singed hide mixed with lichen " ; another time the horns and bones of a dead deer were fried with some old shoes and the " putrid carcase of a deer that had died the previous spring was demolished by the starving men."

At last things grew so bad that Franklin and the most vigorous of his party pushed on to Fort Enterprise to get and send back food if possible to Richardson and Hood, who were now almost too weak and ill to get along at all. Bitter disappointment awaited them.

" At length," says Franklin, " we reached Fort Enterprise, and to our infinite disappointment and grief found it a perfectly desolate habitation. There were no provisions—no Indians. It would be impossible for me to describe our sensations after entering this miserable abode and discovering how we had been neglected; the whole party shed tears, not so much for our own fate as for that of our friends in the rear, whose lives depended entirely on our sending immediate relief from this place." A few old bones and skins of reindeer were collected for supper and the worn-out explorers sat round a fire made by pulling up the flooring of the rooms. It is hardly a matter of surprise to find the following entry in Franklin's journal : " When I arose the following morning my body and limbs were so swollen that I was unable to walk more than a few yards."

Before November arrived another tragedy happened. Hood was murdered by one of the party almost mad with hunger and misery. One after another now dropped down

FRANKLIN'S EXPEDITION TO THE POLAR SEA ON THE ICE.

From a drawing, by Wm. Back, in Franklin's *Journey to the Polar Sea*, 1823.

and died, and death seemed to be claiming Franklin, Richardson, Back, and Hepburn when three Indians made their appearance with some dried deer and a few tongues. It was not a moment too soon. The Indians soon got game and fish for the starving men, until they were sufficiently restored to leave Fort Enterprise and make their way to Moose Deer Island, where, with the Hudson Bay officers, they spent the winter recovering their health and strength and spirits.

When they returned to England in the summer of 1822 they had accomplished five thousand five hundred and fifty miles. They had also endured hardships unsurpassed in the history of exploration. When Parry returned to England the following summer and heard of Franklin's sufferings he cried like a child. He must have realised better than any one else what those sufferings really were, though he himself had fared better.

While Franklin had been making his way to the Copper Mine River, Parry on board the *Fury*, accompanied by the *Hecla*, started for Hudson's Strait, by which he was to penetrate to the Pacific, if possible. Owing to bad weather, the expedition did not arrive amid the icebergs till the middle of June. Towering two hundred feet high, the explorers counted fifty-four at one time before they arrived at Resolution Island at the mouth of Hudson Strait. There were already plenty of well-known landmarks in the region of Hudson's Bay, and Parry soon made his way to Southampton Island and Frozen Strait (over which an angry discussion had taken place some hundred years before). He was rewarded by discovering " a magnificent bay," to which he gave the name of the " Duke of York's Bay." The discovery, however, was one of little importance as there was no passage. The winter was fast advancing, the navigable season was nearly over, and the explorers seemed to be only at the beginning of their work. The voyage had been dangerous, harassing, unproductive.

They had advanced towards the Behring Strait; they had discovered two hundred leagues of North American coast, and they now prepared to spend the winter in these icebound regions. As usual Parry arranged both for the health and amusement of his men during the long Arctic months—even producing a " joint of English roast beef " for Christmas dinner, preserved " by rubbing the outside with salt and hanging it on deck covered with canvas." There were also Eskimos in the neighbourhood, who proved a never-ceasing source of interest.

One day in April—snow had been falling all night, news spread that the Eskimos " had killed something on the ice." " If the women," says Parry, " were cheerful before, they were now absolutely frantic. A general shout of joy re-echoed through the village ; they ran into each others' huts to communicate the welcome intelligence,

AN ESKIMO WATCHING A SEAL HOLE.

From a drawing in Parry's *Second Voyage for a North-West Passage*, 1824.

and actually hugged one another in an ecstasy of delight. When the first burst of joy had at last subsided the women crept one by one into the apartment where the sea-horses had been conveyed. Here they obtained blubber enough to set all their lamps alight, besides a few scraps of meat for their children and themselves. Fresh cargoes were continually arriving, the principal part being brought in by the dogs and the rest by the men, who tied a thong round their waist and dragged in a portion. Every lamp was now swimming with oil, the huts exhibited a blaze of light, and never was there a scene of more joyous festivity than while the cutting up of the walruses continued." For three solid hours the Eskimos appeared to be eating walrus flesh. "Indeed, the quantity they continued to get rid of is almost beyond belief."

It was not till early in July that the ship could be moved out of their winter's dock to renew their efforts towards a passage. They were not a little helped by Eskimo charts, but old ice blocked the way, and it was the middle of August before Parry discovered the Strait he called after his two ships, " the Strait of the Fury and Hecla," between Melville Peninsula and Cockburn Island. Confident that the narrow channel led to the Polar seas, Parry pushed on till " our progress was once more opposed by a barrier of the same impenetrable and hopeless ice as before." He organised land expeditions, and reports, "The opening of the Strait into the Polar sea was now so decided that I considered the principal object of my journey accomplished."

September had come, and once more the ships were established in their winter quarters. A second month in among the ice must have been a severe trial to this little band of English explorers, but cheerfully enough they built a wall of snow twelve feet high round the *Fury* to keep out snowdrifts. The season was long and severe, and it was August before they could get free of ice. The prospect of a third winter in the ice could not be safely faced, and Parry resolved to get home. October found them at the Shetlands, all the bells of Lerwick being set ringing and the town illuminated with joy at the arrival of men who had been away from all civilisation for twenty-seven months. On 14th November 1823 the expedition arrived home in England.

Still the restless explorer was longing to be off again ; he was still fascinated by the mysteries of the Arctic regions, but on his third voyage we need not follow him, for the results were of no great importance. The *Fury* was wrecked amid the ice in Prince Regent's Inlet, and the whole party had to return on board the *Hecla* in 1825.

CHAPTER LIII

FRANKLIN'S LAND JOURNEY TO THE NORTH

THE northern shores of North America were not yet explored, and Franklin proposed another expedition to the mouth of the Mackenzie River, where the party was to divide, half of them going to the east and half to the west. Nothing daunted by his recent sufferings, Franklin accepted the supreme command, and amid the foremost volunteers for service were his old friends, Back and Richardson. The officers of the expedition left England in February 1825, and, travelling by way of New York and Canada, they reached Fort Cumberland the following June; a month later they were at Fort Chipewyan on the shores of Lake Athabasca, and soon they had made their way to the banks of the Great Bear Lake River, which flows out of that lake into the Mackenzie River, down which they were to descend to the sea. They decided to winter on the shores of the Bear Lake; but Franklin could never bear inaction, so he resolved to push on to the mouth of the Great River with a small party in order to prospect for the coming expedition.

So correct had been Mackenzie's survey of this Great River, as it was called, that Franklin, " in justice to his memory," named it the Mackenzie River after its " eminent discoverer," which name it has borne ever since. In a little English boat, with a fair wind and a swift current, Franklin accomplished three hundred and twelve miles in about sixty hours. The saltness of the water, the

sight of a boundless horizon, and the appearance of porpoises and whales were encouraging signs. They had
reached the Polar sea at last—the " sea in all its majesty,
entirely free from ice and without any visible obstruction
to its navigation."

On reaching the coast a silken Union Jack worked by
Franklin's dying wife was unfurled. She had died a
few days after he left England, but she had insisted on
her husband's departure in the service of his country,

FORT FRANKLIN, ON THE GREAT BEAR LAKE, IN THE WINTER.
From a drawing in Franklin's *Second Expedition to the Polar Sea*, 1828.

only begging him not to unfurl her flag till he arrived at
the Polar shores. As it fluttered in the breeze of these
desolate shores, the little band of Englishmen cheered
and drank to the health of the King.

"You can imagine," says Franklin, "with what
heartfelt emotion I first saw it unfurled ; but in a short
time I derived great pleasure in looking at it."

It was too late to attempt navigation for this year,
although the weather in August was " inconveniently
warm," so on 5th September, Franklin returned to winter

quarters on the Great Bear Lake. During his absence a comfortable little settlement had grown up to accommodate some fifty persons, including Canadian and Indian hunters with their wives and children. In honour of the commander it had been called Fort Franklin, and here the party of explorers settled down for the long months of winter.

"As the days shortened," says Franklin, "it was necessary to find employment during the long evenings for those resident at the house, and a school was established from seven to nine for their instruction in reading, writing, and arithmetic, attended by most of the British party. Sunday was a day of rest, and the whole party attended Divine Service morning and evening. If on other evenings the men felt the time tedious, the hall was at their service to play any game they might choose, at which they were joined by the officers. Thus the men became more attached to us, and the hearts and feelings of the whole party were united in one common desire to make the time pass as agreeably as possible to each other, until the return of spring should enable us to resume the great object of the expedition."

April brought warmer weather, though the ground was still covered with snow, and much boat-building went on. In May swans had appeared on the lake, then came geese, then ducks, then gulls and singing birds. By June the boats were afloat, and on the 24th the whole party embarked for the Mackenzie River and were soon making their way to the mouth. Here the party divided. Franklin on board the *Lion*, with a crew of six, accompanied by Back on board the *Reliance*, started westwards, while Richardson's party was to go eastwards and survey the coast between the mouth of the Mackenzie River and the Copper Mine. On 7th July, Franklin reached the sea, and, with flags flying, the *Lion* and the *Reliance* sailed forth on the unknown seas, only to ground a mile from shore. Suddenly some three hundred canoes full of Eskimos crowded towards them. These people had never seen a white man before, but when it was explained to them that the English had come to find a channel for large ships to come and trade with them, they "raised the most deafening shout of applause." They still crowded round the little English boats, till at last, like others of their race, they began to steal things from the boats. When detected they grew furious and brandished knives, they tore the buttons

FRANKLIN'S EXPEDITION CROSSING BACK'S INLET.

From a drawing, by Lieut. Back, in Franklin's *Second Expedition to the Polar Sea*, 1828.

off the men's coats, and for a time matters looked serious till the English showed their firearms, when the canoes paddled away and the Eskimos hid themselves.

With a fair wind the boats now sailed along the coast westward, till stopped by ice, which drove them from the shore. Dense fogs, stormy winds, and heavy rain made this Polar navigation very dangerous; but the explorers pushed on till, on 27th July, they reached the mouth of a broad river which, " being the most westerly river in the British dominions on this coast and near the line of demarcation between Great Britain and Russia, I named it

25

the Clarence," says Franklin, " in honour of His Royal Highness the Lord High Admiral." A box containing a royal medal was deposited here, and the Union Jack was hoisted amid hearty cheers.

Still fogs and storms continued ; the farther west they advanced, the denser grew the fog, till by the middle of August, winter seemed to have set in. The men had suffered much from the hard work of pulling and dragging the heavy boats; they also endured torments from countless swarms of mosquitoes. They were now some three hundred and seventy-four miles from the mouth of the Mackenzie River and only half-way to Icy Cape; but Franklin, with all his courage and with all his enthusiasm, dared not risk the lives of his men farther. " Return Reef " marks his farthest point west, and it was not till long after that he learnt that Captain Beechey, who had been sent in the *Blossom* by way of Behring Strait, had doubled Icy Cape and was waiting for Franklin one hundred and sixty miles away.

On 21st September, Fort Franklin was reached after three months' absence. Dr. Richardson had already returned after a successful coast voyage of some eight hundred miles.

When he had left Franklin he had, on board the *Dolphin*, accompanied by the *Union*, sailed along the unknown coast eastward. Like Franklin's party, his expedition had also suffered from fogs, gales, and mosquitoes, but they had made their way on, naming inlets, capes, and islands as they passed. Thus we find Russell Inlet, Point Bathurst, Franklin's Bay, Cape Parry, the Union and Dolphin Straits, named after the two little ships, where the *Dolphin* was nearly wrecked between two masses of ice. They had reached Fort Franklin in safety just before Franklin's party, and, being too late to think of getting home this year, they were all doomed to another winter at the Fort. They reached England on 26th September 1827, after an absence of two years and a half.

Franklin had failed to find the North-West Passage, but he and Richardson had discovered a thousand miles of North American coast, for which he was knighted and received the Paris Geographical Society's medal for " the most important acquisition to geographical knowledge " made during the year. It was a curious coincidence that the two Arctic explorers, Franklin and Parry, both arrived in England the same month from their various expeditions, and appeared at the Admiralty within ten minutes of one another.

CHAPTER LIV

PARRY'S POLAR VOYAGE

PARRY had left England the preceding April in an attempt to reach the North Pole by means of sledges over the ice. To this end he had sailed to Spitzbergen in his old ship the *Hecla*, many of his old shipmates sailing with him. They arrived off the coast of Spitzbergen about the middle of May 1827. Two boats had been specially built in England, covered with waterproof canvas and lined with felt. The *Enterprise* and *Endeavour* had bamboo masts and paddles, and were constructed to go on sledges, drawn by reindeer, over the ice.

"Nothing," says Parry, "can be more beautiful than the training of the Lapland reindeer. With a simple collar of skin round his neck, a single trace of the same material attached to the sledge and passing between his legs, and one rein fastened like a halter round his neck, this intelligent and docile animal is perfectly under the command of an experienced driver, and performs astonishing journeys over the softest snow. Shaking the rein over his back is the only whip that is required."

Leaving the *Hecla* in safe harbour on the Spitzbergen coast, Parry and James Ross, a nephew of John Ross, the explorer, with food for two months, started off in their two boat-sledges for the north. They made a good start; the weather was calm and clear, the sea smooth as a mirror—walruses lay in herds on the ice, and, steering due north, they made good progress.

Next day, however, they were stopped by ice. Instead

of finding a smooth, level plain over which the reindeer could draw their sledges with ease, they found broken, rugged, uneven ice, which nothing but the keen enthusiasm of the explorer could have faced. The reindeer were useless, and they had to be relinquished; it is always supposed that they were eaten, but history is silent on this point. The little party had to drag their own boats over the rough ice. They travelled by night to save snow-blindness, also that they could enjoy greater warmth during the hours of sleep by day.

THE BOATS OF PARRY'S EXPEDITION HAULED UP ON THE ICE FOR THE NIGHT.
From a drawing in Parry's *Attempt to Reach the North Pole*, 1828.

Parry describes the laborious journey: " Being ' rigged ' for travelling," he says, " we breakfasted upon warm cocoa and biscuit, and after stowing the things in the boats we set off on our day's journey, and usually travelled about five and a half hours, then stopped an hour to dine, and again travelled five or six hours. After this we halted for the night as we called it, though it was usually early in the morning, selecting the largest surface of ice we happened to be near for hauling the boats on. The boats were placed close alongside each other, and the sails supported by bamboo masts placed over them as awnings. Every man then put on dry socks and fur boots and went to supper. Most of the officers and men then smoked their pipes, which served to dry the awnings. We then concluded our day with prayers and, having put on our fur dresses, lay down to sleep," alone in the great ice desert. Progress was slow and very tedious. One day it took them four hours to cover half a mile. On 1st July they were still labouring forward; a foot of soft snow on the ground made travelling very exhausting. Some of the hummocks of ice were as much as twenty-five feet above sea-level; nothing was to be seen but ice and sky, both often hidden by dense fog. Still the explorers pushed on, Parry and Ross leading the way and the men dragging the boat-sledges after. July 12th was a brilliant day, with clear sky overhead—" an absolute luxury." For another fortnight they persevered, and on 23rd July they reached their farthest point north. It was a warm, pleasant day, with the thermometer at thirty-six in the shade; they were a hundred and seventy-two miles from Spitzbergen, where the *Hecla* lay at anchor.

" Our ensigns and pendants were displayed during the day, and severely as we regretted not having been able to hoist the British flag in the highest latitude to which we had aspired, we shall perhaps be excused in having felt some little pride in being the bearers of it to a parallel considerably beyond that mentioned in any other well-authenticated record." On 27th July they reluctantly turned to the south, and on 21st August they arrived on board the *Hecla* after an absence of sixty-one days, every one of the party being in good health. Soon after they sailed for England, and by a strange coincidence arrived in London at the same time as Franklin.

Many an attempt was yet to be made to reach the North Pole, till at last it was discovered by Peary, an American, in 1909.

CHAPTER LV

THE SEARCH FOR TIMBUKTU

IT is a relief to turn from the icy north to the tropical climate of Central Africa, where Mungo Park had disappeared in 1805. The mystery of Timbuktu and the Niger remained unsolved, though more than one expedition had left the coast of Africa for the " mystic city " lying " deep in that lion-haunted inland." Notwithstanding disaster, death, and defeat, a new expedition set forth from Tripoli to cross the great Sahara Desert. It was under Major Denham, Lieutenant Clapperton, and Dr. Oudney. They left Tripoli in March 1822. " We were the first English travellers," says Denham, " who had determined to travel in our real character as Britons and Christians, and to wear our English dress : the buttons on our waistcoats and our watches caused the greatest astonishment." It was the end of November before they were ready to leave the frontier on their great desert journey. The long enforced stay in this unhealthy border town had undermined their health; fever had reduced Denham, Dr. Oudney was suffering from cough and pains in his chest, Clapperton was shivering with ague—a state of health " ill-calculated for undertaking a long and tedious journey." A long escort of men and camels accompanied them into the merciless desert, with its burning heat and drifting sands—" the Sea of Sahara " as the old cartographer calls it. December found them still slowly advancing over the billowy sand, deeply impressed and horrified at the number of slave skeletons that lay about the wind-swept desert. The new year brought little relief. " No wood, no water," occurs constantly in Denham's journal. "Desert as yesterday ; high sandhills." Still they persevered, until, on 4th February 1823, they were rewarded by seeing a sheet of water, " the great Lake Tchad, glowing with the golden rays of the sun in its strength." Was this, after all, the source of the Niger ? Its low shores were surrounded with reedy marshes and clumps of white water-lilies, there were flocks of wild ducks and geese, birds with beautiful plumage were feeding on the margin of the lake, pelicans, cranes, immense white spoonbills, yellow-legged plover—all were dwelling undisturbed in this peaceful spot. And this most remarkable lake lay eight hundred feet above the Atlantic, between the watersheds of Nile, Niger, and Congo.

But Lake Tchad was not their goal; they must push on over new country where no European had been before. A fortnight later they reached Kukawa, the capital of Bornu, once a great Mohammedan empire. " We were about to become acquainted with a people who had never seen or scarcely heard of a European," says Denham, " and to tread on ground, the knowledge and true situation of which had hitherto been wholly unknown. We advanced towards the town of Kuka in a most interesting state of uncertainty, whether we should find its chief at the head of thousands, or be received by him under a tree, surrounded by a few naked slaves."

Their doubts were soon set at rest by the sight of several thousand cavalry, drawn up in line. They were received by an Arab general, " a negro of noble aspect, dressed in a figured silk robe and mounted on a beautiful horse." They had passed from the region of hidden huts to one of great walled cities, from the naked pagan to the cultivated follower of Mohammed, from superstition to mosques and schools, from ignorance to knowledge.

MAJOR DENHAM AND HIS PARTY RECEIVED BY THE SHEIKH OF BORNU.

From a drawing by Major Denham.

The Sheikh, who received the travellers in a small room with armed negroes on either side, asked the reason of their long and painful journey across the desert. " To see the country," answered the Englishmen, " and to give an account of its inhabitants, produce, and appearance, as our sultan was desirous of knowing every part of the globe."

The Sheikh's hospitality was overwhelming; he had huts built for them, " which," says Denham, " were so crowded with visitors that we had not a moment's peace, and the heat was insufferable." He sent presents of bullocks, camel-loads of wheat and rice, leather skins of butter, jars, and honey. The market of Kuka was famous. It was attended by some fifteen thousand persons from all parts, and the produce sold there was astonishing. Here Clapperton and Dr. Oudney stayed all through the summer months, for both were ill, and Oudney was growing rapidly worse. Denham meanwhile went off on exploring expeditions in the neighbourhood.

On 14th December, Clapperton and Oudney left the friendly Sheikh and made their way to Kano. But the rough travelling proved too much for Oudney; each day found him weaker, but he valiantly journeyed on. On 12th January he ordered the camels to be loaded as usual, and he was dressed by Clapperton, but he was too ill to be lifted on to his camel, and a few hours later he died.

Clapperton was now alone " amid a strange people " in a land " hitherto never trodden by European foot," and very ill himself. But he reached Kano, the famous trading centre of the Haussas, containing some forty thousand inhabitants. Here again the market impressed him deeply, so full was it of cosmopolitan articles from far-distant lands. After a month's stay at Kano, now the capital of the northern province of Nigeria of that name, he set out for Sokoto, though very ill and weak at the time. He was assured of kind treatment by the Sultan. He arrived on 16th March, and " to impress them with my official importance I arrayed myself in my lieutenant's coat trimmed with gold lace, white trousers, and silk stockings, and, to complete my finery, I wore Turkish slippers and a turban." Crowds collected on his arrival, and he was conducted to the Sultan, who questioned him closely about Europe. "I laid before him a present in the name of His Majesty the King of England, consisting of two new blunderbusses, an embroidered jacket, some scarlet breeches, cloves and cinnamon, gunpowder, razors, looking-glasses, snuff-boxes, and compasses."

"Everything is wonderful!" exclaimed the Sultan; "but you are the greatest curiosity of all! What can I give that is acceptable to the King of England?"

"Co-operate with His Majesty in putting a stop to the slave trade," was Clapperton's answer.

"What, have you no slaves in England?" The Englishman replied, "No!" to which the Sultan answered: "God is great; you are a beautiful people." But when Clapperton asked for leave in order to solve the mystery of the Niger, the Sultan refused, and he was obliged to return to Kuka, where he arrived on 8th July. A week later he was joined by Denham. "It was nearly eight months since we had separated," says Denham, "and I went immediately to the hut where he was lodged; but so satisfied was I that the sunburnt, sickly person that lay extended on the floor, rolled in a dark-blue shirt, was not my companion, that I was about to leave the place, when he convinced me of my error by calling me by my name. Our meeting was a melancholy one, for he had buried his companion. Notwithstanding the state of weakness in which I found Captain Clapperton, he yet spoke of returning to Sudan after the rains." But this was not to be, and a month later we find the two explorers turning homewards to Tripoli, where they arrived at the end of January.

But, with all his long travelling in Africa, Clapperton

had not seen the Niger, and, although the effects of his fever had not worn away, he spent but two months in England before he was off again. This time he sailed to the Gulf of Guinea, and from a place on the coast near the modern Lagos he started by a new and untried route to reach the interior of the great Dark Continent. It was September 1825 when he left the coast with his companions. Before the month was over, the other Europeans had died from the pestilential climate of Nigeria, and Clapperton, alone with his faithful servant, Richard Lander, pushed on. At last he saw the great Niger near the spot where Mungo Park and his companions had perished. At Bussa they made out the tragic story of his end. They had descended the river from Timbuktu to Bussa, when the boat struck upon some rocks. Natives from the banks shot at them with arrows ; the white men then, seeing all was lost, jumped into the river and were drowned. The Niger claimed its explorer in the end, and the words of Mungo Park must have occurred to Clapperton as he stood and watched : " Though I myself were half-dead, I would still persevere ; and if I could not succeed in the object of my journey, I would at least die on the Niger."

From Bussa, Clapperton made his way to Kano and Sokoto ; but on 13th April 1827, broken down by fever, he died in the arms of his faithful servant. With his master's papers and journal, Lander made his way home, thus establishing for the first time a direct connection between Benin and Tripoli, the west coast and the north.

Still the mouth of the Niger had not been found. This discovery was reserved for this very Richard Lander and his brother John.

Just a year after the death of Clapperton a young Frenchman, Réné Caillé, tempted by the offer of ten thousand francs offered by the French Geographical

Society for the first traveller who should reach that
mysterious city, entered Timbuktu 20th April 1829, after
a year's journey from Sierra Leone. And from his pen
we get the first direct account of the once important city.
" At length," he says, " we arrived safely at Timbuktu,
just as the sun was touching the horizon. I now saw this
capital of the Sudan, to reach which had so long been the
object of my wishes. To God alone did I confide my joy.
I looked around and found that the sight before me
did not answer my expectations. I had formed a totally

THE FIRST EUROPEAN PICTURE OF TIMBUKTU.
From a drawing in Caillé's *Tomboctou*, 1829.

different idea of the grandeur and wealth of it. The city
presented nothing but a mass of ill-looking houses, built
of earth. Nothing was to be seen in all directions but
immense plains of quicksand of a yellowish white colour.
The sky was a pale red as far as the horizon, all nature
wore a dreary aspect, and the most profound silence prevailed : not even the warbling of a bird was to be heard.
The heat was oppressive; not a breath of air freshened the
atmosphere. This mysterious city, which has been the
object of curiosity for many ages, and of whose civilisation, population, and trade with the Sudan such exagger-

ated notions have prevailed, is situated in an immense plain of white sand, having no vegetation but stunted trees and shrubs, and has no other resources save its trade in salt."

It is curious to note what a burst of interest was aroused in England at this time with regard to Timbuktu. Thackeray wrote in 1829—

> " In Africa (a quarter of the world)
> Men's skins are black, their hair is crisp and curl'd;
> And somewhere there, unknown to public view,
> A mighty city lies, called Timbuktu."

while the same year Tennyson's poem on Timbuktu won for him the prize at Cambridge University for the best poem of the year.

CHAPTER LVI

RICHARD AND JOHN LANDER DISCOVER THE MOUTH OF THE NIGER

LANDER, the "faithful attendant of the late Captain Clapperton," as he is called in his instructions, was burning to be off again to explore further the mysterious Niger. No pecuniary reward was to be his; he was a poor man, and just for the love of exploring the unknown he started off. He had inspired his brother with a desire to solve the great mystery; so on 22nd February 1830 the two brothers arrived at Cape Coast Castle and made their way to Bussa, which place they entered on 18th June. Sitting on a rock overlooking the spot where Mungo Park had perished, the brothers resolved to " set at rest for ever the great question of the course and termination of the great Niger."

It was 20th September before preparations were completed for the eventful voyage from Bussa to the mouth of the Niger. For provisions they took three large bags of corn and one of beans, a couple of fowls, and two sheep to last a month, while the king added rice, honey, onions, and one hundred pounds of vegetable butter. Then in two native canoes the Landers embarked on the great river, the "Dark Water" as it was more often called, while the crowds who came down to the riverside to bid them farewell knelt with uplifted hands, imploring for the explorers the protection of Allah and their prophet. It was indeed a perilous undertaking; sunken reefs were an ever-present danger, while the swift current ran them dangerously near many jagged rocks. For nearly a month they paddled onward with their native guides in anxiety and suspense, never knowing what an hour might bring forth. On 7th October a curious scene took place when the King of the Dark Water came forth in all his pomp and glory to see the white strangers who were paddling down the great river. Waiting under the shade of a tree, for the morning was very hot, the Landers observed a large canoe paddled by twenty young black men singing as they rowed. In the centre of the boat a mat awning was erected: in the bows sat four little boys "clad with neatness and propriety," while in the stern sat musicians with drums and trumpets. Presently the king stepped forth. He was coal black, dressed in an Arab cloak, Haussa trousers, and a cap of red cloth, while two pretty little boys about ten years of age, acting as pages, followed him, each bearing a cow's tail in his hand to brush away flies and other insects. Six wives, jet black girls in neat country caps edged with red silk, accompanied him. To make some impression on this pompous king, Lander hoisted the "Union flag." "When unfurled and waving in the wind, it looked extremely pretty, and it made our hearts glow with pride and enthusiasm as we looked at the solitary little banner. I put on an old naval uniform coat, and my brother dressed himself in as grotesque and gaudy a manner as our resources would afford; our eight attendants also put on new white Mohammedan robes." Other canoes joined the royal procession and the little flotilla moved down the river. "Never did the British flag lead so extraordinary a squadron," remarks Lander. As the King of the Dark Water stepped on shore the Englishmen fired a salute, which frightened him not a little till the honour was explained. Having now exchanged their two canoes for one of a larger size, they continued their journey down the river.

On 25th October they found the waters of the Niger were joined by another large river known to-day as the Benue, the Mother of Waters, flowing in from the east. After this the banks of the river seemed to grow hilly, and villages were few and far between. " Our canoe passed smoothly along the Niger, and everything was silent and solitary ; no sound could be distinguished save our own

RICHARD AND JOHN LANDER PADDLING DOWN THE NIGER.
From a drawing in the account of Lander's *Travels*, 1835.

voices and the plashing of the paddles with their echoes ; the song of birds was not heard, nor could any animal whatever be seen ; the banks seemed to be entirely deserted, and the magnificent Niger to be slumbering in its own grandeur."

" One can imagine the feelings," says a modern writer, " in such circumstances of the brothers, drifting they knew not whither, in intolerable silence and loneliness on the bosom of a river which had caused the death of so many men who had endeavoured to wrest from it its secret." Two days later a large village appeared, and suddenly a cry rang through the air : "Holloa, you Englishmen ! You come here !" It came from a "little squinting fellow" dressed in an English soldier's jacket, a messenger from the Chief of Bonney on the coast, buying slaves for his master. He had picked up a smattering of English from the Liverpool trading ships which came to Bonney for palm-oil from the river. There was no longer any doubt that the mouth of the Niger was not far off, and that the many-mouthed delta was well known to Europeans under the name of the " Oil Rivers " flowing into the Bight of Benin.

Lander pushed on till he had paddled down the Brass River, as one of the many branches was called, when he heard " the welcome sound of the surf on the beach."

The mystery of the Niger, after a lapse of two thousand five hundred years since its existence had been recorded by Herodotus, was solved at last.

CHAPTER LVII

ROSS DISCOVERS THE NORTH MAGNETIC POLE

THE first attempt to discover the North-West Passage by means of steam instead of sail was made by Captain Ross, who, since his expedition in 1819, had been burning to set off again for the Arctic regions. The reward of £20,000 held out to the discoverer of a north-west passage had been repealed, but an old friend, Felix Booth, decided to finance Ross, the Government having refused. " After examining various steamships advertised for sale," says Ross, " I purchased the *Victory*, which had been once employed as a packet." With food and fuel for one thousand days, and accompanied by his nephew, James Ross, who had been with Parry on his recent Polar voyage, he left England the end of May 1829, not to return for many a long year. Disasters soon began. The *Victory* began to leak, her engines were defective, and there was nothing for it but to heave up her paddles and trust to sail. Sailing to the northward, they found the sea smooth and the weather so warm that they could dine without a fire and with the skylights off. Entering Lancaster Sound, they sailed up Prince Regent's Inlet. They soon discovered the spot where the *Fury* had been wrecked four years before and abandoned by Captain Parry with whom was James Ross, who now found the stores which had been safely hidden on that occasion. As they made their way up the inlet, strong currents and vast masses of ice hard and solid as granite more than once threatened them with destruction.

"Imagine," says Captain Ross, "these mountains hurled through a narrow strait by a rapid tide, meeting with the noise of thunder, breaking from each other's precipices huge fragments, till, losing their former equilibrium, they fall over headlong, lifting the sea around in breakers and whirling it in eddies."

Escaping these perils, Ross entered a fine harbour. Here he landed, hoisted the colours, and took possession of the new land he had found, and, drinking the King's health, called the land Boothia, after his patron. For the next two months, August and September, he carefully explored the coast of this newly discovered Boothia for some three hundred miles, naming points and capes and islands after friends at home and on board. Heavy squalls of snow and ever-thickening ice pointed out the necessity of winter quarters, and 1st October found the *Victory* imprisoned by thick immovable ice. "The prison door was shut upon us for the first time," says Ross sadly. "Nothing was to be seen but one dazzling, monotonous extent of snow. It was indeed a dull prospect. Amid all its brilliancy, this land of ice and snow has ever been, and ever will be, a dull, dreary, heart-sinking, monotonous waste, under the influence of which the very mind is paralysed. Nothing moves and nothing changes, but all is for ever the same—cheerless, cold, and still."

The explorers little thought that this was to be their home for the next three years. They spent a fairly cheerful Christmas with mince pies and "iced cherry brandy" taken from the stores of the *Fury*, and early in 1830 the monotony was broken by the appearance of Eskimos. These were tremendously dressed up in furs, a shapeless mass, and Ross describes one as resembling "the figure of a globe standing on two pins." They soon

ROSS'S WINTER QUARTERS IN FELIX HARBOUR.

THE FIRST COMMUNICATION WITH ESKIMOS AT BOOTHIA FELIX, JANUARY 1830.
SIR JOHN ROSS'S EXPEDITION TO THE NORTH MAGNETIC POLE, 1829-1833.

From Drawings by Ross in his *Narrative of a Second Voyage in Search of a North-West Passage.*

became friendly, taking the Englishmen to see their snow huts, drawing them charts of Boothia Gulf beyond Felix Harbour, while in exchange the explorers taught English to the little Eskimo children and ministered to their ailments, the ship's carpenter even making a wooden leg for one of the natives.

So the long winter passed away. A few land journeys with sledges only ended in disappointment, but at last the vessel was free of ice and joyfully they hoisted her sails. But worse disappointment was in store. She had sailed for three miles when they met a ridge of ice, and a solid sea forbade any further advance. In vain did they try to saw through the ice. November found the poor *Victory* hopelessly icebound and her crew doomed to another winter in the same region.

It was not till May that a journey across the land of Boothia to the west coast was possible. Ross and his nephew had been calculating the position of the North Magnetic Pole all the long winter, and with signs of spring they set forth.

" Our journey had a very new appearance. The mother of two Eskimos led the way with a staff in her hand, my sledge following with the dogs and one of the children, guided by one of the wives with a child on her back. After a native sledge came that of Commander Ross, followed by more Eskimos. Many halts were made, as our burdens were heavy, the snow deep, and the ice rough."

After a fortnight's travelling past the chain of great lakes—the woman still guiding them—the Rosses, uncle and nephew, separated. James Ross now made for the spot where the Magnetic Pole was supposed to be. His own account shows with what enthusiasm he found it. " We were now within fourteen miles of the calculated position of the Magnetic Pole and now commenced a rapid march, and, persevering with all our might, we reached the calculated place at eight in the morning of the 1st of June. I must leave it to others to imagine the elation of mind with which we found ourselves now at length arrived at this great object of our ambition. It almost seemed as if we had accomplished everything that we had come so far to see and to do ; as if our voyage and all its labours were at an end, and that nothing remained for us but to return home and be happy for the rest of our days. Amid mutual congratulation we fixed the British flag on the spot and took possession of the North Magnetic Pole and its adjoining territory in the name of Great Britain and King William IV. We had plenty of materials for building, and we therefore erected a cairn of some magnitude under which we buried a canister containing a record of the interesting fact." Another fortnight found the successful explorers staggering back to the *Victory* with their great news, after an absence of twenty-eight days.

Science has shown that the Magnetic Pole revolves, and that Ross's cairn will not again mark its exact position for many a long year to come.

By the end of August the ice had broken and the *Victory* was once more in full sail, but gales of wind drove her into harbour, which she never left again. Despite their colossal efforts, it soon became apparent that yet another winter would have to be passed in the frozen seas. The entries in Ross's journal become shorter and more despondent day by day. " The sight of ice to us is a plague, a vexation, a torment, an evil, a matter of despair. Could we have skated, it would not have been an amusement ; we had exercise enough and, worst of all, the ice which surrounds us obstructed us, imprisoned us, annoyed us in every possible manner, had become odious to our sight." By October there was no open water to be seen ; " the hopeful did not hope more, and the despondent continued to despair."

This was their third winter in the ice—food was growing scarce, the meat was so hard frozen that it had to be cut with a saw or thawed in warm cocoa. Snow-blindness afflicted many of the men badly. At last came the summer of 1833, but the *Victory* was still fast in her winter quarters, and all attempts to release her had failed. They now decided to abandon her and to drag their boats

THE ROSSES ON THEIR JOURNEY TO THE NORTH MAGNETIC POLE.

From a drawing in Ross's *Second Voyage for a North-West Passage*, 1835.

over the ice to the wreck of the *Fury*, replenishing their stores and trusting to some whaler to take them home. We get a pathetic picture. "The colours were hoisted," says Ross, "and nailed to the mast, we drank a parting glass to our poor old ship, and, having seen every man out, I took my own adieu of the *Victory* in the evening. She had deserved a better fate. It was like parting with an old friend."

On 23rd April the weary explorers began dragging their boats and the last month's provisions over the ice in the face of wind and snow. The journey was painful and distressing. They found Barrow's Strait full of impenetrable ice, and resolved to pass the winter on Fury beach, which seemed almost like home to the half-starved men. Erecting a house which they called " Somerset House," they prepared for a fourth winter. For severity it was unequalled, the crew developed scurvy, and all were suffering sorely when, in the following August, the unfortunate party was rescued by the whaler, " *Isabella* of Hull, once commanded by Captain Ross." It was the ship in which Ross had made his first Arctic exploration. At first the mate refused to believe the story of these " bear-like " men. The explorers and Ross had been lost these two years. But, almost frantic with delight, the explorers climbed on board the *Isabella* to be received with the heartiest of cheers when their identity was disclosed. " That we were a repulsive-looking people, none could doubt," says poor Ross, " unshaven since I know not when, dirty, dressed in rags of wild beasts, and starved to the very bones, our gaunt and grim looks, when contrasted with those of the well-dressed and well-fed men around us, made us all feel what we really were, as well as what we seemed to others." Then followed a wild scene of " washing, dressing, shaving, eating, all intermingled," while in the midst of all there were questions to be asked and the news from England to be heard. Long accustomed to a cold bed on the hard snow or the bare rock, few of them could sleep that night in the comfort of the new accommodation.

They were soon safely back in England, large crowds collecting to get a glimpse of Captain Ross. His own words best end the account of his travels. " On my arrival in London," he says, " on the 20th of October 1833, it became my first duty to repair to the royal palace at Windsor, with an account of my voyage, and to lay at the feet of His Majesty the British flag which had been hoisted on the Magnetic Pole."

"SOMERSET HOUSE," ROSS'S WINTER QUARTERS ON FURY BEACH.
From a drawing in Ross's *Second Voyage for a North-West Passage,* 1835.

CHAPTER LVIII

FLINDERS NAMES AUSTRALIA

WE must now return to Australia, as yet so imperfectly explored, and take up the story of the young colony at Sydney.

For seven years it thrived under the careful management of Governor Phillips, who was then replaced by one Hunter. With the new governor from England arrived two young men destined to distinguish themselves in the exploration of New South Wales. They were midshipman Matthew Flinders and surgeon George Bass. The reading of *Robinson Crusoe* had created in young Flinders a passion for sea-adventure, and no sooner had the *Reliance* anchored in Sydney harbour than the two young friends resolved on an exploring expedition to the south. For there were rumours afloat that Van Diemen's Land did not join the main continent of New South Wales. Little enough help was forthcoming for the expedition, and the friends had to content themselves with a little boat eight feet long— the *Tom Thumb*—and only a boy to help them. But with all the eager enthusiasm of youth they sailed from Port Jackson on 25th March 1796. It is impossible to follow all their adventures as they attempted the survey of the coast. A storm on the 29th nearly swallowed up the little *Tom Thumb* and her plucky sailors.

"At ten o'clock," says Flinders, " the wind, which had been unsettled and driving electric clouds in all directions, burst out in a gale. In a few minutes the waves began to break, and the extreme danger to which this exposed our little bark was increased by the darkness of the night and the uncertainty of finding any place of shelter. Mr. Bass kept the sheet of the sail in his hand, drawing in a few inches occasionally, when he saw a particularly heavy sea following. I was steering with an oar. A single wrong movement or a moment's inattention would have sent us to the bottom. After running near an hour in this critical manner, some huge breakers were distinguished ahead ; it was necessary to determine what was to be done at once, for our bark could not live ten minutes longer. On coming to what appeared to be the extremity of the breakers, the boat's head was brought to the wind, the mast and sail taken down, and the oars taken out. Pulling then towards the reef during the intervals of the heaviest seas, in three minutes we were in smooth water—a nearer approach showed us the beach of a well-sheltered cove in

MATTHEW FLINDERS.

which we anchored for the rest of the night. We thought Providential Cove a well-adapted name for the place."

Important local discoveries were made by the young explorers, and their skill and courage earned for them a better equipment for further exploration. A whale-boat provisioned for six weeks, and a crew of six, were placed at the disposal of Bass in order that he might discover whether Van Diemen's Land was joined to the mainland or whether there was a strait between. Cook had declared that there was no strait. Flinders now tells the story of his friend's triumphant success in finding the straits that now bear his name. He tells how Bass found the coast turning westward exposed to the billows of a great ocean, of the low sandy shore, of the spacious harbour which " from its relative position to the hitherto known parts of the coasts was called Port Western." His provisions were now at an end and, though he was keen to make a survey of his new discovery, he was obliged to return. This voyage of six hundred miles in an open boat on dangerous and unknown shores is one of the most remarkable on record. It added another three hundred miles of known coast-line, and showed that the shores of New Holland were divided from Van Diemen's Land. So highly did the colonists appreciate this voyage of discovery that the whale-boat in which Bass sailed was long preserved as a curiosity.

A small boat of twenty-five tons, provisioned for twelve weeks, was now put at the disposal of the two friends, Flinders and Bass, to complete the survey of Van Diemen's Land, and in October 1798 they sailed for the south. With gales and strong winds blowing across the channel now known as Bass Strait, they made their way along the coast—the northern shores of Van Diemen's Land—till they found a wide inlet. Here they found a quantity of black swans, which they ate with joy, and also kangaroos, mussels, and oysters. This inlet they called Port Dalrymple, after the late hydrographer to the Admiralty in England. On 9th December, still coasting onward, they passed Three-Hummock Island and then a whole cluster of islands, to which, " in honour of His Excellency the Governor of New South Wales, I gave the title of Hunter's Isles." And now a long swell was noticed from the south-west. " It broke heavily upon a small reef and upon all the western shores, but, although it was likely to prove troublesome and perhaps dangerous, Mr. Bass and myself hailed it with joy and mutual congratulation, as announcing the completion of our long-wished-for discovery of a passage into the southern Indian Ocean."

Calling the point where the island coast turned Cape Grime, they sailed along the western shores, their little boat exposed to the swell of the southern ocean. Sailing joyfully from point to point and naming them at will, the two explorers reached the extreme west, which they called South-West Cape. This had been already sighted by one of Cook's party in 1773. South Cape and Tasman's Head had been likewise charted as points at the extreme south of New South Wales. So the explorers sailed right round the island on which Tasman had landed one hundred and fifty-six years before, and after an absence of five months they reached Sydney with their important news. Bass now disappears from the annals of exploration, but his friend Flinders went off to England and found in our old friend Banks a powerful friend. He was given a stout north-country ship, H.M.S. *Investigator* of three hundred and thirty-four tons, with orders to return to New Holland and make a complete survey of the coast, and was off again in July 1801 with young John Franklin, his nephew, aboard.

The *Investigator* arrived at Cape Leuwin in December and anchored in King George's Sound, discovered by Vancouver some ten years before. By the New Year he was ready to begin his great voyage round the Terra Australis, as the new country was still called. Indeed, it was Flinders who suggested the name of Australia for the tract of land hitherto called New Holland. His voyage can easily be traced on our maps to-day. Voyaging westward through the Recherches group of islands, Flinders passed the low, sandy shore to a cape he named Cape Pasley, after his late Admiral; high, bleak cliffs now rose to the height of some five hundred feet for a distance of four hundred and fifty miles—the great Australian Bight. Young Franklin's name was given to one island, Investigator to another, Cape Catastrophe commemorated a melancholy accident and the drowning of several of the crew. Kangaroo Island speaks for itself. Here they killed thirty-one dark-brown kangaroos. " The whole ship's company was employed this afternoon skinning and cleaning the kangaroos, and a delightful regale they afforded after four months' privation from almost any fresh provisions. Half a hundredweight of heads, forequarters, and tails were stewed down into soup for dinner, and as much steaks given to both officers and men as they could consume by day and night."

In April 1802 a strange encounter took place, when suddenly there appeared a " heavy-looking ship without any top-gallant masts up," showing a French ensign. Flinders cleared his decks for action in case of attack, but the strangers turned out to be the French ship *Le Géographe*, which, in company with *Le Naturaliste*, had left France, 1800, for exploration of the Australian coasts.

Now it was well known that Napoleon had cast longing eyes upon the Terra Australis—indeed, it is said that he took with him to Egypt a copy of *Cook's Voyages*. Flinders, too, knew of this French expedition, but he was not specially pleased to find French explorers engaged on the same work as himself. The commanders met as friends, and Baudin, the French explorer, told how he had landed also near Cape Leuwin in May 1801, how he had given the names of his two ships to Cape Naturaliste and Géographe Bay, and was now making his way round the coast. Flinders little guessed at this time that the French were going to claim the south of New South Wales as French territory under the name of Terra Napoleon, though it was common knowledge that this discovery was made by Englishmen.

"Ah, captain," said one of the French crew to Flinders, "if we had not been kept so long picking up shells and catching butterflies at Van Diemen's Land you would not have discovered this coast before us."

When Baudin put in at Port Jackson a couple of months later, he inquired of the Governor the extent of British claims in the Pacific.

"The whole of Tasmania and Australia are British territory," was the firm answer.

After this encounter Flinders discovered and named

CAPE CATASTROPHE.
From Flinders' *Voyages*.

Port Phillip, at the head of which stands the famous city of Melbourne to-day, and then made his way on to Port Jackson. He had managed his crews so well that the inhabitants of Port Jackson declared they were reminded of England by the fresh colour of the men amongst the *Investigator* ship's company. The Frenchmen had not fared so well. One hundred and fifty out of one hundred and seventy were down with scurvy and had to be taken to the hospital at Sydney.

Before the end of July, Flinders was off again, sailing northwards along the eastern coast of New South Wales.

October found him passing the Great Barrier reefs, and on the 21st he had reached the northernmost point, Cape York. Three days of anxious steering took the *Investigator* through Torres Strait, and Flinders was soon sailing into the great Gulf of Carpentaria. Still hugging the coast, he discovered a group of islands to the south of the gulf, which he named the Wellesley Islands, after General Wellesley, afterwards Duke of Wellington. Here he found a wealth of vegetation; cabbage palm was abundant, nutmegs plentiful, and a sort of sandal-wood was growing freely. He spent one hundred and five days exploring the gulf; then he continued his voyage round the west coast and back to Port Jackson by the south. He returned after a year's absence with a sickly crew and a rotten ship. Indeed, the *Investigator* was incapable of further service, and Flinders decided to go back to England for another ship. As passenger on board the *Porpoise*, early in August 1802, he sailed from Sydney for the Torres Strait accompanied by two returning transports. All went well for the first four days, and they had reached a spot on the coast of Queensland, when a cry of "Breakers ahead!" fell on the evening air. In another moment the ship was carried amongst the breakers and struck upon a coral reef. So sudden was the disaster that there was no time to warn the other ships closely following. As the *Porpoise* rolled over on her beam ends, huge seas swept over her and the white foam leapt high. Then the mast snapped, water rushed in, and soon the *Porpoise* was a hopeless wreck. A few minutes later, one of the transports struck the coral reef: she fell on her side, her deck facing the sweeping rollers, and was completely wrecked. The other transport escaped, sailed right away from the scene of disaster, and was never seen again by the crew of the *Porpoise*. The dawn of day showed the shipwrecked crew a sandbank, to which some ninety-four men made their way and soon set sailcloth tents on the barren shore. They had saved enough food for three months. Flinders as usual was the moving spirit. A fortnight later in one of the ship's boats, with twelve rowers and food for three weeks, he left Wreck Reef amid ringing cheers to get help from Sydney for the eighty men left on the sandbank.

" The reader," says the hero of this adventure, " has perhaps never gone two hundred and fifty leagues at sea in an open boat or along a strange coast inhabited by savages ; but, if he recollect the eighty officers and men upon Wreck Reef, and how important was our arrival to their safety and to the saving of the charts, journals, and papers of the *Investigator's* voyage, he may have some idea of the pleasure we felt, particularly myself, at entering our destined port."

Half-starved, unshaven, deplorable indeed were the men when they staggered into Sydney, and " an involuntary tear started from the eye of friendship and compassion " when the Governor learnt how nearly Flinders and his friends had lost their lives.

A few days later Flinders left Sydney for the last time, in a little home-built ship of twenty-nine tons, the *Cumberland*. It was the first ship ever built in the colony, and the colonists were glad it should be of use to the man who had done so much for their country. With all his papers and his beloved journals, Flinders put to sea accompanied by a ship to rescue the men left on Wreck Reef. Three months later, owing to the leaky condition of the ship, he landed at Mauritius. Here he was taken prisoner and all his papers and journals were seized by the French. During his imprisonment a French *Voyage of Discovery* was issued, Napoleon himself paying a sum of money to hasten publication. All the places discovered by Flinders, or " Monsieur Flinedore " as the French called him, were

called by French names. Fortunately before reaching
Mauritius, Flinders had sent duplicate copies of his charts
home, and the whole fraud was exposed. Flinders did
not reach home till 1810. A last tragedy awaited him.
For he died in 1814, on the very day that his great
book, *The Voyage to Terra Australis*, was published.
Flinders was a true explorer, and as he lay dying he
cried, "I know that in future days of exploration my
spirit will rise from the dead and follow the exploring
ship!"

THE HUTS OF THE CREW OF THE *PORPOISE* ON THE SANDBANK, WRECK REEF.
From Flinders' *Voyages*.

CHAPTER LIX

STURT'S DISCOVERIES IN AUSTRALIA

SINCE the days of Flinders, much discovery had been done in the great new island-continent of Australia. The Blue Mountains had been crossed, and the river Macquarie discovered and named after the governor of that name. But Sturt's famous discovery of the river Darling and his descent of the Murray River rank among the most note-worthy of a bewildering number of lesser expeditions.

Captain Sturt landed with his regiment, the 39th, at Sydney in the year 1827, "to guard the convicts." His first impressions of Sydney are interesting. "Cornfield and orchard," he says, "have supplanted wild grass and brush; on the ruins of the forest stands a flourishing town; and the stillness of that once desert shore is now broken by the bugle and by the busy hum of commerce. It is not unusual to see from thirty to forty vessels from every quarter of the globe riding at anchor at one time."

Sir Ralph Darling, Governor of New South Wales, soon formed a high opinion of Sturt's ability, and when an expedition was proposed into the interior for further exploration, he appointed him leader.

There was a universal opinion in the colony that in the middle of the unknown continent lay a large inland sea. Oxley had made his way to a shallow ocean of reeds where the river Macquarie disappeared; natives spoke of "large waters" containing "great fish." To open up the country and to ascertain the truth of these rumours were the objects of this new expedition which left Sydney in November 1828. It consisted of Hamilton Hume, the first Australian-born explorer, two soldiers, eight convicts, fifteen horses, ten bullocks, and a small boat on a wheeled carriage. Across the roadless Blue Mountains they started, followed the traces of Oxley, who had died just a week before they started, and about Christmas time they passed his last camp and began to break new ground. Through thickets of reeds and marshy swamps they pushed on; the river Macquarie had entirely disappeared, but on 2nd February they suddenly found a large river some eighty yards broad enclosing an unbroken sheet of deep water. " Our surprise and delight," says Sturt, " are better imagined than described. Our difficulties seemed at an end. The banks were too steep to allow of watering the cattle, but the men eagerly descended to quench a thirst increased by the powerful sun. Never shall I forget their cry of amazement, nor the terror and disappointment with which they called out that the water was too salt to drink ! Leaving his party, Sturt pushed on, but no fresh water was to be found, so he named the river the Darling, after the Governor, and returned, but not till he had discovered brine springs in the bed of the river, which accounted for its saltness. Sturt had found no inland sea, but in the Darling he had discovered a main channel of the western watershed.

He now proposed to follow the line of the Murrumbidgee, " a river of considerable size and impetuous current," and to trace it if possible into the interior. Several of his old party again joined him, and once more he rode out of Sydney on this new quest.

The journey to the banks of the Murrumbidgee lay through wild and romantic country, but as they journeyed farther, broad reed belts appeared by the river, which was soon lost in a vast expanse of reeds. For a moment or two Sturt was as one stunned; he could neither sleep nor rest till he had regained the river again. When at last he did so he found the water was deep, the current rapid, and the banks high. But he turned on all hands to build the whale-boat which he had designed at Sydney for the purpose. Early in January he writes home : " I was checked in my advance by high reeds spreading as far as the eye can reach. The Murrumbidgee is a magnificent stream. I do not yet know its fate, but I have taken to the boats. Where I shall wander to God only knows. I have little doubt, however, that I shall ultimately make the coast."

By 6th January the boat was ready and Sturt started on his memorable voyage. After passing the junction of the Lachlan, the channel gradually narrowed; great trees had been swept down by the floods and navigation rendered very dangerous. Still narrower grew the stream, stronger the current. " On a sudden, the river took a general southern direction. We were carried at a fearful rate down its gloomy banks, and at such a moment of excitement had little time to pay attention to the country through which we were passing. At last we found we were approaching a junction, and within less than a minute we were hurried into a broad and noble river. It is impossible to describe the effect upon us of so instantaneous a change. We gazed in silent wonder on the large channel we had entered."

The Murrumbidgee had joined the great Murray River as Sturt now called it, after Sir George Murray of the Colonial Department.

To add to the unknown dangers of the way, numbers of natives now appeared in force on the banks of the river, threatening the white men with " dreadful yells and with the beating of spears and shields."

Firearms alone saved the little crew, and the rage of the natives was turned to admiration as they watched the white men paddling on their great river while some seventy black men swam off to the boat like " a parcel of seals."

The explorers now found a new and beautiful stream flowing into the Murray from the north, up which the boat was now turned, natives anxiously following along the grassy banks, till suddenly a net stretched across the stream checked their course. Sturt instinctively felt he was on the river Darling again. " I directed that the Union Jack should be hoisted, and we all stood up in the boat and gave three distinct cheers. The eye of every native was fixed upon that beautiful flag as it waved over us in the heart of a desert."

While they were still watching, Sturt turned the head of the boat and pursued his way down the great Murray River. Stormy weather at the end of January set in; though they were yet one hundred and fifteen miles from the coast, the river increased in breadth, cliffs towered above them, and the water dashed like sea-waves at their base.

On the 5th of February they were cheered by the appearance of sea-gulls and a heavy swell up the river, which they knew must be nearing the sea. On the twenty-third day of their voyage they entered a great lake. Crossing to the southern shore, they found to their bitter grief that shoals and sandbanks made it impossible for them to reach the sea. They found that the Murray flowed into Encounter Bay, but thither they could not pass. The thunder of the surf upon the shore brought no hope to the tired explorers. They had no alternative but to turn back and retrace their way. Terrible was the task that lay before them. On half-rations and with hostile natives to encounter they must fight their way against wind and

stream.   And they did it.   They reached the camp on
the Murrumbidgee just seventy-seven days after leaving
it, but to their dismay it was deserted.   The river, too, had
risen in flood and " poured its turbid waters with great
violence."

" For seventeen days," says Sturt, " we pulled against
stream with determined perseverance, but in our short
daily journeys we made but trifling way against it."

CAPTAIN STURT AT THE JUNCTION OF THE RIVERS DARLING AND MURRAY.
From the *Narrative of Sturt's Expedition.*

The effects of severe toil were painfully evident.   The men
lost the muscular jerk with the oars.   Their arms were
nerveless, their faces haggard, their persons emaciated,
their spirits wholly spent.   From sheer weariness they
fell asleep at the oar.   No murmur, however, escaped
them.

" I must tell the captain to-morrow," said one, thinking
that Sturt was asleep, " that I can pull no more."   But

when the morrow came he said no word, but pulled on with his remaining strength. One man went mad. The last ounce of flour was consumed when relief arrived, and the weary explorers at last reached Sydney with their great news.

The result of this discovery was soon seen. In 1836 a shipload of English emigrants arrived off Kangaroo Island, and soon a flourishing colony was established at the mouth of the Murray River, the site of the new capital being called Adelaide, after the wife of William IV.

After this Sturt tried to cross Australia from south to north; but though he opened up a good deal of new country, he failed to reach the coast. He was rewarded by the President of the Royal Geographical Society, who described him as " one of the most distinguished explorers and geographers of our age."

The feat of crossing Australia from south to north, from shore to shore, was reserved for an Irishman called Burke in the year 1861. The story of his expedition, though it was successful, is one of the saddest in the history of discovery. The party left Melbourne in the highest spirits. No expense had been spared to give them a good outfit; camels had been imported from India, with native drivers, and food was provided for a year. The men of Melbourne turned out in their hundreds to see the start of Burke with his four companions, his camels, and his horses. Starting in August 1860, the expedition arrived at Cooper's Creek in November with half their journey done. But it was not till December that the party divided, and Burke with his companions, Wills, King, and Gray, six camels, and two horses, with food for three months, started off for the coast, leaving the rest at Cooper's Creek to await their return in about three months. After hard going they reached a channel with tidal waters flowing into the Gulf of Carpentaria on

28th March, but they could not get a view of the open ocean because of boggy ground.

They accomplished their task, but the return journey was disastrous. Short rations soon began to tell, for they had taken longer than they had calculated, and no food was to be found by the way. Gray was the first to fail and to die. Heavy rains made the ground impossibly heavy, and the camels sank to the ground exhausted.

THE BURKE AND WILLS EXPEDITION LEAVING MELBOURNE, 1860.
From a drawing by Wm. Strutt, an acquaintance of Burke.

Finally they had to be killed and eaten. Then the horses went. At long last the three weary men and two utterly worn-out camels dragged themselves to Cooper's Creek, hoping to find their companions and the food they had left there four months ago. It was 21st April. Not a soul was to be seen!

" King," cried Wills, in utter despair, " they are *gone* ! "

As the awful truth flashed on them, Burke—their leader—threw himself on to the ground, realising their terrible situation. They looked round. On a tree they saw the word " Dig." In a bottle they found a letter : " We leave the camp to-day, 21st April 1861. We have left you some food. We take camels and horses."

Only a few hours ago the party had left Cooper's Creek ! And the explorers were too weak and tired to follow ! They ate a welcome supper of oatmeal porridge and then, after resting a couple of days, they struggled on their

BURKE AND WILLS AT COOPER'S CREEK.

From a woodcut in a contemporary Australian account of the expedition.

way, three exhausted men and two tired camels. Their food was soon finished, and they had to subsist on a black seed like the natives called " nardoo." But they grew weaker and weaker, and the way was long. The camels died first. Then Wills grew too ill to walk, and there was nothing for it but to leave him and push on for help. The natives were kind to him, but he was too far gone, and he died before help could arrive. Burke and King sadly pushed on without him, but a few days later Burke died, and in the heart of Australia the one white man, King, was left alone. It was not till the following September that he was found " sitting in a hut that the blacks had made for him. He presented a melancholy appearance, wasted to a shadow and hardly to be distinguished as a civilised being except by the remnants of clothes on him."

So out of that gay party of explorers who left Melbourne in the summer of 1860 only one man returned to tell the story of success and the sadder story of suffering and disaster.

CHAPTER LX

ROSS MAKES DISCOVERIES IN THE ANTARCTIC SEAS

Now, while explorers were busy opening up Australian
inland, Ross was leaving the Australian waters for his
voyage to the south. Four years after the return of the
Ross polar expedition, Sir John Franklin had been made
Governor of Van Diemen's Land, where he was visited by
the ships sent out from England on the first Antarctic
expedition under the command of Sir James Ross, who
had returned to find himself famous for his discovery of
the North Magnetic Pole.

An expedition had been fitted out, consisting of the
Erebus and the *Terror*—ships which later on made history,
for did they not carry Sir John Franklin to his doom
in the Arctic regions some years later? The ships sailed
in the autumn of 1839 by way of the Cape of Good Hope,
and excited great interest at Hobart Town, where the
commanders, Ross and Crozier, were warmly received by
the Governor. In a bay, afterwards called Ross Cove,
the ships were repaired after the long voyage, while an
observatory was built by the convicts under the personal
supervision of Sir John Franklin. Interesting news
awaited the explorers, too, at Hobart Town. Exploration had taken place in the southern regions by a French
expedition under D'Urville and an American, Lieutenant
Wilkes—both of which had made considerable discoveries.
Ross was somewhat surprised at this, for, as he said,
" England had ever *led* the way of discovery in the

southern as well as in the northern regions," but he decided to take a more easterly course, and, if possible, to reach the South Magnetic Pole.

On 5th November 1840 the ships were off again, shaping their course for Auckland Island, nine hundred miles from Hobart Town. The island had been discovered in 1806 by Captain Bristow. He had left some pigs, whose rapid increase filled the explorers with surprise. Christmas Day found them still sailing south, with strong gales, snow, and rain. The first iceberg was seen a few days later, and land on 11th January.

" It was a beautifully clear evening," says Ross, " and we had a most enchanting view of the two magnificent ranges of mountains whose lofty peaks, perfectly covered with eternal snow, rose to elevations of ten thousand feet above the level of the ocean." These icy shores were in-hospitable enough, and the heavy surf breaking along its edge forbade any landing. Indeed, a strong tide carried the ships rapidly and dangerously along the coast among huge masses of ice. "The ceremony of taking possession of these newly discovered lands in the name of our Most Gracious Sovereign Queen Victoria was proceeded with, and on planting the flag of our country amid the hearty cheers of our party, we drank to the health, long life, and happiness of Her Majesty and His Royal Highness Prince Albert."

The end of the month found them farther south than any explorer had sailed before. Everything was new, and they were suddenly startled to find two volcanoes, one of which was active ; steam and smoke rising to a height of two thousand feet above the crater and descending as mist and snow. Mount Erebus and Mount Terror, Ross called them, in memory of his two ships. They sailed on, but soon were stopped by a huge barrier of solid ice like a great white wall, one thousand feet thick and one hundred and eighty feet above sea-level. They knew now they could get no farther this season—they had reached a point one hundred and sixty miles from the Pole. Could they but have wintered here "in sight of the brilliant burning mountain and at so short a distance from the Magnetic Pole," they might easily have reached it the following spring,—so they thought,—but reluctantly Ross had to turn. "Few can understand the deep feelings of regret with which I felt myself compelled to abandon the perhaps too ambitious hope I had so long cherished of being permitted to plant the flag of my country on both Magnetic Poles of our globe."

The whole of the great southern land they had discovered received the name of Queen Victoria, which name it keeps to-day. They had been south of the Antarctic Circle for sixty-three days, when they recrossed it on 4th March. A few days later they narrowly escaped shipwreck. An easterly wind drove them among some hundreds of icebergs. "For eight hours," says Ross, "we had been gradually drifting towards what to human eyes appeared inevitable destruction; the high waves and deep rolling of our ships rendered towing with boats impossible, and our situation was the more painful from our inability to make any effort to avoid the dreadful calamity that seemed to await us. The roar of the surf, which extended each way as far as we could see, and the dashing of the ice fell upon the ear with painful distinctness as we contemplated the awful destruction that threatened in one short hour to close the world and all its hopes and joys and sorrows upon us for ever. In this deep distress we called upon the Lord . . . and our cry came before Him. A gentler air of wind filled our sails; hope again revived, and before dark we found ourselves far removed from every danger."

April found them back again in Van Diemen's land, and though Ross sailed again the following autumn into

southern latitudes, he only reached a point some few miles
farther than before—being again stopped by a great wall
barrier of thick ice.   After this he took his ship home by
way of Cape Horn, and " the shores of Old England came
into view on the 2nd of September 1843."   After an absence
of four years Ross was welcomed home, and honours were
showered on him, including the award of the Gold Medal of
the Royal Geographical Society of Paris.

> " Till then they had deemed that the Austral earth,
>   With a long, unbroken shore,
>   Ran on to the Pole Antarctic,
>   For such was the old sea lore."

PART OF THE GREAT SOUTHERN ICE BARRIER, 450 MILES LONG, 180 FEET ABOVE
SEA-LEVEL, AND 1000 FEET THICK.

From Ross's *Voyage in Antarctic Regions.*

CHAPTER LXI

FRANKLIN DISCOVERS THE NORTH-WEST PASSAGE

THE whole coast-line of North America had now been charted, but the famous North-West Passage, for which so many lives had been laid down, had yet to be found. Sir John Barrow, " the father of modern Arctic discovery," Secretary to the Admiralty, now decided to dispatch another expedition to forge this last link and to connect, if possible, the chain of all former discoveries.

Many were the volunteers who came forward to serve in the new Arctic expedition. But Sir John Franklin claimed the command as his special right.

" No service," he declared, " is nearer to my heart."

He was reminded that rumour put his age at sixty, and that after a long life of hard work he had earned some rest.

" No, no ! " cried the explorer; " I am only fifty-nine ! "

This decided the point, and Franklin was appointed to the *Erebus* and *Terror*, recently returned from the Antarctic expedition of Sir James Ross. The ships were provisioned for three years, and with a crew of one hundred and twenty-nine men and several officers, Sir John Franklin left England for the last time on 19th May 1845. He was never seen again !

All were in the highest spirits, determined to solve the mystery of the North-West Passage once and for all ! So certain were they of success that one of the officers wrote to a friend : " Write to Panama and the Sandwich Islands every six months."

On 4th July the ships anchored near the island of Disco on the west coast of Greenland. After which all is silence. The rest of the story, " one of the saddest ever told in connection with Arctic exploration," is dovetailed together from the various scraps of information that have been collected by those who sailed in search of the lost expedition year by year.

In 1848, Sir James Ross had sailed off in search of his missing friend, and had reached a spot within three hundred miles of the *Erebus* and *Terror* four months after they had been abandoned, but he returned with no news of Franklin.

Then Sir John Richardson started off, but found no trace! Others followed. The Government offered £20,000, to which Lady Franklin added £3000, to any one who should bring news of Franklin. By the autumn of 1850 there were fifteen ships engaged in the search. A few traces were found. It was discovered that Sir John Franklin had spent his first winter (1845–46) at Beechey Island. Captain M'Clure sailed along the north coast of America and made his way from the Pacific to the Atlantic Ocean—thus showing the existence of a north-west passage, for which he and his men were highly rewarded, for at this time no one knew that Franklin had already found a passage though he had not lived to tell the story of triumph and success. But it was not till after years of silence that the story of the missing expedition was cleared up. Lady Franklin purchased and fitted out a little steam yacht, the *Fox*, of one hundred and seventy-seven tons. The command was given to Captain M'Clintock, known to be an able and enthusiastic Arctic navigator. He was to rescue any " possible survivor of the *Erebus* and *Terror*, and to try and recover any records of the lost expedition."

The 12th August found the little *Fox* in Melville Bay made fast to an iceberg, and a few days later she was frozen

28

firmly into an ice-pack. For two hundred and forty-two days she was beset, drifting all through the long, bitter winter with the ice, till on 25th April 1858, after having been carried over a thousand miles, she was released. M'Clintock, undaunted by danger, turned northwards, and by May he had reached Melville Bay. Thence up Lancaster Sound, he reached Beechey Island in August and found

ESKIMOS AT CAPE YORK WATCHING THE APPROACH OF THE *FOX*.
From M'Clintock's *Voyage in Search of Franklin.*

there three lonely graves of three sailors from the *Erebus* and *Terror*. Here the English commander erected a tablet sent out by Lady Franklin.

On the morning of 16th August, M'Clintock sailed from Beechey Island, but the short summer was passing quickly and they had no fresh news of the Franklin expedition. Half-way through Bellot Strait the *Fox* was again ice-bound, and another long winter had to be faced. By the middle of February 1859 there was light enough to start some sledging along the west coast of Boothia Felix. Days passed and M'Clintock struggled on to the south, but no Eskimos appeared and no traces of the lost explorers were to be found. Suddenly they discovered four men walking after them.

A naval button on one of the Eskimos attracted their attention.

THE THREE GRAVES ON BEECHEY ISLAND.

From M'Clintock's *Voyage in Search of Franklin.*

" It came," said the Eskimo, " from some white people who were starved upon an island where there are salmon, but none of them had seen the white men."

Here was news at last—M'Clintock travelled on some ten miles to Cape Victoria, where the Eskimos built him a " commodious snow-hut in half an hour." Next morning the entire village of Eskimos arrived—some forty-five people—bringing relics of the white men. There were silver spoons, part of a gold chain, buttons, knives made of

the iron and wood of the wrecked ships. But none of
these people had seen the white men—one man said he
had seen their bones upon the island where they died, but
some were buried. They said a ship " having three masts
had been crushed by the ice out in the sea to the west
of King William's Island." One old man made a rough
sketch of the coast-line with his spear upon the snow; he
said it was eight journeys to where the ship sank.

M'Clintock hastened back to the ship with his news—
he had by his sleigh-journey added one hundred and twenty
miles to the old charts and " completed the discovery of
the coast-line of Continental America."

On 2nd April more sledge-parties started out to reach
King William's Island—the cold was still intense, the glare
of the sun painful to their eyes. The faces and lips of
the men were blistered and cracked; their fingers were
constantly frostbitten. After nearly three weeks'
travelling they found snow-huts and Eskimos at Cape
Victoria. Here they found more traces of Franklin's
party—preserved meat tins, brass knives, a mahogany
board. In answer to their inquiries, they heard that two
ships had been seen by the natives of King William's
Island; one had been seen to sink in deep water, the other
was forced on shore and broken up. " It was in the fall
of the year (August or September)," they said, when the
ships were destroyed, that all the white people went away
to the large river, taking a boat with them, and that in the
following winter their bones were found there.

M'Clintock now made his way to the opposite coast of
King William's Island. Here he found Eskimos with pieces
of silver-plate bearing the crest and initials of Sir John
Franklin and some of his officers. They said it was five
days' journey to the wreck, of which little now remained.
There had been many books, said the Eskimos, but they had
been destroyed by the weather. One woman volunteered

EXPLORING PARTIES STARTING FROM THE *FOX*.

From M'Clintock's *Voyage of the "Fox" in Search of Franklin*.

a statement. " Many of the white men," she said,
" dropped by the way as they went to the Great River.
Some were buried and some were not. Their bodies
were discovered during the winter following." Moving
onwards, M'Clintock reached the Great Fish River on the
morning of 12th May. A furious gale was raging and the
air was heavy with snow, but they encamped there to
search for relics. With pickaxes and shovels they searched
in vain. No Eskimos were to be found, and at last in despair
the little party of explorers faced homewards. M'Clintock
was slowly walking near the beach, when he suddenly
came upon a human skeleton, lying face downwards, half
buried in the snow. It wore a blue jacket with slashed
sleeves and braided edging and a greatcoat of pilot-cloth.

The old woman was right. "They fell down and died as
they walked along." And now the reward of the explorers
was at hand. On the north-west coast of King William's
Island was found a cairn and a blue ship's paper, weather-
worn and ragged, relating in simple language, written by one
of the ship's officers, the fate of the Franklin expedition.
The first entry was cheerful enough. In 1846 all was
well. His Majesty's ships, *Erebus* and *Terror*, wintered in
the ice—at Beechey Island, after having ascended Wellington Channel and returned to the west side of
Cornwallis Island. Sir John Franklin was commanding
the expedition. The results of their first year's labour
was encouraging. In 1846 they had been within twelve
miles of King William's Island, when winter stopped them.
But a later entry, written in April 1848, states that the
ships were deserted on 22nd April, having been beset
in ice since September 1846—that Sir John Franklin
had died on 11th June 1847, and that Captain Crozier was
in command.

Then came the last words, " And start to-morrow
twenty-sixth for Back's Fish River." That was all.

After a diligent search in the neighbourhood for journals or relics, M'Clintock led his party along the coast, till on 30th May they found another relic in the shape of a large boat, with a quantity of tattered clothing lying in her. She had been evidently equipped for the ascent of the Great Fish River. She had been built at Woolwich Dockyard; near her lay two human skeletons, a pair of worker slippers, some watches, guns, a *Vicar of Wakefield*, a small Bible, New Testament, and Prayer Book, seven or eight pairs of boots, some silk handkerchiefs, towels, soap, sponge, combs, twine, nails, shot, and cartridges, needle and thread cases, some tea and chocolate, and a little tobacco.

Everything was carefully collected and brought back to the ship, which was reached on 19th June. Two months later the little *Fox* was free from ice and M'Clintock reached London towards the end of September, to make known his great discovery.

The rest of the story is well known. Most of us know the interesting collection of Franklin relics in the United Service Institution in London, and the monument in Waterloo Place to " the great navigator and his brave companions who sacrificed their lives in completing the discovery of the North-West Passage."

It was acknowledged " that to Sir John Franklin is due the priority of discovery of the North-West Passage— that last link to forge which he sacrificed his life."

And on the marble monument in Westminster Abbey, Tennyson, a nephew of Sir John Franklin, wrote his well-known lines—

" Not here, the white north hath thy bones, and thou,
    Heroic Sailor Soul,
  Art passing on thy happier voyage now
    Towards no earthly pole."

CHAPTER LXII

DAVID LIVINGSTONE

" I SHALL open up a path to the interior or perish."

Such were the words of one of the greatest explorers of Africa in the nineteenth century. Determination was the keynote of his character even as a young boy. At the age of ten he was at work in a cotton factory in Scotland : with his first week's wages he bought a Latin grammar. Fourteen hours of daily work left little time for reading, but he educated himself, till at nineteen he was resolved to be a medical missionary.

" In the glow of love which Christianity inspires, I resolved to devote my life to the alleviation of human misery." He was accepted for service by the London Missionary Society, and in the year 1840 he sailed for South Africa. After a voyage of three months he arrived at Cape Town and made his way in a slow ox-waggon seven hundred miles to Kuruman, a small mission station in the heart of Bechuanaland where Dr. Moffat had laboured for twenty years. He did well, and two years later he was sent north to form another mission station at Mabotsa (Transvaal). Having married Moffat's daughter Mary, he worked in these parts till June 1849, when, with his wife and three children, he started with oxen and waggon for a journey northwards. Across the great Kalahari Desert moved the exploring family, till they came

LIVINGSTONE, WITH HIS WIFE AND FAMILY, AT THE DISCOVERY OF LAKE NGAMI.

From Livingstone's *Missionary Travels.*

to the river called Zouga, which, said the natives, led to a large lake named Lake Ngami. In native canoes, Livingstone and his little family ascended this beautifully wooded river, " resembling the river Clyde above Glasgow," till on 1st August 1849, Lake Ngami appeared, " and for the first time," says Livingstone, " this fine sheet of water was beheld by Europeans." The lake was two thousand eight hundred feet above the sea, but the climate was terribly unhealthy. The children grew feverish, and mosquitoes made life a misery to them, while the tsetse fly made further exploration for the moment impossible. So the family journeyed back to headquarters for a time. But Livingstone was unsatisfied, and once more in 1851 we find him starting again with wife and children to seek the great river Zambesi, known to exist in central Africa, though the Portuguese maps represented it as rising far to the east of Livingstone's discovery.

" It was the end of June 1851," he tells us, " that we were rewarded by the discovery of the Zambesi in the centre of the continent. This was an important point, for that river was not previously known to exist there at all. As we were the very first white men the inhabitants had ever seen, we were visited by prodigious numbers of Makololo in garments of blue, green, and red baize." Livingstone wanted to know more of this unknown river, but he now decided that exploring with a wife and family was not only perilous, but difficult, so he returned to the coast, put them on a homeward-bound ship for England, and returned to central Africa to continue his work of exploration alone.

It was 11th November 1853 when Livingstone left the town of Linyanti in the very heart of central Africa for his great journey to the west coast to trace the course of the Zambesi.

"The Zambesi. Nobody knows
Whence it comes and whither it goes."

So ran an old canoe-song of the natives.

With twenty-seven faithful black Makololos, with "only a few biscuits, a little tea and sugar, twenty pounds of coffee and three books," with a horse rug and sheepskin for bedding and a small gipsy tent and a tin canister, fifteen inches square, filled with a spare shirt, trousers, and shoes for civilised life, and a few scientific instruments, the English explorer started for a six months' journey. Soon his black guides had embarked in their canoes and were making their way up the Zambesi. "No rain has fallen here," he writes on 30th November, "so it is excessively hot. The atmosphere is oppressive both in cloud and sunshine." Livingstone suffered badly from fever during the entire journey. But the blacks took fatherly care of him. "As soon as we land," he says, "the men cut a little grass for my bed, while the poles of my little tent are planted. The bed is made and boxes ranged on each side of it, and then the tent pitched over all. Two Makololos occupy my right and left both in eating and sleeping as long as the journey lasts, but my head boatman makes his bed at the door of the tent as soon as I retire."

As they advanced up the Barotse valley, rains had fallen and the woods had put on their gayest hue. Flowers of great beauty grew everywhere. "The ground begins to swarm with insect life, and in the cool, pleasant mornings the place rings with the singing of birds."

On 6th January 1854 they left the river and rode oxen through the dense parts of the country through which they had now to pass. Through heavy rains and with very little food, they toiled on westward through miles and miles of swamp intersected by streams flowing southward to the Zambesi basin. One day Livingstone's ox, Sindbad, threw him, and he had to struggle wearily forward on foot. His strength was failing. His meagre fare varied by boiled zebra and dried elephant, frequent wettings and constant fever, were reducing him to a mere skeleton. At last on 26th March he arrived at the edge of the high land over which he had so long been travelling. " It is so steep," he tells us, " that I was obliged to dismount, and I was so weak that I had to be led by my companions to prevent my toppling over in walking down. Below us lay the valley of the Kwango in glorious sunlight." Another fortnight and they were in Portuguese territory. The sight of white men once more and a collection of traders' huts was a welcome sight to the weary traveller. The commandant at once took pity on Livingstone, but after a refreshing stay of ten days the English explorer started off westward to the coast. For another month he pursued his way. It was 31st May 1854. As the party neared the town of Loanda, the black Makololos began to grow nervous. " We have stood by each other hitherto and will do so to the last," Livingstone assured them, as they all staggered into the city by the seashore. Here they found one Englishman sent out for the suppression of the slave trade, who at once gave up his bed to the stricken and emaciated explorer. " Never shall I forget," he says, " the luxury I enjoyed in feeling myself again on a good English bed after six months' sleeping on the ground."

Nor were the Makololos forgotten. They were entertained on board an English man-of-war lying off the coast. Livingstone was offered a passage home, but he tells us : " I declined the tempting offers of my friends, and resolved to take back my Makololo companions to their Chief, with a view of making a path from here to the east coast by means of the great river Zambesi."

With this object in view, he turned his back on home and comfort, and on 20th September 1854 he left Loanda and " the white man's sea," as the black guides called the Atlantic Ocean that washes the shores of West Africa. Their way lay through the Angola country, rich in wild coffee and cotton plantations. The weather was as usual still and oppressive, but slowly Livingstone made his way eastward. He suffered badly from fever as he had done on the outward journey. It had taken him six months to reach Loanda from central Africa ; it took a year to complete the return journey, and it was September 1855 before Linyanti was again reached. Waggons and goods left there eighteen months before were safe, together with many welcome letters from home. The return of the travellers after so long an absence was a cause of great rejoicing. All the wonderful things the Makololos had seen and heard were rehearsed many times before appreciative audiences. Livingstone was more than ever a hero in their eyes, and his kindness to his men was not forgotten. He had no difficulty in getting recruits for the journey down the Zambesi to the sea, for which he was now making preparations.

On 3rd November he was ready to resume his long march across Africa. He was much better equipped on this occasion ; he rode a horse instead of an ox, and his guide, Sekwebu, knew the river well. The first night out they were unfortunately caught in a terrific thunderstorm accompanied by sheet-lightning, which lit up the whole country and flooded it with torrents of tropical rain.

A few days' travelling brought the party to the famous Zambesi Falls, called by the natives " where smoke sounds," but renamed by Livingstone after the Queen of England, Victoria. The first account of these now famous Falls is very vivid. " Five columns of vapour, appropriately named smoke, bending in the direction of the wind, appeared to mingle with the clouds. The whole scene was extremely beautiful. It had never been seen before by European eyes. When about half a mile from the Falls, I left the canoe and embarked in a lighter one with men well acquainted with the rapids, who brought me to an island in the middle of the river and on the edge of the lip over which the water rolls. Creeping with care to the verge, I peered down into a large rent which had been made from bank to bank of the broad Zambesi. In looking down into the fissure one sees nothing but a dense white cloud; from this cloud rushed up a great jet of vapour exactly like steam, and it mounted two or three hundred feet high."

Livingstone now continued his perilous journey with his hundred men along the Zambesi, the country once densely populated, now desolate and still. The Bakota tribes, "the colour of coffee and milk," were friendly, and "great numbers came from all the surrounding villages and expressed great joy at the appearance of a white man and harbinger of peace." They brought in large supplies of food, and expressed great delight when Livingstone doctored their children, who were suffering from whooping-cough. As they neared the coast, they became aware of hostile forces. This was explained when they were met by a Portuguese half-caste "with jacket and hat on," who informed them that for the last two years they had been fighting the natives. Plunging thus unconsciously into the midst of a Kafir war rendered travelling unpleasant and dangerous. In addition, the party of explorers found their animals woefully bitten by the tsetse fly, rhinoceroses and elephants were too plentiful to be interesting, and the great white ant made itself tiresome.

It was 3rd March before Livingstone reached Tete, two hundred and sixty miles from the coast. The last stages of the journey had been very beautiful. Many of the hills were of pure white marble, and pink marble formed the

THE "SMOKE" OF THE ZAMBESI (VICTORIA) FALLS.

After a drawing in Livingstone's *Missionary Travels*.

bed of more than one of the streams. Through this country the Zambesi rolled down toward the coast at the rate of four miles an hour, while flocks of water-fowl swarmed upon its banks or flew over its waters. Tete was the farthest outpost of the Portuguese. Livingstone was most kindly received by the governor, but fever again laid him low, and he had to remain here for three weeks before he was strong enough to start for the last stage of his journey to the coast. He left his Makololos here, promising to return some day to take them home again. They believed in him implicitly, and remained there three years, when he returned according to his word. Leaving Tete, he now embarked on the waters of the Zambesi, high with a fourth annual rise, which bore him to Sena in five days. So swift is the current at times that twenty-four hours is enough to take a boat from Tete to Sena, whereas the return journey may take twenty days.

"I thought the state of Tete quite lamentable," says Livingstone, but that of Sena was ten times worse. "It is impossible to describe the miserable state of decay into which the Portuguese possessions here have sunk."

Though suffering badly from fever, Livingstone pushed on; he passed the important tributary of the Zambesi, the Shire, which he afterwards explored, and finally reached Quilimane on the shores of the Indian Ocean. It was now 20th May 1856, just four years after he had left Cape Town on his great journey from west to east, since when he had travelled eleven thousand miles. After waiting six weeks on the " great mud bank, surrounded by extensive swamps and rice grounds," which form the site of Quilimane, Livingstone embarked on board a gunboat, the *Frolic*, for England. He had one Makololo with him—the faithful Sekwebu. The poor black man begged to be allowed to follow his master on the seas.

" But," said Livingstone, " you will die if you go to such a cold country as mine."

" Let me die at your feet," pleaded the black man.

He had not been to Loanda, so he had never seen the sea before. Waves were breaking over the bar at Quilimane and dashing over the boat that carried Sekwebu out to the brig. He was terribly alarmed, but he lived to reach Mauritius, where he became insane, hurled himself into the sea, and was drowned !

On 12th December 1856, Livingstone landed in England after an absence of sixteen years. He had left home as an obscure missionary ; he returned to find himself famous. The Royal Geographical Society awarded him its gold medal; France and Scotland hastened to do him honour. Banquets and receptions were given for him, and finally this " plain, single-minded man, somewhat attenuated by years of toil, and with his face tinged by the sun of Africa," was received by the Queen at Windsor. The enthusiasm aroused by this longest expedition in the history of African travel was unrivalled, and the name of Livingstone was on every lip. But meanwhile others were at work in central Africa, and we must turn from the discoveries of Livingstone for the moment.

CHAPTER LXIII

BURTON AND SPEKE IN CENTRAL AFRICA, 1856

LIVINGSTONE had just left Loanda and was making his way across Africa from west to east, when an English expedition set forth to find the Great Lakes still lying solitary and undiscovered, although they were known to exist. If we turn to the oldest maps of Africa, we find, rudely drawn and incorrectly placed, large inland waters, that may nevertheless be recognised as these lakes just about to be revealed to a wondering world. Ptolemy knew of them, the Arabs spoke of them, Portuguese traders had passed them, and a German missionary had caught sight of the Mountains of the Moon and brought back strange stories of a great inland lake.

The work of rediscovering the lakes was entrusted to a remarkable man named Richard Burton, a man whose love of adventure was well known. He had already shown his metal by entering Mecca disguised as a Persian, and disguised as an Arab he had entered Harar, a den of slave traders, the "Timbuktu of Eastern Africa." On his return he was attacked by the Somalis; one of his companions was killed, another, Speke, escaped with terrible spear-wounds, and he himself was badly wounded.

Such were the men who in 1856 were dispatched by the Royal Geographical Society for the exploration of the mysterious lakes in the heart of central Africa. Speke gives us an idea of the ignorance prevailing on this subject only fifty-six years ago: " On the walls of the Society's rooms there hung a large diagram constructed by two missionaries carrying on their duties at Zanzibar. In this section map, swallowing up about half of the whole area of the ground included in it, there figured a lake of such portentous size and such unseemly shape, representing a gigantic slug, that everybody who looked at it incredulously laughed and shook his head—a single sheet of sweet water, upwards of eight hundred miles long by three hundred broad, equal in size to the great salt Caspian."

It was April 1857 before Burton and Speke had

BURTON IN A DUG-OUT ON LAKE TANGANYIKA.
After a drawing by Burton.

collected an escort and guides at Zanzibar, the great slave market of East Africa, and were ready to start for the interior. "We could obtain no useful information from the European merchants of Zanzibar, who are mostly ignorant of everything beyond the island," Burke wrote home on 22nd April.

At last on 27th June, with thirty-six men and thirty donkeys, the party set out for the great malarious coast-belt which had to be crossed before Kaze, some five hundred miles distant, could be reached. After three months' arduous travelling—both Burton and Speke were badly stricken with fever—they reached Kaze. Speke now spread open the map of the missionaries and inquired of the natives where the enormous lake was to be found. To their intense surprise they found the missionaries had run three lakes into one, and the three lakes were Lake Nyassa, Tanganyika, and Victoria Nyanza. They stayed over a month at Kaze, till Burton seemed at the point of death, and Speke had him carried out of the unhealthy town. It was January before they made a start and continued their journey westward to Ujiji.

"It is a wonderful thing," says Drummond, "to start from the civilisation of Europe, pass up these mighty rivers, and work your way alone and on foot, mile after mile, month after month, among strange birds and beasts and plants and insects, meeting tribes which have no name, speaking tongues which no man can interpret, till you have reached its sacred heart and stood where white man has never trod before."

As the two men tramped on, the streams began to drain to the west and the land grew more fertile, till one hundred and fifty miles from Kaze they began to ascend the slope of mountains overhanging the northern half of Lake Tanganyika. "This mountain mass," says Speke, "I consider to be the True Mountains of the Moon." From the top of the mountains the lovely Tanganyika Lake could be seen in all its glory by Burton. But to Speke it was a mere mist. The glare of the sun and oft-repeated fever had begun to tell on him, and a kind of inflammation had produced almost total blindness. But they had reached the lake and they felt sure they had found the source of the Nile. It was a great day when Speke crossed the lake in a long canoe hollowed out of the trunk of a tree and manned by twenty native savages under the command of a captain in a "goatskin uniform." On the

far side they encamped on the opposite shore, Speke being
the first white man to cross the lake.

Having retired to his hut for the night, Speke proceeded to light a candle and arrange his baggage, when to
his horror he found the whole interior swarming with
black beetles. Tired of trying to brush them away, he
put out his light and, though they crawled up his sleeves
and down his back, he fell asleep. Suddenly he woke to
find one crawling into his ear, and in spite of his frantic
efforts it crept in farther and farther till it reached the

BURTON AND HIS COMPANIONS ON THE MARCH TO THE VICTORIA NYANZA.

From a humorous sketch by Burton.

drum, which caused the tired explorer intense agony.
Inflammation ensued, his face became drawn, he could
with difficulty swallow a little broth, and he was quite
deaf. He returned across the lake to find his companion,
Burton, still very ill and unfit for further exploration.

So Speke, although still suffering from his ear, started
off again, leaving Burton behind, to find the great northern
lake spoken of as the sea of Ukerewe, where the Arabs
traded largely in ivory. There was a great empire beyond
the lake, they told him, called Uganda.

But it was July 1858 when the caravan was ready to start from Kaze. Speke himself carried Burton's large elephant gun. " I commenced the journey," he says, " at 6 p.m., as soon as the two donkeys I took with me to ride were caught and saddled. It was a dreary beginning. The escort who accompanied me were sullen in their manner and walked with heavy gait and downcast countenance. The nature of the track increased the general gloom.

" For several weeks the caravan moved forward, till on 3rd August it began to wind up a long but gradually inclined hill, until it reached its summit, when the vast expanse of the pale blue waters of the Nyanza burst suddenly upon my eyes ! It was early morning. The distant sea-line of the north horizon was defined in the calm atmosphere, but I could get no idea of the breadth of the lake, as an archipelago of islands, each consisting of a single hill rising to a height of two or three hundred feet above the water, intersected the line of vision to the left. A sheet of water extended far away to the eastward. The view was one which even in a well-known country would have arrested the traveller by its peaceful beauty. But the pleasure of the mere view vanished in the presence of those more intense emotions called up by the geographical importance of the scene before me. I no longer felt any doubt that the lake at my feet gave birth to that interesting river (Nile), the source of which has been the subject of so much speculation and the object of so many explorers. This is a far more extensive lake than Tanganyika ; it is so broad that you could not see across it, and so long that nobody knew its length. This magnificent sheet of water I have ventured to name Victoria after our gracious sovereign."

Speke returned to Kaze after his six weeks' eventful journey, having tramped no less than four hundred and fifty-two miles. He received a warm welcome from Burton, who had been very uneasy about his safety, for rumours of civil war had reached him. " I laughed over the matter," says Speke, " but expressed my regret that he did not accompany me, as I felt quite certain in my mind I had discovered the source of the Nile."

Together the two explorers now made their way to the coast and crossed to Aden, where Burton, still weak and ill, decided to remain for a little, while Speke took passage in a passing ship for home.

When he showed his map of Tanganyika and Victoria Nyanza to the President of the Royal Geographical Society in London, Sir Roderick Murchison was delighted.

" Speke, we must send you there again," he said enthusiastically.

And the expedition was regarded as " one of the most notable discoveries in the annals of African discovery."

CHAPTER LXIV

LIVINGSTONE TRACES LAKE SHIRWA AND NYASSA

BURTON and Speke had not yet returned from central Africa, when Livingstone left England on another expedition into the interior, with orders " to extend the knowledge already attained of the geography of eastern and central Africa and to encourage trade." Leaving England on 10th March 1858, he reached the east coast the following May as British Consul of Quilimane, the region which lies about the mouth of the Zambesi. Livingstone had brought out with him a small steam-launch called by the natives the *Ma-Robert* after Mrs. Livingstone, the mother of Robert, their eldest child. In this little steam-launch he made his way up the Shire River, which flows into the Zambesi quite near its mouth. " The delight of threading out the meanderings of upwards of two hundred miles of a hitherto unexplored river must be felt to be appreciated," says Livingstone in his diary. At the end of this two hundred miles further progress became impossible because of rapids which no boat could pass. " These magnificent cataracts we called the Murchison Cataracts, after one whose name has already a world-wide fame," says Livingstone. Leaving their boat here, they started on foot for the Great Lake described by the natives. It took them a month of hard travelling to reach their goal. Their way lay over the native tracks which run as a network over this part of the world. " They are veritable footpaths, never over a foot in breadth, beaten as hard as adamant by centuries of native traffic. Like the roads of the old Romans, they run straight on over everything, ridge and mountain and valley."

On 18th April, Lake Shirwa came into sight, " a considerable body of bitter water, containing leeches, fish, crocodiles, and hippopotami. The country around is very beautiful," adds Livingstone, " and clothed with rich vegetation, and the waves breaking and foaming

THE *MA-ROBERT* ON THE ZAMBESI.

After a drawing in Livingstone's *Expedition to the Zambesi*.

over a rock, added to the beauty of the picture. Exceedingly lofty mountains stand near the eastern shore."

No white man had gazed at the lake before. Though one of the smaller African lakes, Shirwa is probably larger than all the lakes of Great Britain put together. Returning to Tete, the explorer now prepared for his journey to the farther Lake Nyassa. This was to be no new discovery. The Portuguese knew the locality of Lake Shirwa, and at the beginning of the seventeenth century Nyassa was familiar to them under another name. Landing at the same spot on the Shire banks as before,

Livingstone, with thirty-six Makololo porters and two native guides, ascended the beautiful Shire Highlands, some twelve hundred feet above sea-level, and crossed the range on which Zomba, the residence of the British Commissioner for Nyassaland, now stands. When within a day's march of their goal they were told that no lake had ever been heard of in the neighbourhood, but, said the natives, the river Shire stretched on, and it would take two months to reach the end, which came out of perpendicular rocks which towered almost to the skies.

"Let us go back to the ship," said the followers; "it is no use trying to find the lake."

But Livingstone persevered, and he was soon rewarded by finding a sheet of water, which was indeed the beginning of Lake Nyassa. It was 16th September 1859.

" How far is it to the end of the lake ? " he asked.

" The other end of the lake ? Who ever heard of such a thing ? Why, if one started when a mere boy to walk to the other end of the lake, he would be an old grey-headed man before he got there," declared one of the natives. Livingstone knew that he had opened up a great waterway to the interior of Africa, but the slave trade in these parts was terrible, gangs being employed in carrying the ivory from countries to the north down to the east coast. The English explorer saw that if he could establish a steamer upon this Lake Nyassa and buy ivory from the natives with European goods he would at once strike a deadly blow at the slave trade. His letters home stirred several missionaries to come out and establish a settlement on the banks of the Shire River. Bishop Mackenzie and a little band of helpers arrived on the river Shire two years later, and in 1862 Mrs. Livingstone joined them, bringing out with her a little new steamer to launch on the Lake Nyassa. But the unhealthy season was at its height, and " the surrounding low land, rank with vegetation and reeking from the late rainy season, exhaled the malarious poison in enormous quantities." Mrs. Livingstone fell ill, and in a week she was dead. She was buried under a large baobab tree at Shapunga, where her grave is visited by many a traveller passing through this once solitary region first penetrated by her husband.

The blow was a crushing one for Livingstone, and for a time he was quite bewildered. But when his old energy returned he superintended the launching of the little steamer, the *Lady Nyassa*. But disappointment and failure awaited him, and at last, just two years after the death of his wife, he took the *Lady Nyassa* to Zanzibar by the Rovuma River and set forth to reach Bombay, where he hoped to sell her, for his funds were low.

On the last day of April 1864 he started on his perilous journey. Though warned that the monsoon would shortly break, he would not be deterred. And after sailing two thousand five hundred miles in the little boat built only for river and lake, " a forest of masts one day loomed through the haze in Bombay harbour," and he was safe. After a brief stay here, Livingstone left his little launch and made his way to England on a mail-packet.

But no one realised at this time the importance of his new discoveries. No one foresaw the value of " Nyassaland " now under British protectorate. Livingstone had brought to light a lake fifteen hundred and seventy feet above the sea, three hundred and fifty miles long and forty broad, up and down which British steamers make their way to-day, while the long range of mountains lining the eastern bank, known as the Livingstone range, testify to the fact that he had done much, even if he might have done more.

CHAPTER LXV

EXPEDITION TO VICTORIA NYANZA

WHILE Livingstone was discovering Lake Nyassa, Speke was busy preparing for a new expedition to find out more about the great sheet of water he had named Victoria Nyanza and to solve the vexed question : Was this the source of the Nile ?

In April 1860, accompanied by Captain Grant, an old friend and brother sportsman, he left England, and by way of the Cape reached Zanzibar some five months later. The two explorers started for their great inland journey early in October, with some hundred followers, bound for the great lake. But it was January 1861 before they had covered the five hundred miles between the coast and Kaze, the old halting-station of Burton and Speke. Through the agricultural plains known as Uzarana, the country of Rana, where many negro porters deserted, because they believed the white men were cannibals and intended to eat them when safe away from the haunts of men ; through Usagara, the country of Gara, where Captain Grant was seized with fever ; through Ugogo's great wilderness, where buffalo and rhinoceros abounded, where the country was flooded with tropical rains, on to the land of the Moon, three thousand feet above sea-level, till the slowly moving caravan reached Kaze. Here terrible accounts of famine and war reached them, and, instead of following Speke's route of 1858, they turned north-west and entered the

Uzinza country, governed by two chieftains of Abyssinian descent. Here Speke was taken desperately ill. His cough gave him no rest day or night; his legs were " reduced to the appearance of pipe-sticks." But, emaciated as he was, he made his way onwards, till the explorers were rewarded by finding a " beautiful sheet of water lying snugly within the folds of the hills," which they named the Little Windermere, because they thought it was so like " our own English lake of that name. To do royal honours to the king of this charming land, I ordered my men," says Speke, " to put down their loads and fire a volley."

The king, whom they next visited, was a fine-looking man, who, with his brother, sat cross-legged on the ground, with huge pipes of black clay by their sides, while behind them, " squatting quiet as mice," were the king's sons, six or seven lads, with little dream-charms under their chins ! The king shook hands in true English fashion and was full of inquiries. Speke described the world, the proportions of land and water, and the large ships on the sea, and begged to be allowed to pass through his kingdom to Uganda. The explorers learnt much about the surrounding country, and spent Christmas Day with a good feast of roast beef. The start for Uganda was delayed by the serious illness of Grant, until at last Speke reluctantly decided to leave him with the friendly king, while he made his way alone to Uganda and the Lake Victoria Nyanza. It was the end of January 1861 when the English explorer entered the unknown kingdom of Uganda. Messengers from the king, M'tesa, came to him. " Now," they said, " you have really entered the kingdom of Uganda, for the future you must buy no more food. At every place that you stop for the day, the officer in charge will bring you plantains."

The king's palace was ten days' march; the way lay along the western coast of the Lake Victoria Nyanza, the roads were "as broad as our coach roads cut through the long grass straight over the hills and down through the woods. The temperature was perfect. The whole land was a picture of quiescent beauty, with a boundless sea in the background."

On 13th February, Speke found a large volume of water going to the north. "I took off my clothes," he says, "and jumped into the stream, which I found was twelve yards broad and deeper than my height. I was delighted beyond measure, for I had, to all appearance, found one of the branches of the Nile's exit from the Nyanza."

M'TESA, KING OF UGANDA.

From Speke's *Journey to Discover the Source of the Nile.*

But he had not reached the Nile yet. It was not till the end of July that he reached his goal.

"Here at last," he says, "I stood on the brink of the Nile, most beautiful was the scene, nothing could surpass it—a magnificent stream from six hundred to seven hundred yards wide, dotted with islets and rocks, the former occupied by fishermen's huts, the latter by crocodiles basking in the sun. I told my men they ought to bathe in the holy river, the cradle of Moses."

Marching onwards, they found the waterfall, which

Speke named the Ripon Falls, "by far the most interesting sight I had seen in Africa." The arm of the
water from which the Nile issued he named "Napoleon
Channel," out of respect to the French Geographical
Society for the honour they had done him just before
leaving England in presenting their gold medal for the
discovery of Victoria Nyanza.

The English explorers had now spent six months in
Uganda. The civilisation in this country of M'tesa's

THE RIPON FALLS ON THE VICTORIA NYANZA.
From Speke's *Journey to Discover the Source of the Nile.*

has passed into history. Every one was clothed, and
even little boys held their skin-cloaks tightly round
them lest their bare legs might by accident be seen!
Everything was clean and orderly under the all-powerful
ruler M'tesa. Grant, who arrived in the end of May,
carried in a litter, found Speke had not yet obtained
leave from the king to " open the country to the north,
that an uninterrupted line of commerce might exist
between England and Uganda by means of the Nile."
But at last on 3rd July he writes with joy: "The

moment of triumph has come at last and suddenly the road is granted."

The explorers bid farewell to M'tesa. "We rose with an English bow, placing the hand on the heart, whilst saying adieu ; and whatever we did M'tesa in an instant mimicked with the instinct of a monkey."

In five boats of five planks each tied together and caulked with rags, Speke started with a small escort and crew to reach the palace of the neighbouring king, Kamrasi, "father of all the kings," in the province of Unyoro. After some fierce opposition they entered the palace of the king, a poor creature. Rumours had reached him that these two white men were cannibals and sorcerers. His palace was indeed a contrast to that of M'tesa. It was merely a dirty hut approached by a lane ankle-deep in mud and cow-manure. The king's sisters were not allowed to marry; their only occupation was to drink milk from morning to night, with the result that they grew so fat it took eight men to lift one of them, when walking became impossible. Superstition was rife, and the explorers were not sorry to leave Unyoro *en route* for Cairo. Speke and Grant now believed that, except for a few cataracts, the waterway to England was unbroken. The Karuma Falls broke the monotony of the way, and here the party halted a while before plunging into the Kidi wilderness across which they intended to march to save a great bend of the river. Their path lay through swampy jungles and high grass, while great grassy plains, where buffaloes were seen and the roar of lions was heard, stretched away on every side.

Suddenly they reached a huge rock covered with huts, in front of which groups of black men were perched like monkeys, evidently awaiting the arrival of the white men. They were painted in the most brilliant colours, though without clothes, for the civilisation of Uganda had been left far behind. Pushing on, they reached the Madi country, where again civilisation awaited them in the shape of Turks. It was on 3rd December that they saw to their great surprise three large red flags carried in front of a military procession which marched out of camp with drums and fifes playing.

"A very black man named Mohammed, in full Egyptian regimentals, with a curved sword, ordered his regiment to halt, and threw himself into my arms endeavouring to kiss me," says Speke. "Having reached his huts, he gave us two beds to sit upon, and ordered his wives to advance on their knees and give us coffee."

CAPTAINS SPEKE AND GRANT.

"I have directions to take you to Gondokoro as soon as you come," said Mohammed.

Yet they were detained till 11th January, when in sheer desperation they started off, and in two days reached the Nile. Having no boats, they continued their march overland till 15th February, when the masts of Nile boats came in sight, and soon after the two explorers walked into Gondokoro. Then a strange thing happened. "We saw hurrying on towards us the form of an Englishman, and the next moment my old friend Baker, famed for his sports in Ceylon, seized me by the

30

hand. What joy this was I can hardly tell. We could not talk fast enough, so overwhelmed were we both to meet again. Of course we were his guests, and soon learned everything that could be told. I now first heard of the death of H.R.H. the Prince Consort. Baker said he had come up with three vessels fully equipped with armed men, camels, horses, donkeys; and everything necessary for a long journey, expressly to look after us. Three Dutch ladies also, with a view to assist us (God bless them!); had come here in a steamer, but were driven back to Khartum by sickness. Nobody had dreamt for a moment it was possible we could come through."

Leaving Baker to continue his way to central Africa, Speke and Grant made their way home to England, where they arrived in safety after an absence of three years and fifty-one days, with their great news of the discovery of Uganda and their further exploration of Victoria Nyanza. When Speke reached Alexandria he had telegraphed home : " The Nile is settled." But he was wrong. The Nile was not settled, and many an expedition was yet to make its way to the great lakes before the problem was to be solved.

CHAPTER LXVI

BAKER FINDS ALBERT NYANZA

BAKER had not been long at Gondokoro when the two English explorers arrived from the south.

" In March 1861," he tells us, " I commenced an expedition to discover the sources of the Nile, with the hope of meeting the East African expedition of Captains Speke and Grant that had been sent by the English Government from the south *via* Zanzibar for that object. From my youth I had been inured to hardship and endurance in tropical climates, and when I gazed upon the map of Africa I had a wild hope that I might by perseverance reach the heart of Africa."

These are the opening lines of the published travels of Samuel Baker, famous as an elephant-hunter in Ceylon and engineer of the first railway laid down in Turkey. Like Livingstone, in his early explorations, Baker took his wife with him. " It was in vain that I implored her to remain, and that I painted the difficulties and perils still blacker than I supposed they really would be ; she was resolved to share all dangers and to follow me through each rough footstep of the wild life before me."

On 15th April 1861, Baker and his wife left Cairo to make their way southward to join the quest for the source of the Nile. They reached Korosko in twenty-six days, and crossed the Nubian desert on camels; a "very wilderness of scorching sand, the simoon in full force and the thermometer in the shade standing at 114° Fahr." By

Abu Hamed and Berber they reached Atbara. It now occurred to Baker that without some knowledge of Arabic he could do little in the way of exploration, so for a whole year he stayed in northern Abyssinia, the country explored by Bruce nearly ninety years before.

It was therefore 18th December 1862 before he and Mrs. Baker left Khartum for their journey up the Nile through the slave-driven Sudan. It was a fifty days' voyage to Gondokoro. In the hope of finding Speke and Grant, he took an extra load of corn as well as twenty-two donkeys, four camels, and four horses. Gondokoro was reached just a fortnight before the two explorers returned from the south.

Baker's account of the historical meeting between the white men in the heart of Africa is very interesting : " Heard guns firing in the distance—report that two white men had come from the sea. Could they be Speke and Grant ? Off I ran and soon met them ; hurrah for Old England. They had come from the Victoria Nyanza from which the Nile springs. The mystery of ages solved ! With a heart beating with joy I took off my cap and gave a welcome hurrah as I ran towards them ! For the moment they did not recognise me ; ten years' growth of beard and moustache had worked a change, and my sudden appearance in the centre of Africa appeared to them incredible. As a good ship arrives in harbour battered and torn by a long and stormy voyage, so both these gallant travellers arrived in Gondokoro. Speke appeared to me the more worn of the two. He was excessively lean ; he had walked the whole way from Zanzibar, never having ridden once during that wearying march. Grant was in rags, his bare knees projecting through the remnants of trousers."

Baker was now inclined to think that his work was done, the source of the Nile discovered, but after looking at the map of their route, he saw that an important part of the Nile still remained undiscovered, and though there were dangers ahead he determined to go on his way into central Africa.

" We took neither guide nor interpreter," he continues. " We commenced our desperate journey in darkness about an hour after sunset. I led the way, Mrs. Baker riding by my side and the British flag following close behind us as a guide for the caravan of heavily laden camels and

BAKER AND HIS WIFE CROSSING THE NUBIAN DESERT.
From Baker's *Travels.*

donkeys. And thus we started on our march in central Africa on the 26th of March 1863."

It would take too long to tell of their manifold misfortunes and difficulties before they reached the lake they were in search of on 16th March 1864. How they passed through the uncivilised country so lately traversed by Speke and Grant, how in the Obbo country all their porters deserted just a few days before they reached the Karuma Falls, how Baker from this point tried to follow the Nile to the yet unknown lake, how fever seized both the explorer and his wife and they had to live on the common food of the natives and a little water, how suddenly Mrs. Baker fell down with a sunstroke and was carried for seven days quite unconscious through swamp and jungle, the rain descending in torrents all the time, till Baker, "weak as a reed," worn out with anxiety, lay on the ground as one dead.

It seemed as if both must die, when better times dawned and they recovered to find that they were close to the lake.

Baker's diary is eloquent: "The day broke beautifully clear, and, having crossed a deep valley between the hills, we toiled up the opposite slope. I hurried to the summit. The glory of our prize burst suddenly upon me! There, like a sea of quicksilver, lay far beneath us the grand expanse of water, a boundless sea-horizon on the south and south-west, glittering in the noonday sun, while at sixty miles' distance, blue mountains rose from the lake to a height of about seven thousand feet above its level. It is impossible to describe the triumph of that moment; here was the reward for all our labour! England had won the sources of the Nile! I looked from the steep granite cliff upon those welcome waters, upon that vast reservoir which nourished Egypt, upon that great source so long hidden from mankind, and I determined to honour it with a great name. As an imperishable memorial of one loved and mourned by our gracious Queen, I called this great lake 'the Albert Nyanza.' The Victoria and the Albert Lakes are the two sources of the Nile."

Weak and spent with fever, the Bakers descended tottering to the water's edge. "The waves were rolling upon a white pebbly beach. I rushed into the lake and, thirsty with heat and fatigue, I drank deeply from the sources of the Nile. My wife, who had followed me so devotedly, stood by my side pale and exhausted—a wreck

upon the shores of the great Albert Lake that we had long
striven to reach. No European foot had ever trod upon
its sand, nor had the eyes of a white man ever scanned its
vast expanse of water."

After some long delay, the Bakers procured canoes,
" merely single trees neatly hollowed out," and paddled
along the shores of the newly found lake. The water was
calm, the views most lovely. Hippopotami sported in the

BAKER'S BOAT IN A STORM ON LAKE ALBERT NYANZA.

From Baker's *Albert Nyanza.*

water; crocodiles were numerous. Day after day they
paddled north, sometimes using a large Scotch plaid as
sail. It was dangerous work. Once a great storm nearly
swamped them. The little canoe shipped heavy seas;
terrific bursts of thunder and vivid lightning broke over
the lake, hiding everything from view. Then down came
the rain in torrents, swept along by a terrific wind. They
reached the shore in safety, but the discomforts of the

voyage were great, and poor Mrs. Baker suffered severely. On the thirteenth day they found themselves at the end of the lake voyage, and carefully examined the exit of the Nile from the lake. They now followed the river in their canoe for some eighteen miles, when they suddenly heard a roar of water, and, rounding a corner, "a magnificent sight suddenly burst upon us. On either side of the river were beautifully wooded cliffs rising abruptly to a height of three hundred feet and rushing through a gap that cleft the rock. The river pent up in a narrow gorge roared furiously through the rock-bound pass, till it plunged in one leap of about one hundred and twenty feet into a dark abyss below. This was the greatest waterfall of the Nile, and in honour of the distinguished President of the Royal Geographical Society I named it the Murchison Falls." Further navigation was impossible, and with oxen and porters they proceeded by land. Mrs. Baker was still carried in a litter, while Baker walked by her side. Both were soon attacked again with fever, and when night came they threw themselves down in a wretched hut. A violent thunderstorm broke over them, and they lay there utterly helpless, and worn out till sunrise. Worse was to come. The natives now deserted them, and they were alone and helpless, with a wilderness of rank grass hemming them in on every side. Their meals consisted of a mess of black porridge of bitter mouldy flour " that no English pig would notice " and a dish of spinach. For nearly two months they existed here, until they became perfect skeletons.

" We had given up all hope of Gondokoro," says Baker, " and I had told my headman to deliver my map and papers to the English Consul at Khartum."

But they were not to die here. The king, Kamrasi, having heard of their wretched condition, sent for them, treated them kindly, and enabled them to reach Gondokoro, which they did on 23rd March 1865, after an absence of two years. They had long since been given up as lost, and it was an immense joy to reach Cairo at last and to find that, in the words of Baker, " the Royal Geographical Society had awarded me the Victoria Gold Medal at a time when they were unaware whether I was alive or dead and when the success of my expedition was unknown."

CHAPTER LXVII

LIVINGSTONE'S LAST JOURNEY

In the year 1865 "the greatest of all African travellers" started on his last journey to central Africa.

" I hope," he said, " to ascend the Rovuma, and shall strive, by passing along the northern end of Lake Nyassa and round the southern end of Lake Tanganyika, to ascertain the watershed of that part of Africa."

Arrived at Zanzibar in January 1866, he reached the mouth of the Rovuma River some two months later, and, passing through dense thickets of trees, he started on his march along the northern bank. The expedition consisted of thirteen sepoys from Bombay, nine negroes from one of the missions, two men from the Zambesi, Susi, Amoda, and others originally slaves freed by Livingstone. As beasts of burden, they had six camels, three Indian buffaloes, two mules, four donkeys, while a poodle took charge of the whole line of march, running to see the first man in the line and then back to the last, and barking to hasten him up.

" Now that I am on the point of starting on another trip into Africa," wrote Livingstone from Rovuma Bay, " I feel quite exhilarated. The mere animal pleasure of travelling in a wild, unexplored country is very great. Brisk exercise imparts elasticity to the muscles, fresh and healthy blood circulates through the brain, the mind works well, the eye is clear, the step firm, and a day's exertion makes the evening's repose thoroughly enjoyable."

But misfortunes soon began. As they marched along the banks of the Rovuma the buffaloes and camels were badly bitten by the tsetse fly, and one after another died. The cruelty of the followers to the animals was terrible. Indeed, they were thoroughly unsatisfactory.

One day a party of them lagged behind, killed the last young buffalo, and ate it. They told Livingstone that it had died and tigers had come and devoured it.

" Did you see the stripes of the tiger ? " asked Livingstone.

Yes; all declared that they had seen them distinctly— an obvious lie, as there are no striped tigers in Africa.

On 11th August, Livingstone once more reached Lake Nyassa. " It was as if I had come back to an old home I never expected again to see, and pleasant it was to bathe in the delicious waters again. I feel quite exhilarated."

Having sent word to the Arab chief of Kota-Kota on the opposite coast, and having received no reply to his request to be ferried across the lake, he started off and marched by land round the southern end, crossing the Shire River at its entrance. He continued his journey round the south-western gulf of Lake Nyassa, till rumours of Zulu raids frightened his men. They refused to go any farther, but just threw down their loads and walked away. He was now left with Susi and Chuma and a few boys with whom he crossed the end of a long range of mountains over four thousand feet in height, and, pursuing a zigzag track, reached the Loangwa River on 16th December 1866, while his unfaithful followers returned to the coast to spread the story that Livingstone had been killed by the Zulus !

Meanwhile the explorer was plodding on towards Lake Tanganyika. The beauty of the way strikes the lonely explorer. The rainy season had come on in all its force, and the land was wonderful in its early green. " Many gay flowers peep out. Here and there the scarlet lily, red, yellow, and pure white orchids, and pale lobelias. As we ascended higher on the plateau, grasses which have pink and reddish brown seed-vessels were grateful to the eye."

Two disasters clouded this month of travel. His poor poodle was drowned in a marsh and his medicine-chest was stolen. The land was famine-bound too; the people were living on mushrooms and leaves. " We get some elephants' meat, but it is very bitter, and the appetite in this country is always very keen and makes hunger worse to bear, the want of salt probably making the gnawing sensation worse."

On 28th January, Livingstone crossed the Tshambezi, " which may almost be regarded as the upper waters of the Congo," says Johnstone, though the explorer of 1867 knew it not.

" Northwards," says Livingstone, " through almost trackless forest and across oozing bogs "; and then he adds the significant words, " I am frightened at my own emacia- tion." March finds him worse. " I have been ill of fever; every step I take jars in my chest, and I am very weak ; I can scarcely keep up the march." At last, on 1st April, " blue water loomed through the trees." It was Lake Tanganyika lying some two thousand feet below them. Its " surpassing loveliness " struck Livingstone. " It lies in a deep basin," he says, " whose sides are nearly per- pendicular, but covered well with trees, at present all green; down some of these rocks come beautiful cascades, while buffaloes, elephants, and antelopes wander and graze on the more level spots, and lions roar by night. In the morning and evening huge crocodiles may be observed quietly making their way to their feeding-grounds, and hippopotami snort by night."

Going westwards, Livingstone met a party of Arabs

amongst whom he remained for over three months, till he
could make his way on to Lake Meoro, reported to be only
three days' journey. It took him sixteen days to reach it.
" Lake Meoro seems of goodly size," he says, " and is
flanked by ranges of mountains on the east and west. Its
banks are of coarse sand and slope gradually down to the
water. We slept in a fisherman's cottage on the north
shore."

After a stay of six weeks in the neighbourhood, Livingstone returned to the Arabs, until the spring of 1868,
when he decided to explore the Lake Bangweolo. In
spite of opposition and the desertion of more men, he
started with five attendants and reached this—one of the
largest of the central African lakes—in July. Modestly
enough he asserts the fact. " On the 18th I saw the
shores of the lake for the first time. The name Bangweolo
is applied to the great mass of water, though I fear that our
English folks will bogle at it or call it Bungyhollow. The
water is of a deep sea-green colour. It was bitterly cold
from the amount of moisture in the air."

This moisture converted the surrounding country into
one huge bog or sponge, twenty-nine of which Livingstone
had to cross in thirty miles, each taking about half an hour
to cross.

The explorer was still greatly occupied on the problem
of the Nile. " The discovery of the sources of the Nile,"
he says, " is somewhat akin in importance to the discovery
of the North-West Passage." It seemed to him not impossible that the great river he found flowing through
these two great lakes to the west of Tanganyika might
prove to be the Upper Nile.

It was December before he started for Tanganyika.
The new year of 1868 opened badly. Half-way, he became
very ill. He was constantly wet through; he persistently
crossed brooks and rivers, wading through cold water up

to his waist. "Very ill all over," he enters in his diary; "cannot walk. Pneumonia of right lung, and I cough all day and all night. I am carried several hours a day on a frame. The sun is vertical, blistering any part of the skin exposed, and I try to shelter my face and head as well as I can with a bunch of leaves."

On 14th February 1869 he arrived on the western shores of the lake, and after the usual delay he was put into a canoe for Ujiji. Though better, he was still very ill, and we get the pathetic entry, " Hope to hold out to Ujiji."

At last he reached the Arab settlement on the eastern shores, where he found the goods sent to him overland from Zanzibar, and though much had been stolen, yet warm clothes, tea, and coffee soon revived him. After a stay of three months he grew better, and turned westwards for the land of the Manyuema and the great rivers reported to be flowing there.

He was guided by Arabs whose trade-route extended to the great Lualaba River in the very heart of Africa some thousand miles west of Zanzibar. It was an unknown land, unvisited by Europeans when Livingstone arrived with his Arab escort at Bambarra in September 1869.

" Being now well rested," he enters in his diary, " I resolved to go west to Lualaba and buy a canoe for its exploration. The Manyuema country is all surpassingly beautiful. Palms crown the highest heights of the mountains, and the forests about five miles broad are indescribable. Climbers of cable size in great numbers are hung among the gigantic trees, many unknown wild fruits abound, some the size of a child's head, and strange birds and monkeys are everywhere."

With the Arab caravan he travelled almost incessantly zigzagging through the wonderful Manyuema country until, after a year's wandering, he finally reached the banks of the Lualaba (Congo) on 31st March 1871.

THE DISCOVERY OF LAKE BANGWEOLO, 1868 : LIVINGSTONE ON THE LAKE WITH HIS MEN.

From Livingstone's *Last Journals*, by permission of Mr. John Murray.

It was a red-letter day in his life. " I went down," he says, " to take a good look at the Lualaba here. It is a mighty river at least three thousand yards broad and always deep. The banks are steep; the current is about two miles an hour away to the north." Livingstone was gazing at the second-largest river in the world—the Congo. But he thought it was the Nile, and confidently relates how it overflows all its banks annually as the Nile does.

At Nyangwe, a Manyuema village, Livingstone stayed for four months. The natives were dreadful canni- bals. He saw one day a man with ten human jaw-bones hung by a string over his shoulder, the owners of which he had killed and eaten. Another day a terrible massacre took place, arising from a squabble over a fowl, in which some four hundred perished. The Arabs too disgusted him with their slave-raiding, and he decided that he could no longer travel under their protection. So on 20th July 1871 he started back for Ujiji, and after a journey of seven hundred miles, accomplished in three months, he arrived, reduced to a skeleton, only to find that the rascal who had charge of his stores had stolen the whole and made away.

But when health and spirit were failing, help was at hand. The meeting of Stanley and Livingstone on the shores of the Lake Tanganyika is one of the most thrilling episodes in the annals of discovery. Let them tell their own story : " When my spirits were at their lowest ebb," says Livingstone, " one morning Susi came running at the top of his speed and gasped out, " An Englishman ! I see him ! " and off he darted to meet him. The American flag at the head of a caravan told of the nationality of the stranger. Bales of goods, baths of tin, huge kettles, and cooking-pots made me think, " This must be a luxurious traveller and not one at his wits' end, like me."

It was Henry Morton Stanley, the travelling correspondent of the *New York Herald*, sent at an expense of more than £4000 to obtain accurate information about Dr. Livingstone if living, and if dead to bring home his bones.

And now Stanley takes up the story. He has entered Ujiji and heard from the faithful Susi that the explorer yet lives. Pushing back the crowds of natives, Stanley

LIVINGSTONE AT WORK ON HIS JOURNAL.

From a sketch by H. M. Stanley.

advanced down " a living avenue of people " till he came to where "the white man with the long grey beard was standing."

"As I advanced slowly towards him," says Stanley, " I noticed he was pale, looked worried, wore a bluish cap with a faded gold band round it, had on a red-sleeved waistcoat and a pair of grey tweed trousers. I walked

31

deliberately to him, took off my hat, and said, 'Dr. Livingstone, I presume?'

"'Yes,' said he, with a kind smile, lifting his cap slightly.

"Then we both grasp hands and I say aloud, 'I thank God, Doctor, I have been permitted to see you.'

"'You have brought me new life—new life,' murmured the tired explorer," and for the next few days it was enough for the two Englishmen to sit on the mud verandah of Livingstone's house, talking. Livingstone soon grew better, and November found the two explorers surveying the river flowing from the north of Tanganyika and deciding that it was not the Nile.

Stanley now did his best to persuade Livingstone to return home with him to recruit his shattered health before finishing his work of exploration. But the explorer, tired and out of health though he was, utterly refused. He must complete the exploration of the sources of the Nile before he sought that peace and comfort at home for which he must have yearned.

So the two men parted—Stanley to carry Livingstone's news of the discovery of the Congo back to Europe, Livingstone to end his days on the lonely shores of Lake Bangweolo, leaving the long-sought mystery of the Nile sources yet unsolved.

On 25th August 1872 he started on his last journey. He had a well-equipped expedition sent up by Stanley from the coast, including sixty men, donkeys, and cows. He embarked on his fresh journey with all his old eagerness and enthusiasm, but a few days' travel showed him how utterly unfit he was for any more hardships. He suffered from intense and growing weakness, which increased day by day. He managed somehow to ride his donkey, but in November his donkey died and he struggled along on foot. Descending into marshy regions north of Lake

LIVINGSTONE ENTERING THE HUT AT ILALA ON THE NIGHT THAT HE DIED.

From Livingstone's *Last Journals*, by permission of Mr. John Murray.

Bangweolo, the journey became really terrible. The rainy season was at its height, the land was an endless swamp, and starvation threatened the expedition. To add to the misery of the party, there were swarms of mosquitoes, poisonous spiders, and stinging ants by the way. Still, amid all the misery and suffering, the explorer made his way on through the dreary autumn months. Christmas came and went; the new year of 1873 dawned. He could not stop. April found him only just alive, carried by his faithful servants. Then comes the last entry in his diary, 27th April: " Knocked up quite. We are on the banks of R. Molilamo."

THE LAST ENTRIES IN LIVINGSTONE'S DIARY.

They laid him at last in a native hut, and here one night he died alone. They found him in the early morning, just kneeling by the side of the rough bed, his body stretched forward, his head buried in his hands upon the pillow. The negroes buried his heart on the spot where he died in the village of Ilala on the shores of Lake Bangweolo under the shadow of a great tree in the still forest. Then they wrapped his body in a cylinder of bark wound round in a piece of old sailcloth, lashed it to a pole, and a little band of negroes, including Susi and Chuma, set out to carry their dead master to the coast. For hundreds of miles they tramped with their precious burden, till they reached the sea and could give it safely to his fellow-countrymen, who conveyed it to England to be laid with other great men in Westminster Abbey.

> " He needs no epitaph to guard a name
> Which men shall praise while worthy work is done.
> He lived and died for good, be that his fame.
> Let marble crumble : this is living-stone."

SUSI, LIVINGSTONE'S SERVANT.

From a sketch by H. M. Stanley.

CHAPTER LXVIII

THROUGH THE DARK CONTINENT

THE death of Livingstone, the faithfulness of his native servants in carrying his body and journals across hundreds of miles of wild country to the coast, his discovery of the great river in the heart of Africa, and the great service in Westminster Abbey roused public interest in the Dark Continent and the unfinished work of the great explorer. " Never had such an outburst of missionary zeal been known, never did the cause of geographical exploration receive such an impetus."

The dramatic meeting between Livingstone and Stanley on the shores of Lake Tanganyika in 1871 had impressed the public in England and America, and an expedition was now planned by the proprietors of two great newspapers, the *London Daily Telegraph* and the *New York Herald*. Stanley was chosen to command it. And perhaps there is hardly a better-known book of modern travels than *Through the Dark Continent*, in which he has related all his adventures and discoveries with regard to the Congo. Leaving England in August 1874 with three Englishmen and a large boat in eight sections, the *Lady Alice*, for the navigation of lake and river, the little exploring party reached Zanzibar a few weeks later and started on their great inland journey. The way to Victoria Nyanza lay through what is now known as German East Africa. They reached Ugogo safely and turned to the north-west, entering an immense and silent bush-field, where no food was obtainable.   On the eighth day five people died of starvation and the rest of the expedition was only saved by the purchase of some grain from a distant village.   But four more died and twenty-eight miles under a hot sun prostrated one of the white men, who died a few days later.   Thus they entered Ituru, "a land of naked people, whose hills drained into a marsh, whence issue the southernmost waters of the Nile."

Here they were surrounded by angry savages on whom they had to fire, and from whose country they were glad to escape.

On 27th February 1875, after tramping for one hundred and three days, they arrived at their destination.   One of the white men who was striding forward suddenly waved his hat, and with a beaming face shouted out, " I have seen the lake, sir; it is grand."

Here, indeed, was the Victoria Nyanza, " which a dazzling sun transformed into silver," discovered by Speke sixteen years before, and supposed to be the source of the Nile.   The men struck up a song of triumph—

> " Sing, O friends, sing; the journey is ended.
> Sing aloud, O friends; sing to the great Nyanza.
> Sing all, sing loud, O friends, sing to the great sea;
> Give your last look to the lands behind, and then turn to the sea.
> Lift up your heads, O men, and gaze around.
> Try if you can to see its end.
> See, it stretches moons away,
> This great, sweet, fresh-water sea."

" I thought," says Stanley, " there could be no better way of settling, once and for ever, the vexed question, than by circumnavigating the lake."

So the *Lady Alice* was launched, and from the shores of Speke Gulf, as he named the southern end, the explorer set forth, leaving the two remaining Englishmen in charge of the camp.

"The sky is gloomy," writes Stanley, "the rocks are bare and rugged, the land silent and lonely. The rowing of the people is that of men who think they are bound to certain death; their hearts are full of misgivings as slowly we move through the dull dead waters." The waters were not dead for long. A gale rose up and the lake became wild beyond description. "The waves hissed as we tore along, the crew collapsed and crouched into the bottom of the boat, expecting the end of the wild venture, but the *Lady Alice* bounded forward like a wild courser and we floated into a bay, still as a pond."

So they coasted along the shores of the lake. Their guide told them it would take years to sail round their sea, that on the shores dwelt people with long tails, who preferred to feed on human beings rather than cattle or goats. But, undaunted, the explorer sailed on, across the Napoleon Channel, through which flowed the superfluous waters of the lake rushing northward as the Victoria Nile. "On the western side of the Channel is Uganda, dominated by an Emperor who is supreme over about three millions of people. He soon heard of my presence on the lake and dispatched a flotilla to meet me. His mother had dreamed the night before that she had seen a boat sailing, sailing like a fish-eagle over the Nyanza. In the stern of the boat was a white man gazing wistfully towards Uganda."

On reaching the port a crowd of soldiers, "arrayed in crimson and black and snowy white," were drawn up to receive him. "As we neared the beach, volleys of musketry burst out from the long lines. Numerous kettles and brass drums sounded a noisy welcome, flags and banners waved, and the people gave a great shout."

Such was Stanley's welcome to M'tesa's wonderful kingdom of Uganda, described by Speke sixteen years before. The twelve days spent at the court of this

STANLEY AND HIS MEN MARCHING THROUGH UNYORO.

From a sketch, by Stanley, in *Through the Dark Continent.*

monarch impressed Stanley deeply. Specially was the king interested in Christianity, and the English explorer told the story of the Creation and the birth of the Messiah to this intelligent pagan and his courtiers. " Ten days after we left the genial court, I came upon the scene of a tragedy. We were coasting the eastern side of a large island, having been thirty-six hours without food, looking for a port where we could put in and purchase provisions. Natives followed our movements, poising their spears, stringing their bows, picking out the best rocks for their slings. We were thirteen souls, they between three and four hundred. Seeing the boat advance, they smiled, entered the water, and held out inviting hands. The crew shot the boat towards the natives ; their hands closed on her firmly, they ran with her to the shore and dragged her high and dry about twenty yards from the lake. Then ensued a scene of rampant wildness and hideous ferocity of action beyond description. The boat was surrounded by a forest of spears and two hundred demons contended for the first blow. I sprang up to kill and be killed, a revolver in each hand, but as I rose to my feet the utter hopelessness of our situation was revealed to me."

To make a long story short, the natives seized the oars, and, thinking the boat was now in their power, they retired to make their plans. Meanwhile Stanley commanded his crew to tear the bottom boards up for paddles, and, pushing the boat hastily into the water, they paddled away, their commander firing the while with his elephant rifle and explosive bullets. They were saved.

On 6th May the circumnavigation was finished and the *Lady Alice* was being dragged ashore in Speke Gulf with shouts of welcome and the waving of many flags. But sad news awaited him. He could see but one of his white companions.

" Where is Barker ? " he asked Frank Pocock.

" He died twelve days ago," was the melancholy answer.

Stanley now took his whole expedition to Uganda, and after spending some months with the King he passed on to Lake Tanganyika, crossing to Ujiji, where he arrived in May 1876. Here five years before he had found Livingstone.

" We launched our boat on the lake and, circumnavigating it, discovered that there was only a periodical outlet to it. Thus, by the circumnavigation of the two lakes, two of the geographical problems I had undertaken to solve were settled. The Victoria Nyanza had no connection with the Tanganyika. There now remained the grandest task of all. Is the Lualaba, which Livingstone had traced along a course of nearly thirteen hundred miles, the Nile, the Niger, or the Congo ? I crossed Lake Tanganyika with my expedition, lifted once more my gallant boat on our shoulders, and after a march of nearly two hundred and twenty miles arrived at the superb river. Where I first sighted it, the Lualaba was fourteen hundred yards wide, pale grey in colour, winding slowly from south and by east. We hailed its appearance with shouts of joy, and rested on the spot to enjoy the view. I likened it to the Mississippi as it appears before the impetuous, full-volumed Missouri pours its rusty brown water into it. A secret rapture filled my soul as I gazed upon the majestic stream. The great mystery that for all these centuries Nature had kept hidden away from the world of science was waiting to be solved. For two hundred and twenty miles I had followed the sources of the Livingstone River to the confluence, and now before me lay the superb river itself. My task was to follow it to the ocean."

Pressing on along the river, they reached the Arab

city of Nyangwe, having accomplished three hundred and thirty-eight miles in forty-three days. And now the famous Arab Tippu-Tib comes on the scene, a chief with whom Stanley was to be closely connected hereafter. He was a tall, black-bearded man with an intelligent face and gleaming white teeth. He wore clothes of spotless white, his fez was smart and new, his dagger resplendent with silver filigree. He had escorted Cameron across the river to the south, and he now confirmed Stanley in his idea that the greatest problem of African geography, " the discovery of the course of the Congo," was still untouched.

" This was momentous and all-important news to the expedition. We had arrived at the critical point in our travels," remarks Stanley. " What kind of a country is it to the north along the river ? " he asked.

" Monstrous bad," was the reply. " There are large boa-constrictors in the forest suspended by their tails, waiting to gobble up travellers. You cannot travel without being covered by ants, and they sting like wasps. There are leopards in countless numbers. Gorillas haunt the woods. The people are man-eaters. A party of three hundred guns started for the forest and only sixty returned."

Stanley and his last remaining white companion, Frank Pocock, discussed the somewhat alarming situation together. Should they go on and face the dwarfs who shot with poisoned arrows, the cannibals who regarded the stranger as so much meat, the cataracts and rocks—should they follow the " great river which flowed northward for ever and knew no end " ?

" This great river which Livingstone first saw, and which broke his heart to turn away from, is a noble field," argued Stanley. " After buying or building canoes and floating down the river day by day, either to the Nile or to some vast lake in the far north or to the Congo and the Atlantic Ocean."

" Let us follow the river," replied the white man.

So, accompanied by Tippu-Tib, with a hundred and forty guns and seventy spearmen, they started along the banks of the river which Stanley now named the Livingstone River.

" On the 5th of November 1876," says Stanley, " a force of about seven hundred people, consisting of Tippu-Tib's slaves and my expedition departed from the town of Nyangwe and entered the dismal forest-land north. A straight line from this point to the Atlantic Ocean would measure one thousand and seventy miles; another to the Indian Ocean would measure only nine hundred and twenty miles; we had not reached the centre of the continent by seventy-five miles.

" Outside the woods blazed a blinding sunshine; underneath that immense roof-foliage was a solemn twilight. The trees shed continual showers of tropic dew. As we struggled on through the mud, the perspiration exuded from every pore; our clothes were soon wet and heavy. Every man had to crawl and scramble as he best could. Sometimes prostrate forest-giants barred the road with a mountain of twigs and branches. For ten days we endured it; then the Arabs declared they could go no farther. I promised them five hundred pounds if they would escort us twenty marches only. On our way to the river we came to a village whose sole street was adorned with one hundred and eighty-six human skulls. Seventeen days from Nyangwe we saw again the great river and, viewing the stately breadth of the mighty stream, I resolved to launch my boat for the last time. Placing thirty-six of the people in the boat, we floated down the river close to the bank along which the land-party marched. Day after day passed on and we found the natives increasing in wild rancour and unreasoning hate of strangers. At every curve and bend they ' telephoned ' along the river warning signals ; their huge wooden drums sounded the muster for fierce resistance ; reed arrows tipped with poison were shot at us from the jungle as we glided by. On the 18th of December our miseries culminated in a grand effort of the savages to annihilate us. The cannibals had manned the topmost branches of the trees above the village of Vinya Njara to shoot at us."

A camp was hastily constructed by Stanley in defence, and for several days there was desperate fighting, at the end of which peace was made. But Tippu-Tib and his escort refused to go a step farther to what they felt was certain destruction. Stanley alone was determined to proceed. He bought thirty-three native canoes and, leading with the *Lady Alice*, he set his face towards the unknown country. His men were all sobbing. They leant forward, bowed with grief and heavy hearts at the prospect before them. Dense woods covered both banks and islands. Savages with gaily feathered heads and painted faces dashed out of the woods armed with shields and spears, shouting, " Meat ! meat ! Ha ! ha ! We shall have plenty of meat ! "

" Armies of parrots screamed overhead as they flew across the river ; legions of monkeys and howling baboons alarmed the solitudes ; crocodiles haunted the sandy points ; hippopotami grunted at our approach ; elephants stood by the margin of the river ; there was unceasing vibration from millions of insects throughout the livelong day. The sun shone large and warm ; the river was calm and broad and brown."

By January 1877 the expedition reached the first cataract of what is now known as the Stanley Falls. From this point for some sixty miles the great volume of the Livingstone River rushed through narrow and lofty banks in a series of rapids. For twenty-two days he toiled along the banks, through jungle and forest, over cliffs and rocks exposed all the while to murderous attacks by cannibal savages, till the seventh cataract was passed and the boats were safely below the falls. "We hastened away down river in a hurry, to escape the noise of the cataracts which for many days and nights had almost

"TOWARDS THE UNKNOWN": STANLEY'S CANOES STARTING FROM VINYA NJARA.

From *Through the Dark Continent.*

stunned us with their deafening sound. We were once more afloat on a magnificent stream, nearly a mile wide, curving north-west. 'Ha! Is it the Niger or Congo?' I said."

But day after day as they dropped down stream new enemies appeared, until at last, at the junction of the Aruwimi, a tributary as large as the main stream, a determined attack was made on them by some two thousand warriors in large canoes. A monster canoe led the way, with two rows of forty paddlers each, their bodies swaying to a barbarous chorus. In the bow were ten prime young warriors, their heads gay with the feathers of the parrot, crimson and grey : at the stern eight men with long paddles decorated with ivory balls guided the boat, while ten chiefs danced up and down from stem to stern. The crashing of large drums, a hundred blasts from ivory horns, and a song from two thousand voices did not tend to assure the little fleet under Stanley. The

THE SEVENTH CATARACT, STANLEY FALLS.
From *Through the Dark Continent.*

Englishman coolly anchored his boats in mid-stream and received the enemy with such well-directed volleys that the savages were utterly paralysed, and with great energy they retreated, pursued hotly by Stanley's party.

"Leaving them wondering and lamenting, I sought the mid-channel again and wandered on with the current. In the voiceless depths of the watery wilderness we encountered neither treachery nor guile, and we floated down, down, hundreds of miles. The river curved west-

THE FIGHT BELOW THE CONFLUENCE OF THE ARUWIMI AND THE LIVINGSTONE RIVERS.

From a sketch, by Stanley, in *Through the Dark Continent*.

32

ward, then south-westward. Ah, straight for the mouth of the Congo. It widened daily. The channels became numerous."

Through the country of the Bangala they now fought their way. These people were armed with guns brought up from the coast by native traders. It was indeed an anxious moment when, with war-drums beating, sixty-three " beautiful but cruel canoes " came skimming towards Stanley with some three hundred guns to his forty-four. For nearly five hours the two fleets fought until the victory rested with the American. " This," remarks Stanley, " was our thirty-first fight on the terrible river, and certainly the most determined conflict we had endured."

They rowed on till the 11th of March; the river had grown narrower and steep, wooded hills rose on either side above them. Suddenly the river expanded, and the voyagers entered a wide basin or pool of three hundred square miles. "Sandy islands rose in front of us like a sea-beach, and on the right towered a long row of cliffs white and glistening, like the cliffs of Dover."

"Why not call it Stanley Pool and those cliffs Dover Cliffs ?" suggested Frank Pocock. And these names may be seen on our maps to-day. Passing out of the Pool, the roar of a great cataract burst upon their ears. It was the first of a long series of falls and rapids which continued for a distance of one hundred and fifty-five miles. To this great stretch of cataracts and rapids Stanley gave the name of the " Livingstone Falls." At the fifth cataract Stanley lost his favourite little native page-boy, Kalulu. The canoe in which he was rowing shot suddenly over the rapids, and in the furious whirl of rushing waters poor little Kalulu was drowned. He had been born a prince and given to Stanley on his first expedition into Africa. Stanley had taken him to

Europe and America, and the boy had repaid his kindness by faithful and tender devotion till that fatal day, when he went to his death over the wild Livingstone Falls. Stanley named the rapid after him, Kalulu Falls.

But a yet more heart-rending loss was in store for him. Progress was now very slow, for none of the cataracts or rapids could be navigated; canoes as well as stores had to be dragged over land from point to point. Frank Pocock had fallen lame and could not walk with the rest. Although accidents with the canoes were of daily occurrence, although he might have taken warning by the death of Kalulu, he insisted that his crew should try to shoot the great Massassa Falls instead of going round by land. Too late he realised his danger. The canoe was caught by the rushing tide, flung over the Falls, tossed from wave to wave, and finally dragged into the swirling whirlpool below. The " little master " as he was called was never seen again ! Stanley's last white companion was gone ! Gloom settled down on the now painfully reduced party.

" We are all unnerved with the terrible accident of yesterday," says Stanley. " As I looked at the dejected woe-stricken servants, a choking sensation of unutterable grief filled me. This four months had we lived together, and true had been his service. The servant had long ago merged into the companion ; the companion had become the friend."

Still Stanley persevered in his desperate task, and in spite of danger from cataracts and danger from famine, on 31st July he reached the Isangila cataract. Thus far in 1816 two explorers had made their way from the ocean, and Stanley knew now for certain that he was on the mighty Congo. He saw no reason to follow it farther, or to toil through the last four cataracts. " I therefore announced to the gallant but wearied followers that we should abandon the river and strike overland for Boma, the nearest European settlement, some sixty miles across country."

At sunset on 31st July they carried the *Lady Alice* to the summit of some rocks above the Isangila Falls and abandoned her to her fate.

"Farewell, brave boat!" cried Stanley; "seven thousand miles up and down broad Africa thou hast accompanied me. For over five thousand miles thou hast been my home. Lift her up tenderly, boys—so tenderly—and let her rest."

Then, wayworn and feeble, half starved, diseased, and suffering, the little caravan of one hundred and fifteen men, women, and children started on their overland march to the coast.

"Staggering, we arrived at Boma on 9th August 1877; a gathering of European merchants met me and, smiling a warm welcome, told me kindly that I had done right well. Three days later I gazed upon the Atlantic Ocean and saw the powerful river flowing into the bosom of that boundless, endless sea. But grateful as I felt to Him who had enabled me to pierce the Dark Continent from east to west, my heart was charged with grief and my eyes with tears at the thought of the many comrades and friends I had lost."

The price paid had indeed been great; he had lost his three English companions and one hundred and seventy natives besides. But for years and years to come, in many a home at Zanzibar, whither Stanley now took his party by sea, the story of this great journey was told, and all the men were heroes and the refrain of the natives was chanted again and again—

"Then sing, O friends, sing: the journey is ended;
Sing aloud, O friends, sing to this great sea."

Stanley had solved the problem of the Congo River at last.

CHAPTER LXIX

NORDENSKIÖLD ACCOMPLISHES THE NORTH-EAST PASSAGE

THE North-West Passage, for the accomplishment of which so many brave lives had been laid down, had been discovered. It now remained for some explorer to sail round the North-East Passage, which was known to exist, but which, up to this time, no man had done.

Nordenskiöld the Swede was to have this honour. Born in 1832 in Finland, he had taken part in an Arctic expedition in 1861, which attempted to reach the North Pole by means of dog-sledges from the north coast of Spitzbergen. Three years later he was appointed to lead an expedition to Spitzbergen, which succeeded in reaching the highest northern latitude which any ship had yet attained. In 1870 his famous journey to Greenland took place, and two years later he left Sweden on another Polar expedition; but misfortunes beset the expedition, and finally the ships were wrecked. The following year he commanded a reconnoitring expedition. He passed Nova Zembla and reached the mouth of the Yenisei. This was the first time that a ship had accomplished the voyage from the Atlantic Ocean. Thus Nordenskiöld had gained considerable knowledge of the Northern Seas, and he was now in a position to lay a plan of his schemes before King Oscar, who had always interested himself in Arctic discovery. His suggestions to the King are of singular interest.

" It is my intention," he says, " to leave Sweden in July 1878 in a steamer specially built for navigation among ice, which will be provisioned for two years at most. The course will be shaped for Nova Zembla, where a favourable opportunity will be awaited for the passage of the Kara Sea. The voyage will be continued to the mouth of the Yenisei, which I hope to reach in the first half of August. As soon as circumstances permit, the expedition will continue its voyage along the coast to Cape Chelyuskin, where the expedition will reach the only part of the proposed route which has not been traversed by some small vessel, and is rightly considered as that which it will be most difficult for a vessel to double during the whole North-East Passage; but our vessel, equipped with all modern appliances, ought not to find insuperable difficulties in doubling this point, and if that can be accomplished, we will probably have pretty open water towards Behring's Straits, which ought to be reached before the end of September. From Behring Strait the course will be shaped for some Asiatic port and then onwards round Asia to Suez."

King Oscar and others offered to pay the expenses of the expedition, and preparations were urged forward. The *Vega* of 300 tons, formerly used in walrus-hunting in northern waters, was purchased, and further strengthened to withstand ice. On 22nd June all was ready, and with the Swedish flag with a crowned O in the middle, the little *Vega*, which was to accomplish such great things, was " peacefully rocking on the swell of the Baltic as if impatient to begin her struggle against waves and ice." She carried food for thirty people for two years, which included over three thousand pounds of bacon, nine thousand pounds of coffee, nine thousand pounds of biscuits. There were pemmican from England, potatoes from the Mediterranean, cranberry juice from Finland. Fresh bread was made during the whole expedition. A few days later the *Vega* reached Copenhagen and steamed north in the finest weather.

" Where are you bound for ? " signalled a passing ship.

" To Behring Sea," was the return signal, and the Swedish crew waved their caps, shouting their joyful news.

At Gothenburg they took on eight sledges, tents, and cooking utensils, also two Scotch sheep dogs and a little coal-black kitten, which lived in the captain's berth till it grew accustomed to the sea, when it slept in the forecastle by day and ran about stealing the food of the sleeping sailors by night.

On 16th July they crossed the Polar Circle. " All on board feel they are entering upon a momentous period of their life," says the explorer. " Were we to be the fortunate ones to reach this goal, which navigators for centuries had striven to reach ? "

The south-west coast of Nova Zembla was reached on 28th July, but the weather being calm and the sea completely free of ice, Nordenskiöld sailed onwards through the Kara Strait or Iron Gates, which during the winter was usually one sheet of ice, until they anchored outside the village of Khabarova. The " village " consisted of a few huts and tents of Russian and Samoyedes pasturing their reindeer on the Vaygets Island. On the bleak northern shores stood a little wooden church, which the explorers visited with much interest. It seemed strange to find here brass bas-reliefs representing the Christ, St. Nicholas, Elijah, St. George and the Dragon, and the Resurrection ; in front of each hung a little oil lamp. The people were dressed entirely in reindeer skin from head to foot, and they had a great collection of walrus tusks and skins such as Othere had brought centuries before to King Alfred.

Nordenskiöld's account of a short drive in a reindeer sledge is amusing. " Four reindeer were put side by side to each sledge," he says. "Ivan, my driver, requested me to hold tight; he held the reins of all four reindeer in one hand, and away we went over the plain ! His request to keep myself tight to the sledge was not unnecessary; at one moment the sledge jumped over a big tussock, the next it went down into a pit. It was anything but a comfortable drive, for the pace at which we went was very great."

On 1st August the *Vega* was off again, and soon she had entered the Kara Sea, known in the days of the Dutch explorers as the "ice-cellar." Then past White Island and the estuary of the great Obi River, past the mouth of the Yenisei to Dickson Island, lately discovered, she sailed. Here in this "best-known haven on the whole north coast of Asia they anchored and spent time in bear and reindeer hunting." "In consequence of the successful sport we lived very extravagantly during these days; our table groaned with joints of venison and bear-hams."

They now sailed north close bound in fog, till on 20th August "we reached the great goal, which for centuries had been the object of unsuccessful struggles. For the first time a vessel lay at anchor off the northernmost cape of the Old World. With colours flying on every mast and saluting the venerable north point of the Old World with the Swedish salute of five guns, we came to an anchor ! "

The fog lifting for a moment, they saw a white Polar bear standing "regarding the unexpected guests with surprise."

When afterwards a member of the expedition was asked which moment was the proudest of the whole voyage, he answered, without hesitation : " Undoubtedly the moment when we anchored off Cape Chelyuskin."

It had been named thus by the " Great Northern Expedition " in 1742 after Lieutenant Chelyuskin, one of the Russian explorers under Laptieff, who had reached this northern point by a land journey which had entailed terrible hardships and suffering.

" Next morning," relates Nordenskiöld, " we erected a cairn on the shore, and in the middle of it laid a tin box with the following document written in Swedish : ' The

NORDENSKIÖLD'S SHIP, THE *VEGA*, SALUTING CAPE CHELYUSKIN, THE MOST NORTHERLY POINT OF THE OLD WORLD.

From a drawing in Hovgaard's *Nordenskiöld's Voyage.*

Swedish Arctic Expedition arrived here yesterday, the 19th of August, and proceeds in a few hours eastward. The sea has been tolerably free from ice. Sufficient supply of coals. All well on board.

"'A. E. NORDENSKIÖLD.'

And below in English and Russian were the words, ' Please forward this document as soon as possible to His Majesty the King of Sweden.'"

Nordenskiöld now attempted to steam eastwards towards the New Siberian Islands, but the fog was thick, and they fell in with large ice-floes which soon gave place to ice-fields. Violent snowstorms soon set in and " aloft everything was covered with a crust of ice, and the position in the crow's nest was anything but pleasant." They reached Khatanga Bay, however, and on 27th August the *Vega* was at the mouth of the Lena.

" We were now in hopes that we should be in Japan in a couple of months; we had accomplished two-thirds of our way through the Polar sea, and the remaining third had been often navigated at different distances."

So the *Vega* sailed on eastwards with an ice-free sea to the New Siberian Islands, where lie embedded " enormous masses of the bones and tusks of the mammoth mixed with the horns and skulls of some kind of ox and with the horns of rhinoceros."

All was still clear of snow, and the New Siberian Islands lying long and low in the Polar seas were safely passed. It was not till 1st September that the first snows fell ; the decks of the *Vega* were white with snow when the Bear Islands were reached. Fog now hindered the expedition once more, and ice was sighted.

" Ice right ahead ! " suddenly shouted the watch on the forecastle, and only by a hair's-breadth was the *Vega* saved. On 3rd September a thick snowstorm came on, the Bear Islands were covered with newly fallen snow, and though the ice was growing more closely packed than any yet encountered they could still make their way along a narrow ice-free channel near the coast. Snowstorms, fog, and drifting ice compelled careful navigation, but a pleasant change occurred early in September by a visit from the natives. We have already heard of the Chukches from Behring—the Chukches whom no man had yet vanquished, for when Siberia was conquered by a Kossack chief in 1579, the Chukches in this outlying north-eastern corner of the Old World, savage, courageous, resolute, kept the conquerors at bay. For the last six weeks the explorers had not seen a human being on that wild and desolate stretch of coast, so they were glad enough to see the little Chukches with their coal-black hair and eyes, their large mouths and flat noses. " Although it was only five o'clock in the morning, we all jumped out of our berths and hurried on deck to see these people of whom so little was known. The boats were of skin, fully laden with laughing and chatter-ing natives, men, women, and children, who indicated by cries and gesticulations that they wished to come on board. The engine was stopped, the boats lay to, and a large number of skin - clad, bare - headed beings climbed up over the gunwale and a lively talk began. Great gladness pre-vailed when tobacco and

MENKA, CHIEF OF THE CHUKCHES.

Dutch clay pipes were distributed among them. None of them could speak a word of Russian; they had come in closer contact with American whalers than with Russian traders." The Chukches were all very short and dressed in reindeer skins with tight-fitting trousers of seal-skin, shoes of reindeer-skin with seal-skin boots and walrus-skin soles. In very cold weather they wore hoods of wolf fur with the head of the wolf at the back.

But Nordenskiöld could not wait long. Amid snow and ice and fog he pushed on, hoping against hope to get through to the Pacific before the sea was completely frozen over. But the ice was beginning to close. Large blocks were constantly hurled against the ship with great violence, and she had many a narrow escape of destruction.

At last, it was 28th September, the little *Vega* was finally and hopelessly frozen into the ice, and they made her fast to a large ice-block. Sadly we find the entry : " Only one hundred and twenty miles distant from our goal, which we had been approaching during the last two months, and after having accomplished two thousand four hundred miles. It took some time before we could accustom ourselves to the thought that we were so near and yet so far from our destination."

Fortunately they were near the shore and the little settlement of Pitlekai, where in eight tents dwelt a party of Chukches. These little people helped them to pass the long monotonous winter, and many an expedition inland was made in Chukche sledges drawn by eight or ten wolf-like dogs. Snowstorms soon burst upon the little party of Swedish explorers who had made the *Vega* their winter home. "During November we have scarcely had any daylight," writes Nordenskiöld; " the storm was generally howling in our rigging, which was now enshrouded in a thick coat of snow, the deck was full of large snowdrifts, and snow penetrated into every corner of the ship where it was possible for the wind to find an opening. If we put our heads outside the door we were blinded by the drifting snow."

Christmas came and was celebrated by a Christmas tree made of willows tied to a flagstaff, and the traditional rice porridge.

By April large flocks of geese, eider-ducks, gulls, and little song-birds began to arrive, the latter perching on the rigging of the *Vega*, but May and June found her still ice-bound in her winter quarters.

It was not till 18th July 1879 that " the hour of deliverance came at last, and we cast loose from our faithful ice-block, which for two hundred and ninety-four days had protected us so well against the pressure of the ice and stood westwards in the open channel, now about a mile wide. On the shore stood our old friends, probably on the point of crying, which they had often told us they would do when the ship left them."

THE *VEGA* FROZEN IN FOR THE WINTER.

From a drawing in Hovgaard's *Nordenskiöld's Voyage.*

For long the Chukches stood on the shore—men, women, and children—watching till the "fire-dog," as they called the *Vega*, was out of sight, carrying their white friends for ever away from their bleak, inhospitable shores.

"Passing through closely packed ice, the *Vega* now rounded the East Cape, of which we now and then caught a glimpse through the fog. As soon as we came out of the ice south of the East Cape, we noticed the heavy swell of the Pacific Ocean. The completion of the North-East Passage was celebrated the same day with a grand dinner, and the *Vega* greeted the Old and New Worlds by a display of flags and the firing of a Swedish salute. Now for the first time after the lapse of three hundred and thirty-six years was the North-East Passage at last achieved."

Sailing through the Behring Strait, they anchored near Behring Island on 14th August. As they came to anchor, a boat shot alongside and a voice cried out in Swedish, " Is it Nordenskiöld ? " A Finland carpenter soon stood in their midst, and they eagerly questioned him about the news from the civilised world !

There is no time to tell how the *Vega* sailed on to Japan, where Nordenskiöld was presented to the Mikado, and an Imperial medal was struck commemorating the voyage of the *Vega*, how she sailed right round Asia, through the Suez Canal, and reached Sweden in safety. It was on 24th April 1880 that the little weather-beaten *Vega*, accompanied by flag-decked steamers literally laden with friends, sailed into the Stockholm harbour while the hiss of fireworks and the roar of cannon mingled with the shouts of thousands. The Royal Palace was ablaze with light when King Oscar received and honoured the successful explorer Nordenskiöld.

CHAPTER LXX

THE EXPLORATION OF TIBET

PERHAPS no land in the world has in modern times exercised a greater influence over the imagination of men than the mysterious country of Tibet. From the days of Herodotus to those of Younghusband, travellers of all times and nations have tried to explore this unknown country, so jealously guarded from Europeans. Surrounded by a " great wilderness of stony and inhospitable altitudes " lay the capital, Lhasa, the seat of the gods, the home of the Grand Lama, founded in 639 A.D., mysterious, secluded, sacred. Kublai Khan, of Marco Polo fame, had annexed Tibet to his vast Empire, and in 1720 the mysterious land was finally conquered by the Chinese. The history of the exploration of Tibet and the adjoining country, and of the various attempts to penetrate to Lhasa, is one of the most thrilling in the annals of discovery.

We remember that Benjamin of Tudela in the twelfth century, Carpini and William de Rubruquis in the thirteenth, all assert that they passed through Tibet, but we have no certain records till several Italian Capuchin friars succeeded in reaching Lhasa. There they lived and taught for some thirty-eight years, when they were withdrawn. And the little " Tibetan Mission," as it was called, came to an end.

It was yet early in the eighteenth century. England was taking up her great position in India, and Warren

Hastings was anxious to open up friendly relations with Tibet beyond the great Himalaya ranges. To this end he sent an Englishman, George Bogle, with these instructions : " I desire you will proceed to Lhasa. The design of your mission is to open a mutual and equal communication of trade between the inhabitants of Tibet and Bengal. You will take with you samples, for a trial of such articles of commerce as may be sent from this country. And you will diligently inform yourself of the manufactures, productions, and goods which are to be procured in Tibet. The following will also be proper subjects for your inquiry, the nature of the roads between the borders of Bengal and Lhasa and the neighbouring countries. I wish you to remain a sufficient time to obtain a complete knowledge of the country. The period of your stay must be left to your discretion."

Bogle was young; he knew nothing of the country, but in May 1774 his little expedition set off from Calcutta to do the bidding of Warren Hastings. By way of Bhutan, planting potatoes at intervals according to his orders, Bogle proceeded across the eastern Himalayas toward the Tibetan frontier, reaching Phari, the first town in Tibet, at the end of October. Thence they reached Gyangtse, a great trade centre now open to foreigners, crossed the Brahmaputra, which they found was "about the size of the Thames at Putney," and reached the residence of the Tashi Lama, the second great potentate of Tibet. This great dignitary and the young Englishman made great friends.

" On a carved and gilt throne amid cushions sat the Lama, cross-legged. He was dressed in a mitre-shaped cap of yellow broadcloth with long bars lined with red satin, a yellow cloth jacket without sleeves, and a satin mantle of the same colour thrown over his shoulders. On one side of him stood his physician with a bundle of perfumed sandal-wood rods burning in his hand; on the other stood his cup-bearer."

Such was this remarkable man as first seen by the English, "venerated as God's vice-regent through all the eastern countries of Asia." He had heard much of the power of the "Firinghis," as he called the English. "As my business is to pray to God," he said to Bogle, "I was afraid to admit any Firinghis into the country. But I have since learned that they are a fair and just people."

THE POTALA AT LHASA: A SEVENTEENTH-CENTURY VIEW.

From Kircher's *China Illustrata*. The only good representation of the Potala until photographs were obtainable in the twentieth century.

Bogle would have proceeded to Lhasa, the home of the Grand Lama, but this permission was refused, and he had to return to India with the information he had collected.

The next Englishman to enter Tibet was Thomas Manning, the first to reach the sacred city of Lhasa. He was a private adventurer, who had lived in China and learnt the language. Attended by a Chinese servant, and wearing a flowing beard of singular length, he left Calcutta, crossed into Bhutan, and arrived at the Tibetan

33

border in October 1811. Then he crossed the Brahmaputra in a large ferry-boat, and arrived within seven
miles of Lhasa. On 9th December the first European
entered the sacred city since the expulsion of the Capuchin
friars. The view of the famous Potala, the lofty towering palace, filled him with admiration, but the city of
which Europe, knowing nothing, had exalted into a
magnificent place, was very disappointing.

"We passed under a large gateway," says Manning,
"whose gilded ornaments were so ill-fixed that some
leaned one way and some another. The road as it winds
round the palace is royally broad; it swarmed with monks,
and beggars were basking in the sun. There is nothing
striking in its appearance; the habitations are begrimed
with smut and dirt. The avenues are full of dogs—in
short, everything seems mean and gloomy. Having
provided himself with a proper hat, Manning went to
the Potala to salute the Grand Lama, taking with him
a pair of brass candlesticks with two wax candles, some
'genuine Smith's lavender water, and a good store of
Nankin tea, which is a rare delicacy at Lhasa. Ushered
into the presence of the Grand Lama, a child of seven,
he touched his head three times on the floor, after the
custom of the country, and, taking off his hat, knelt to
be blessed by the little monarch.' He had the simple
and unaffected manners of a well-educated princely
child. His face was affectingly beautiful—his beautiful
mouth was perpetually unbending into a graceful smile,
which illuminated his whole countenance."

Here Manning spent four months, at the end of which
time he was recalled from Pekin, and reluctantly he was
obliged to return the way he came.

The next man to reach the forbidden city was a Jesuit
missionary, the Abbé Huc, who reached Lhasa in 1846
from China. He had adopted the dress of the Tibetan

Lama—the yellow cap and gown—and he piloted his little caravan across the wide steppes on horseback, while his fellow-missionary, Gabet, rode a camel and their one Tartar retainer rode a black mule. It took them a year and a half to reach the sacred city of Lhasa, for many and great were the difficulties of the way. Their first difficulty lay in crossing the Yellow River, which was in flood.

" It is quite impossible to cross the Yellow River," they were told. " Eight days ago the river overflowed its banks and the plains are completely flooded."

" The Tartars only told us the truth," remarked Huc sadly. " The Yellow River had become a vast sea, the limits of which were scarcely visible : houses and villages looked as though they were floating upon the waves. What were we to do ? To turn back was out of the question. We had vowed that, God willing, we would go to Lhasa whatever obstacles impeded."

And so they did. The camels were soon up to their knees in a thick slimy compost of mud and water, over which the poor animals slid on their painful way. Their courage was rewarded, native ferry-boats came to their rescue, and they reached the other side in safety. They were now on the main caravan route to the Tibetan frontier and the Koko-Nor. Immense caravans were met, with strings of camels extending for miles in length. Three times between the Yellow River and the Koko-Nor Lake did they pass the Great Wall built in 214 A.D. After over four months of travel Huc arrived at the monastery of Kunkum on the borderland of Tibet. This was the home of four thousand Lamas all clothed in red dresses and yellow mitres, and thither resorted the worshippers of Buddha from all parts of Tartary and Tibet.

" The site is one of enchanting beauty," says Huc. " Imagine in a mountain-side a deep, broad ravine adorned with fine trees and alive with the cawing of rooks and yellow-beaked crows and the amusing chatter of magpies. On the two sides of the ravine and on the slopes of the mountain rise the white dwellings of the Lamas. Amid the dazzling whiteness of these modest habitations rise numerous Buddhist temples with gilt roofs, sparkling with a thousand brilliant colours. Here the travellers stayed for three months, after which they made their way on to the Koko-Nor Lake.

"As we advanced," says Huc, "the country became more fertile, until we reached the vast and magnificent pasturage of Koko-Nor. Here vegetation is so vigorous that the grass rose up to the stomachs of our camels. Soon we discovered far before us what seemed a broad silver riband. Our leader informed us that this was the Blue Sea. We urged on our animals, and the sun had not set when we planted our tent within a hundred paces of the waters of the great Blue Lake. This immense reservoir of water seems to merit the title of sea rather than merely that of lake. To say nothing of its vast extent, its waters are bitter and salt, like those of the ocean."

After a month spent on the shores of the Blue Lake, an opportunity offered for the advance. Towards the end of October they found that an embassy from Lhasa to Pekin was returning in great force. This would afford Huc and his companion safe travelling from the hordes of brigands that infested the route through Tibet. The caravan was immense. There were fifteen hundred oxen, twelve hundred horses, and as many camels, and about two thousand men. The ambassador was carried in a litter. Such was the multitude which now started for the thousand miles across Tibet to Lhasa.

After crossing the great Burkhan Buddha range, the caravan came to the Shuga Pass, about seventeen thousand feet high, and here their troubles began.

" When the huge caravan first set itself in motion,"
says Huc, " the sky was clear, and a brilliant moon lit
up the great carpet of snow with which the whole country
was covered. We were able to attain the summit by
sunrise. Then the sky became thickly overcast with
clouds and the wind began to blow with a violence which
became more and more intense."

Snow fell heavily and several animals perished. They
marched in the teeth of an icy wind which almost choked
them, whirlwinds of snow blinded them, and when they
reached the foot of the mountain at last, M. Gabet found
that his nose and ears were frostbitten. As they proceeded, the cold became more intense. " The demons of
snow, wind, and cold were set loose on the caravan with
a fury which seemed to increase from day to day."

" One cannot imagine a more terrible country," says
poor Huc.

Not only were the animals dying from cold and exposure, but men were beginning to drop out and die.
Forty of the party died before the plateau of Tangla
had been crossed, a proceeding which lasted twelve days.
The track, some sixteen thousand feet above the sea,
was bordered by the skeletons of mules and camels, and
monstrous eagles followed the caravan. The scenery
was magnificent, line upon line of snow-white pinnacles
stretched southward and westward under a bright sun.
The descent was "long, brusque, and rapid, like the
descent of a gigantic ladder." At the lower altitude
snow and ice disappeared. It was the end of January
1846, when at last our two travellers found themselves
approaching the longed-for city of Lhasa.

" The sun was nearly setting," says Huc, "when we
found ourselves in a vast plain and saw on our right
Lhasa, the famous metropolis of the Buddhist world.
After eighteen months' struggle with sufferings and

obstacles of infinite number and variety, we were at length arrived at the termination of our journey, though not at the close of our miseries."

Huc's account of the city agrees well with that of Manning : "The palace of the Dalai Lama," he says, "merits the celebrity which it enjoys throughout the world. Upon a rugged mountain, the mountain of Buddha, the adorers of the Lama have raised the magnificent palace wherein their Living Divinity resides in the flesh. This place is made up of various temples; that which occupies the centre is four storeys high; it terminates in a dome entirely covered with plates of gold. It is here the Dalai Lama has set up his abode. From the summit of his lofty sanctuary he can contemplate his innumerable adorers prostrate at the foot of the divine mountain. But in the town all was different—all are engaged in the grand business of buying and selling, all is noise, pushing, excitement, confusion."

Here Huc and his companion resided for two and a half months, opening an oratory in their house and even making a few Christian converts. But soon they were ordered to leave, and reluctantly they travelled back to China, though by a somewhat different route.

After this the Tibetans guarded their capital more zealously than before. Przhevalsky, "that grand explorer of Russian nationality," spent years in exploring Tibet, but when within a hundred and sixty miles of Lhasa he was stopped, and never reached the forbidden city.

Others followed. Prince Henri of Orleans got to within one hundred miles of Lhasa, Littledale and his wife to within fifty miles. Sven Hedin, the "Prince of Swedish explorers," who had made so many famous journeys around and about Tibet, was making a dash for the capital disguised as a Mongolian pilgrim when he, too, was stopped.

" A long black line of Tibetan horsemen rode towards us at full gallop," he relates. " It was not raining just at that moment, so there was nothing to prevent us from witnessing what was in truth a very magnificent spectacle. It was as though a living avalanche were sweeping down upon us. A moment more and we should be annihilated ! We held our weapons ready. On came the Tibetans in one long line stretching across the plain. We counted close upon seventy in all. In the middle rode the chief on a big handsome mule, his staff of officers all dressed in their finest holiday attire. The wings consisted of soldiers armed to the teeth with gun, sword, and lance. The great man, Kamba Bombo, pulled up in front of our tent. After removing a red Spanish cloak and hood he " stood forth arrayed in a suit of yellow silk with wide arms and a little blue Chinese skull-cap. His feet were encased in Mongolian boots of green velvet. He was magnificent."

" You will not go another step towards Lhasa," he said. " If you do you will lose your heads. It doesn't the least matter who you are or where you come from. You must go back to your headquarters."

So an escort was provided and sorrowfully Sven Hedin turned his back on the jealously guarded town he had striven so hard to reach.

The expedition, or rather mission, under Colonel Younghusband in 1904 brings to an end our history of the exploration of Tibet. He made his way to Lhasa from India; he stood in the sacred city, and " except for the Potala " he found it a " sorry affair." He succeeded in getting a trade Treaty signed, and he rode hastily back to India and travelled thence to England. The importance of the mission was accentuated by the fact that the flag, a Union Jack bearing the motto, " Heaven's Light our Guide," carried by the expedition and placed on the table when the Treaty was signed in Lhasa, hangs to-day in the Central Hall at Windsor over the statue of Queen Victoria.

The veil so long drawn over the capital of Tibet had been at last torn aside, and the naked city had been revealed in all its " weird barbarity." Plans of the " scattered and ill-regulated " city are now familiar, the Potala has been photographed, the Grand Lama has been drawn, and if, with the departure of Younghusband, the gates of Lhasa were once more closed, they did not remain closed, and voices from beyond the snowy Himalayas were heard again ere long.

THE WORLD'S MOST MYSTERIOUS CITY UNVEILED : LHASA AND THE POTALA

From a photograph by a member of Younghusband's expedition to Tibet and Lhasa, 1904.

CHAPTER LXXI

NANSEN REACHES FARTHEST NORTH

No names are better known in the history of Arctic exploration than those of Nansen and the *Fram,* and although others have done work just as fine, the name of Nansen cannot be omitted from our *Book of Discovery.*

Sven Hedin had not long returned from his great travels through eastern Turkestan and Tibet when Nansen was preparing for his great journey northwards.

He had already crossed Greenland from east to west, a brilliant achievement only excelled by Peary, who a few years later, crossed it at a higher latitude and proved it to be an island.

Now the movement of ice drift in the Arctic seas was occupying the attention of explorers at this time. A ship, the *Jeannette,* had been wrecked in 1881 off the coast of Siberia, and three years later the débris from the wreck had been washed up on the south-west coast of Greenland. So it occurred to Nansen that a current must flow across the North Pole from Behring Sea on one side to the Atlantic Ocean on the other. His idea was therefore to build a ship as strong as possible to enable it to withstand the pressure of the ice, to allow it to become frozen in, and then to drift as the articles from the *Jeannette* had drifted. He reckoned that it would take three years for the drift of ice to carry him to the North Pole.

Foolhardy and impossible as the scheme seemed to some, King Oscar came forward with £1000 toward expenses. The *Fram* was then designed. The whole success of the expedition lay in her strength to withstand the pressure of the ice. At last she was ready, even fitted with electric light. A library, scientifically prepared food, and instruments of the most modern type were on board. The members of the expedition numbered thirteen, and on Midsummer Day, 1893, " in calm summer weather, while the setting sun shed his beams over the land, the *Fram* stood out towards the blue sea to get its first roll in the long, heaving swell." Along the coast of Norway, past Bergen, past Trondhjem, past Tromsö, they steamed, until in a north-westerly gale and driving snow they lost sight of land. It was 25th July when they sighted Nova Zembla plunged in a world of fog. They landed at Khabarova and visited the little old church seen fifteen years before by Nordenskiöld, anxiously inquiring about the state of the ice in the Kara Sea. Here, amid the greatest noise and confusion, some thirty-four dogs were brought on board for the sledges. On 5th August the explorer successfully passed through the Yugor Strait into the Kara Sea, which was fairly free from ice, and five weeks later sailed past Cape Chelyuskin, the northernmost point of the Old World.

" The land was low and desolate," says Nansen. " The sun had long since gone down behind the sea; only one star was to be seen. It stood straight above Cape Chelyuskin, shining clearly and sadly in the pale sky. Exactly at four o'clock our flags were hoisted and our last three cartridges sent out a thundering salute over the sea."

The *Fram* was then turned north to the west of the New Siberian Islands. " It was a strange thing to be sailing away north," says Nansen, " to unknown lands, over an open rolling sea where no ship had been before. On to the north, steadily north with a good wind, as fast as steam and sail can take us through unknown regions."

They had almost reached 78 degrees north when they saw ice shining through the fog, and a few days later the *Fram* was frozen in. "Autumn was well advanced, the long night of winter was approaching, there was nothing to be done except prepare ourselves for it, and we converted our ship as well as we could into comfortable winter quarters."

By October the ice was pressing round the *Fram* with a noise like thunder. "It is piling itself up into long walls and heaps high enough to reach a good way up the *Fram's* rigging : in fact, it is trying its very utmost to grind the *Fram* into powder."

Christmas came and went. The New Year of 1894 dawned with the thermometer 36 degrees below zero. By February the *Fram* had drifted to the 80th degree of latitude. "High festival in honour of the 80th degree," writes Nansen. "Hurrah! Well sailed! The wind is whistling among the hummocks, the snow flies rustling through the air, ice and sky are melted into one, but we are going north at full speed, and are in the wildest of gay spirits. If we go on at this rate we shall be at the Pole in fifty months."

On 17th May the 81st degree of latitude was reached. Five months passed away. By 31st October they had drifted to the 82nd. "A grand banquet to-day," says Nansen, "to celebrate the 82nd degree of latitude. We are progressing merrily towards our goal; we are already half-way between the New Siberian Islands and Franz Josef Land, and there is not a soul on board who doubts that we shall accomplish what we came out to do; so long live merriment."

Now Nansen planned the great sledge journey, which has been called "the most daring ever undertaken."

The winter was passed in peaceful preparation for a start in the spring. When the New Year of 1895 dawned the *Fram* had been firmly frozen in for fifteen months. A few days later, the ship was nearly crushed by a fresh ice pressure and all prepared to abandon her if necessary, but after an anxious day of ice roaring and crackling—" an ice pressure with a vengeance, as if Doomsday had come," remarked Nansen—it quieted down. They had now beaten all records, for they had reached 83 degrees latitude.

And now preparations for the great sledge journey were complete. They had built kayaks or light boats to sail in open water, and these were placed on the sledges and drawn by dogs. Nansen decided only to take one companion, Johansen, and to leave the others with the *Fram*.

" At last the great day has arrived. The chief aim of the expedition is to push through the unknown Polar sea from the region around the New Siberian Islands, north of Franz Josef Land and onward to the Atlantic Ocean near Spitzbergen or Greenland." Farewells were said, and then the two men bravely started off over the unknown desert sea with their sledges and twenty-eight dogs. For the first week they travelled well and soon reached 85 degrees latitude. " The only disagreeable thing to face now is the cold," says Nansen. " Our clothes are transformed more and more into complete suits of ice armour. The sleeve of my coat actually rubbed deep sores in my wrists, one of which got frostbitten; the wound grew deeper and deeper and nearly reached the bone. At night we packed ourselves into our sleeping-bags and lay with our teeth chattering for an hour before we became aware of a little warmth in our bodies."

Steadily, with faces to the north, they pressed on

over the blocks of rough ice, stretching as far as the horizon, till on 8th April further progress became impossible. Nansen strode on ahead and mounted one of the highest hummocks to look around. He saw "a veritable chaos of ice-blocks, ridge after ridge, and nothing but rubble to travel over." He therefore determined to turn and make for Franz Josef Land some four hundred and fifty miles distant. They had already reached 86 degrees of latitude, farther north than any expedition had reached before.

DR. NANSEN.
After a photograph.

As they travelled south, they rejoiced in the warmth of the sun, but their food was growing scarce, and they had to kill a dog every other day to feed the others, till by May they had only thirteen dogs left. June found them having experienced tremendous snowstorms with only seven dogs left. Although they were in the latitude of Franz Josef Land, no welcome shores appeared. It was now three months since they had left the *Fram*; the food for the dogs was quite finished and the poor creatures were beginning to eat their harness of sailcloth. Mercifully before the month ended they managed to shoot a seal which provided them with food for a month. "It is a pleasing change," says Nansen, "to be able to eat as much and as often as we like. Blubber is excellent, both raw and fried. For dinner I fried a highly successful steak, for supper I made blood-pancakes fried in blubber with sugar, unsurpassed in flavour. And here we lie up in the far north, two grim, black, soot-stained barbarians, stirring a mess of soup in a kettle, surrounded on all sides by ice—ice covered with impassable snow."

A bear and two cubs were shot and the explorers stayed on at " Longing Camp " as they named this dreary spot, unable to go on, but amply fed.

On 24th July we get the first cheerful entry for many a long day : " Land ! land ! after nearly two years we again see something rising above that never-ending white line on the horizon yonder—a new life is beginning for us ! "

Only two dogs were now left to drag the sledges, so the two explorers were obliged to help with the dragging. For thirteen days they proceeded in the direction of land, dragging and pushing their burdens over the ridges of ice with thawing snow. At last on 7th August they stood at the edge of the ice. Behind lay their troubles; before was the waterway home. Then they launched their little kayaks, which danced over the open waters, the little waves splashing against their sides. When the mist cleared they found themselves on the west coast of Franz Josef Land, discovered by an Austro-Hungarian expedition in 1874.

They were full of hope, when a cruel disappointment damped their joy. They had landed and were camping on the shore, when a great storm arose and the wind blew the drift ice down till it lay packed along the coast. The little ships were frozen in, and there was no hope of reaching home that winter. Here they were doomed to stay. Fortunately there were bears and walrus, so they could not starve, and with magnificent pluck they set to work to prepare for the winter. For many a long day they toiled at the necessary task of skinning and cutting up walrus till they were saturated with blubber, oil, and blood, but soon they had two great heaps of blubber and meat on shore well covered over with walrus hides.

September was occupied in building a hut amid the frost and snow with walrus hides and tusks, warmed inside with train-oil lamps. Here under bear skins they slept

THE SHIP THAT WENT FARTHEST NORTH: THE *FRAM*.
From a photograph.

and passed the long months of winter. In October the sun disappeared, the days grew darker. Life grew very monotonous, for it was the third Polar winter the explorers had been called on to spend. They celebrated Christmas Day, Nansen by washing himself in a " quarter of a cup of warm water," Johansen by turning his shirt. The weather outside was stormy and almost took their breath away with its icy coldness. They longed for a book, but they wiled away the hours by trying to calculate how far the *Fram* could have drifted and when she was likely to reach home. They were distressed at the dirt of their clothes, and longed to be able to throw away the heavy oily rags that seemed glued to their bodies. They had no soap, and water had no effect on the horrible grease. It was May before the weather allowed them to leave the hut at last. Hopefully they dragged their kayaks over the snow, the sledge runners fastened on to their feet, and so made their way southwards down Franz Josef Land.

Once Nansen was very nearly drowned. The explorers had reached the south of the Islands, and, having moored their little boats together, they ascended a hummock close by, when to their horror they saw the kayaks were adrift. Nansen rushed down, threw off some clothes, and sprang into the water after them. He was none too soon, for already the boats were drifting rapidly away. The water was icy cold, but it was a case of life or death. Without the boats they were lost men. " All we possessed was on board," says Nansen, " so I exerted myself to the utmost. I redoubled my exertions though I felt my limbs gradually stiffening; at last I was able to stretch out my hand to the edge of the kayak. I tried to pull myself up, but the whole of my body was stiff with cold. After a time I managed to swing one leg up on to the edge and to tumble up. Nor was it easy to paddle in the double vessel ; the gusts of wind seemed to go right through me as I stood there in my wet woollen shirt. I shivered, my teeth chattered, and I was numb all over. At last I managed to reach the edge of the ice. I shook and trembled all over, while Johansen pulled off the wet things and packed me into the sleeping-bag. The critical situation was saved."

And now came one of those rare historic days in the history of exploration. It was 17th June 1896. Nansen was surveying the lonely line of coast, when suddenly the barking of a dog fell on his ear, and soon in front he saw the fresh tracks of some animal. " It was with a strange mixture of feelings," he says, " that I made my way among the numerous hummocks towards land. Suddenly I thought I heard a human voice—the first for three years. How my heart beat and the blood rushed to my brain as I hallooed with all the strength of my lungs. Soon I heard another shout and saw a dark form moving among the hummocks. It was a man. We approached one another quickly. I waved my hat; he did the same. As I drew nearer I thought I recognised Mr. Jackson, whom I remembered once to have seen. I raised my hat; we extended a hand to one another with a hearty 'How do you do?' Above us a roof of mist, beneath our feet the rugged packed drift ice."

" Ar'n't you Nansen ? " he said.

" Yes, I am," was the answer.

And, seizing the grimy hand of the Arctic explorer, he shook it warmly, congratulating him on his successful trip. Jackson and his companions had wintered at Cape Flora, the southern point of Franz Josef Land, and they were expecting a ship, the *Windward,* to take them home. On 26th July the *Windward* steamed slowly in, and by 13th August she reached Norway, and the news of Nansen's safe arrival was made known to the whole world. A week later the little *Fram,* " strong and broad and weather-beaten," also returned in safety. And on 9th September 1896, Nansen and his brave companions on board the *Fram* sailed up Christiania Fjord in triumph.

He had reached a point farthest North, and been nearer to the North Pole than had any explorer before.

34

CHAPTER LXXII

PEARY REACHES THE NORTH POLE, 1909

THE 6th April 1909 is a marked day in the annals of exploration, for on that day Peary succeeded in reaching the
North Pole, which for centuries had defied the efforts
of man; on that day he attained the goal for which the
greatest nations of the world had struggled for over four
hundred years. Indeed, he had spent twenty-three years
of his own life labouring toward this end.

He was mainly inspired by reading Nordenskiöld's
Exploration of Greenland, when a lieutenant in the United
States Navy. In 1886 he got leave to join an expedition
to Greenland, and returned with the Arctic fever in
his veins and a scheme for crossing that continent as
far north as possible. This after many hardships he
accomplished, being the first explorer to discover that
Greenland was an island. Peary was now stamped as
a successful Arctic explorer. The idea of reaching the
North Pole began to take shape, and in order to raise
funds the enthusiastic explorer delivered no less than
one hundred and sixty-eight lectures in ninety-six days.
With the proceeds he chartered the *Falcon* and left
the shores of Philadelphia in June 1893 for Greenland.
His wife, who accompanied him before, accompanied him
again, and with sledges and dogs on board they made
their way up the western coast of Greenland. Arrived
at Melville Bay, Peary built a little hut; here a little
daughter was born who was soon "bundled in soft warm

Arctic furs and wrapped in the Stars and Stripes." No
European child had ever been born so far north as this;
the Eskimos travelled from long distances to satisfy themselves she was not made of snow, and for the first six
months of her life the baby lived in continuous lamp-
light.

But we cannot follow Peary through his many Polar
expeditions; his toes had been frozen off in one, his leg
broken in another, but he was enthusiastic enough when
all preparations were complete for the last and greatest
expedition of all.

The *Roosevelt,* named after the President of the United
States, had carried him safely to the north of Greenland
in his last expedition, so she was again chosen, and in
July 1908, Peary hoisted the Stars and Stripes and steamed
from New York.

" As the ship backed out into the river, a cheer went
up from the thousands who had gathered on the piers
to see us off. It was an interesting coincidence that
the day on which we started for the coldest spot on earth
was about the hottest which New York had known for
years. As we steamed up the river, the din grew louder
and louder; we passed President Roosevelt's naval yacht,
the *Mayflower,* and her small gun roared out a parting
salute—surely no ship ever started for the ends of the
earth with more heart-stirring farewells."

President Roosevelt had himself inspected the ship
and shaken hands with each member of the expedition.

" I believe in you, Peary," he had said, " and I believe
in your success, if it is within the possibility of man."
So the little *Roosevelt* steamed away; on 26th July the
Arctic Circle was crossed by Peary for the twentieth
time, and on 1st August, Cape York, the most northerly
home of human beings in the world, was reached. This
was the dividing line between the civilised world on

one hand and the Arctic world on the other. Picking up several Eskimo families and about two hundred and fifty dogs, they steamed on northwards.

"Imagine," says Peary—"imagine about three hundred and fifty miles of almost solid ice, ice of all shapes and sizes, mountainous ice, flat ice, ragged and tortured ice; then imagine a little black ship, solid, sturdy, compact, strong, and resistant, and on this little ship are sixty-nine human beings, who have gone out into the crazy, ice-tortured channel between Baffin Bay and the Polar sea —gone out to prove the reality of a dream in the pursuit of which men have frozen and starved and died."

The usual course was taken, across Smith's Sound and past the desolate wind-swept rocks of Cape Sabine, where, in 1884, Greely's ill-fated party slowly starved to death, only seven surviving out of twenty-four.

Fog and ice now beset the ship, and on 5th September they were compelled to seek winter quarters, for which they chose Cape Sheridan, where Peary had wintered before in 1905. Here they unloaded the *Roosevelt*, and two hundred and forty-six Eskimo dogs were at once let loose to run about in the snow. A little village soon grew up, and the Eskimos, both men and women, went hunting as of yore. Peary had decided to start as before from Cape Columbia, some ninety miles away, the most northerly point of Grant Land, for his dash to the Pole.

On 12th October the sun disappeared and they entered cheerfully into the " Great Dark."

"Imagine us in our winter home," says Peary, "four hundred and fifty miles from the North Pole, the ship held tight in her icy berth one hundred and fifty yards from the shore, ship and the surrounding world covered with snow, the wind creaking in the rigging, whistling and shrieking around the corners of the deck houses, the temperature ranging from zero to sixty below, the ice-pack in the channel outside us groaning and complaining with the movement of the tides."

Christmas passed with its usual festivities. There were races for the Eskimos, one for the children, one for the men, and one for the Eskimo mothers, who carried babies in their fur hoods. These last, looking like " animated walruses," took their race at a walking pace.

At last, on 15th February 1909, the first sledge-party left the ship for Cape Columbia, and a week later Peary himself left the *Roosevelt* with the last loads. The party assembled at Cape Columbia for the great journey north, which consisted of seven men of Peary's party, fifty-nine Eskimos, one hundred and forty dogs, and twenty-eight sledges. Each sledge was complete in itself; each had its cooking utensils, its four men, its dogs and provisions for fifty or sixty days. The weather was " clear, calm, and cold."

On 1st March the cavalcade started off from Cape Columbia in a freezing east wind, and soon men and dogs became invisible amid drifting snow. Day by day they went forward, undaunted by the difficulties and hardships of the way, now sending back small parties to the dépôt at Cape Columbia, now dispatching to the home camp some reluctant explorer with a frostbitten heel or foot, now delayed by open water, but on, on, till they had broken all records, passed all tracks even of the Polar bear, passed the 87th parallel into the region of perpetual daylight for half the year. It was here, apparently within reach of his goal, that Peary had to turn back three years before for want of food.

Thus they marched for a month; party after party had been sent back, till the last supporting party had gone and Peary was left with his black servant, Henson, and four Eskimos. He had five sledges, forty picked dogs, and supplies for forty days when he started off alone to dash the last hundred and thirty-three miles to the Pole itself. Every event in the next week is of thrilling interest. After a few hours of sleep the little party started off shortly after midnight on 2nd April 1909. Peary was leading.

" I felt the keenest exhilaration as I climbed over the ridge and breasted the keen air sweeping over the mighty ice, pure and straight from the Pole itself."

They might yet be stopped by open water from reaching the goal. On they went, twenty-five miles in ten hours, then a little sleep, and so on again, then a few hours' rest and another twenty miles till they had reached latitude 89 degrees.

Still breathlessly they hurried forward, till on the 5th they were but thirty-five miles from the Pole.

" The sky overhead was a colourless pall, gradually deepening to almost black at the horizon, and the ice was a ghastly and chalky white."

On 6th April the Pole was reached.

" The Pole at last ! " writes Peary in his diary. " The prize of three centuries ! My dream and goal for twenty years. Mine at last ! I cannot bring myself to realise it. It all seems so simple and commonplace."

Flags were at once hoisted on ice lances, and the successful explorer watched them proudly waving in the bright Arctic sunlight at the Pole. Through all his perilous expeditions to the Arctic regions, Peary had worn a silken flag, worked by his wife, wrapped round his body. He now flew it on this historic spot, " which knows no North, nor West, nor East."

Not a vestige of land was to be seen; nothing but ice lay all around. They could not stay long, for provisions would run short, and the ice might melt before their return journey was accomplished.

So after a brief rest they started off for Cape Columbia,

PEARY'S FLAG FLYING AT THE NORTH POLE, APRIL 1909.

By the courteous permission of Admiral Peary, from his book *The North Pole*, published by Messrs. Hodder & Stoughton.

which they reached after a wild rush of sixteen days. It had taken them thirty-seven days to cover the four hundred and seventy-five miles from Cape Columbia to the Pole, from which they had returned at the rate of thirty miles a day.

The whole party then started for the *Roosevelt*, and on 18th July she was taken from her winter quarters and turned towards home. Then came the day when wireless telegraphy flashed the news through the whole of the civilised world: " Stars and Stripes nailed to the North Pole."

The record of four hundred years of splendid self-sacrifice and heroism unrivalled in the history of exploration had been crowned at last.

CHAPTER LXXIII

THE QUEST FOR THE SOUTH POLE

An American had placed the Stars and Stripes on the North Pole in 1909. It was a Norwegian who succeeded in reaching the South Pole in 1911. But the spade-work which contributed so largely to the final success had been done so enthusiastically by two Englishmen that the expeditions of Scott and Shackleton must find a place here before we conclude this *Book of Discovery* with Amundsen's final and brilliant dash.

The crossing of the Antarctic Circle by the famous *Challenger* expedition in 1874 revived interest in the far South. The practical outcome of much discussion was the design of the *Discovery*, a ship built expressly for scientific exploration, and the appointment of Captain Scott to command an Antarctic expedition.

In August 1901, Scott left the shores of England, and by way of New Zealand crossed the Antarctic Circle on 3rd January 1902. Three weeks later he reached the Great Ice Barrier which had stopped Ross in 1840. For a week Scott steamed along the Barrier. Mounts Erebus and Terror were plainly visible, and though he could nowhere discover Parry Mountains, yet he found distant land rising high above the sea, which he named King Edward VII.'s Land. Scott had brought with him a captive balloon in which he now rose to a height of eight hundred feet, from which he saw an unbroken glacier stream of vast extent stretching to the south. It was now time to seek for winter quarters, and Scott, returning to M'Murdo Bay named by Ross, found that it was not a bay at all, but a strait leading southward. Here they landed their stores, set up their hut, and spent the winter, till on 2nd November 1902 all was ready for a sledge-journey to the south. For fifty-nine days Scott led his little land-party of three, with four sledges and nineteen dogs, south. But the heavy snow was too much for the dogs, and one by one died, until not one was left and the men had to drag and push the sledges themselves. Failing provisions at last compelled them to stop. Great mountain summits were seen beyond the farthest point reached.

"We have decided at last we have found something which is fitting to bear the name of him whom we most delight to honour," says Scott, "and Mount Markham it shall be called in memory of the father of the expedition."

It was 30th December when a tremendous blizzard stayed their last advance. "Chill and hungry," they lay all day in their sleeping-bags, miserable at the thought of turning back, too weak and ill to go on. With only provisions for a fortnight, they at last reluctantly turned home, staggering as far as their dépôt in thirteen days. Shackleton was smitten with scurvy; he was growing worse every day, and it was a relief when on 2nd February they all reached the ship alive, "as near spent as three persons can well be." But they had done well: they had made the first long land journey ever made in the Antarctic; they had reached a point which was farthest south; they had tested new methods of travel; they had covered nine hundred and sixty miles in ninety-three days. Shackleton was now invalided home, but it was not till 1904 that the *Discovery* escaped from the frozen harbour to make her way home.

Shackleton had returned to England in 1903, but the

mysterious South Pole amid its wastes of ice and snow still called him back, and in command of the *Nimrod* he started forth in August 1907 on the next British Antarctic expedition, carrying a Union Jack, presented by the Queen, to plant on the spot farthest south. He actually placed it within ninety-seven miles of the Pole itself!

With a petrol motor-car on board, Eskimo dogs, and Manchurian ponies, he left New Zealand on 1st January 1908, watched and cheered by some thirty thousand of his fellow-countrymen. Three weeks later they were in sight of the Great Ice Barrier, and a few days later the huge mountains of Erebus and Terror came into sight. Shackleton had hoped to reach King Edward VII.'s Land for winter quarters, but a formidable ice-pack prevented this, and they selected a place some twenty miles north of the *Discovery's* old winter quarters. Getting the wild little Manchurian ponies ashore was no light job; the poor little creatures were stiff after a month's constant buffeting, for the *Nimrod's* passage had been stormy. One after another they were now led out of their stalls into a horse-box and slung over the ice. Once on *terra firma* they seemed more at home, for they immediately began pawing the snow as they were wont to do in their far-away Manchurian home.

The spacious hut, brought out by Shackleton, was soon erected. Never was such a luxurious house set up on the bleak shores of the Polar seas. There was a dark room for developing, acetylene gas for lighting, a good stove for warming, and comfortable cubicles decorated with pictures. The dark room was excellent, and never was a book of travels more beautifully illustrated than Shackleton's *Heart of the Antarctic.*

True, during some of the winter storms and blizzards the hut shook and trembled so that every moment its

SHACKLETON'S SHIP, THE *NIMROD*, AMONG THE ICE IN McMURDO SOUND, THE WINTER LAND QUARTERS
OF THE BRITISH ANTARCTIC EXPEDITION.

By Sir Ernest Shackleton's permission from his book "The Heart of the Antarctic," published by Mr. Heinemann.

occupants thought it would be carried bodily away, but it stood its ground all right. The long winter was spent as usual in preparing for the spring expedition to the south, but it was 29th October 1908 before the weather made it possible to make a start. The party consisted of Shackleton, Adams, Marshall, and Wild, each leading a pony which dragged a sledge with food for ninety-one days.

"A glorious day for our start," wrote Shackleton in his diary, " brilliant sunshine and a cloudless sky. As we left the hut where we had spent so many months in comfort we had a feeling of real regret that never again would we all be together there. A clasp of the hands means more than many words, and as we turned to acknowledge the men's cheer, and saw them standing on the ice by the familiar cliffs, I felt we must try to do well for the sake of every one concerned in the expedition."

New land in the shape of ice-clad mountains greeted the explorers on 22nd November. " It is a wonderful place we are in, all new to the world," says Shackleton; " there is an impression of limitless solitude about it that makes us feel so small as we trudge along, a few dark specks on the snowy plain."

They now had to quit the Barrier in order to travel south. Fortunately they found a gap, called the Southern Gateway, which afforded a direct line to the Pole. But their ponies had suffered badly during the march; they had already been obliged to shoot three of them, and on 7th December the last pony fell down a crevasse and was killed. They had now reached a great plateau some seven thousand feet above the sea; it rose steadily toward the south, and Christmas Day found them " lying in a little tent, isolated high on the roof of the world, far from the ways trodden by man." With forty-eight degrees of frost, drifting snow, and a biting wind, they spent the next few days hauling their sledges up a steep incline. They had now only a month's food left. Pressing on with reduced rations, in the face of freezing winds, they reached a height of ten thousand and fifty feet.

It was the 6th of January, and they were in latitude 88 degrees, when a "blinding, shrieking blizzard" made all further advance impossible. For sixty hours the four hungry explorers lay in their sleeping-bags, nearly perished with cold. "The most trying day we have yet spent," writes Shackleton, "our fingers and faces being continually frostbitten. To-morrow we will rush south with the flag. It is our last outward march."

The gale breaking, they marched on till 9th January, when they stopped within ninety-seven miles of the Pole, where they hoisted the Union Jack, and took possession of the great plateau in the King's name.

"We could see nothing but the dead-white snow plain. There was no break in the plateau as it extended towards the Pole. I am confident that the Pole lies on the great plateau we have discovered miles and miles from any outstanding land."

And so the four men turned homewards. "Whatever our regret may be, we have done our best," said the leader somewhat sadly. Blinding blizzards followed them as they made their way slowly back. On 28th January they reached the Great Ice Barrier. Their food was well-nigh spent; their daily rations consisted of six biscuits and some horse-meat in the shape of the Manchurian ponies they had shot and left the November before. But it disagreed with most of them, and it was four very weak and ailing men who staggered back to the *Nimrod* toward the end of February 1909.

Shackleton reached England in the autumn of 1909 to find that another Antarctic expedition was to leave our shores in the following summer under the command

of Scott, in the *Terra Nova*. It was one of the best-
equipped expeditions that ever started ; motor-sledges
had been specially constructed to go over the deep snow,
which was fatal to the motor-car carried by Shackleton.
There were fifteen ponies and thirty dogs. Leaving
England in July 1910, Scott was established in winter
quarters in M'Murdo Sound by 26th January 1911. It
was November before he could start on the southern
expedition.

" We left Hut Point on the evening of 2nd November.
For sixty miles we followed the track of the motors (sent
on five days before). The ponies are going very steadily.
We found the motor party awaiting us in latitude 80½
degrees south. The motors had proved entirely satisfactory, and the machines dragged heavy loads over the
worst part of the Barrier surface, crossing several crevasses.
The sole cause of abandonment was the overheating of
the air-cooled engines. We are building snow cairns at
intervals of four miles to guide homeward parties and
leaving a week's provisions at every degree of latitude.
As we proceeded the weather grew worse, and snowstorms were frequent. The sky was continually overcast,
and the land was rarely visible. The ponies, however,
continued to pull splendidly."

As they proceeded south they encountered terrific
storms of wind and snow, out of which they had constantly
to dig the ponies. Christmas passed and the New Year of
1912 dawned. On 3rd January when one hundred and
fifty miles from the Pole, " I am going forward," says Scott,
" with a party of five men with a month's provisions, and
the prospect of success seems good, provided that the
weather holds and no unforeseen obstacles arise."

Scott and his companions successfully attained the
object of their journey. They reached the South Pole on
17th January only to find that they had been forestalled

by others ! And it is remarkable to note that so correct were their observations, the two parties located the Pole within half a mile of one another.

Scott's return journey ended disastrously. Blinding blizzards prevented rapid progress ; food and fuel ran short ; still the weakened men struggled bravely forward till, within a few miles of a depôt of supplies, death overtook them.

Scott's last message can never be forgotten. "I do not regret this journey which has shown that Englishmen can endure hardship, help one another, and meet death with as great fortitude as ever in the past. . . . Had we lived, I should have had a tale to tell of the hardihood, endurance, and courage of my companions which would have stirred the heart of every Englishman. These rough notes and our dead bodies must tell the tale ; but surely, surely, a great, rich country like ours will see that those who are dependent upon us are properly provided for."

It was on 14th December 1911 that Captain Amundsen had reached the Pole. A Norwegian, fired by the example of his fellow-countryman, Nansen, Amundsen had long been interested in both Arctic and Antarctic exploration. In a ship of only forty-eight tons, he had, with six others, made a survey of the North Magnetic Pole, sailed through the Behring Strait, and accomplished the North-West Passage, for which he was awarded the Royal Medal of the Royal Geographical Society. On his return he planned an expedition to the North Pole. He had made known his scheme, and, duly equipped for North Polar expedition in Nansen's little *Fram*, Amundsen started. Suddenly the world rang with the news that Peary had discovered the North Pole, and that Amundsen had turned his prow southwards and was determined to make a dash for the South Pole. Landing in Whales Bay some four hundred miles to the east of Scott's winter quarters, his first visitors were the Englishmen on board the *Terra Nova*, who were taking their ship to New Zealand for the winter.

Making a hut on the shore, Amundsen had actually started on his journey to the Pole before Scott heard of his arrival.

"I am fully alive to the complication in the situation arising out of Amundsen's presence in the Antarctic," wrote the English explorer, "but as any attempt at a race might have been fatal to our chance of getting to the Pole at all, I decided to do exactly as I should have done had not Amundsen been here. If he gets to the Pole he will be bound to do it rapidly with dogs, and one foresees that success will justify him."

Although the Norwegian explorer left his winter quarters on 8th September for his dash to the Pole, he started too early; three of his party had their feet frostbitten, and the dogs suffered severely, so he turned back, and it was not till 20th October, just a week before Scott's start, that he began in real earnest his historic journey. He was well off for food, for whales were plentiful on the shores of the Bay, and seals, penguins, and gulls abounded. The expedition was well equipped, with eight explorers, four sledges, and thirteen dogs attached to each.

"Amundsen is a splendid leader, supreme in organisation, and the essential in Antarctic travel is to think out the difficulties before they arise." So said those who worked with him on his most successful journey.

Through dense fog and blinding blizzards the Norwegians now made their way south, their Norwegian skis and sledges proving a substantial help. The crevasses in the ice were very bad; one dog dropped in and had to be abandoned; another day the dogs got across, but the sledge fell in, and it was necessary to climb down the crevasse, unpack the sledge, and pull up piece by piece till it was possible to raise the empty sledge. So intense was the cold that the very brandy froze in the bottle and was served out in lumps.

" It did not taste much like brandy then," said the men, " but it burnt our throats as we sucked it."

The dogs travelled well. Each man was responsible for his own team ; he fed them and made them fond of him. Thus all through November the Norwegians travelled south, till they reached the vast plateau described by Shackleton. One tremendous peak, fifteen thousand feet high, they named " Frithjof Nansen."

On 14th December they reached their goal; the weather was beautiful, the ground perfect for sledging.

" At 3 p.m. we made halt," says Amundsen. " According to our reckoning, we had reached our destination. All of us gathered round the colours—a beautiful silken flag; all hands took hold of it, and, planting it on the spot, we gave the vast plateau on which the Pole is situate the name of ' The King Haakon VII.' It was a vast plain, alike in all directions, mile after mile."

Here in brilliant sunshine the little party camped, taking observations till 17th December, when, fastening to the ground a little tent with the Norwegian flag and the *Fram* pennant, they gave it the name " Polheim " and started for home.

So the North and South Poles yielded up their well-hoarded secrets after centuries of waiting, within two and a half years of one another.

They had claimed more lives than any exploration had done before, or is ever likely to do again.

And so ends the last of these great earth-stories—stories which have made the world what it is to-day—and we may well say with one of the most successful explorers of our times, " The future may give us thrilling stories of the conquest of the air, but the spirit of man has mastered the earth."

CAPTAIN ROALD AMUNDSEN TAKING SIGHTS AT THE SOUTH POLE.

From a photograph, by permission of Mr. John Murray and the *Illustrated London News.*

DATES OF CHIEF EVENTS

35*

INDEX

PRINTED IN GREAT BRITAIN AT THE PRESS OF THE PUBLISHERS

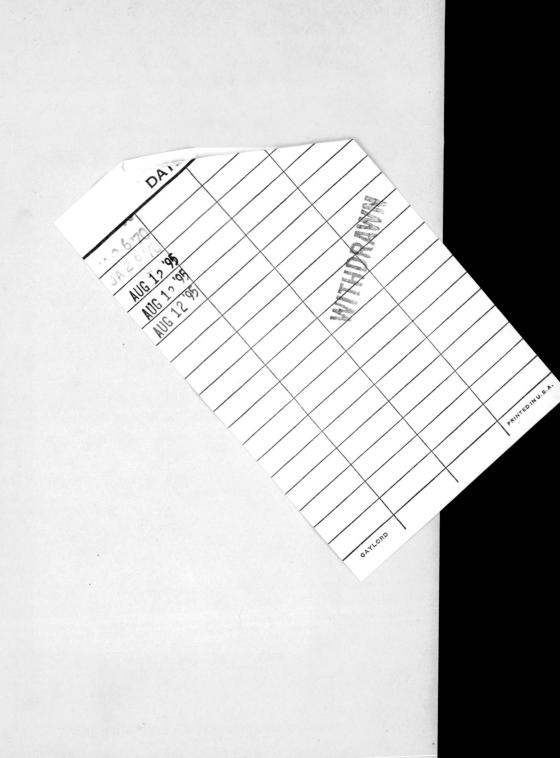